Entrepreneurship in Small Island States and Territories

Entrepreneurship in Small Island States and Territories is the first publication ever to consider the "creative" side of enterprise in small island states and territories. Rather than playing out as remote, vulnerable, and dependent backwaters of neocolonialism, the world's small island states and territories (with resident populations of less than 1 million) show considerable resourcefulness in facing up to the very real challenges of their predicament.

The creative endeavors of their residents, facilitated by adroit public policy, have created economic and investment opportunities that translate into private-sector employment and decent livelihoods for many. Their ingenuity, coupled with strategic investments and the support of the diaspora, has led to a suite of (sometimes unlikely) products and services: from citizenship and higher-level Internet domain names to place-branded foods and beverages; from electronic gaming to niche manufacturing.

There is much more to small island survival than subsistence farming, aid, remittances, and public-sector workfare. *Entrepreneurship in Small Island States and Territories* helps to dispel this myth, showcasing an aspect of life in small island states and territories that is rarely documented or critically reviewed.

Godfrey Baldacchino is Professor of Sociology, Department of Sociology, and chairman of the board of the Centre for Labour Studies, both at the University of Malta, Malta. He is an Island Studies Teaching Fellow at the University of Prince Edward Island (UPEI), Canada.

Routledge Studies in Entrepreneurship

Edited by Susan Marlow and Janine Swail
(University of Nottingham, UK)

This series extends the meaning and scope of entrepreneurship by capturing new research and enquiry on economic, social, cultural, and personal value creation. Entrepreneurship as value creation represents the endeavors of innovative people and organizations in creative environments that open up opportunities for developing new products, new services, new firms, and new forms of policy making in different environments seeking sustainable economic growth and social development. In setting this objective, the series includes books that cover a diverse range of conceptual, empirical, and scholarly topics that both inform the field and push the boundaries of entrepreneurship.

Entrepreneurship in Small Island States and Territories

Edited by Godfrey Baldacchino

Routledge
Taylor & Francis Group

LONDON AND NEW YORK

First published 2015
by Routledge

2 Park Square, Milton Park, Abingdon, Oxfordshire OX14 4RN
711 Third Avenue, New York, NY 10017

Routledge is an imprint of the Taylor & Francis Group, an informa business

First issued in paperback 2018

Library of Congress Cataloging-in-Publication Data
Entrepreneurship in small island states and territories / edited by
    Godfrey Baldacchino. — First Edition.
        pages cm. — (Routledge studies in entrepreneurship)
    Includes bibliographical references and index.
    1. Entrepreneurship—Case studies.   2. Islands—Economic conditions.
3. States, Small—Economic conditions.   I. Baldacchino, Godfrey.
    HB615.E633485 2015
    338′.0409142—dc23
    2015000926

ISBN: 978-1-138-78998-2 (hbk)
ISBN: 978-1-138-61704-9 (pbk)

Typeset in Sabon
by Apex CoVantage, LLC

Contents

PART 3
Tourism Segments

PART 4
Other Intangibles

PART 5
Island Entrepreneurship: A Personal Testimony

PART 6
Epilogue

Tables

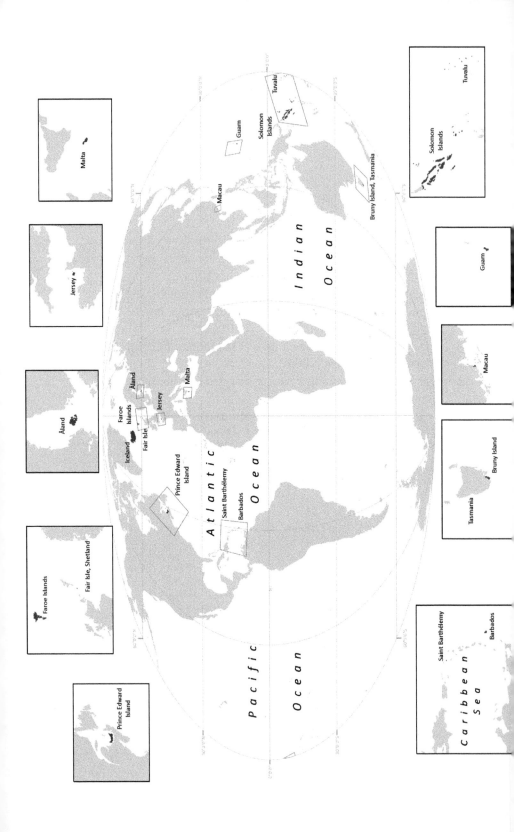

Acknowledgments

Is it perhaps because I am, let's face it, an academic entrepreneur? I have always been interested in the spirit of enterprise, and while most of my early work dealt with supporting trade unions and cooperative societies, I maintained and nurtured a soft spot for those enterprising individuals who manage to run away with an idea and transform it into a viable business. While attached to the University of the South Pacific in Suva, Fiji, in 1997, I explored and wrote about Mokosoi, a local soap company, with papers appearing in 1999 in the *Journal of Pacific Studies, 23*(1), the *International Journal of Employment Studies, 7*(2), and the *Journal of Small Business Management, 37*(4). Still in 1999, while summering on Prince Edward Island, Canada, I researched the specifics of the Island Preserve Company, writing about the case in the *Journal of Small Business Management* (2002). During 2002 to 2004, I was the academic coordinator of the NISSOS project, involving 11 partners from five countries looking at successful small businesses from small islands. The project spawned various teaching manuals in different languages, plus at least three academic papers.

With his 1988 edited book *Island Entrepreneurs: Problems and Performances in the Pacific*, Te'o I. J. Fairbairn inspired me to continue working in this field, and together we edited a special issue of the *Journal of Small Business & Entrepreneurship, 19*(4), 2006. I thank Léo-Paul Dana, the contributor of this volume's epilogue, who encouraged me to develop and collate another special journal issue, focusing this time on small island brands, which appeared as the *International Journal of Entrepreneurship and Small Business, 9*(4), 2010. I also thank Geoff Bertram, who has been a great mentor during my PhD travails and eventually a coauthor and coresearcher. He has nudged me in pursuit of the idiosyncrasies of small island development. Finally, I also wish to acknowledge the work of my colleague and Maltese conational, Lino Briguglio. He has been significant in establishing small island vulnerability as an issue of global concern, helping put small island states squarely on the map. This text is also, in a way, a critical and never boring conversation with his arguments.

This book project was launched soon after I returned full time to the University of Malta (UoM) in Malta in October 2013 after a 10-year spell as

Canada Research Chair in Island Studies at the University of Prince Edward Island (UPEI), Charlottetown, Canada. I continue to benefit from an association with both UoM and UPEI, and I am grateful for the powerful intellectual synergies and collegial relations this double affiliation has provided. Long may it continue.

My special thanks go to the various contributors to the chapters of this volume. Securing a global coverage of the topic at hand was not easy; the contributors have been patient with my editorial exhortations and suggestions and not least my reminders about deadlines, style guides, and focus of the argument. I also thank David Varley and Jabari LeGendre, my commissioning editors at Taylor & Francis/Routledge, for believing in this project and closely supporting the editorial process.

The map of the world showing the location of the various case studies has been kindly drawn by Nikoleta Koukourouvli at the Laboratory of Local and Island Development, University of the Aegean, Lesvos, Greece.

I remain responsible for any errors of omission or commission that may be found in this book and for which I humbly apologize.

Godfrey Baldacchino
Marsaskala, Malta—January 4, 2015

Contributors

Gylfi Dalmann Aðalsteinsson is associate professor of human resource management and employment relations and deputy head, School of Business, University of Iceland. His research interests lie mainly in the area of human resource management and industrial relations. Recent publications in the *Icelandic Review of Politics and Administration* include: "Legislation intervening strikes in Iceland 1985–2010; grounds for legal intervention" (2010, with F. Friðriksson); "Icelandic organizational culture; Clear and effective policy but lack of coordination and integration" (2010, with Þórhallur Örn Guðlaugsson and Ester Rós Gústavsdóttir); "Icelandic National Culture in Relation to Hofstede's Five Dimensions" (2011, with Þ. Ö. Guðlaugsson and Svala Guðmundsdóttir); "Comparison of the recruitment process when appointing officials in Iceland before and after the economic collapse" (2014, with B. Möller). Articles in the *International Journal of Business Research* include: "The Germanic and Anglo Cultural Cluster Compared to Icelandic National Culture By Using VSM94" (2014, with S. Guðmundsdóttir and Þ. Ö. Guðlaugsson) and "The Nordic Cultural Cluster: A Relative Comparisons Using VSM94" (2014, with Þ. Ö. Guðlaugsson and S. Guðmundsdóttir). Gylfi is also a consultant to both public and private organizations. He holds a bachelor's degree in political science from the University of Iceland and an MA (Industrial Relations) from the University of Warwick, UK.

Krystyna Adams is a PhD student in the Faculty of Health Sciences at Simon Fraser University (SFU) in British Columbia, Canada. She is a member of the SFU Medical Tourism Research Group and completed her master's degree working with this group, writing her thesis on the potential impacts of an information sheet regarding ethical considerations in medical tourism on patient decision making. Her PhD dissertation looks at medical tourism, particularly in the Caribbean region, with a focus on examining potentially exploitative relationships in medical tourism planning and development in this region.

Mario Aloisio is lecturer in computing at the University of Malta Junior College, Malta. He started his computing career in 1979 with Imperial Chemical Industries plc at their research laboratories in Runcorn,

Cheshire, UK. After graduating in applied physics (from the former Preston Polytechnic, now the University of Central Lancashire, UK), he spent many years involved in software design and development, following which he moved into academia. He completed a PhD in computer science at the University of Warwick, UK. His main area of research is the history of computing, but he is also interested in information and communications technology (ICT) policy, object-oriented programming, machine vision, and computer simulation of physical systems. He is author of two books, including *Plugging the Microstate: A History of Technology Adoption, ICT Policy* (2012), and *Software Development in the Small Island State of Malta* (2012), and various articles in peer-reviewed journals. He has mostly lived and worked in Malta but for some years also worked in Libya, the UK, and Germany.

Godfrey Baldacchino is professor of sociology at the University of Malta, Malta; Island Studies Teaching Fellow and outgoing Canada Research Chair (Island Studies) at the University of Prince Edward Island, Charlottetown, Canada; and Visiting Professor of Island Tourism at the Università di Corsica Pasquale Paoli, France. He is founding executive editor of *Island Studies Journal*, president of the International Small Islands Studies Association (ISISA), council member of the Islands Commission of the International Geographical Union (IGU), and a director for Global Islands Network (GIN). Recently published books include *Island Enclaves: Offshoring Strategies, Creative Governance and Subnational Island Jurisdictions* (2010); *Island Futures: Conservation and Development Across the Asia-Pacific* (2011, with D. Niles); *Extreme Heritage Management: Practices and Policies From Densely Populated Islands* (2011); *Island Songs: A Global Repertoire* (2011); *A Taste of Islands* (2012, with A. Baldacchino); *The International Political Economy of Divided Islands* (2012); *Independence Movements From Subnational Island Jurisdictions* (2013, with E. Hepburn); and *Archipelago Tourism: Principles and Practices* (2015).

Carola Betzold is a postdoctoral researcher at the University of Gothenburg, Sweden, and fellow at the Gothenburg Centre for Globalization and Development. Prior to coming to Sweden, Carola obtained a PhD from ETH Zurich, Switzerland. Her research focuses on environmental and especially climate-change politics, in particular in relation to small island states. For her thesis, she analyzed disadvantaged actors in international climate-change negotiations, including nongovernmental organizations and the Alliance of Small Island States (AOSIS). In her current position, she is interested in adaptation and aid, again with a particular focus on small island states.

Michael Lujan Bevacqua graduated from the University of Guam with a BA in art and literature in 2001 and an MA in Micronesian studies in 2004.

He completed an MA in ethnic studies from the University of California, San Diego, in 2007 and was conferred a PhD degree in 2010. He is currently an instructor of Chamorro studies at the University of Guam. Bevacqua's research deals with the impact of colonization on Chamorros in Guam and theorizes the possibilities for the decolonization of their lands and lives. In 2011, he led a faculty task force in successfully creating a Chamorro studies BA program at the University of Guam. He is a passionate advocate for the revitalization of the Chamorro language and has translated manga comic books, rock songs, and even Beethoven's "Ode to Joy" into Chamorro. Bevacqua is a member of Nasion Chamoru, the Association of Asian American Studies, the National Association of Ethnic Studies and the National Pacific Islander Education Network and is a founding member of the Chamorro Information Activists and Famoksaiyan.

Richard W. Butler is emeritus professor of international tourism, Strathclyde University, Glasgow, UK. He holds degrees in geography and spent 30 years at the University of Western Ontario in Canada before joining the University of Surrey, UK (1997 to 2005) and then moving to Strathclyde. He has published numerous journal articles and book chapters and 16 books on tourism. For many years, he served as editor of the *Journal of Tourism and Hospitality Research*. His principal research interests are the development of tourist destinations and the impacts of tourism. He is a former president of the International Academy for the Study of Tourism. He is possibly best known for having developed the tourism area life cycle model in 1980.

Valorie A. Crooks is associate professor in the Department of Geography at Simon Fraser University, Canada. She holds the Canada Research Chair in Health Service Geographies and a Scholar Award from the Michael Smith Foundation for Health Research. She is a health geographer who specializes in health services research. In 2009, she formed the SFU Medical Tourism Research Group and currently leads a number of studies examining equity, ethical, and safety issues associated with this global health services practice.

Léo-Paul Dana read his BA and MBA degrees at McGill University and his PhD from the Ecole des Hautes Etudes Commerciales, Montreal, Canada. He is professor at Montpellier Business School, France, and was formerly tenured at the University of Canterbury, New Zealand. He also served as visiting professor of entrepreneurship at INSEAD Business School and deputy director of the International Business MBA Programme at Nanyang Business School, both in Singapore. He has published extensively in many leading journals, including *British Food Journal, Cornell Quarterly, Entrepreneurship & Regional*

Development, Entrepreneurship, Theory & Practice, Journal of Small Business Management, Journal of World Business, and *Small Business Economics.* His research interests focus on cultural issues, including the internationalization of entrepreneurship and the nature of indigenous entrepreneurship. He is editor emeritus of the *Journal of International Entrepreneurship.* His recent edited projects include the *World Encyclopedia of Entrepreneurship.*

Michael Entwistle has been a visiting lecturer at Highlands College, Jersey, since 2006, leading two modules for the BSc social sciences degree program. His areas of academic interest include public policy and the governance of small islands/microstate jurisdictions. Originally qualified as a biomedical scientist in Bristol, UK, he coauthored chapters in a scientific publication. After taking up a post in Jersey, Channel Islands, he pursued management qualifications, gaining an MBA (health executive) from Keele University, UK, in 1998, and had responsibilities for Jersey's health policy and strategy. He moved from the health service to take up a post in international relations in Jersey's Chief Minister's Department in 2003 and is now Deputy Director in the new Ministry of External Relations, with particular responsibilities for implementing international sanctions and compliance with international aviation and maritime conventions.

Hermon Farahi is a prototypical polymath: artist, scholar, filmmaker, musician, designer and entrepreneur. He is the co-founder of Circle Group, an integrated creative agency. A cultural anthropologist cum agency creative director, he brings a rare academic expertise to the creative world. He completed an interdisciplinary Master's Degree in Anthropology, International Development Studies and Documentary Filmmaking at George Washington University, USA. He has conducted ethnographic research and directed documentary films in challenging environments in many developing countries, working with indigenous communities, Fortune 500 companies, and international organizations. He has published research on Sub-Saharan African migration in Morocco, and directed creative campaigns and documentary film for clients that include the World Bank and USAID. An active adventurer, Hermon recently filmed the journey to Mt. Everest with The Love Hope Strength Cancer Foundation; and shot a documentary with aboriginal communities in the Arctic. Hermon is currently an affiliate with George Washington University's Global Gender Program.

Katarina Fellman is head of research at Statistics and Research Åland (ÅSUB) Åland Islands. She has a master's degree in social sciences and holds degrees in economics. She has been responsible for a wide range of research projects within regional development, demography, knowledge economy, entrepreneurship, economic growth, labor market, and evaluation of policy measures and has published many reports and book chapters. She is especially interested in comparative studies and in combining quantitative and qualitative research methods. Through the work of the Åland Islands Peace Institute, where she is member of the board of directors, she is also engaged in research in the fields of autonomy, minorities, and integration. She is a member of Nordregio board of directors, an international Nordic research institute in the field of regional studies.

Nick Haddow is the owner of Bruny Island Cheese Co., a business located on Bruny Island, off the southeast coast of Tasmania, Australia. His business has received several awards, including the 2013 Telstra Australian Business of the Year and Small Business of the Year. Nick has had a long fascination with the unique economies and communities of islands; his work and travels have taken him to many islands around the world. He was awarded a Winston Churchill Memorial Fellowship in 2013 to investigate the use of destination branding as a driver for economic and community development in small island economies, which was carried out in Iceland, Shetlands, Prince Edward Island, and the islands off British Columbia. In his capacity as a cheese maker, he has been awarded the Prud Homme Medal from the International Guilde du Fromage (2013), the Goddard Sapin-Jaloustre Trust Scholarship (2004), the ISS/Richard Pratt Fellowship (2006), and a Queen's Trust Scholarship (1995). Nick is a member of the Brand Tasmania Council and is on the board of several community and professional organizations. Nick also has a busy media career as copresenter of the very successful *Gourmet Farmer* television series and has coauthored two books on food.

Gestur Hovgaard is associate professor and director of studies in social sciences at the University of the Faroe Islands. He holds a master's degree in public administration and a PhD in social science from Roskilde University, Denmark. He has been a researcher and director at the Centre for Local and Regional Development (Faroe Islands) and assistant professor in business administration at Roskilde University. His publications cover local and regional development and planning, innovation, and public-sector organization, mainly in a North Atlantic context. His recent research focuses on educational planning, work-related mobility, and social history of the Faroe Islands.

Rory Johnston is a PhD candidate in the Department of Geography at Simon Fraser University, Canada. A health services researcher, his work focuses on the challenges arising from internationalizing health systems and the uptake of medical tourism as a policy direction among Caribbean health planners and providers.

Ilan Kelman is a reader in risk, resilience and global health at University College London, UK, and senior research fellow at the Norwegian Institute of International Affairs, Oslo, Norway. His overall research interest is linking disasters and health, including the integration of climate change, into disaster and health research. He covers three main areas of inquiry: disaster diplomacy and health diplomacy, island sustainability involving safe and healthy communities in isolated locations, and risk education for health and disasters. His books, papers, and chapters include these topics as well as climate change adaptation, disaster anthropology, infrastructure damage from natural hazards, tourism research, and postdisaster shelter and settlement.

Jouko Kinnunen is researcher with Statistics and Research Åland (ÅSUB), Åland Islands. He gained his doctoral degree in economics in 2005 from Aalto University School of Business. Before joining ÅSUB in 1997, he worked for several Finnish research institutes and for the United Nations International Drug Control Program in Bolivia and Austria. Apart from doing research and statistics on the economy of Åland, he has participated in several national and international research projects as an expert in computable general equilibrium modeling. The countries covered by his research include Finland, Sweden, Uganda, Moldova, and Pakistan.

Bjarne Lindström (PhLic) is the outgoing director of Statistics and Research Åland (ÅSUB), Åland Islands. During his professional career, he has worked as a regional planner, lecturer, researcher, and policy advisor. He has been assistant professor at the Department of Regional Planning, Royal Institute of Technology (KTH) in Stockholm and the director of the Nordic Institute of Regional Research (NordREFO) in Stockholm and Copenhagen. He has held positions as a member of a number of international and Scandinavian expert groups, research program committees, scientific councils, and assessment teams on regional and urban policy. He has also been responsible for appraisals of research projects/programs submitted to the national research council of Norway. He has evaluated EU programs and national growth policies in Åland, Sweden, and Denmark. His research focuses on spatial development and regional policy issues in connection with theories of region building and regional autonomy.

Colin S. Mellor is a chartered professional engineer and international consultant with long years of professional experience on major economic/ infrastructure projects, trade/investment planning, and policy analysis in many parts of the world. He is an experienced team leader, in addition to undertaking numerous specialist team member roles. He has successfully undertaken an extensive range of professional consulting assignments with international and regional agencies (AusAID, ADB, AfDB, World Bank, IFC, UNDP, FAO, UNCTAD, UNIDO, ILO, USAID, EC, EIB, DFID, ComSec, KfW, JICA, CIDA, NZAid, ForumSec, ASEAN, ESCAP, SPC), governments (national, provincial, local), NGOs, and the private sector.

Keith Nurse is the executive director of UWI Consulting Inc. and the incumbent World Trade Organization Chair at the University of the West Indies (UWI). He is the former director of the Shridath Ramphal Centre (SRC) for International Trade Law, Policy and Services, UWI, Barbados, and formerly taught at the Institute of International Relations and the University of Ottawa, Canada. He currently lectures on trade policy and innovation governance at the SRC and the Arthur Lok Jack Graduate School of Business (Trinidad and Tobago). He has published scholarly articles and books on a broad range of topics including trade policy, migration and diasporas, creative economy, tourism, innovation governance, and climate change. He is former president of the Association of Caribbean Economists and founding member of the World Economics Association. Dr. Nurse has served as consultant and advisor to several governments and regional and international organizations, including the WTO Chairs program, the ACP/IOM Intra-regional Migration Observatory, the MA in Technology Governance at the University of Tallinn, Estonia, and the OECD Knowledge Networks and Markets project. He is executive producer of the documentary *Forward Home: The Power of the Caribbean Diaspora*, which has been screened to wide acclaim at multiple festivals, events, and organizations around the world.

Michael J. Oliver is senior lecturer in finance at the Open University, UK, cofounder of Global Partnership Family Offices, associate of Lombard Street Research (which boasts some of the most original, rigorous, and consistently accurate comment and analysis on the world's markets), and member of the advisory board of the Official Monetary and Financial Institutions Forum. Michael has spent almost 25 years teaching at various universities in the UK, France, and the United States. He has combined this with a practical application of finance and economics to offer executive education, workshops, and a broad range of consultancy for high-profile corporations and family offices. Michael is also an economic advisor to the corporate services scrutiny panel on the island jurisdiction of Jersey, where he lives. He has published extensively on macroeconomic policy, exchange rate regimes, and monetary history. His edited book *Economic Disasters of the Twentieth Century* (2007) has attracted widespread critical acclaim.

Karen L. Orengo Serra is professor of international business at the Graduate School of Business Administration, University of Puerto Rico, Río Piedras Campus, USA. Her research interests deal with the internationalization of SMEs, business networks, and family entrepreneurship. She holds a PhD from the Université de la Sorbonne, France. She serves as member of the International Editorial Board of the *Journal of Small Business Management*. Her most recent work is published in the *Journal of Innovation Management in Small & Medium Enterprise* (2013), *ACRN Journal of*

Entrepreneurship Perspectives (2013), *AD-minister* (2012), and *Small Enterprise Research Journal* (2010), Her books include *Empresas Puertorriquenas a la Hora de La Integracion Regional* (2007) and *L'Industrie Pharmaceutique dans l'Economie de Porto Rico* (2012).

Richard Palmer is a researcher at Statistics and Research Åland (ÅSUB), Åland Islands. He received his PhD in economic history at Stockholm University in 2001 and worked there as a researcher before assuming his current position in 2005. His research has been in the areas of long-term globalization of businesses from small, open economies. In his current position, he carries out applied economic research commissioned by the government of Åland, and he has recently studied the economic and demographic development of the Nordic autonomies. His publications include *Historical Patterns of Globalization: The Growth of Outward Linkages of Swedish Longstanding Transnational Corporations, 1980s–1990s* (2001); *Outpost, Land in Between, Bridge* (2009, with S. Spiliopoulou-Åkerberg and others); and *The Significance of Duty-Free Sales on Board Ferries and the Transnational Transport System in the Baltic Sea Region* (2011, with B. Lindström).

James E. Randall is professor and coordinator of the master of arts (island studies) program at the University of Prince Edward Island, Charlottetown, Canada. He has held numerous academic administrative positions at three Canadian universities, including serving as vice-president academic, provost, dean and head. While at the University of Saskatchewan, he was cofounder and codirector of the Community-University Institute for Social Research. His academic credentials are in economic and human geography. He teaches and publishes in the subject areas of island studies, economic geography, quality-of-life indicators, community economic development, and the role of universities in communities.

Cheney Shreve is a senior research assistant for the TACTIC (Tools, Methods and Training for Communities and Society to better prepare for a Crisis) project at Northumbria University, UK. Her primary research interests center around questions of scale and interdisciplinary methods for engaging in human–environment and disasters research. She has a research background in environmental sciences, remote sensing/geographical information systems, and climate and vulnerability topics. She has also published on cost-benefit analysis for disaster risk reduction.

Runólfur Smári Steinþórsson is professor of strategy and management and head, School of Business, University of Iceland. He led the establishment of graduate studies at the School of Business and is cofounder and former director of its executive MBA program. He is currently chairman of the Nordic Academy of Management, the Center of Strategy and Competitiveness,

University of Iceland, and the editorial board of *The Icelandic Journal of Business and Economics*. Recent publications include a book chapter in *Advancing Research on Projects and Temporary Organizations* (Editors: Rolf Lundin and Markus Hällgren) on relating temporary organizations to strategy concepts (2014) and articles in the *Icelandic Review of Politics and Administration*: "Do Reactions to Volcanic Eruptions Give Insight Into Crisis Management: An Example From Icelandair" (2013, with Regína Ásdísardóttir); *Organizational Structure in Icelandic Companies 2004– 2007* (2012, with Einar Svansson), and *Strategy in Icelandic Organizations* (2011, with Ingi Rúnar Eðvarðsson and Helgi Gestsson). Runólfur Smári holds a Cand. Oecon degree from the University of Iceland and a Cand. Merc and PhD in business administration from Copenhagen Business School, Denmark.

Sopheap Theng is a PhD candidate in economics and tourism studies at the Université des Antilles, French West Indies. Her research focuses on strategies for tourism development in island and coastal areas, with comparative approaches between Southeast Asia and the Lesser Antilles. She works on planning, positioning, and attractiveness of tourist destinations. She is involved in the setting up of an observatory of experimental tourism in small Caribbean island territories. She is also secretary of *Caribbean Studies Journal*. Her recent publications focus on the relationship among cruise tourism, poverty, and luxury goods in the context of community development. Recently published papers include *Destination Saint-Barth: Lorsque le luxe s'invite* (2014), *Cruise Tourism: Global Logic and Asian Perspectives* (2014, with O. Dehoorne & C. Tatar), and *Tourisme et pauvreté: Le champ des possibles* (2014, with O. Dehoorne & C. Tatar).

Ricardo Chi Sen Siu is associate professor of business economics at the University of Macau, Macao Special Administrative Region, China. He served as the program coordinator of economics and international finance (2001– 2004) and gaming management (2005–2009), as well as the acting head of the Department of Finance and Business Economics (2011–2012) at the Faculty of Business Administration of the University of Macau. He is an internationally known scholar in the field of casino gaming, specializing in the areas of public policy and evolution of casino gaming in Macao and other Asian jurisdictions. His scholarly articles have appeared in the *Journal of Economic Issues, Journal of Gambling Studies, International Gaming Studies, Journal of Gambling Business and Economics, UNLV Gaming Research and Review Journal, Gaming Law Review, Economics, Casino & Gaming International*, and *The Oxford Handbook of the Economics of Gambling*.

Rebecca Whitmore is an MA candidate in the Department of Geography at Simon Fraser University, Canada. Her MA research is focused on learning more about the caregiving experiences of the friends and family members who accompany medical tourists abroad. She is also a member of the SFU Medical Tourism Research Group and assisted with a project examining health equity impacts of medical tourism in Barbados.

IpKin Anthony Wong is an assistant professor at the Institute for Tourism Studies, Macau. His current research interests include tourism and hospitality marketing, service quality management, international marketing, corporate social responsibility, green marketing and tourism, casino management and gambling behaviors, branding and destination image, and human resource management. He has authored more than 100 publications as referred journal articles, book chapters, and conference papers, including those that have appeared in *Tourism Management, Journal of Travel Research, Journal of Business Research, Journal of Sustainable Tourism, International Journal of Hospitality Management, Journal of Hospitality & Tourism Research, International Journal of Contemporary Hospitality Management,* and *Journal of Travel & Tourism Marketing.* He serves as coordinating editor of *International Journal of Hospitality Management.* He is on the editorial boards of *Cornell Hospitality Quarterly* and *International Journal of Contemporary Hospitality Management.*

1 Editorial

Small Island States and Territories: Vulnerable, Resilient, but Also Doggedly Perseverant and Cleverly Opportunistic

Godfrey Baldacchino

INTRODUCTION

This introduction frames this volume in the context of the unfolding literature about small island states and territories: "small" here meaning having resident populations of up to 1 million. This collection argues for a *more* optimistic ontology of the small island state and territory: one that departs from an acknowledgement of a savvy, smart, and entrepreneurial resident population and institutions and government that nimbly exploit the opportunities provided by small size and islandness, as and when they may arise. The "more" is an important signifier here. It would be rash and irresponsible to discount the many ways in which most states and territories navigate a world in which they must willy-nilly either accept decisions taken elsewhere and/or bear the brute force of natural or economic events that can have catastrophic consequences. However, the literature has been driven so much by such considerations of economic and environmental vulnerability that even increasingly more proactive talk of resilience and capacity building departs from the structural doom and gloom of given handicaps. For a change, and hopefully a *welcome* change, this volume will stand out by bucking this trend. Here, islandness and smallness, along with the often associated attributes of remoteness and peripherality, will be shown to serve *also* as opportunities, qualities that permit some island-based businesses to emerge, thrive, and survive.

Agreed: a swallow does not make a summer: a few cases of success and a few entrepreneurial islanders leading them need not infer that the overall negative assessment of the predicament of the small island jurisdiction is unwarranted. And one should take note that even some of the principles of the so-called successes can be questioned and their morality debated (Kelman & Shreve, this volume). Does selling postage stamps, offering flags of convenience, or proposing money parking facilities, as many small island jurisdictions still do, constitute more than "pseudo development" strategies (Baldacchino, 1993)? But then, even larger mainland states have their own dubious practices. We should definitely not pick out small island candidates for special moral treatment.

In any case, it is high time to open a new paradigmatic front for contemplating the predicament of the small island state and territory. We do so at a time when the differences between small island *states* (most but not all under the UN–driven nomenclature of "small island developing states," or SIDS) and small island *territories* that enjoy a measure of political autonomy—what are referred to as "subnational island jurisdictions," or SNIJs—increasingly deserve a comparative ear and assessment (Baldacchino & Milne, 2009). Sovereignty and independent statehood have created a rationale for looking at states *qua* states. However, various recent practices have eroded what may have appeared as a clear dividing line between SIDS and SNIJs. Measures of political autonomy and rights of diplomatic representation granted to nonsovereign jurisdictions, from the Cook Islands to Greenland, from the Isle of Man to Bermuda, and from Montserrat to Hong Kong, can rival the suite of decision-making powers held by states even as notionally sovereign states themselves surrender powers to larger national or supranational entities (as with Nauru becoming a *de facto* suzerainty of Australia in processing the latter's asylum seekers; or with various countries becoming members of trade blocs or economic communities like the European Union). This is why this scholarly collection compares and contrasts examples from SIDSs and SNIJs together, possibly for the first and hopefully not for the last time.

ISLAND ENTREPRENEURSHIP

An entrepreneur is a person who, driven by urge and opportunity, conceives and manages a business idea and assumes its risk, often for the sake of profit (Guralnik, 1980). This definition, however, tells us nothing about how this practice may play out in particular geographical, regional, socioeconomic, or cultural contexts. Nor does it tell us whether the act of being an entrepreneur renders this activity exceptional, habitual, or anywhere in between for the members of a particular social group. Are entrepreneurial skills really scarce by definition? And can the experience, nature, and overall challenges of entrepreneurship be somehow patterned in terms of scale and geographical context?

The focus of our particular concern here is with small island jurisdictions, be they states or territories. These often have to contend with various implications of their islandness when it comes to "doing business": limited land area and finite resources; limited domestic markets and client bases; a physical isolation that implies that significant transport costs come into play in order to access distant alternative markets or source raw material; and with local consumer tastes—often managed by a powerful local mercantile elite—that prefer metropolitan imports to locally made commodities. Even where small island jurisdictions have good-quality and competitive products, there may be difficulties in securing effective research and development capability, skilled human resources, suitable terms for financing, and/or appropriate technology. Moreover, a more common strategy and attitude among islanders is to favor *intra*preneurship, in which individuals seek to become innovative and creative *within* the confines and protection of an existing public or private organization (Armstrong et al., 1993; Dolman, 1985; Doumenge, 1985, p. 86; Encontre, 1999; Fischer & Encontre, 1998; Payne, 1987). Note that these observations apply generally to *all* island societies, increasingly so with decreasing size of the resident island population, and irrespective of whether these islands are listed as having developed or developing economies.

BEYOND INTRINSIC VULNERABILITY

Even with the inherent benefits of modern information and communication technologies, setting up and operating a business from a small island jurisdiction involves specific challenges. The given conditions of isolation, remoteness, marginalization, absence of economies of scale, tightly networked communities, the obligation to export or perish, and ubiquitous (often meddlesome) government, in their various combinations and with their various implications, do not simply melt away just because we are living in a digital age. Indeed, recent decades have been progressively *concentrating* development, privileging metropoles and city-regions (Danson & De Souza, 2012, pp. 11–12). Meanwhile, the "development" agenda of small island states has been gripped by a paradigm of vulnerability for at least three decades, though a recognition of resilience has now become mainstream (Briguglio & Cordina, 2004; Briguglio & Kisanga, 2004). Such disarming discourse vindicates the concerns of many observers and scholars with the presumed nonviability of small island polities and economies, expressed both before and after the wave of small state sovereignty took off in the 1960s (Cyprus in 1960; [Western] Samoa in 1962; Malta in 1964; Maldives in 1965) and also propelled by the collapse of the West Indies Federation (starting with the independence of Jamaica in 1962). Independence for the small island territory was deemed extravagant or dangerous (Commonwealth Consultative Group, 1985; Diggines, 1985; Harden, 1985) and even a recipe for a "failed state" (Kabutaulaka, 2004) or a "security threat" (Griffith, 2004).

So much talk about inherent vulnerability has its limits. With challenges also come opportunities. When wealth is defined in GNP or GDP (at purchasing power parity) standards, and in spite of how badly such statistical tools serve small islands, many small island states and territories score exceptionally well. In their analytic critiques, Armstrong and colleagues (1998, p. 644), Easterly and Kraay (2000, p. 2015), and Armstrong and Read (2002) agree that small (and mainly island) jurisdictions actually perform economically *better* than larger (mainly continental) states. Comparative research has also shown that nonsovereign island territories tend to be richer *per capita* than sovereign ones (Bertram, 2004; Poirine, 1998). Most of these nonsovereign territories benefit from some form of stable *asymmetrical federalism* with(in) a much larger state (Stevens, 1977). It should come as no surprise, therefore, that most of the world's lingering imperial remnants—places like Aruba, Bermuda, the Cook Islands, and Puerto Rico—would much rather prefer autonomy within the purview of a larger, richer state than fully fledged independence, with the associated glamour and prestige but also the economic threats and insecurities that this status brings (Baldacchino, 2010).

Rather than playing out as remote, vulnerable, and dependent backwaters of neocolonialism, the world's small island jurisdictions—consisting of some 35 sovereign states and around 110 territories (each with resident populations of less than 1 million)—do show considerable resourcefulness in facing up to the very real challenges of their predicament. The creative endeavors of their residents, facilitated by adroit public policy, have created economic and investment opportunities that translate into private-sector employment and decent livelihoods for many. Their ingenuity (at national, sectoral, and household levels), coupled with strategic investments, the support of the island diaspora, and perhaps some doses of good fortune and serendipity, has led to a suite of (sometimes unlikely) products and services being developed, marketed, and sold or rented. These range from citizenship schemes and rents from top-level Internet domain names to place-branded foods and beverages, from electronic gaming to niche manufacturing, and from processed fish products to offshore finance. As Dana wryly observes (epilogue, this volume), there is much more to small island survival than subsistence farming, aid, remittances, and public sector workfare. This book will help to dispel this myth, showcasing an aspect of life in small island states and territories that is rarely documented or critically reviewed but is (we think) worth celebrating.

THE STATE OF PLAY

While the notion of a small state is an old one, and most jurisdictions have been small for much of recorded history, very few of these are known to have been small islands or island clusters. The exceptions have been places like Venice, Crete, and Tonga, which were island-based maritime powers in their respective regions.[1] And so practically all small islands entered the 20th century as appendages to larger political blocks. Iceland was the pioneer small island state, securing its independence from Nazi-occupied Denmark during the Second World War in 1944, and became the first of 35 independent postcolonial island states (at the time of writing) with populations of less than five million, and with 28 of these having resident populations below even the 1 million mark.[2] Iceland remains very much the exception of this family of small island states, being to this day the world's only cold-water island state. All the others are located in temperate or tropical zones. *Most of these small island states secured independence following a long period of* colonialism, and they have been thus categorized by the international community as SIDSs.[3] We say "most" because four fairly successful European small, postcolonial island states—Cyprus, Malta, Iceland, along with not-as-small Ireland—plus archipelagic New Zealand, are *not* considered as SIDSs. Meanwhile, around 100 subnational island jurisdictions (SNIJs) persist as lingering fragments of empire (Bermuda, Caymans, Falklands, French Polynesia, Montserrat, St. Pierre et Miquelon, Turks and Caicos, Pitcairn, Wallis et Futuna), special components of larger states (Åland, American Samoa, Channel Islands, Cook Islands, Hong Kong, Isle of Man, Jeju, Macao, Okinawa), or island jurisdictions of large, continental federated states (Hawai'i, Prince Edward Island, Tasmania). Enjoying varying levels of autonomy and self-determination, a few of these island jurisdictions may yet become independent (Baldacchino & Milne, 2009).

But *only four* small island territories have actually secured full sovereignty since Brunei did so on January 1, 1984. (These countries include East Timor, independent since 2002, and whose resident population has exceeded 1 million since 2006, should we wish to include that case; the other three cases—Palau, Marshall Islands, and Federated States of Micronesia—are discussed in what follows). This factual observation merits some careful scrutiny, since there is neither a shortage of candidates nor a reticence from the lingering colonial powers—particularly Denmark, the Netherlands, and the United Kingdom—to judge this motley set of candidates as fit to graduate to sovereignty. Indeed, while a comparative quantitative analysis reveals that SIDSs exhibit better economic indicators than larger developing states (e.g., Anklesaria Aiyar, 2008; Armstrong et al., 1998; Easterly & Kraay, 2000; Rezvani, 2014), SNIJs are even more economically developed, socially advanced, and demographically progressive than independent small island states. McElroy and Pearce (2006) suggest that this differential performance is perhaps best encapsulated in the disparate migration experiences characteristic of the two distinct small island profiles. On the one hand, the average independent island state is typically a society experiencing slow economic growth, labor surplus, and chronic out-migration. On the other hand, the typical SNIJ is an immigrant society with labor shortages and which benefits from being attached to a larger and richer metropolitan power.

AN IMPRESSIVE CREATIVITY

Most small island states continue to impress with a wily and adroit commercialization of "resources" that boggles the mind. These include bilateral and multilateral aid, offshore banking and financial services, the receipt of remittances, the sale of citizenship, Internet domains, philately, generic drugs, aggressively place-branded food and drink, plus various rent-driven geostrategic services (tourism, second-home residences, telecommunications infrastructure, military bases, detention facilities, transshipment depots . . .). Many such revenue-generating schemes were already in place by the early 1990s. For small island states and territories, life continues to be a scramble to exploit one niche or opportunity, then another, moving as nimbly as possible from one to the next or from one crisis to the next as one dries up and (hopefully) another presents itself (Baldacchino, 2009; Guillaumont, 2010). There is no elegant progression from primary to secondary to tertiary economic activity; no evolution of economic capacity; no macro-level diversification; no hoped-for economic viability as may have been envisaged by industrialization-led development models. The "input-output" Leontief tables of these jurisdictions, if they appear at all as part of their economic statistics, are largely composed of empty cells. With very few exceptions, industrialization strategies in small island states have failed (e.g., Kaplinsky, 1983). Generic environmental, economic, and social problems ensue from a dependence on producing a narrow range of cash crops—the typical suspects being banana, cocoa, coffee, copra, ginger, guano/phosphate, sugar, tobacco, and vanilla—for sale in the world economy, plus out-migration and remittances, and foreign aid. For many small island states, opportunities for development are typically regarded as minimal because of fragile ecosystems and a shortage of land, fresh water, and local energy supplies (Macpherson, 2000). These were not just Lilliputian actors on the world stage; they were minnows who defied the logic of economic development and transitioned as best they could from one calamity to another, often with very limited formal private-sector activity; hardly a recipe for "sustainable development" (Bertram, 1986). They eked an existence as MIRAB economies, also called MIRAGE economies: household-to-household MIgration, which fuels Remittances; and state-to-state Aid that supports a Bureaucracy, or Government Expenditure (or Employment) (Bertram & Watters, 1985; Connell, 1991). Was this existential bubble about to burst? Could anything better than "aid with dignity" (Connell, 1988) be secured and save these jurisdictions some embarrassment?

NEGATIVITY GALORE

Small island states were met with considerable skepticism by the established great powers in the post–Second World War and Cold War epochs; their presumed economic viability was clearly in doubt, and their naiveté in messing up the global and high-stakes superpower game was of concern (Keohane, 1969; Plischke, 1977). Meanwhile, given their sheer numbers on the world stage, and especially at the United Nations and a number of its agencies, small island states received collective recognition (as SIDSs): they secured their own version of the 1992 "Agenda 21" Rio Summit and aftermaths (in Barbados in 1994, Mauritius in 2005, Samoa in 2014) and enhanced their global visibility in the context of climate-change debates, thanks to the setting up and lobbying of the 39-full-member Alliance of Small Island States (AOSIS) as from 1991, and so well documented at, for example, the COP

15 meeting in Copenhagen in 2009 (Parker et al., 2012). The tone of such historical commentary, championed by such agencies as the United Nations Development Program (UNDP) and the Commonwealth Secretariat, has been particularly one of a deep-rooted vulnerability and fragility predicated on islandness and small scale, somewhat toned down later with some recognition of agency, resilience, capacity building, and otherwise good governance as the suitable human and institutional response to such a structural, chronic, and irrevocable weakness. "Descriptions of islands as fragile, small, peripheral and dependent are often taken for granted, reiterated within a discourse of 'vulnerability'" (Amoamo, 2011, p. 69).

It is easy to accept the deterministic mantra of small island state vulnerability. An unavoidable openness to all things external (markets, prices, investments, tourists, financiers, environmental hazards, military invasions, epidemics, and now global warming and sea level rise) renders such small island jurisdictions inherently fragile and highly elastic, liable to large oscillations of economic fortune and collapse. There are no cushions, no robust economic differentiation, no economies of scale, no physical, economic, or psychological hinterland to absorb any such shocks: a dismal string of deficit discourse. Any economic graph would show dizzy ups and downs, phenomenally steep booms and troughs, often traceable to discrete events: the purchase of a ship, the bankruptcy of a cannery, the closure of a military base (Carse, 1998). Their higher per-capita economic indicators were illusory; they could plummet overnight with the arrival of a hurricane, a bad harvest, or the departure of a major investment. The records for the highest and lowest per-capita income enjoyed by any sovereign state in the world are held by the same small island state: Nauru (Connell, 2006a; Gowdy & McDaniel, 1999).

The deficit and belittling discourse surrounding the representation of such islands—and their citizens—lends credence to these enduring negative tropes. Small island states have been summarily "aestheticized, sanitized and anaesthetized" (Connell, 2003, p. 568), weighed down by the multiple baggage of paradise (an unspoiled Eden waiting to be discovered and consumed), exoticity (a sensuous and lush natural and human garden that effuses pleasure) but also alarmism and fragility (high-risk environments, with fickle livelihoods, so: handle with care) . . . These are seemingly contradictory tropes, yet all may be deemed necessary to fulfill the promise of tourism for visitors and to instruct donors about the deceptive basis of any local economic wealth. Small island states suffer—just as they do on maps— the imperial arrogance and paternalism of those who would either neglect them—the tyranny of exclusion—or else paint them in bizarre hues—the tyranny of the inset. All too often, one is here faced with a situation in which the *subject* matter—the island, the islander, the islanders—becomes *object* matter: a "looked at" reference group; stages for the enactment of processes dictated from elsewhere; mere props of various *dei ex machina*, so many Gullivers landing in Lilliput and becoming self-appointed experts on domestic affairs (Warrington, 1998). These would have been mainly explorers, missionaries, traders, or colonial administrators in the past, but they have now been replaced by consultants, economists, and journalists in more recent years, and now climatologists (Baldacchino, 2008, pp. 38–39). In a recent book that reviews island environments and economies, the reader can be quite overwhelmed by the continuous assault of negative language on the senses, whether in the form of dramatic action nouns (collapses, catastrophes, departures, eruptions, extinctions, extirpations, hazards, insecurities, threats, uncertainties) or in the form of adjectives (absent, corrupt, lacking, powerless, unsustainable, vulnerable, weak). No fault of the author: all these words are lifted from the titles of the books, reports, and articles listed in the reference section (Connell, 2013).

The hyperbole may have gotten even worse of late, with the looming doomsday scenarios exacerbated by the effects of sea level rise. The discourse of drowning, disappearing, and sinking has been added to the litany of woes. A sinister, hedonistic, and bizarre dark tourism marketing has emerged, encouraging visitors to visit places like the Maldives before they cannot be visited any more: "So come here fast, before it disappears. This is a paradise faced with extinction," proposes a BBC journalist (Bryant, 2004). In the process, long-haul tourists contribute to the same greenhouse gases that are causing the waters to expand and rise. This is victimization writ large: small, fragile islanders facing the inexorable impact of "development": not so much their own but that of the developed world and industrializing countries with their high-carbon footprints. The locals are not always amused (e.g., Farbotko, 2010, on Tuvalu); and the current near-obsession with "sustainable development" and its focus on "livable futures" does not always pay adequate attention to what may be more pressing issues for a livable present (Baldacchino & Kelman, 2014). Indeed, the official script in the Maldives has now changed: the current president is arguing that the island country *can* be saved: talk about the inevitability of sinking had been scaring away most foreign investment (*Orange County Register*, 2012).

Such small island states and their communities continue to survive. Granted, they seem to be bobbing up and down, not moving forward. But nor are they moving back, lapsing to some kind of doomsday scenario. The development bubble has not burst—well, not yet. Even tiny Pitcairn, the world's smallest jurisdiction—with a population of 51, at the last count—and which has been expected to fold up some years back (Connell, 1988; Winchester, 2003)—is still in business, is contemplating a niche tourism industry (Amoamo, 2013), and may soon usher in the world's largest marine park (*The Economist*, 2013a).

ALTERNATIVE DEVELOPMENT TRAJECTORIES

Generalizations are odious, and I resort to them at my peril. However, small island states appear to survive in the 21st century mainly because of a combination of factors that can be still described as "pseudodevelopment" strategies that nevertheless generate revenue and support livelihoods. Small island states have shied away from a commitment to industrialization, with only Barbados, Fiji, Malta, and Mauritius having some success there, while others have tried to lure foreign industrial capital but only managed to do so for a limited time at best. Instead, they have found themselves pursuing some very different alternative development routes. These include (1) heavy international out-migration, often circular or cyclical, which supports sustained remittance transfers (increasingly important, as aid has fallen to record historic lows); (2) rich and vibrant subsistence and noncash economies, which provide safeguards and welfare nets; (3) the export of niche products, including some manufactures, that secure high value added in select export markets; (4) tourism, in its various forms and segments beyond mass market generics; and (5) other "geostrategic rents" and including offshore finance, in spite of the strong attacks this sector has faced of late from the governments of cash- and tax-starved, developed countries. Overall, we are talking about a deployment of what Foucault (1991a) calls "governmentality" in the judicious management of extraterritorial opportunities (Baldacchino, 2012b). By this, we mean a "strategy game" whereby small island states and territories play out their international relations, especially with respect to one particular larger and richer country (typically, their current or former colonial power and/or the regional hegemon) and to the federal and regional entities and agreements of which they form part (Rezvani, 2014). Small island states and subnational island jurisdictions are, in this context, both victims and actors of these "procedures, techniques and methods" (Foucault, 1991b, p. 75). Different spaces are constituted as policy fields, and different agents and target groups are assembled as amenable to being "worked on." Thus, even a mini-jurisdiction like Pitcairn has been able to survive, mainly by its successful claims and overtures—what Foucault would call "bio-politics'—to British taxpayers, American stamp collectors, and Filipino sailors: "the only cash economy of Pitcairn is the sale of stamps and the sale of handicrafts to passing ships" (Ridgell, 1995, p. 149).

Let us now move from theory and rhetoric to actual examples. We do so by examining the main sectors that comprise the economies of small island states and territories, starting with the extraterritorial link, represented by migration (outward or circular) and remittances, followed by the nonmonetized sector and the practice of economies of scope. Next are local products meant for export: these would traditionally be cash crops or fish; but, ideally, products that involve some processing and higher value added and that thus command higher prices in niche markets. Tourism is the next sector: such an important driver on its own right and with strong economic linkages with various other activities. Finally, a consideration of "intangibles": services that have no weight and occupy no physical space and are thus not handicapped by small size, islandness, and remoteness and which are somehow connected to an island's geostrategic location and specificity. In all these cases, we are reminded that there is no economics, only political economy (Bertram & Poirine, 2007): the identification and exploitation of particular economic activities is as much a result of creative endeavor and risk taking on the part of island entrepreneurs as of opportunistic and flexible politicians or state officials who craft suitably attractive policy and regulatory tools in support (Baldacchino and Bertram, 2009).

Migration and Remittances

Intranational or international emigration often becomes the response to the gamut of economic vulnerabilities faced by small islands. Labor becomes the "monocrop" to be exported to the global market, possibly replacing cash crops (e.g., Schneider & Schneider, 1976). For the world's smaller islands, the end result is often a MIRAB economic model in which islanders survive thanks to the remittances transferred by emigrants from abroad and the state aid flows that support the domestic public bureaucracy and its wage bill (Bertram, 2006; Bertram & Poirine, 2007; Bertram & Watters, 1985).

Moreover, high population density and its strain on finite resources (land, water, beaches, energy) along with the intense psychosocial atmosphere in which everybody may know everybody else may reach a tipping point, aligning elements of the local population to consider or crave emigration, for work, education, or just freedom and adventure (Connell, 2007; King, 2009, p. 58). Most islands would today have a diaspora more numerous than the resident population. Many first-generation emigrants would maintain close ties with their island of birth, especially the family they left behind. They send substantial remittances, write emails, connect via social media, smart phone, and Skype, send gift packages, and visit as frequently as possible (Connell & King, 1999). These migrants are therefore very much socially present in these island societies, being part of wide-ranging fields of relations and investments that extend from islands of origin to overseas migration destinations. From a social and economic point of view, therefore, island territories should not be viewed as isolated archipelagos surrounded by the sea but rather as critical anchors in vast webs of relations linking migrant and local islanders. These webs are flexible, resilient, and adaptive, being based on personal interrelationships of loyalty and obligation toward close kin yet also premised on the somewhat contradictory feelings of strong emotional attachments to island homes on the part of migrants and possibly equally strong desires to explore global opportunities on the part of those left behind. For many generations, this sea of relationships has made small islands what they are, and it is likely to continue to do so in the future (Olwig, 1993). Return migration may cushion the long-term demographic and economic decline somewhat, but much depends on the age of the returnees, the financial and human capital they bring back, and what they earmark it for (King, 2009, p. 58). With low-cost airlines and dual citizenship, cyclical or circular migration is now increasingly common, as individuals try to strategically exploit the best of multiple worlds for themselves and their dependents (Baldacchino, 2006; Nurse, this volume).

Subsistence, Noncash, and Odd Jobs

Given the obvious absence of economies of scale, small islander behavior is often grounded in economies of scope and the flexible and opportunist operation in monetized, nonmonetized, public, and intermediate (gray) economies, both local and foreign, for economic gain.

Consider, for example, Isaac Caines, from the Caribbean island state of St. Kitts-Nevis (profiled in Richardson, 1983, pp. 54–55); Kawagl, from the Melanesian South Pacific (in Brookfield, 1972, pp. 67–68); and Marshy, a street vendor from Kingston, Jamaica (in Wardle, 2002). Each of the three has a broad skill set; yet would focus on a particular set of tasks at any point in time. Moreover, when looked at longitudinally, each of these individuals demonstrates an uncanny skill repertoire that includes entrepreneurship, public-sector employment, and stints abroad. "Flexible specialization" (Poon, 1990) and "multifunctionality" (Farrugia & Attard, 1989) are the key attributes of small island economies as much as of their constituent citizens, households, and firms (Baldacchino, 2001; Bertram & Poirine, 2007, p. 368; Schmitz, 1989). As Carnegie (1982, p. 12) observes:

> Even people with very secure jobs often have part-time occupations or get training in other trades to develop other marketable skills . . . It is commonplace to have several sources of income and systematically to maintain each one, even if some may bring in very little cash.

Thus, individuals, households, or business units strategically spread their risks, not in spite but *because* of the small economy's overall macro-dependence on one or a few exogenous sources of income. Any synchronic "snapshot" might easily suggest a precariously specialized economy; however, a diachronic "video" would reveal a more dynamic and diversified portfolio, with considerable articulations between formal and informal (including nonmonetized) activity. For more on "subsistence affluence," see Baldacchino and Mellor (this volume).

Local Products for Niche Export Markets

The next cluster of examples relates to *products whose essential raw materials are typically sourced locally* and therefore lend themselves to some clever branding that aligns the product to the island where it is made and to the tropes surrounding that island. Sourcing locally available ingredients—ranging from fruit, glass, grain, leather, sand, shell, skin, and stone to vegetables, wood, wool, even the waste products of other industries, such as agriculture and fisheries—means that such material is both less costly to secure (does not have to be imported, unlike much of everything else) and is more naturally aligned with the island brand and its evocations. Moreover, once this provenance is well defined, the final product—which could consist in just the raw material itself—can be addressed to specific niche markets, where it could command a higher price and a narrower clientele (including the island diaspora). "These [specialized niche] markets are based on differentiation, not cost/price; smaller producers with relatively high costs can be competitive, and sales of small numbers at high margins can be profitable (Punnett & Morrison, 2006, p. 351).

Iceland's long and proud association with the sea, its fisheries industry, and its maritime culture promote the branding of Iceland as a reliable provider of fish- or marine-related products and derivatives, as are the omega-3 marine oil products of **LYSI**. Moreover, the tourism industry in Iceland is also showing off its product as a unique destination with very high standards of natural beauty, purity, cleanliness, and general good health, all of which are useful sales pitches to **LYSI**'s health-related products (Aðalsteinsson & Steinþórsson, this volume). Another clear link with the sea and the availability of clean water at regular temperatures are at the basis of the winning climatic combination that now supports a thriving aquaculture industry for Atlantic salmon (*Salmo salar*) in the Faroe Islands. Within this sector, now globalized and fully vertically integrated, **Bakkafrost** is a dominant player; while **Luna**, via its brand name Hiddenfjord, seeks to target upscale consumers overseas with its gourmet products (Hovgaard, this volume). Similarly, Malta's tourism profile is heavily themed with notions of a hardworking and flexiskilled Mediterranean race; the skill involved in developing the decorative ware of **Mdina Glass** is thus a way of congealing in time both contemporary labor and its historical past, as are other products, such as gold and silver filigree or hand-crafted decorative lace (Baldacchino, 2005). Well-branded Barbados rum products—like **Mount Gay**—are more than a drink: they are a concept and a lifestyle; and this is clearly associated with the favorable, Caribbean "fun and frolic" sense of islandness that is attached to them and that is key to a successful enhancement of these brands and their competitiveness (Pounder, 2006). Tasmania's gentle climate, advantage of isolation, and tight regulations have secured it the production of the pharmaceutical industry's most important raw material: extract of the **opium poppy** (*Papaver somniferum*; Bradsher, 2014; Williams, 2010) as well as landing it the envious position of being able to export **tulips** *to* Amsterdam during the antipodean spring (Cica, 2010). **Fiji Water** is the second best-selling bottled water in the United States, after Evian. While the water is from Fiji, the company is not Fijian, however, and has run into problems with the Fijian state over its environmental record (Connell, 2006b; Kaplan, 2007). The Comoros is the world's leading producer of **ylang-ylang** (*Cananga odorata*), much of it finding its way to the fragrance Chanel N° 5, "the world's most famous perfume" (Mazzeo, 2011). Grenada produces one fifth of the world's total supply of nutmeg (*Myristica fragrans*), and this ingredient serves as the basis to various branded products (Nurse, this volume); Fair Isle sweaters, named after the island of their origin in Shetland, Scotland, were catapulted to upmarket status via an association with the British Royal Family, and they continue to fetch high prices (Butler, this volume). **Cultured pearls** from the black-lipped pearl oyster (*Pinctada margaritifera*) have been important sources of export revenue in various island jurisdictions, especially in the Pacific. Pearl farming can stem outer-island emigration and can provide critical economic alternatives. In the Federated States of Micronesia, pearl farming now complements the lost income that artisanal reef fishing communities have to incur with the introduction of no-fishing zones and marine protected areas. This new source of income has created an incentive for conservation by reducing pressure on reef fish stocks, and it is increasing the resilience of local communities in the face of climate change (Cartier et al., 2012). Locally produced (but not necessarily locally owned) **beers** from many small island states—from Samoa's **Vailima** (now owned by the Coca-Cola company) to **Kalik** in the Bahamas (owned by Heineken)—could easily represent the largest (or sole) locally owned manufacturing capacity in these jurisdictions and typically peddle an explicit affiliation with the island locality; they are sought after by locals, tourists, and the island diaspora (Baldacchino, 2010). In Fiji, small-scale farmers have contributed to the exports of **kava**, the dried root of the pepper plant (*Piper methysticum forster*) from which a slightly narcotic and anesthetic drink can be concocted. The product is increasingly used for medicinal purposes on a commercial scale. This venture has had positive benefits on farmer livelihoods (Prasad & Raj, 2006).

This list goes on and is getting lengthier: many governments and chambers of commerce (and not just on islands) are now promoting quality labels that identify local products in synch with the specific locality and *terroir* of their provenance. This association and "place branding" initiative, so much easier to conceive on islands, mainly applies to food items (olive oils, cheeses, pastries, fish, salad marinades, jam, honey) and beverages (wine, brandy, liqueurs, beer, whisky), as well as some cosmetics and health products, such as Ligne St. Barth from St. Barthélemy (Orengo Serra & Theng, this volume), clothing products, and many souvenirs. Many an island is already deeply wedded to an existing, iconic image typically connected to some locally available species, practice, craft, or material with high levels of local input. Agrofood and drink brands, in particular, seek a "valorization of milieu" (Amin & Thrift, 1992) by ". . . articulating and representing particular, spatially embedded cultural forms and meanings of goods and services as sources of value" (Pike, 2009, p. 194). Examples (apart from the ones already mentioned, and not just in terms of food and drink) include Bahamian conch, Chios mastic, Corsican *brocciu*, Faroese lamb, Gozo lace, Guernsey cows, Islay whisky, Kinmen knives, Shetland ponies, Texel sheep, and Trinidad hot sauce (Baldacchino, 2012a; Zhang, 2010).

These initiatives go beyond conventional import substitution, in which locally available products can replace more expensive exports, as with the use of coconut oil as biofuel in the Solomon Islands (Betzold, this volume). They also go beyond the exceptional cases of competitive high-tech companies, when their small island locations are at times felt best not to brag about (Baldacchino & Vella Bonnici, 2005; Randall, this volume).

Tourism

Niche product manufacture finds a significant partner in *tourism*: when tourists buy locally made island products, they incur the full costs, risk, and hassle of packaging and transportation involved in the product's export. Moreover, the evocative nature of specific island products is more likely to resonate with visitors who cherish this association and can connect with island products in a more immediate, multisensorial, and experiential manner. The products described in the previous section and other similar offerings may depend on such tourist markets—involving physical contact or via remote, online purchase—for their survival.

Meanwhile, tourism is now one of the world's largest and still-growing industries and an obvious attraction to small island states and territories that can flaunt their sea, sun, and sand credentials. It is claimed that tourism "offers the best chance for development in terms of creating growth and employment, generating foreign exchange and reducing poverty" (Croes, 2006, p. 455). So pervasive and dominant has tourism become that one of three general classifications of island economies has been called SITEs: small island tourist economies (McElroy & Hamma, 2010). And yet, the industry is highly sensitive to perceptions and acts of civil unrest and to shifts in investment flows; landscapes can be transformed and eroded with the arrival of too many guests; and local tourism may ironically depend on wide-ranging imports that span from furniture to food and expatriate management. In such cases, the local economy may largely benefit from a range of seasonal and low-skilled service jobs. Then there is competition: island destinations have sought to move away from a bland and generic coastal resort appeal—and its tough, cut-throat prices—that fails to distinguish one "sun, sand, and sea" jurisdiction from another, leaving each at the mercy of travel agents and low-cost airlines. Ecotourism, in places like the Azores, Dominica, and the Seychelles, offers a real opportunity for ". . . some kind of authentic, sustainable tourism strategy . . . in harmony with the island's society and environment" (Bishop, 2010, p. 109), and where what had been seen as backward and underdeveloped become strong green credentials (Ancharaz, 2014; Dehoorne & Tătar, 2013; Silva, 2013). Scuba diving in the Maldives (Sathiendrakumar & Tisdell, 1989), music tourism in Cape Verde (Carter & Aulette, 2009), "learning English as an additional language" tourism in Malta (Language Course, 2014), military tourism in the Falklands (Royle, 2006), cultural tourism in Guam (Farahi & Bevacqua, this volume), festival tourism in the Bahamas (Hampton & Jeyacheja, 2013), meetings and conventions tourism in Trinidad and Tobago, medical tourism in Barbados (Adams et al., this volume), and gaming and casino tourism in Macau (Wong & Siu, this volume)—these are just some of the many strategies resorted to by small island states and territories to carve out and exploit specific segments in the mature global or regional tourist market in order to rise above the noise of the competition while moving up the value chain (Lewis-Cameron & Roberts, 2010).

Geostrategic Rents

Another cluster of economic activity relates to *geostrategic economic rents*: revenue that accrues from the purchase or rent of property, facilities, or natural assets that secure consumer appeal and interest largely by virtue of their geographic location (e.g., Bertram & Poirine, 2007). Tourism is, in a way, one such industry, but it has become so rampant and sophisticated to warrant its separate entry here. Additional rent-generating activity includes second-home properties, military bases, detention centers, refueling stations, fishing licenses, shipping registries, communication facilities, test installations, transshipment sites, low-tax regimes, financial services, and Internet domain names. In many cases, an island jurisdiction that is poorly endowed in natural resources is more likely to pursue such an economic trajectory. In these and similar geostrategic services, extraterritorial clients use the island's location and its territorial integrity as a sovereign jurisdiction mainly to "park" assets, be they industrial or technological facilities, trawlers, ships, immigrants, military materiel, trendy business addresses, or corporate finance. Even in a post–Cold War era, the maintenance of military bases in various parts of the world, particularly for the United States, remains impressive at around 900 overseas bases (Lutz, 2009). Where small island states are concerned, this is especially so in the Middle East (with extensive U.S. facilities in Bahrain) and the Western Pacific (where the United States has the right to operate military bases in Palau, Marshall Islands, and the Federated States of Micronesia). Three percent of the land area of Cyprus consists of British Sovereign Bases, while Turkey maintains a military presence in North Cyprus. Over the course of a decade after the Second World War, the United States conducted scores of nuclear tests on the Bikini and Enewetak atolls, in the Marshall Islands. Bikini and neighboring Rongelap remain uninhabitable (DeLoughrey, 2013; *The Economist*, 2013b). The Tuvalu government secures considerable revenue from the sale of the use of its dot tv top-level Internet domain (Tasner, 2010; Wilson, 2001; Baldacchino & Mellor, this volume). Nauru runs a detention center for undocumented migrants and asylum seekers caught in Australian waters; this center provides one fifth of all employment on that island country (Hasmath & McKenzie, 2013). Some island states provide "flags of convenience": the Marshall Islands boasts the world's third-largest ship registry, run out of Reston, Virginia, USA (Palan, 2003, p. 53); the Bahamas, Cyprus, Malta, Vanuatu, and São Tomé y Príncipe are also involved in this business (Baldacchino, 2010, p. 6; Connell, 2013, p. 113; Kelman, 2011). Electronic gaming is a growing sector, and Malta is the premier jurisdiction for this service within the European Union (Aloisio, this volume). Iceland, with its steady temperatures and cheap geothermal energy, beckons as an attractive location for housing Internet servers and as a haven for whistleblowers (Gaedtke, 2014). Differently contentious is the operation of international finance centers: regimes offering a sophisticated range of products:—such as the reinsurance and captive insurance markets operating out of Bermuda (Bruner, 2013) or fund management in Jersey (Entwistle & Oliver, this volume). There have been attempts to vilify the industry as unjust by virtue of cheating states of precious tax revenues and jeopardizing welfare systems (e.g., Hampton & Christensen, 2002). Whereas island jurisdictions retort that there is no morality in the market; similar mechanisms exist within developed countries (such as Delaware in the United States) and that they are merely exploiting one of their very few current competitive advantages (Cobb, 2001; Rose & Spiegel, 2007).

DISCUSSION

These sets of activities have been taking over more traditional, subsistence based farming and fishing as well as colonial economic activity that was organized around mining or monoplantation agriculture. Lucrative terrestrial or marine species—from cod in the North Atlantic to sea cucumber in the Pacific and from old-growth hardwood on Prince Edward Island, Canada, to moas (*Dinornithiformes*) in New Zealand—have been harvested or hunted to near or total extinction (e.g., Kurlansky, 2011; Anderson et al., 2011; MacQuarrie and Lacroix, 2003; Anderson, 1989, respectively). The strategy of transforming islands into wholesale plantation monocrop economies—first involving tobacco but then mainly sugar as the key cash crop—was very profitably pursued with the indiscriminate use of slave and indentured labor, and while Europe had a huge craving for all things sweet (Grove, 1995; Mintz, 1985; Strachan, 2002). More recent large-scale agricultural production, as in bananas for Grenada, Dominica, St. Lucia, and St. Vincent, benefited from trade protectionism with privileged access to European Union markets; but eventually these socioeconomic systems collapsed in the wake of a more neoliberal, World Trade Organization–driven regime that rewarded more efficient producers from larger (and non–small island) states (Mlachila et al., 2010). Copra production has likewise disappeared from most of the Federated States of Micronesia, the Marshall Islands, Tonga, and Tuvalu (Connell, 2013, p. 63).

Of course, there are problems and challenges with these "pseudodevelopment strategies." Success in exported products and manufactures can breed failure when growth is unmanaged, quality is not guaranteed, and domestic product regulation remains inexistent or lax (e.g., Prasad & Raj, 2006). Customer loyalty to specific place-based (and more expensive) commodities needs to be assiduously earned and then carefully maintained. Local companies may fly under the radar of the big corporate players but, once successful, they can attract their attention and eventually can get bought out by the stronger competition. A successful firm could also encourage other local service providers to enter the field, quickly saturating the small local market and threatening both quality and profitability. Meanwhile, tourism, for all its promises, is no silver bullet: various small island states have developed a particular kind of tourism industry that remains externally controlled, dependent on external financing, and incongruent with island society or ecology (Bishop, 2010, p. 101). Is this much different from the monocrop agricultural economy it has replaced (McElroy, 2004)? Some of these "development strategies" may also be deemed to be verging on the criminal and illegal: interested in a passport from Tonga, Samoa, the Marshall Islands, Vanuatu, or Nauru (van Fossen, 2007)? When does offshore banking become money laundering (Hampton & Levi, 1999)? When does a flag of convenience become a euphemism for clandestine arms trafficking (*Sydney Morning Herald*, 2003)?

Small island state governments have sought to rebut such accusations. But the greatest challenge of all remains the fact that success depends on extraterritorial take-up, be this made up of governments, tourists, investors, consumers, or a combination of these. Should things change in the receiving country—a change in defense, economic, marine, taxation, trade, migration, or detention policy, for example—the source of revenue can disappear and can do so quite suddenly, too. Indeed, this is the very same argument making the case for the structural vulnerability of small island states. Openness is a double-edged sword:

> Small states, particularly island ones, tend to be more economically vulnerable than other groups of countries, due mostly to a high degree of economic openness and a high degree of export concentration. These lead to exposure to exogenous shocks, which could constitute a disadvantage to economic development by magnifying the element of risk in growth processes.
>
> (Briguglio et al., 2006, p. 1; *also* Briguglio, 1995)

Quite so. And yet:

> Hyper-specialization, openness, reliance upon external sources of finance, living with cycles of volatility, all go with the territory and do not in themselves carry any necessary connotation of weakness, fragility, or vulnerability . . . Paradoxically, the often-cited openness to international trade (one of the key components of the vulnerability index), with its associated volatility, is a source of strength rather than weakness for small economies, obliging them to be internationally competitive on open markets and preventing them from collapsing into anarchy or protectionism on economic terms.
>
> (Baldacchino, 2009, *passim*)

Many small jurisdictions have deployed their regulatory powers to facilitate favorable transborder activity, enacting laws and regulations intended and aimed *exclusively* at individuals and institutions located beyond their borders (Conrad, 1973, p. 633, my emphasis; *also* Alesina & Spolaore, 2003; Armstrong & Read, 2004, pp. 214, 217–218). Small island states, some more than others, have managed to compensate effectively for their small size by "optimal endogenous policy formulation and implementation" and via a successful "international political economy" (Armstrong & Read, 1998, p. 13). Beyond public policy considerations, small entrepôt economies remain prone to such additional contingencies as regional wars, natural disasters, accidents, security threats, epidemics, tourism consumer shifts, market shocks, or technological obsolescence. Lacking a hinterland under their own control, these states cannot count on the material, fiscal, food, or even human resource reserves available to larger countries. Yet, paradoxically, they must tap these pools to survive. Even Singapore, with its solid reputation as a robust and successful economy, needs to negotiate with neighboring Malaysia for its water requirements (Sprake et al., 2004).

Perhaps this is why, ultimately, many small subnational jurisdictions, islanded and otherwise, have decided *not* to graduate to full sovereignty. If survival depends on transborder activity, then is it not easier to access, secure, and consolidate such a flow by operating from *inside* a larger, wealthier state rather than from *outside* (Rezvani, 2014)? True: the status of a distinct sovereign state may be notionally more prestigious and dignified—with the flag, national anthem, UN seat, and head of state that accompanies sovereignty—yet could it not be economically much more dubious and fickle (Baldacchino, 2009)?

Would this rationale explain why so many candidates for sovereignty have opted *not* to take the step to full independence over the past 40 years? And if that is so, then what has changed since the mid-1980s to warrant such a hesitation? Or, to reverse the question, "Given the significant and long-lasting material advantage of nonsovereign over sovereign islands, why would so many of the latter have opted for independence prior to 1984?" (McElroy & Parry, 2012, p. 418). It is probably not just that the rhetoric of self-determination and sovereignty has worn off from the heydays of decolonization of the late 1950s and mid-1960s. More significantly, neoliberalism and an enhanced cross-boundary openness to trade and finance capital flows may have significantly improved the economic fortunes of subnational jurisdictions, particularly in terms of revenues from tourism and offshore finance, spectacularly transforming these spaces from the policy-neglected, labor-sending, and remittance-fuelled societies of just a few decades ago. For example, Bertram and Poirine (2007, pp. 334–335) recount the transition of the Cayman Islands from its dependence on remittances from off-island seafaring labor in the early 1960s to the much more sophisticated tourism destination, in-migration hub, and offshore financial center it has become today.

Consider the three small island states that secured independence since 1984: the Federated States of Micronesia, Marshall Islands, and Palau. These three Pacific states have secured a status of independence in principle: all three are full members of the United Nations. And yet they are "hybrid jurisdictions" (Levine & Roberts, 2005, pp. 276–279), representing attempts at exploiting the advantages of both full sovereignty and of an autonomy supported by a benign patron state, in this case the United States, via an ongoing series of Compact Agreements that effectively cede international relations and defense to the United States in exchange for payment. These agreements also afford the citizens of these three Pacific SIDSs with the opportunity to live and work in the United States, should they choose to (Baldacchino, 2010, p. 46).

CONCLUSION

In his grand sweep of 16th-century Mediterranean history, French historian Braudel (1972, p. 154) claimed that "the great problem" of the islands, never or only partly solved, was how to live off their own resources: soil, orchards, flocks, fish stocks, and "if that was not possible, to look outwards" (ibid.). In spite of the mantra of sustainable and self-reliant development, islands fare best economically when they lure revenue from elsewhere, and the performance of small island politicians is often appraised at home by how well they manage to secure such largesse. Those small island territories that have, for some reason, been obliged to live off their own resources would have morphed themselves as plantation (and often largely monocrop) economies, providing nonessential goods to the kitchens of the West. But, without the economies of scale of larger continental competitors, this business model has been shown to fail without the scaffolding of those protectionist policies whose heyday looks very much like a thing of the past.

If this extraterritorial turn is the key to small island survival, then sovereignty may lose its legitimate appeal. This then is a strong case for non-sovereignty: a SNIJ political economy that secures autonomy but maintains the vital lifelines with larger, richer economies and their labor markets. And these links are especially significant in a post–9/11 scenario in which the option to migrate is increasingly fraught by the regulations of the receiving countries, wary of heightened security concerns, stagnant economic growth, and rising xenophobia. This approach may not sound like a "development" strategy, but it has been, in its own right, a sustainable one.

In any case, for those territories that have made the unequivocal jump to full sovereignty, there is continued evidence of a smart deployment of jurisdiction as an economic resource (Baldacchino & Milne, 2001). It is unfortunate that the successful European small island state quartet—Cyprus, Iceland, Ireland, Malta—is largely invisible from small state discussions, since they have "graduated" beyond SIDS status. New Zealand never featured as a

SIDS. And while Singapore clings to that grouping, it recognizes its heft in this assemblage and has committed its resources to help support other SIDS, mainly through the Small Island Developing States Technical Cooperation Programme (SIDSTEC).

Contrary to widely held beliefs, small island countries have many lessons to offer to other countries and the world community in terms of their development strategies. Even in the current heyday of globalization and neo-liberal ideology and perhaps *because* of this context, small island countries have expertly worked around the rules of the game, showcasing a distinct form of intrapreneurship. As minions in the global system, these countries have also used their sovereignty and nonmarket options to their advantage, scouring for opportunities and potential for derogations, exceptions, and special arrangements (Prasad, 2004). Even as Tuvalu and Kiribati use "moral power," appeals to common interest (Betzold, 2010), and diplomatic channels to alert the world to their likely total submersion because of global warming, they have been differently proactive, with many of their citizens having secured access to the labor markets of Australia and New Zealand (Shen & Binns, 2012; Smith, 2013). The "extraordinary successes" (Bruner, 2013, p. 5) achieved by certain small island jurisdictions call out for viable explanation.

In this volume, we offer a case study of the Åland islands, a Swedish-speaking autonomy within the state of Finland with some 27,000 residents, as an example of a successful SNIJ, with a gross domestic product per capita (at purchasing power parity) of US$38,000. Three "keys to island prosperity" are suggested: (1) the ability to transform the geophysical condition of being an island into an economic opportunity; (2) a focus on niche markets instead of economies of scale in the production of island-branded, high-quality goods and services; and (3) making creative use of the islands' special political and institutional status (Fellman et al., this volume).

We could not conclude this collection without at least one commentary from an actual island entrepreneur (Haddow, this volume). Here is testimony to the ingenuity of a producer based on Bruny (year-round population: about 700), an island off an island (Tasmania) off the Australian mainland. Nick Haddow has been described as a "renaissance man: cook, writer, marketer, television personality, cheese judge and retailer" (Lethlean, 2012, n.p.), the quintessential multifunctional small island entrepreneur. He could be echoing the sentiment of many (including Fellman et al. on Åland, this volume) when saying:

> There are much better places to start a small business, making a hand-made and highly perishable product, than a small island off the south coast of Tasmania. It is tempting to say that, *despite* our location, we have achieved success in our business. I suspect, though, the truth is that we have been successful *because* of our location.
>
> (emphasis in original)

We augur that this collection helps spread and share such "truths," reversing some of the bad press and deficit discourse that has come to be associated with small island jurisdictions. It also hopes that the argument for comparisons between small island states and subnational island jurisdictions is a valid one. Perhaps stories of island entrepreneurship, dogged perseverance, and clever opportunism can be better noted and sustained from a palimpsest of what has been for too long a script of acute vulnerability and its presumed corollary, resilience. Indeed, for those living in small states and territories where risks, hazards, and uncertainties are part of life, small island entrepreneurs and their canny political leaders can tell us much about the political economy of the present era of uncertainty (Pugh, 2014).

NOTES

1. Britain was the preeminent global maritime power for many decades, but it is not a small state. Japan secured its own empire in the mid-20th century, but then, again, it is not a small state.
2. As of January 2015, there are 28 small island states with a resident population of up to 1 million. Of these, 12 are in the Pacific Ocean, 8 in the Caribbean Sea, 3 in the Indian Ocean, 2 in the Mediterranean Sea, 2 in the Eastern mid-Atlantic, and 1 in the North Atlantic. The Turkish Republic of Northern Cyprus (TRNC) is recognized as a sovereign state only by Turkey. There are also seven island states with populations between 1 and 5 million: Bahrain, East Timor, Ireland, Jamaica, Mauritius, New Zealand, and Trinidad and Tobago. Apart from the TRNC, Brunei and East Timor share their island territory with other states: Brunei shares Borneo with Indonesia and Malaysia; East Timor shares Timor with Indonesia.
3. But note that this nomenclature is subject to political opportunism. The 38 SIDSs that are UN member states (and therefore sovereign states) include Belize, Guinea Bissau, Guyana, and Suriname (which are not islands); Cuba, Dominican Republic, Haiti, and Papua New Guinea (which are not small, with resident populations larger than the world's mean of 5.3 million); and Singapore (not a developing country, and also with a resident population of more than 5 million).

REFERENCES

Alesina, A., & Spolaore, E. (2003). *The size of nations.* Cambridge, MA: MIT Press.

Amin, A., & Thrift, N. (1992). Neo-Marshallian nodes in global networks. *International Journal of Urban and Regional Research, 16*(4), 571–587.

Amoamo, M. (2011). The mitigation of vulnerability: Mutiny, resilience and reconstitution. A case study of Pitcairn Island. *Shima: The International Journal of Research into Island Cultures, 5*(1), 69–93.

Amoamo, M. (2013). Development on the periphery: A case study of the sub-national island jurisdiction of Pitcairn Island. *Asia Pacific Viewpoint, 54*(1), 91–108.

Ancharaz, V. (2014). The political economy of transitioning to a green economy in Seychelles. In N. Smith, A. Halton, & J. Strachan (Eds.), *Transitioning to a green economy: Political economy of approaches in small states* (pp. 196–213). London: Commonwealth Secretariat.

Anderson, A. (1989). Mechanics of overkill in the extinction of New Zealand moas. *Journal of Archaeological Science, 16*(2), 137–151.

Anderson, S. C., Flemming, J. M., Watson, R., & Lotze, H. K. (2011). Serial exploitation of global sea cucumber fisheries. *Fish and Fisheries, 12*(3), 317–339.

Anklesaria Aiyar, S. S. (2008). Small states: Not handicapped and under-aided, but advantaged and over-aided. *Cato Journal, 28*(3), 449–478.

Armstrong, H. W., De Kervenoael, R. J., Li, X., & Read, R. (1998). A comparison of the economic performance of different micro-states, and between micro-states and larger countries. *World Development, 26*(4), 639–656.

Armstrong, H., Johnes, G., Johnes, J., & Macbean, A. (1993). The role of transport costs as a determinant of price level differentials between the Isle of Man and the United Kingdom, 1989. *World Development, 21*(2), 311–318.

Armstrong, H. W., & Read, R. (1998). *The international political economy of micro-states: An overview.* Paper presented at 5th Islands of the World Conference, Mauritius, University of Mauritius, July.

Armstrong, H. W., & Read, R. (2002). The phantom of liberty? Economic growth and the vulnerability of small states. *Journal of International Development, 14*(4), 435–458.

Armstrong, H. W., & Read, R. (2004). Small states and island states: Implications of size, location and isolation for prosperity. In J. Poot (Ed.), *On the edge of the global economy* (pp. 191–223). Cheltenham, UK: Edward Elgar.

Baldacchino, G. (1993). Bursting the bubble: The pseudo-development strategies of microstates. *Development and Change, 24*(1), 29–51.

Baldacchino, G. (2001). Human resource management strategies for small territories: An alternative proposition. *International Journal of Educational Development, 21*(3), 205–215.

Baldacchino, G. (2005). Successful small scale manufacturing from small islands: Comparing firms benefiting from local raw material input. *Journal of Small Business & Entrepreneurship, 18*(1), 21–38.

Baldacchino, G. (2006). The brain rotation and brain diffusion strategies of small islanders: Considering "movement" in lieu of "place." *Globalisation, Societies & Education, 4*(1), 143–154.

Baldacchino, G. (2008). Studying islands: On whose terms? Some epistemological and methodological challenges to the pursuit of island studies. *Island Studies Journal, 3*(1), 37–56.

Baldacchino, G. (2010). Islands and beers: Toasting a discriminatory approach to small island manufacturing. *Asia Pacific Viewpoint, 51*(1), 61–72.

Baldacchino, G. (2012a). The lure of the island: A spatial analysis of power relations. *Journal of Marine and Island Cultures, 1*(2), 55–62.

Baldacchino, G. (2012b). Governmentality is all the rage: The strategy games of small jurisdictions. *The Round Table: Commonwealth Journal of International Affairs, 101*(3), 235–251.

Baldacchino, G., & Bertram, G. (2009). The beak of the finch: Insights into the economic development of small economies. *The Round Table: Commonwealth Journal of International Affairs, 98*(401), 141–160.

Baldacchino, G., & Bray, M. (Eds.). (2001). Human resource issues in small states. *International Journal of Educational Development, 21*(2), 203–291, special issue.

Baldacchino, G., & Kelman, I. (2014). Critiquing the pursuit of island sustainability: Blue and green with hardly a colour in between. *Shima: The International Journal of Research into Island Cultures, 8*(2), 1–21.

Baldacchino, G., & Milne, D. (Eds.). (2000). *Lessons from the political economy of small islands: The resourcefulness of jurisdiction.* New York: St. Martin's Press.

Baldacchino, G., & Milne, D. (Eds.). (2009). *The case for non-sovereignty: Lessons from subnational island jurisdictions.* London: Routledge.

Baldacchino, G., & Vella Bonnici, J. (2005). *Small business from small islands: Real stories of real people. A training manual.* Marsa, Malta: Malta Enterprise.

Bertram, G. (1986). "Sustainable development" in Pacific micro-economies. *World Development, 14*(7), 809–822.

Bertram, G. (2004). On the convergence of small island economies with their metropolitan patrons. *World Development, 32*(2), 343–364.

Bertram, G. (2006). The MIRAB model in the twenty-first century. *Asia Pacific Viewpoint, 47*(1), 1–14.

Bertram, G., & Poirine, B. (2007). Island political economy. In G. Baldacchino (Ed.), *A world of islands: An island studies reader* (pp. 325–378). Charlottetown, PE, and Luqa, Malta: University of Prince Edward Island and Agenda Academic.

Bertram, G., & Watters, R. F. (1985). The MIRAB economy in the South Pacific microstates. *Pacific Viewpoint, 26*(3), 497–520.

Betzold, C. (2010). "Borrowing" power to influence international negotiations: AOSIS in the climate change regime, 1990–1997. *Politics, 30*(3), 131–148.

Bishop, M. L. (2010). Tourism as a small-state development strategy: Pier pressure in the Eastern Caribbean? *Progress in Development Studies, 10*(2), 99–114.

Bradsher, K. (2014). Shake-up on Opium Island. *The New York Times.* July 20. Retrieved from www.nytimes.com/2014/07/20/business/international/tasmania-big-supplier-to-drug-companies-faces-changes.html?_r=0

Braudel, F. (1972). *The Mediterranean and the Mediterranean world in the age of Philip II.* Translated by S. Reynolds. London: Collins.

Briguglio, L. (1995). Small island states and their economic vulnerabilities. *World Development, 23*(9), 1615–1632.

Briguglio, L., & Cordina, G. (Eds.). (2004). *Competitiveness strategies for small states.* Malta: Formatek, for Commonwealth Secretariat.

Briguglio, L., Cordina, G., Bugeja, S., & Farrugia, N. (2006). *Conceptualizing and measuring economic resilience.* Mimeograph. Malta: Economics Department, University of Malta. Retrieved from www.um.edu.mt/__data/assets/pdf_file/0013/44122/resilience_index.pdf

Briguglio, L., & Kisanga, E. J. (Eds.). (2004). *Economic vulnerability and resilience of small states.* Malta: Formatek, for Commonwealth Secretariat.

Brookfield, H. C. (1972). *Colonialism, development and independence: The case of the Melanesian islands in the South Pacific.* Cambridge, UK: Cambridge University Press.

Bruner, C. M. (2013). *Market-dominant small jurisdictions in a globalizing financial world.* Washington & Lee Legal Studies Paper No. 2013–19. Retrieved from http://ssrn.com/abstract=2343111

Bryant, N. (2004). Maldives: Paradise soon to be lost. *BBC News.* 28th July. Retrieved from http://news.bbc.co.uk/2/hi/south_asia/3930765.stm

Carnegie, C. V. (1982). Strategic flexibility in the West Indies: A social psychology of Caribbean migration. *Caribbean Review, 11*, 10–13, 54.

Carse, S. (1998). Sustaining small island development: Isle of Man. In G. Baldacchino & R. Greenwood (Eds.), *Competing strategies of socio-economic development for small islands* (pp. 268–291). Charlottetown, PE: Institute of Island Studies, University of Prince Edward Island.

Carter, K., & Aulette, J. (2009). Creole in Cape Verde: Language, identity and power. *Ethnography, 10*(2), 213–236.

Cartier, L. E., Krzemnicki, M. S., & Ito, M. (2012). Cultured pearl farming and production in the Federated States of Micronesia. *Gems & Gemology, 48*(2), 108–122.

Cica, N. (2010). Tulips to Amsterdam. *Griffith Review, 27*, Autumn, 70–74.

Cobb, S. C. (2001). Globalization in a small island context: Creating and marketing competitive advantage for offshore financial services. *Geografiska Annaler B, 83*(4), 161–174.

Commonwealth Consultative Group. (1985). *Vulnerability: Small states in the global society*. London: Commonwealth Secretariat.

Connell, J. (1988). The end ever nigh: Contemporary population change on Pitcairn Island. *GeoJournal, 16*(2), 193–200.

Connell, J. (1991). Island microstates: The mirage of development. *The Contemporary Pacific, 3*(2), 251–287.

Connell, J. (2003). Island dreaming: The contemplation of Polynesian paradise. *Journal of Historical Geography, 29*(4), 554–581.

Connell, J. (2006a). Nauru: The first failed Pacific state? *The Round Table: Commonwealth Journal of International Affairs, 95*(383), 47–63.

Connell, J. (2006b). "The taste of paradise": Selling Fiji and Fiji Water. *Asia Pacific Viewpoint, 47*(3), 342–350.

Connell, J. (2007). Island migration. In G. Baldacchino (Ed.), *A world of islands: An island studies reader* (pp. 455–482). Charlottetown, Canada, and Luqa, Malta: University of Prince Edward Island and Agenda Academic.

Connell, J. (2013). *Islands at risk? Environments, economies and contemporary change*. Cheltenham, UK: Edward Elgar.

Connell, J., & King, R. (1999). Island migration in a changing world. In R. King & J. Connell (Eds.), *Small worlds, global lives: Islands and migration* (pp. 1–26). London: Pinter.

Conrad, A. F. (1973). An overview of the laws of corporations. *Michigan Law Review, 4*, 623–690.

Croes, R. R. (2006). A paradigm shift to a new strategy for small island economies: Embracing demand side economics for value enhancement and long term economic stability. *Tourism Management, 27*(3), 453–465.

Dawson, M., & De Souza, P. (Eds.). (2012). *Regional development in Northern Europe: Peripherality, marginality and border issues*. London: Routledge.

Dehoorne, O., & Tătar, C. (2013). Ecotourism at the heart of development strategies: Elements for reflections based on the Caribbean experience. *Tourismos: An International Multidisciplinary Journal of Tourism, 8*(1), 213–231.

DeLoughrey, E. M. (2013). The myth of isolates: Ecosystem ecologies in the nuclear Pacific. *Cultural Geographies, 20*(2), 167–184.

Diggines, C. E. (1985). The problems of small states. *The Round Table, 74*(295), 191–205.

Dolman, A. J. (1985). Paradise lost? The past performance and future prospects of small island developing countries. In E. C. Dommen & P. L. Hein (Eds.), *States, microstates and islands* (pp. 40–69). London: Croom Helm.

Doumenge, F. (1985). The viability of small, inter-tropical islands. In E. C. Dommen & P. L. Hein (Eds.), *States, microstates and islands* (pp. 70–118). London: Croom Helm.

Easterly, W. & Kraay, A. C. (2000). Small states, small problems? Income, growth and volatility in small states. *World Development, 28*(11), 2013–2027.

The Economist. (2013a). Pitcairn's bounty. October 26th. Retrieved from www.economist.com/news/asia/21588420-south-pacific-about-get-worlds-biggest-national-park-pitcairns-bounty

The Economist. (2013b). Sea change: A gathering of Pacific leaders worries about climate change. August 31st. Retrieved from www.economist.com/news/asia/21584396-gathering-pacific-leaders-worries-about-climate-change-sea-change

Encontre, P. (1999). The vulnerability and resilience of small island developing states in the context of globalization. *Natural Resources Forum, 23*(2), 261–270.

Farbotko, C. (2010). "The global warming clock is ticking so see these places while you can": Voyeuristic tourism and model environmental citizens on Tuvalu's disappearing islands. *Singapore Journal of Tropical Geography, 31*(2), 224–238.

Farrugia, C.J., & Attard, P.A. (1989). *The multifunctional administrator*. London: Commonwealth Secretariat.

Fischer, G., & Encontre, P. (1998). The economic disadvantages of island developing countries: Problems of smallness, remoteness and economies of scale. In G. Baldacchino & R. Greenwood (Eds.), *Competing strategies of economic development for small islands* (pp. 69–87). Charlottetown, Canada: Institute of Island Studies, University of Prince Edward Island.

Foucault, M. (1991a). Governmentality. In G. Burchell, C. Gordon, & P. Miller (Eds.), *The Foucault effect: Studies in governmentality* (pp. 87–104). Chicago, IL: University of Chicago Press.

Foucault, M. (1991b). Questions of method. In G. Burchell, C. Gordon, & P. Miller (Eds.), *The Foucault effect: Studies in governmentality* (pp. 73–86). Chicago, IL: University of Chicago Press.

Gaedtke, F. (2014, December 30). Can Iceland become the Switzerland of data? *Aljazeera*. Retrieved from www.aljazeera.com/indepth/features/2014/12/can-iceland-become-switzerland-data-20141228113345770287.html

Gowdy, J.M., & McDaniel, C.N. (1999). The physical destruction of Nauru: An example of weak sustainability. *Land Economics, 75*(2), 333–338.

Griffith, I. L. (Ed.). (2004). *Caribbean security in the age of terror: Challenge and change*. Kingston, Jamaica: Ian Randle Publishers.

Grove, R.H. (1995). *Green imperialism: Colonial expansion, tropical island Edens and the origins of environmentalism, 1600–1860*. Cambridge: Cambridge University Press.

Guillaumont, P. (2010). Assessing the economic vulnerability of small island developing states and the least developed countries. *Journal of Development Studies, 46*(5), 828–854.

Guralnik, D. B. (Ed.). (1980). *Webster's new world dictionary of the American language*. Cleveland, OH: Simon & Schuster.

Hampton, M. P., & Christensen, J. (2002). Offshore pariahs? Small island economies, tax havens, and the re-configuration of global finance. *World Development, 30*(9), 1657–1673.

Hampton, M. P., & Jeyacheya, J. (2013). *Tourism and inclusive growth in small island developing states*. London: Commonwealth Secretariat.

Hampton, M. P., & Levi, M. (1999). Fast spinning into oblivion? Recent developments in money-laundering policies and offshore finance centres. *Third World Quarterly, 20*(3), 645–656.

Harden, S. (1985). *Small is dangerous: Microstates in a macro world*. London: Frances Pinter.

Hasmath, R., & McKenzie, J. (2013). Deterring the "boat people": Explaining the Australian government's people swap response to asylum seekers. *Centre on Migration, Policy and Society, University of Oxford Working Paper Series, 13*(103), 1–22.

Kabutaulaka, T. T. (2004). Solomon Islands. *The Contemporary Pacific, 16*(2), 393–401.

Kaplan, M. (2007). Fijian water in Fiji and New York: Local politics and a global commodity. *Cultural Anthropology, 22*(4), 685–706.

Kaplinsky, R. (1983). Prospering at the periphery, a special case: The Seychelles. In R. Cohen (Ed.), *African islands and enclaves* (pp. 195–215). London: Sage.

Kelman, I. (2011). Dealing with climate change on small island developing states. *Practising Anthropology, 33*(1), 28–32.

Keohane, R. O. (1969). Lilliputians' dilemmas: Small states in international politics. *International Organization, 23*(2), 291–310.

King, R. (2009). Geography, islands and migration in an era of global mobility. *Island Studies Journal, 4*(1), 53–84.

Kurlansky, M. (2011). *Cod: A biography of the fish that changed the world.* New York, NY: Random House.

Language Course. (2014). English language schools in Malta. Retrieved from www.languagecourse.net/schools—malta.php3

Lethlean, J. (2012, June 23). Nick finds the raw stuff. *The Australian.* Retrieved from www.theaustralian.com.au/executive-living/food-drink/nick-haddow-finds-the-raw-stuff/story-fn86jbrr-1226401410057

Levine, S., & Roberts, N. S. (2005). The constitutional structures and electoral systems of Pacific island states. *Commonwealth & Comparative Politics, 43*(3), 276–295.

Lewis-Cameron, A., & Roberts, S. (Eds.). (2010). *Marketing island destinations: Concepts and cases.* London: Routledge.

Lutz, C. (Ed.). (2009). *The bases of empire: The global struggle against US military posts.* New York, NY: New York University Press.

Macpherson, C. (2000). Oasis or mirage: The farming of black pearl in the northern Cook Islands. *Pacific Studies, 23*(3), 33–55.

MacQuarrie, K., & Lacroix, C. (2003). The upland hardwood component of Prince Edward Island's remnant Acadian forest: Determination of depth of edge and patterns of exotic plant invasion. *Canadian Journal of Botany, 81*(11), 1113–1128.

Mazzeo, T. J. (2011). *The secret of Chanel N°. 5: The intimate history of the world's most famous perfume.* New York, NY: Harper Collins.

McElroy, J. L. (2004). Global perspectives of Caribbean tourism. In D. Duval (Ed.), *Tourism in the Caribbean: Trends, development, prospects* (pp. 39–56). London: Routledge.

McElroy, J. L., & Parry, C. E. (2012). The long-term propensity for political affiliation in island microstates. *Commonwealth & Comparative Politics, 50*(4), 403–421.

McElroy, J. L., & Pearce, K. B. (2006). The advantages of political affiliation: Dependent and independent small-island profiles. *The Round Table: Commonwealth Journal of International Affairs, 95*(386), 529–539.

McElroy, J. L., & Hamma, P. E. (2010). SITEs revisited: Socioeconomic and demographic contours of small island tourist economies. *Asia Pacific Viewpoint, 51*(1), 36–46.

Mintz, S. W. (1985). *Sweetness and power.* New York, NY: Penguin.

Mlachila, M., Cashin, P., & Haines, C. (2010). Caribbean bananas: The macroeconomic impact of trade preference erosion. *IMF Working Papers*, WP 10/59. Retrieved from www.imf.org/external/pubs/ft/wp/2010/wp1059.pdf

Olwig, K. F. (1993). *Global culture, island identity.* London: Harwood Academic Press.

Orange County Register. (2012). Global warming sinking the Maldives? Not exactly. August 24. Retrieved from www.ocregister.com/orangepunch/maldives-491386-president-global.html

Palan, R. (2003). *The offshore world: Sovereign markets, virtual places and nomad millionaires.* Ithaca, NY: Cornell University Press.

Parker, C. F., Karlsson, C., Hjerpe, M., & Linnér, B. O. (2012). Fragmented climate change leadership: Making sense of the ambiguous outcome of COP-15. *Environmental Politics, 21*(2), 268–286.

Payne, T. (1987). Economic issues. In C. Clarke & T. Payne (Eds.), *Politics, security and development in small states* (pp. 50–62). London: Allen & Unwin.

Pike, A. (2009). Brand and branding geographies. *Geography Compass, 3*(1), 190–213.

Plischke, E. (1977). *Microstates in world affairs: Policy problems and options.* Washington, DC: American Enterprise Institute for Public Policy Research.

Poirine, B. (1998). Should we hate or love MIRAB? *The Contemporary Pacific, 10*(1), 65–105.

Poon, A. (1990). Flexible specialization and small size: The case of Caribbean tourism. *World Development, 18*(1), 109–123.

Pounder, P. (2006). Branding: A Caribbean perspective on rum manufacturing competitiveness. *International Journal of Entrepreneurship and Small Business, 9*(4), 394–406.

Prasad, N. (2004). Escaping regulation, escaping convention. *World Economics, 5*(1), 41–65.

Prasad, N., & Raj, S. (2006). The perils of unmanaged export growth: The case of kava in Fiji. *Journal of Small Business & Entrepreneurship, 9*(4), 381–393.

Pugh, J. (2014). Resilience, complexity and post-liberalism. *Area*. First published online. DOI: 10.1111/area 12118

Punnett, B. J., & Morrison, A. (2006). Niche markets and small Caribbean producers: A match made in heaven? *Journal of Small Business and Entrepreneurship, 9*(4), 341–354.

Rezvani, D. A. (2014). *Surpassing the sovereign state: The wealth, self-rule, and security advantages of partially independent territories*. Oxford: Oxford University Press.

Richardson, B. C. (1983). *Caribbean migrants: Environment and human survival on St. Kitts and Nevis*. Knoxville, TN: University of Tennessee Press.

Ridgell, R. (1995). *Pacific nations and territories: The islands of Micronesia, Melanesia and Polynesia*. Honolulu, HI: Pacific Region Educational Laboratory.

Rose, A. K., & Spiegel, M. M. (2007). Offshore financial centres: Parasites or symbionts? *The Economic Journal, 117*(523), 1310–1335.

Royle, S. A. (2006). The Falkland Islands. In G. Baldacchino (Ed.), *Extreme tourism: Lessons from the world's cold water islands* (pp. 181–192). Amsterdam: Elsevier.

Sathiendrakumar, R., & Tisdell, C. A. (1989). Tourism and the economic development of the Maldives. *Annals of Tourism Research, 16*(2), 254–269.

Schmitz, H. (1989). *Flexible specialization: A new paradigm of small-scale industrialization*. Discussion Paper No. 261. Brighton, UK: Institute of Development Studies, University of Sussex.

Schneider, P., & Schneider, J. (1976). *Culture and political economy in Western Sicily*. New York, NY: Academic Press.

Shen, S., & Binns, T. (2012). Pathways, motivations and challenges: Contemporary Tuvaluan migration to New Zealand. *GeoJournal, 77*(1), 63–82.

Silva, L. (2013). How ecotourism works at the community-level: The case of whale-watching in the Azores. *Current Issues in Tourism* (ahead-of-print), 1–16. DOI: 10.1080/13683500.2013.786027

Smith, R. (2013). Should they stay or should they go? A discourse analysis of factors influencing relocation decisions among the outer islands of Tuvalu and Kiribati. *Journal of New Zealand & Pacific Studies, 1*(1), 23–39.

Sparke, M., Sidaway, J. D., Bunnell, T., & Grundy-Warr, C. (2004). Triangulating the borderless world: Geographies of power in the Indonesia-Malaysia-Singapore growth triangle. *Transactions of the Institute of British Geographers, 29*(4), 485–498.

Stevens, R. M. (1977). Asymmetrical federalism: The federal principle and the survival of the small republic. *Publius, 7*(4), 177–203.

Strachan, I. G. (2002). *Paradise and plantation: Tourism and culture in the Anglophone Caribbean*. Charlottesville, VA: University of Virginia Press.

Sydney Morning Herald. (2003, January 14). The ships that died of shame. Retrieved from www.smh.com.au/articles/2003/01/13/1041990234408.html

Tasner, M. (2010). *Internet TV: Taking video to the next level*. New York, NY: Pearson Education.

Van Fossen, A. (2007). Citizenship for sale: Passports of convenience from Pacific island tax havens. *Commonwealth & Comparative Politics, 45*(2), 138–163.

Wardle, H. (2002). Marshy and friends: Informality, deformalization and West Indian island experience. *Social Identities, 8*(2), 255–270.

Warrington, E. (1998). Gulliver and Lilliput in a new world order: The impact of external relations on the domestic policies and institutions of micro-states. *Public Administration and Development, 18*(2), 101–105.

Williams, S. (2010). On islands, insularity, and opium poppies: Australia's secret pharmacy. *Environment and Planning D: Society and Space, 28*(2), 290–310.

Wilson, M. I. (2001). Location, location, location: The geography of the dot com problem. *Environment and Planning B, 28*(1), 59–72.

Winchester, S. (2003). *Outposts: Journeys to the surviving relics of the British empire.* New York, NY: Harper Collins.

Zhang, J. J. (2010). Of kaoliang, bullets and knives: Local entrepreneurs and the battlefield tourism enterprise in Kinmen (Quemoy), Taiwan. *Tourism Geographies, 12*(3), 395–411.

PRODUCT WEBSITES

Dot TV Domains—Verisign (Tuvalu): www.tv/
Fiji Water (Fiji): www.fijiwater.com/
LYSI (Iceland): www.lysi.eu/
Mdina Glass (Malta): www.mdinaglass.com.mt/
Mount Gay Rum (Barbados): www.mountgayrum.com/
Sustainable Pearls (Federated States of Micronesia): www.sustainablepearls.org/pearls/pearl-farming-around-the-world/micronesia/

Part 1
General Considerations

2 Dark Entrepreneurship in Small Island States and Territories

Ilan Kelman and Cheney M. Shreve

INTRODUCTION

Small states and territories have often been iconized as subsidence-based, small, rural economies, divorced from modern livelihoods; yet an expanding literature challenges that view in two ways (Baldacchino, 2007), first by characterizing livelihoods through models combining dependency on macroscale aid and microscale remittances (Bertram, 2006; Bertram & Watters, 1985) with an almost inevitable sun-sea-sand (and sex?) tourism industry (Butcher, 2003; Oberst & McElroy, 2007; Poirine, 1994). Second, without denying the realities and strengths of these tendencies, others push back against the stereotypes by describing efforts at sustainable island tourism (Graci & Dodds, 2010) and local manufacturing taking advantage of the smallness and uniqueness of the territories including via place branding (Baldacchino, 2005a; 2005b).

This resourcefulness has had various effects. On the positive side, it brings creativity and income to island communities that otherwise might struggle for viability, such as philately from Tristan da Cunha in the South Atlantic and honey from Colonsay, Scotland. The downside is a location being labeled based on its products—for instance, the reputation of King Island, Tasmania, for pristine nature producing top foods, which masks the island's development difficulties such as poor infrastructure, a falling population, and inadequate disaster risk-reduction measures (Khamis, 2007). Irrespective, connectivity is a key element of these entrepreneurial approaches, just as connectivity through ocean travel has long defined Pacific island living and lifestyle (Dening, 2004; Hau'ofa, 1993). That is, although the entrepreneurship of small island states and territories might use isolation, remoteness, and islandness as part of the sell, the existence and success of those livelihoods emerges from strong connections with others.

That does not imply that all such entrepreneurship or its results are laudable. Island tourism has long displayed examples of "dark tourism," referring to visiting sites of death, dying, and memorialization (Foley & Lennon, 1996; Seaton, 1996). Some yield few ethical debates, such as memorializing and teaching about World War II through the museum and monuments at

Pearl Harbor, Hawai'i, a site that is particularly popular with Japanese tourists (Yaguchi, 2005). An uncontroversial example from the UK is battlefield tourism in the Falklands (Royle, 2006), although Argentine tourists travelling to the islands stir up controversy (Royle, 2010). Such examples of dark tourism in island jurisdictions are generally accepted despite intense controversy at times over a site's operationalization, epitomized by the destroyed World Trade Center, called Ground Zero, in Manhattan (Lisle, 2004). Yet other instances of island tourism are not dark tourism but are seen as the darker side of tourism entrepreneurship: disaster tourism in Montserrat (Kelman & Dodds, 2009), child sex tourism in Phuket (Berkman, 1996), and drug tourism in Fiji (Rao, 2002).

Building on such examples, this chapter examines and analyses dark entrepreneurship for small island states and territories, including but not limited to tourism. An overview of defining and theorizing dark entrepreneurship (being quite different from dark tourism) is provided in the next section to guide the discussion of what is and is not considered to be entrepreneurial. Examples of dark island entrepreneurship follow and enable a subsequent discussion of ethics, starting with drivers and mechanisms of entrepreneurship and ending with power dynamics. The conclusions describe the poignancy of small island states and territories in demonstrating challenges and opportunities of entrepreneurship.

THEORIZING DARK ENTREPRENEURSHIP

Schumpeter (1934, pp. 153–154) defines an entrepreneur as someone who "attaches to the creation of new things, to the realization of the future value system. Entrepreneurship is at the same time the child and victim of development." Despite (or because of) a wealth of literature since then, there is no consensus on the definition of an entrepreneur or the activities and processes of entrepreneurship, but a widely accepted definition speaks to the seeking, identification, and usage of previously unknown, unexplored, or unrecognized approaches (Arend, 2007).

Austin and colleagues (2006) note that entrepreneurship and entrepreneurs have been researched from three main, broad approaches: (1) economists exploring the impacts and results of entrepreneurship, for example, as a key process advancing the whole economy (Schumpeter, 1934); (2) psychologists and sociologists examining the entrepreneurs themselves (Collins & Moore, 1964; McClelland, 1961); and (3) business studies focusing on the entrepreneurial management process (Stevenson & Harmeling, 1990). A fourth research stream is presented by Stevenson (1983) as the "how" of entrepreneurship, defining entrepreneurialism as the pursuit of opportunity beyond the resource base one currently controls or can access. While entrepreneurship has generally been seen as positive, more contemporary work starts to question entrepreneurship ethics.

Dess and colleagues (1997) point out a disconnect between the view of entrepreneurship as inherently positive, driving successful business, and the reality of empirical evidence showing that this is not always the case. Baumol (1990), like Schumpeter (1934), theorizes creative yet destructive entrepreneurship, taking examples from Roman, Chinese, and European history that suggest their entrepreneurship approaches as being parasitical to the economy, harming it in the long run even as individuals make short-term gains. The Roman Empire illustrates this point (Baumol, 1990). Entrepreneurship for wealth acquisition was admired as long as it was not done through technological or commercial innovation, instead focusing on rents, taxes, indemnities, lootings, loans, and political payoffs. These mechanisms are effectively wealth transfer, ultimately at the expense of the Empire's subjects, which is indeed creative entrepreneurship but which discourages creation of wealth and knowledge, potentially contributing to the empire's decay over the long term (Baumol, 1990). There is no dispute that entrepreneurship can be productive for the economy and can be a positive influence on society, but there is no guarantee that it must be either or both.

In exploring harmful possibilities for entrepreneurship, Bakker (2012, p. 1) defines "dark entrepreneurship" as "entrepreneurship that is both illegal and covert," then focusing on empirical cases of armed groups (nominally terrorists) and their networks. Both adjectives in this definition are partial. "Illegal" is limited because different jurisdictions promulgate different laws. Illegal activities in one location might be legal, even encouraged, elsewhere. "Covert" is limited because many ostensibly undesirable activities, including terrorism, happen overtly with such networks being well known and highly publicized.

In this chapter, we mean dark entrepreneurship to refer to livelihoods and economic activities that violate ethical or legal norms across many jurisdictions and are unconcerned with demonstrable resulting harm. As such, this definition is not so restrictive as to assume that the entrepreneurship is literally "dark," being undercover and rarely seen. Nor is it so broad as to encompass livelihoods that balance positive and negative impacts and consequently are debated ethically. Examples of the latter are tourism in the Maldives, which brings needed income through detrimental environmental effects such as the tourists flying there; financial services offered by small jurisdictions such as Jersey (Entwistle & Oliver, this volume); and the Bahamas as a gambling haven (e.g., Paradise Island) and hangout for the rich.

For small island states and territories, many entrepreneurial activities that may be questioned are run by the government of the small island state or territory, interrogating the notion of "entrepreneurship" that is often associated with the private sector, even by governments (Perren & Jennings, 2005). The population size of small island states and territories means that there is usually significant overlap between the private sector and the state. It can be difficult to differentiate who leads and controls specific initiatives. State-led initiatives might have private individuals and business leaders dominating, supporting, instigating, or running the activity. Meanwhile, private-led initiatives in small jurisdictions generally have government backing to enable their functioning. As such, the examples provided here do not differentiate among sectors.

DARK ENTREPRENEURSHIP IN SMALL ISLAND STATES AND TERRITORIES

This section provides examples of dark entrepreneurship in small island states and territories, fleshing out some examples that are illustrative but not comprehensive.

Citizenship

"Economic citizenship" or "citizenship-by-investment programs" allow foreign investors to purchase citizenship and passports. Economic citizenship programs exist globally; however, the fees are usually much higher for purchasing citizenship from wealthier countries such as the United States and Canada, compared to island states such as Dominica and St. Kitts and Nevis. Under the "EB-5 Immigrant Investor" scheme, noncitizen investors can gain a U.S. green card by investing US$1 million (or US$500,000 in high unemployment areas) toward a commercial venture that will employ 10 full-time U.S. employees (with caveats). Investors can apply for permanent residency after 2 years and seek citizenship after 5 years (Department of Homeland Security, 2012). Comparatively, in Dominica, foreign investors can purchase citizenship for US$100,000 for a single person or US$200,000 for a family of four or more (Government of the Commonwealth of Dominica, 2014).

Adding controversy to the disparity in citizenship costs, additional requirements for citizenship, or lack thereof, can potentially make this income-generating opportunity more darkly entrepreneurial. While Malta requires a higher investment than the United States, requesting €1.15 million, the government has strict requirements on how the money is invested and who controls the investment, including allocations in cash, property, and bonds or shares chosen and sanctioned by the government of Malta, in addition to residency requirements (Carrera, 2014). Similarly, for Cyprus, citizenship-by-investment can be completed for a sum as low as €2 million but more commonly costs at least €2.5 million, with strict rules on where the money is placed (PwC Cyprus, 2013). In St. Kitts and Nevis, applicants must invest in "officially approved" real estate development, valued at US$400,000 or more, or make a contribution of US$250,000 to the Sugar Industry Diversification Fund (Department of Information Technology, 2014).

Who is purchasing citizenship, whether they take up long-term residence on the island, and the nature of the investment can significantly impact the small island state or territory. St. Kitts and Nevis is a sovereign state with only 261 km^2 in land area and a resident population of about 52,000. A cohort of 20 millionaires from China, Russia, or Brazil could impact the country's development and culture, as well as the availability and cost of property, especially if they settle on Nevis (population 12,000), compared to them moving to the United States with its 9 million km^2 area and more than 300 million population.

Is economic citizenship ethical? It offers the opportunity for stateless people to resettle and find a home if they are rich enough. Moreover, Larmour (1997) discusses a proposal by Fiji to sell passports to Hong Kong families ostensibly seeking to avoid being ruled by China. Economic citizenship does indeed offer opportunities for entrepreneurs who have succeeded in their home country and who wish to escape political turmoil, harassment, or human rights violations or who wish to escape taxes and interference with their more malfeasant activities. Van Fossen (2007) describes alleged terrorists and criminals using Nauruan passports, one purchased for as little as US$15,025, before Nauru officially stopped the scheme in 2003.

Van Fossen (2007) summarizes the evolution of passport sales in Tonga, Samoa, the Marshall Islands, Vanuatu, and Nauru, including internal and external opposition to the sales. The evidence demonstrates that sales "involve secrecy and corruption which attenuates following exposure by media, opposition politicians, watchdogs and crusaders against international terrorism" (Van Fossen, 2007, p. 138). Additionally, illegal sales and privatization of passport sales minimize the proportion of revenue that small island state and territory governments collect.

Official estimates of revenue from passport sales are limited and hard to find. Van Fossen (2007, p. 141) estimates passport sales across Pacific islands accounted for 6.5% of Tonga's GDP from 1982 to 1996 and 11% of the Marshall Islands' GDP from 1995 to 1996. Wainwright (2003) considers additional uncertainty surrounding the sale of passports using the Solomon Islands as an example: what happens if the state fails or is in crisis? There could be less oversight of passport sales and purchases, although in the case of postphosphate Nauru, there might potentially be improved monitoring of passports given the Australian presence in contributing to governing the country.

Natural Resource Extraction

Many small island states and territories rely on typical natural resource extraction activities. Examples are Bahrain's economy dominated by fossil fuel income (Hamdi & Sbia, 2013), deep-sea fishing for tourists travelling to the Canary Islands (León et al., 2003), and agrotourism such as harvesting olives in the Greek Aegean islands as part of a holiday (Aikaterini et al., 2001). All these are typical livelihood activities enacted around the world, irrespective of ethical debates about the detrimental social and environmental impacts of fossil fuel extraction and natural resource–based tourism.

In other instances, dark entrepreneurship begins to emerge. Nauru became wealthy on mining its phosphate deposits, a legitimate natural-resource activity, but did not think beyond the finite reserves, leaving the country with little when the mining ended (Weeramantry, 1992). Mining phosphate in itself is a common activity, but lack of planning for a postphosphate environmental and social future could be considered somewhat unfair in the sense of entrepreneurship for "now" only, irrespective of what happens afterward. The same analysis could apply to selling fishing rights by island states such as Kiribati (Gagern & van den Bergh, 2013) or overfishing devastating stocks such as around the Galápagos Islands (Baldacchino, 2006). The activity itself is entrepreneurial, and the manner of implementation is dark due to the lack of thinking about the future.

Hunting in small island states and territories is another example some have interpreted as being entrepreneurship of dubious ethics. Polar bear hunting in Baffin Island, Nunavut, entails Inuit guiding rich outsiders to track and shoot polar bears, helping to preserve indigenous culture while bringing significant income to northern island communities (Dowsley, 2009; Freeman & Wenzel, 2006). Some environmentalists see polar bear hunting as having clear moral grounds for criticism, with the NGO Animal First! organizing a petition to the government of Canada to outlaw polar bear hunting.

Tourists can book a whale hunting tour in Lembata Island, Indonesia, hoping to see the locals from Lamalera village use traditional techniques to kill a migrating sperm whale, although the hunters also target orcas, pilot whales, and other sea creatures, including turtles (Egami & Kojima, 2013). The Visit Faroe Islands (2014) website advertises the pilot whale drive as an event of interest for tourists (www.visitfaroeislands.com/be-inspired/in-dept-articles/whaling). In both cases, the locals use the whale catches for subsistence and little goes to waste, so tourism income derived from the whale hunt is a bonus, not the main reason for the hunting. While the vociferous antiwhaling campaign views such income as being of dubious ethics, international protocols (e.g., International Convention for the Regulation of Whaling, 1946) accept indigenous whaling for local needs. Moreover, the tourism income is a sideline to the main reason for the hunts rather than being entrepreneurship *per se*. Consequently, whale hunting illustrates ambiguities of classifying dark entrepreneurship, while hunting with tourists overall represents different interpretations of the ethics of that entrepreneurship.

That is the same for some island mining activities. Fracking in Newfoundland (Brake & Addo, 2014), conservation hotspots encouraging bioprospecting in Madagascar for pharmaceutical development (Neimark & Schroeder, 2009), and deep-sea mineral exploration and extraction in the waters of the Solomon Islands and Papua New Guinea (Van Dover, 2011) are all discussed in their respective citations as representing entrepreneurship opportunities and concerns. Natural resource extraction has dark entrepreneurship dimensions, with small island states and territories providing numerous examples, but the virtue of these activities depends on the viewpoint adopted.

Waste Disposal

Accepting nuclear waste from outside jurisdictions, voluntarily or involuntarily, may negatively impact environmental conditions in islands. "Waste trade" or waste acceptance, like most of the questionable entrepreneurship activities mentioned, is poorly documented, especially with regard to the income earned (Clapp, 1994). Discussions suggest inconclusively and unclearly that circumstances occur where the trade is voluntary and for profit, as well as where the trade is involuntary with little income being derived. Clapp (1994) reports waste trade, assumedly for profit, for Caribbean, Pacific, and African islands, while Williams (1991) documents children playing on toxic waste imported from the United States to the island of Kassa, just offshore from Guinea's capital, Conakry.

E-waste—from devices such as laptops, monitors, and mobile phones—is emerging as the next big waste trade problem (Grossman, 2006). Batam Island, Indonesia, has been identified as accepting e-waste from the United States, recycling it in unsafe conditions, and then sometimes exporting recycled products to other Asian countries (GAO, 2008). Whatever the type of waste, mislabeling is a significant problem for the importing countries (Clapp, 1994), because they might seek nontoxic waste, to gain income as well as for land reclamation, but they do not have the resources to verify that the waste they are being given is what they expect to receive.

The Business of People

Holding asylum seekers might be considered dark entrepreneurship. Australia is the only developed nation practicing the mandatory detention of men, women, and children seeking asylum, perceiving refugees and asylum seekers as threats to national security (Hudson-Rodd, 2011). Refugees and asylum seekers are deterred, intercepted, and detained in extraterritorial islands such as Nauru and Papua New Guinea, outside the Australian legal system. As such, detainees do not receive equal legal rights. One example is the high-security prison constructed on Christmas Island where detainees can be held indefinitely; if the same detainees were held in Cairns or Adelaide, then their applications for asylum would have to be processed within 90 days (Hudson-Rodd, 2011). Nauru and Papua New Guinea are examples in which the island governments are paid by the Australian government to detain asylum seekers and refugees, with potential human rights violations (Briskman et al., 2008; Mountz, 2011).

Additional human rights violations that may arise due to entrepreneurial activities include trafficking humans (as well as weapons, drugs, and animals), as described by Cockayne and Williams (2009) and Souaré (2010) for the Bijagos Islands, Guinea-Bissau, and for remote islands of Cape Verde. With poor law enforcement and hidden airstrips around these islands, smugglers from Latin America have numerous havens to offload their cargo for further transport to Europe. The same occurs on Caribbean islands, with North America included as a final destination (Bartmann, 2007).

Flags of Convenience

In April 2003, Australian police arrested two men who were onshore from the North Korean freighter *Pong Su* and discovered 50 kg of heroin, leading to a 3-day chase of the ship through Australian waters, ending when Australian special forces boarded the ship and arrested the crew (Hurst & Reserve, 2005; Richardson, 2002). It is alleged that the *Pong Su* was part of a drug-smuggling network led by North Korea's government to earn cash. The ship was registered in Tuvalu as a flag of convenience.

Meanwhile, the Marshall Islands was used as a flag of convenience to register the oil rig *Deepwater Horizon*, which was drilling in the Gulf of Mexico when it exploded on April 20, 2010 killing 11 crew members. It sank 2 days later, and led to the largest U.S. offshore oil spill to date (Osofsky, 2011). Reports into the disaster concluded that it occurred due to organizational failures and lack of following proper procedures (Deepwater Horizon Study Group, 2011); there was apparently no oversight of the oil rig from the Marshall Islands.

These two examples illustrate island governments making easy money by registering vessels, which could include aircraft, for anyone who is willing to pay (see also Larmour, 1997). In each case, the registering government suffered few adverse consequences, apart from the loss of income through the vessels not reregistering. Instead, the *Pong Su* incident was between Australia and North Korea, while the reaction to *Deepwater Horizon* vilified the owner, oil company BP. Dark entrepreneurship is epitomized: solid income through creative means with dubious ethics and few consequences for the income earners, even if major consequences result for others.

Geostrategic Uses

Small island states and territories have long been used involuntarily by larger jurisdictions for military and defense purposes. Such practices are much easier to implement on clearly delineated spaces, namely islands, but there are exceptions such as the Golan Heights and Gibraltar. Fifield (1944) explores the geostrategy of location, detailing how river valleys as well as islands hold strategic value, but islands may be more prone to exploitation because of their relative lack of power and low population numbers. Oceans themselves hold strategic value for navigation, military positioning, and natural resource extraction, making islands that much more enticing. In fact,

Gibraltar is littoral and, rather than entire islands being used for geostrategic purposes, cases exist of small parts of larger islands being exploited, such as Guantánamo Bay, which is a U.S. military base in Cuba, and Akrotiri and Dhekelia, which are British sovereign military bases in Cyprus. All three are coastal.

Islanders displaced from their homes for military purposes and forced into poverty include those from (i) Bikini in the Marshall Islands for nuclear bomb testing (DeLoughrey, 2013, who also describes how the islanders were then unwittingly researched to better understand the health effects of nuclear fallout) and (ii) Diego Garcia in the British Indian Ocean Territory for a U.S. military base (Sand, 2009). Baldacchino (2010) and Vine (2004) cite Diego Garcia and several other examples of island inhabitants forced to move or being involuntarily affected so that the United States could use their land for military purposes, including Thule, Greenland; Okinawa, Japan; Naval Station Subic Bay and Clark Air Base in the Philippines until Mount Pinatubo erupted in 1991; and on U.S. territories of Guam, various parts of Hawai'i, and Vieques, Puerto Rico. Vine (2004) explains how the U.S. Navy, after World War II, described the "strategic island concept" for the Indian Ocean which argued that the United States should obtain the rights to as many of the islands as feasible in order to keep them available for future military use. This policy considered but rejected nonisland bases in the countries surrounding the Indian Ocean because it was felt that dealing with the local politics and people would be too difficult. Islands were seen as fair game.

With regard to Ascension Island in the South Atlantic and used by the UK as a military base, Baldacchino (2010) raises interesting questions that can be interpreted in the context of dark entrepreneurship. The island has no indigenous inhabitants, so it was used initially only by the military. People were brought in to serve the military and, eventually, a group settled there, feeling that the island is their home. The UK government does not permit the right of abode or owning property on the island, leading to significant tension, especially as travel for tourism and research increases. The UK government has, in effect, been exploiting the island for its own purposes, creating livelihoods and taking advantage of the military opportunities.

ETHICAL DISCUSSION

Important questions for better understanding the origins and propagation of entrepreneurship include: Who are the entrepreneurs? In which activities do they engage? Which factors or conditions enable or inhibit these activities? What are the interactions among different types of entrepreneurship?

Austin and colleagues (2006) distinguish between two types of entrepreneurship, social and commercial, and discuss activities and drivers of the two. Social entrepreneurship is defined as entrepreneurial activity within an embedded social purpose, creating social value, rather than necessarily financial value, in any sector. Social entrepreneurs can be individuals, governments, for-profit businesses, and nonprofit organizations (Dees & Anderson, 2003; Emerson & Twersky, 1996; Zadek & Thake, 1997). Commercial entrepreneurship engages similar groups and may be facilitated by similar mechanisms, but the defining goal is private financial gain. As the authors note, the two types of entrepreneurship are not dichotomous, often overlapping or serving both purposes simultaneously.

The definition of dark entrepreneurship given here seems to be the antithesis of social entrepreneurship. Indigenous hunting with tourists demonstrates how the same activity can be seen as dark entrepreneurship by those opposing hunting while being accepted as social entrepreneurship due to its social value in maintaining traditional knowledge and viable northern communities.

Ventures beginning as noncontentious social or commercial entrepreneurship may become dark entrepreneurship and vice versa. Lack of alternative livelihood options on postphosphate Nauru—despite being well established as a money-laundering center (Van Fossen, 2003)—led the country toward economic citizenship and housing asylum seekers (Maley, 2003; SBS, 2013). Conversely, activities that might originally have been deemed dark entrepreneurship can become mainstreamed.

This leads to the crux of many of the ethical debates enveloping entrepreneurship: all forms of entrepreneurship, including dark, are inextricably linked to local and global markets that serve social and commercial purposes. Dark entrepreneurship can arise not simply because someone sees an opportunity to try something new that succeeds but also because a clear but need is identified and entrepreneurship is used to satisfy that need while bringing income and/or social value. Notwithstanding all the positive entrepreneurship examples described in other chapters of this book, many small island states and territories might not have obvious means for lucrative livelihoods or might not have the skills or desire to resort to more ethical entrepreneurial activities. As with Nauru, when Australia offers governance support (social value) and income (financial value), both of which are needed for maintaining statehood, in exchange for holding asylum seekers, what incentive exists for Nauruans to (i) decline that opportunity on moral grounds and (ii) work hard to seek, not necessarily successfully, other alternatively viable entrepreneurial livelihood sources and/or be forced to migrate and seek such livelihoods elsewhere?

The same is true of other dark entrepreneurship. Those opposing tourists hunting polar bears or watching whale hunting rarely offer other livelihoods to the locals, particularly livelihoods that make use of the people's culture and knowledge, thereby providing social value. This is not claiming that all tradition is good and ought to be preserved, especially given that definitions of "traditional knowledge" include its dynamism (e.g., Flavier et al., 1995). It does blur the lines regarding the meaning of "dark" with respect to entrepreneurship.

Would those who oppose hunting prefer a MIRAB (migration, remittances, aid, and bureaucracy) economy (Bertram, 2006; Bertram & Watters, 1985)? It has been straightforward for many small islands states and territories to rely on external handouts, living off the taxpayers of larger countries such as Australia, France, the Netherlands, New Zealand, the UK, and the United States, and generating limited social value. For those islanders who choose to survive on remittances and aid, perhaps even on only their own government's welfare payments, are they being lazy or commercially entrepreneurial (e.g., Poirine, 1998)? As Tester (2009, pp. 139–140) writes, "In the census period May to July of 2006, Inuit accounted for 75% of the working-age population in the 10 largest Nunavut communities but only 60% of those employed," pointing out the huge injustices afflicting Inuit in Canada and preventing the Inuit from pursuing fulfilling livelihoods with social value. Instead of that analysis, should the Inuit in Baffin Island be encouraged toward exploiting the welfare system as a form of dark entrepreneurship? Yet many ethical systems—including that of the Inuit themselves—would see such an attitude being as reprehensible as some see the polar bear hunt.

In fact, islanders themselves decry the "handout mentality" they see pervading their culture (Tuiloma-Palesoo, 2004). Would being locked in an "aid and remittance" economic paradigm be a preferable economic base compared to imprisoning asylum seekers or accepting nuclear waste? How would the world react if, instead of handouts or hunting, islanders rented, leased, or sold their islands for military and other geostrategic purposes and sold themselves as test subjects for the effects of nuclear, biological, and chemical weapons? That would be dark commercial entrepreneurship with limited social value. This would be similar to development theory challenging certain participatory processes as "The New Tyranny" (Cooke & Kothari, 2001); the top-down imposition of livelihoods and the external judgment of livelihoods on ethical grounds could be seen as tyrannical.

Consequently, power dynamics emerge between the islanders seeking livelihoods, even through dark entrepreneurship, and those internal or external to the small island states and territories who would morally judge the livelihood choices. For Maltese and Kittitian/Nevisian citizenship, the research is not clear regarding how much is driven by the islanders as entrepreneurship and how much is demand led, with rich externals convincing or cajoling the islanders and their "soft states" (Hyden, 1983) to sell passports. In both cases, economic citizenship is certainly commercial entrepreneurship, but it could arguably be social entrepreneurship as well, in terms of creating innovative jobs, bringing creativity and diversity to the countries, and inspiring locals to be similarly entrepreneurial (if that actually happens).

In contrast, for Nauru, Australia could be seen as both the welcome savior of a broken country and a neoimperialist regime forcing the naïve, exploitable islanders into nefarious, purely commercial deeds. Either view would label the dark entrepreneur being the Australian, rather than the Nauruan, government.

Yet Australia does not gain commercially. Instead, for the Australian government, housing asylum seekers on Nauru is social (dark) entrepreneurship—notwithstanding the Australians who vehemently oppose this policy—while for Nauru, it is commercial (dark) entrepreneurship.

The power dynamics do not absolve those in the jurisdictions who profit from dark entrepreneurship but indicate how nebulous entrepreneurship ethics are. Ultimately, those with the least power tend to suffer the most due to dark entrepreneurship: those affected by disasters from flags of convenience, the asylum seekers and refugees, and islanders who are just trying to feed their family or save for their children's education.

CONCLUSION

Rarity and exclusivity of products and services frequently yields desirability due to uniqueness, as is often exploited for small island states and territories (Baldacchino, 2005a, 2005b). That opens doors to entrepreneurship, which is sometimes as simple as branding a mundane product, such as FIJI water (Connell, 2006), and which is sometimes as complex as providing a dubious service. For the latter, the smallness—and often remoteness—of the territories considered here is advantageous because the lack of prominence of the jurisdictions and the potential difficulty of reaching them can make any perpetrators of unethical practices difficult to track down and inhibit.

Suggestions are also made that the power brokers in small island states and territories might be more trusting, needy, or easier to manipulate. That has some truth, with examples being the siphoning of Tonga's funds (James, 2003) and the mismanagement of Nauru's phosphate profits (Weeramantry, 1992). Yet no studies exist to indicate that the frequency or likelihood of such instances correlates with the jurisdiction's size, remoteness, or islandness or that external exploitation is the only factor leading to these cases.

Highlighting "remoteness from ethics," "naiveté," or "financial incompetence" as inevitable characteristics of small island states and territories is patronizing and inaccurate, especially considering how many prominent nonislanders lost substantial investments in Ponzi schemes (Pozza, Jr. et al., 2009–2010). As with any location and any group of people, needs and temptations to pursue livelihoods exist, leading some to be entrepreneurial and some to be darkly entrepreneurial. The motivation of the latter, ultimately, is to make short-term money without much regard to the consequences, a phenomenon witnessed around the world at all jurisdictional scales (Klein, 2007).

Nevertheless, small island states and territories encapsulate and starkly demonstrate challenges and opportunities common to many other locations. Prasad (2004) details how small jurisdictions frequently bypass or ignore global trade rules for their own advantage, effectively suggesting that these economies are too small for the big players to worry about. That applies to dark entrepreneurship, too. Unless something emerges to make the small island state and territory's activities known, such as environmental campaigners periodically seeking to embarrass the Faroese with gory photos of whale kills, the jurisdictions tend to be too remote and too small to be noticed or to take action against.

Moreover, the specificities of small island states and territories—bounded, isolated, small, and often beyond the horizon of public opinion, media scrutiny, or domestic legislation—tolerate, even encourage, dark entrepreneurship. That provides opportunities to evade many standard norms and rules that could not be avoided in larger, more populous, more regulated locations. As an example, the legal ethics of Guantánamo Bay and of the torture conducted there by American authorities is one of the most noted cases (Kaplan, 2005).

Some of the small islands and territories are also forced into seeking and implementing entrepreneurial activities with negative outcomes due to the challenges of maintaining livelihoods. Notwithstanding the exploitation of large-scale marine resources and the economic advantages of smallness displayed by many island communities, many lack substantive land-based natural resources and do not have the personnel or possibilities to explore economies of scale. Furthermore, livelihood difficulties echoed across many small island states and territories include high transport costs alongside irregular or unreliable transportation options for goods and people. When many common entrepreneurship options are not feasible, it is unsurprising that some island communities seek dark entrepreneurship to give themselves income and opportunities.

Meanwhile, two principal challenges emerge. First, judging entrepreneurs to common and consistent standards is important for equity. Small island states and territories do not necessarily seek equity with their non-island counterparts, nor do they have to, due to the reduced accountability emerging from remoteness. Second, if some forms of entrepreneurship are deemed to be inappropriate and therefore to be stopped, providing alternatives is necessary so that the people's creativity and livelihoods do not suffer. Who determines inappropriateness and who provides the alternative livelihoods is about power relations and the small island states and territories using their geographic position to take and (ab)use the power, which otherwise they could not have, for enacting dark entrepreneurship on their own terms.

REFERENCES

Arend, R. J. (2007). Abandoning (entrepreneur) ship: Children and victims first. *Strategic Organization, 5*(4), 409–422.

Aikaterini, G., Spilanis, I., & Kizos, T. (2001). Is agrotourism "Agro" or "Tourism"? Evidence from agrotourist holdings in Lesvos, Greece. *Anatolia: An International Journal of Tourism and Hospitality Research, 12*(1), 6–22.

Austin, J., Stevenson, H., & Wei-Skillern, J. (2006). Social and commercial entrepreneurship: Same, different, or both? *Entrepreneurship theory and practice, 30*(1), 1–22.

Bakker, R. (2012). *ACE research vignette 019: Exploring the "dark side" of entrepreneurship.* Brisbane, Australia: Queensland University of Technology.

Baldacchino, G. (2005a). Island entrepreneurs: Insights from exceptionally successful knowledge-driven SMEs from 5 European island territories. *Journal of Enterprising Culture, 13*(2), 145–170.

Baldacchino, G. (2005b). Successful small scale manufacturing from small islands: Comparing firms benefiting from local raw material input. *Journal of Small Business and Entrepreneurship, 18*(1), 21–38.

Baldacchino, G. (2006). Warm versus cold water island tourism: A review of policy implications. *Island Studies Journal, 1*(2), 183–200.

Baldacchino, G. (Ed.). (2007). *A world of islands: An island studies reader.* Charlottetown, Canada, and Luqa, Malta: Institute of Island Studies, University of Prince Edward and Agenda Academic.

Baldacchino, G. (2010). *Island enclaves: Offshoring strategies, creative governance, and subnational island jurisdictions.* Montreal, QC: McGill-Queen's University Press.

Bartmann, B. (2007). Island war and security. In Godfrey Baldacchino (Ed.), *A world of islands: An island studies reader* (pp. 295–322). Charlottetown, Canada, and Luqa, Malta: University of Prince Edward Island and Agenda Academic.

Baumol, W.J. (1990). Entrepreneurship: Productive, unproductive, and destructive. *Journal of Political Economy, 98*, 893–921.

Berkman, E.T. (1996). Responses to the international child sex tourism trade notes. *Boston College International & Comparative Law Review, 19*, 397–422.

Bertram, G. (2006). Introduction: The MIRAB model in the twenty-first century. *Asia Pacific Viewpoint, 47*(1), 1–13.

Bertram, G., & Watters, R.F. (1985). The MIRAB economy in South Pacific microstates. *Pacific Viewpoint, 26*(3), 497–519.

Brake, W., & Addo, E. (2014). Tourism and "fracking" in western Newfoundland: Interests and anxieties of coastal communities and companies in the context of sustainable tourism. *International Journal of Marine Science, 4.* doi: 10.5376/ijms.2014.04.0002

Briskman, L., Goddard, C., & Latham, S. (2008). *Human rights overboard: Seeking asylum in Australia.* London: Scribe Publications.

Butcher, J. (2003). *The moralization of tourism: Sun, sand and . . . saving the world.* London: Routledge.

Carrera, S. (2014). *How much does EU citizenship cost? The Maltese citizenship-for-sale affair: A breakthrough for sincere cooperation in citizenship of the union?* Brussels: The Centre for European Policy Studies.

Clapp, J. (1994). The toxic waste trade with less-industrialized countries: Economic linkages and political alliances. *Third World Quarterly, 15*, 505–518.

Cockayne, J., & Williams, P. (2009). *The invisible tide: Towards an international strategy to deal with drug trafficking through West Africa.* New York, NY: International Peace Institute.

Collins, O.F., & Moore, D.G. (1964). *The enterprising man.* East Lansing, MI: Michigan State University.

Connell, J. (2006). The taste of paradise: Selling Fiji and FIJI water. *Asia Pacific Viewpoint, 47*(3), 342–350.

Cooke, B., & Kothari, U. (2001). *Participation: The new tyranny.* London: Zed Books.

Deepwater Horizon Study Group. (2011). *Final report on the investigation of the Macondo well blowout.* Berkeley, CA: Deepwater Horizon Study Group.

Dees, J. G., & Anderson, B. B. (2003). For-profit social ventures. *International Journal of Entrepreneurship Education, 2*(1), 1–26.

DeLoughrey, E. M. (2013). The myth of isolates: Ecosystem ecologies in the nuclear Pacific. *Cultural Geographies, 20*(2), 167–184.

Dening, G. (2004). *Beach crossings: Voyaging across times, cultures and self.* Philadelphia, PA: University of Pennsylvania Press.

Department of Homeland Security. (2012). EB-5 Immigrant Investor. Retrieved from www.uscis.gov/working-united-states/permanent-workers/employment-based-immigration-fifth-preference-eb-5/eb-5-immigrant-investor

Department of Information Technology, Government of St. Christopher (St. Kitts) and Nevis. (2014). St. Kitts & Nevis citizenship by investment program. Retrieved from www.ciu.gov.kn

Dess, G. G., Lumpkin, G. T., & Covin, J. G. (1997). Entrepreneurial strategy making and firm performance: Tests of contingency and configurational models. *Strategic Management Journal, 18*(9), 677–695.

Dowsley, M. (2009). Inuit organized polar bear sport hunting in Nunavut Territory, Canada. *Journal of Ecotourism, 8*(2), 161–175.

Egami, T., & Kojima, K. (2013). Traditional whaling culture and social change in Lamalera, Indonesia: An analysis of the catch record of whaling 1994–2010. *Senri Ethnological Studies, 84*, 155–176.

Emerson, J., & Twersky, F. (Eds.). (1996). *New social entrepreneurs: The success, challenge and lessons of non-profit enterprise creation.* San Francisco, CA: Roberts Foundation, Homeless Economic Development Fund.

Fifield, R. H. (1944). The geostrategy of location. *Journal of Geography, 43*(8), 297–303.

Flavier, J. M., de Jesus, A., & Navarro, C. (1995). The regional program for the promotion of indigenous knowledge in Asia. In D. M. Warren, L. J. Slikkerveer, & David Brokensha (Eds.), *The cultural dimension of development: Indigenous knowledge systems* (pp. 479–487). London: Intermediate Technology Publications.

Foley, M., & Lennon, J. (1996). JFK and dark tourism: Heart of darkness. *Journal of International Heritage Studies, 2*(2), 198–211.

Freeman, M.M.R., & Wenzel, G. W. (2006). The nature and significance of polar bear conservation hunting in the Canadian Arctic. *Arctic, 59*, 21–30.

Gagern, A., & van den Bergh, J. (2013). A critical review of fishing agreements with tropical developing countries. *Marine Policy, 38*, 375–386.

GAO. (2008). *GAO testimony before the subcommittee on Asia, the Pacific, and the global environment, committee on Foreign Affairs, House of Representatives. Electronic waste. Harmful US exports flow virtually unrestricted because of minimal EPA enforcement and narrow regulation. Statement of John B. Stephenson, Director Natural Resources and Environment.* Washington, DC: United States Government Accountability Office.

Government of the Commonwealth of Dominica, Financial Services Unit of the Ministry of Finance. (2014). Policy guidelines and procedural steps for applying for economic citizenship of the commonwealth of Dominica (Guidelines for promoters/agents/applicants). Retrieved from www.dominica.gov.dm/services/how-do-i-apply-for-economic-citizenship-of-the-commonwealth-of-dominica

Graci, S., & Dodds, R. (2010). *Sustainable tourism in island destinations.* London: Earthscan.

Grossman, E. (2006). *High tech trash: Digital devices, hidden toxics, and human health.* Washington, DC: Island Press.

Hamdi, H., & Sbia, R. (2013). Dynamic relationships between oil revenues, government spending and economic growth in an oil-dependent economy. *Economic Modelling, 35*(1), 118–125.

Hau'ofa, E. (1993). *A new Oceania: Rediscovering our sea of islands*. Suva: University of the South Pacific. Retrieved from www.formazione.unimib.it/DATA/Insegnamenti/2_512/materiale/our-sea-of-islands.pdf

Hudson-Rodd, N. (2011). The engineering of detentional landscapes: Australia's asylum seeker island prisons. In S. D. Brunn (Ed.), *Engineering Earth: The impacts of megaengineering projects* (pp. 1723–1748). Berlin: Springer.

Hurst, C. A., & Reserve, U. N. (2005). North Korea: Government-sponsored drug trafficking. *Military Review, 85*(5), 35.

Hyden, G. (1983). *No shortcuts to progress: African development management in perspective*. London: Heinemann.

International Convention for the Regulation of Whaling. (1946). *International convention for the regulation of whaling*. Schedule, as amended by Commission at 64th annual meeting. Panama City, Panama.

James, K. (2003). Tonga. *The Contemporary Pacific, 15*(2), 187–192.

Kaplan, A. (2005). Where Is Guantánamo? *American Quarterly, 57*(3), 831–858.

Kelman, I., & Dodds, R. (2009). Developing a code of ethics for disaster tourism. *International Journal of Mass Emergencies and Disasters, 27*(3), 272–296.

Khamis, S. (2007). Gourmet and green: The branding of King Island. *Shima, 1*(1), 14–29.

Klein, N. (2007). *The shock doctrine: The rise of disaster capitalism*. London: Macmillan.

Larmour, P. (1997). Corruption and governance in the South Pacific. *Pacific Studies, 20*(1), 1–17.

León, C. J., Araña, J. E., & Melián, A. (2003). Tourist use and preservation benefits from big-game fishing in the Canary Islands. *Tourism Economics, 9*(1), 53–65.

Lisle, D. (2004). Gazing at ground zero: Tourism, voyeurism and spectacle. *Journal for Cultural Research, 8*(1), 3–21.

Maley, W. (2003). Asylum-seekers in Australia's international relations. *Australian Journal of International Affairs, 57*(1), 187–202.

McClelland, D. C. (1961). *The achieving story*. Princeton, NJ: D. Van Nostrand.

Mountz, A. (2011). The enforcement archipelago: Detention, haunting, and asylum on islands. *Political Geography, 30*(1), 118–128.

Neimark, B. D., & Schroeder, R. A. (2009). Hotspot discourse in Africa: Making space for bioprospecting in Madagascar. *African Geographical Review, 28*(1), 43–69.

Oberst, A., & McElroy, J. L. (2007). Contrasting socio-economic and demographic profiles of two, small island, economic species: MIRAB versus PROFIT/SITE. *Island Studies Journal, 2*(1), 163–176.

Osofsky, H. M. (2011). Multidimensional governance and the BP Deepwater Horizon oil spill. *Florida Law Review, 63*, 1077–1137.

Perren, L., & Jennings, P. L. (2005). Government discourses on entrepreneurship: Issues of legitimization, subjugation, and power. *Entrepreneurship Theory and Practice, 29*(2), 173–184.

Poirine, B. (1994). Rent, emigration and unemployment in small islands: The MIRAB model and the French overseas departments and territories. *World Development, 22*(12), 1997–2009.

Poirine, B. (1998). Should we hate or love MIRAB? *The Contemporary Pacific, 10*, 65–105.

Pozza, Jr., Clarence L., Cox, T. R., & Mora, R. J. (2010). A review of recent investor issues in the Madoff, Stanford and Forte Ponzi scheme cases. *Journal of Business & Securities Law, 10*(2), 113–131.

Prasad, N. (2004). Escaping regulation, escaping convention: Development strategies in small economies. *World Economics, 5*(1), 41–65.

PwC Cyprus. (2013). *Cyprus citizenship for foreign investors*. Nicosia, Cyprus: PwC (PricewaterhouseCoopers).

Rao, M. (2002). Challenges and issues for tourism in the South Pacific island states: The case of the Fiji Islands. *Tourism Economics, 8*(4), 401–429.

Richardson, M. (2002). Crimes under flags of convenience—in a depressed shipping market, poor nations sell flags for criminal venture. *Maritime Studies, 127*, 22–24.

Royle, S. A. (2006). The Falkland Islands. In G. Baldacchino (Ed.), *Extreme tourism: Lessons from the world's cold water islands* (pp. 181–192). Oxford: Elsevier.

Royle, S. A. (2010). Postcolonial culture on dependent islands. *Space and Culture, 13*(2), 203–215.

Sand, P. H. (2009). Diego Garcia: British-American legal black hole in the Indian Ocean? *Journal of Environmental Law, 21*(1), 113–137.

SBS. (2013). *Australia signs asylum deal with Nauru.* Sydney: Special Broadcasting Service Corporation.

Schumpeter, J. A. (1934). *The theory of economic development: An inquiry into profits, capital, credit, interest, and the business cycle.* Cambridge, MA: Transaction Publishers.

Seaton, A. V. (1996). From thanatopsis to thanatourism: Guided by the dark. *International Journal of Heritage Studies, 2*(4), 234–244.

Souaré, I. K. (2010). *A critical assessment of security challenges in West Africa.* Pretoria: Institute for Security Studies.

Stevenson, H. H. (1983). *A perspective on entrepreneurship.* Boston, MA: Harvard Business School.

Stevenson, H., & Harmeling, S. (1990). Entrepreneurial management's need for a more "chaotic" theory. *Journal of Business Venturing, 5*(1), 1–14.

Tester, F. (2009). Iglutaasaavut (Our new homes): Neither "new" nor "ours." Housing challenges of the Nunavut Territorial Government. *Journal of Canadian Studies, 43*(2), 137–158.

Tuiloma-Palesoo, D. (2004). Handout mentality. *Small Islands Voice Global Forum.* Retrieved from www.sivglobal.org/?read=82

Van Dover, C. L. (2011). Tighten regulations on deep-sea mining. *Nature, 470*(7332), 31–33.

Van Fossen, A. (2003). Money laundering, global financial instability, and tax havens in the Pacific Islands. *The Contemporary Pacific, 15*(2), 237–275.

Van Fossen, A. (2007). Citizenship for sale: Passports of convenience from Pacific island tax havens. *Commonwealth & Comparative Politics, 45*(2), 138–163.

Vine, D. (2004). War and forced migration in the Indian Ocean: The US military base at Diego Garcia. *International Migration, 42*(3), 111–143.

Visit Faroe Islands. (2014). Whales and whaling in the Faroe Islands. Retrieved from www.visitfaroeislands.com/be-inspired/in-dept-articles/whaling

Wainwright, E. (2003). Responding to state failure: The case of Australia and Solomon Islands. *Australian Journal of International Affairs, 57*(3), 485–498.

Weeramantry, C. G. (1992). *Nauru: Environmental damage under international trusteeship.* Melbourne: Oxford University Press.

Williams, J. D. (1991). Trashing developing nations: The global hazardous waste trade. *Buffalo Law Review, 39*, 275–312.

Yaguchi, Y. (2005). War memories across the Pacific: Japanese visitors at the Arizona Memorial. *Comparative American Studies, 3*(3), 345–360.

Zadek, S., & Thake, S. (1997). Send in the social entrepreneurs. *New Statesman, 26*(7339), 31–39.

3 The Diasporic Economy, Trade and Entrepreneurship in the Island Caribbean

Keith Nurse

INTRODUCTION

The diasporic economy is one of the few bright sparks in the contemporary recession-plagued global economy (*The Economist*, 2011). The flows associated with the diasporic economy, particularly remittances, continue to expand and contribute to sending societies such that they have surpassed the traditional sources of external development financing. The importance of the diasporic economy is illustrated by the fact that, for many of the recipient countries, remittances account for a significant share of their foreign exchange reserves and so represent a vital mechanism to stabilize balance of payments and currency markets and securitize external debt (Ratha & Plaza, 2011; World Bank, 2013, pp. 48–51). In addition, remittances and other flows have played a critical role in many developing countries in terms of poverty reduction and bilateral trade (Nurse, 2004a).

These impacts are particularly evident among small island states. This is because the highest emigration rates are generally recorded for small countries (most of which are islands anyway). In 2005/06, one third of persons born in Jamaica were living in Organisation for Economic Co-operation and Development (OECD) countries, and more than 20% of the population originating from Cape Verde, Trinidad and Tobago, Malta and Fiji were in the OECD area (OECD, 2014). As such, small island states have large diasporic communities in relative terms and often have significant diaspora-related trade flows and thus have strategic opportunities in relation to the growth of the diasporic economy.

This chapter argues that the ability of small island states and territories to activate and explore the opportunities in the diasporic economy is the new frontier in global competitiveness, innovation and entrepreneurship. An increasing number of countries in the Caribbean have established departments and units within ministries of foreign affairs, trade and investment to deal specifically with the interests of diasporic communities. However, the economic contribution and developmental potential of diasporic relations and entrepreneurship requires further documentation, measurement and policy coherence. As such, there is a great need to identify ways in which emigration and the growth of island diasporas can be enhanced through a strategic diasporic engagement framework focused on trade and enterprise development.

This chapter examines the emigration and development nexus in relation to the growth of diasporic markets and diasporic entrepreneurship in small island jurisdictions. The rationale is that international migration and the growth of diasporic communities create markets and encourage both trade and entrepreneurship. Migrants, their families and their communities tend to demand niche, specialty, identity and nostalgic goods, services and intellectual property that are often provided by firms and entrepreneurs from the sending countries or from the host societies (e.g., immigrant entrepreneurs). The entrepreneurs may be operating from both jurisdictions and may also not have any identity connections to the diasporic communities or the homelands. Often these ventures are transnational firms that enjoy economies of scale in a particular sector and/or have spotted the opportunities in the diasporic economy and market.

THE DIASPORIC ECONOMY, TRADE AND DEVELOPMENT

The growth of diasporas in the last few decades has led to a new geo-economics of development, with economic flows like financial transfers (remittances) playing a critical role in poverty reduction as well as enterprise development (Nurse, 2004a, 2004b). For many countries, remittances have exceeded traditional modes of external financing. Remittance flows to developing countries are estimated at US$414 billion for 2013 (up 6.3% over 2012) and are expected to experience an annual growth rate of 8% for the period 2013 to 2016 to reach US$540 billion in 2016. Remittance flows to developing countries surpassed official development assistance in the mid-1990s and are currently three times larger (World Bank, 2013). While remittances were affected by the global financial and economic crisis, as exemplified by a drop of 6.1% in 2009 on account of the weak jobs market, they have emerged from the decline to be more resilient and larger than private debt and portfolio equity flows to developing countries (Mohapatra & Ratha, 2010, p. 1). Currently, only flows of foreign direct investment (FDI) outstrip remittances.

However, this is only the tip of the iceberg given that the diasporic economy is wider than financial transfers from remittances. The diasporic economy includes flows associated with sectors like telecoms, tourism, transportation and trade in nostalgic, ethnic or niche goods (Orozco, Lowell, Bump, & Fedewa, 2005). It also includes the monetization of intellectual property through copyrights in the media and creative industries as well as geographic indications embedded in specialty goods. Countries also benefit from diasporas by tapping into networks of trade, scientific and professional diasporas. These economic flows also facilitate investment by diaspora communities and encourage brain circulation (e.g., return migration, mobility of professional services) that redress the challenges associated with brain drain (i.e., the emigration of the tertiary educated; Dawson, 2007).

Migration and the growth of a diasporic economy have emerged to be among the most important strategic economic resources for developing countries in the late 20th and early 21st centuries. Remittances and other economic flows associated with the diasporic economy make a substantial contribution to economic development, poverty reduction, international trade and a more favorable balance-of-payments position in the region when compared to traditional forms of external capital and development assistance such as foreign aid, debt financing and FDI. While there is no denying the importance of the diasporic economy, there remains much concern as to whether the benefits of migration—such as remittances, diasporic exports and the vent of surplus population—redress the loss of economically active workers (i.e., brain drain) and the social investment foregone.

The developmental impact of emigration on sending countries has generated much debate and is generally a contested area of research (Stahl, 1982; Stalker, 2003; Swanson, 1979). From a historical perspective, it is argued that European emigration "did little to raise the real incomes of growing populations or to expand employment opportunities. . .these improvements depended more on the spread of industrialization, technical progress, and the growth of productivity than on a simple loss of population" (Kenwood & Lougheed 1992, p. 55). From another standpoint, European emigration is considered to be one of the key factors in the convergence of wages and living standards of countries like Ireland, Italy and Norway with Britain by the early 20th century (O'Rourke, 2004, p. 10). Based upon this latter diagnosis, "emigration is an incredibly effective way for poor countries to raise their living standards" (O'Rourke, 2004, p. 3).

Trade is also an important feature of the diasporic economy. The literature on trade and migration suggests that there is a positive relationship between bilateral migration and bilateral trade. In a study of the effect of immigration on U.S. trade flows, Mundra (2005) points out that immigrants (1) demand goods and services from their home countries; (2) introduce new products and services to the host countries; (3) introduce new products and services from their host countries to their home countries; and (4) impact business development through the circulation of knowledge and ideas.

Immigrant populations operate in transnational spaces and consequently are uniquely positioned to capitalize on the economic opportunities of both sending and receiving countries. In this regard, Jansen and Piermatini (2009, p. 737) argue that

> Migrants can play a role in reducing information costs. They are in a privileged position to provide information about distribution networks and about demand in their home countries to host country exporters. They are also in a privileged position to provide the same type of information on the host country to home country exporters. In addition, they

can provide understanding about culturally derived negotiating norms, thus reducing negotiating costs between the two sides.

Many developing countries have seized the opportunities embodied in these flows and have reaped huge rewards through strategic diaspora engagement programs. For example, countries like the People's Republic of China, India, Israel, Mexico and El Salvador have targeted their diasporic communities for "brain gain": trade, investment and technology transfer (Kuznetsov, 2006). Similar opportunities are available for small island states and territories, as they tend to have large diasporic communities in relative terms that offer the opportunities to deepen the linkages between small island jurisdictions and global cities (Terrazas, 2010).

There is an emerging discourse, if not consensus, in development circles that the migration and development nexus is a critical resource for inclusive development that needs to be unlocked (GFMD, 2013, p. 3). Diasporic entrepreneurship is considered to be an important element of unlocking this developmental potential. For example, the Migration Policy Institute argues that

Development practitioners and policymakers are beginning to examine the role of diaspora entrepreneurs in gearing investments toward their home countries, thereby creating jobs, spurring innovation, and fostering networks. Compared with remittances or diaspora bonds, entrepreneurial investments give diaspora members more direct control over the use of their funds. Given their ties to their countries of origin, diaspora members are often more willing than non-diaspora investors to risk starting or engaging in business activities in high-risk or emerging markets. Moreover, their knowledge of the local political, economic, and cultural environment, as well as their personal connections and linguistic abilities, may give members of diasporas a "first mover" advantage over others when investing in or starting businesses in their countries of origin.

(Newland & Tanaka, 2010, p. 2)

The diasporic economy and market can be considered as strategic resources in that firms that are able to tap into these markets are able to transcend the limitations of size, which is a structural constraint in small economies. It is also important to note that the diasporic market often offers a bridge into mainstream markets, thus allowing for market presence and the establishment of firms abroad. Diasporic entrepreneurs also tend to have a network base (e.g., hub-to-hub ties) that spans both the sending and receiving countries and as such are often able to overcome the hurdles of doing business or trade between the two jurisdictions. The benefits of such networking tend to be pronounced where the business, trade and financing institutions are weak and hence the barriers to running a successful business are higher. The successful diasporic entrepreneurs therefore act as institutional influencers, able to transform or transcend institutional arrangements in the home country (Kuznetsov, 2006).

Return migration plays a critical role in boosting the entrepreneurial capacities of the home country, especially in a context in which there have been high levels of brain drain among the tertiary-educated and the professional and business classes. This is particularly evident through what are described as social remittances or the flow of ideas, skills, social capital and networks between migrants and their home countries, whether through return migration and tourism or through economic mechanisms like diasporic trade, investment and entrepreneurship. Social remittances are inherently circular as well as cultural because they involve the transfer of ideas, practices, narratives and identities between home and host countries (Levitt, 1998). Indeed, "returning and circulatory elites, embedded in international 'epistemic communities' have long served as conduits for the diffusion of new ideas and paradigms within both domestic and international spheres" (Kapur, 2010, p. 125). But what are the mechanisms by which these migrants make an impact on their home countries? Kapur (2010, p. 149) suggests that the three critical factors to be considered are (1) the institutional configuration in the country of origin and its relative receptivity to accepting new ideas and returning human capital; (2) the willingness of individuals to return; and (3) the reputation and credibility of the migrant's destination.

THE CARIBBEAN DIASPORIC ECONOMY

The Caribbean is a good case study because it has some of the highest remittance/GDP rates in the world along with some of the highest brain drain rates (*Canadian Foreign Policy Journal*, 2011; *also* Baldacchino, 2006). In relative terms, the Caribbean region has a large diasporic community geographically spread across the United States, Canada, the UK, the rest of Europe and the wider Caribbean. As such, there are significant potential growth opportunities, given the size of the diasporic market, if emigration rates, remittances and brain drain rates are used as a proxy.

The Caribbean region has a high level of exposure to the diasporic economy when compared with other developing country regions. Within the "African, Caribbean and Pacific" group of developing countries (ACP), the Caribbean has approximately 25% of the remittances and 22% of the migrant stock in spite of only 4.4% of the population share in the ACP. In comparison, Africa has close to 95% of the population but only close to three quarters of the remittances and migrant shares. The Pacific region has a small share of the population along with low shares of remittances and migrant stocks (see Table 3.1).

Table 3.1   Remittances and Migration in the ACP

Regions/ Indicators	Share of Remittances (%)	Share of Migrants (%)	Share of Population (%)
Africa	73	76	94.5
Caribbean	25.5	22	4.4
Pacific	1.5	2	1.1

Source: Gallina (2010, p. 78).

Remittances

Remittances or money transfers, which are a key indicator of the size of the diasporic economy, have contributed to a more favorable balance-of-payments position in several labor-exporting territories in the Caribbean. Remittances to Barbados exceeded US$81 million, while St. Kitts and St. Lucia had inflows of US$45.1 million and US$29.8 million, respectively in 2010. Caribbean remittances have been stable in recent years in spite of the global financial crisis (Maldonaldo & Hayem, 2013).

Remittances are a major source of external flow to these economies. In most small economies in the Caribbean—such as Antigua and Barbuda, Barbados, St. Kitts and Nevis and St. Vincent and the Grenadines—remittances outstrip overseas development assistance (ODA; see Table 3.2). However, remittances are less impactful than FDI in all territories except for Dominica, which generally has low levels of external flows. Tourism receipts are significantly larger than remittances and the other external flows in Antigua and Barbuda, Barbados and St. Lucia, given the dominance of this sector in these small island economies.

Table 3.2   Selected External Flows, US$ million (2010)

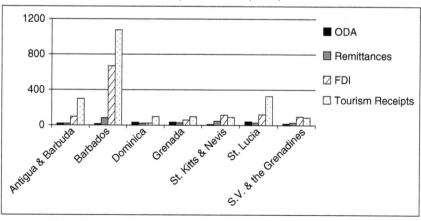

Source: World Bank (2012)

Table 3.3   Top 10 Remittance Recipients as a Percentage of GDP (2009)

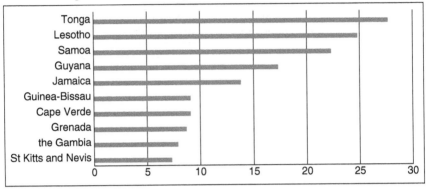

Source: Ratha and Silwal (2012)

Remittances are also a major source of income for many lower-income households around the region. Migration is very much a family decision, and remittances are often seen as part of a bond or contract between remitters and their families and dependents. It is estimated that more than 80% of the funds that are remitted are used for immediate consumption and welfare rather than long-term investment in land, housing, education and productive investments (Nurse, 2004a). Small jurisdictions, including many small island states, lead the pack of top remittance recipients as a percentage of gross domestic product (GDP; see Table 3.3).

Brain Drain

The Caribbean region has one of the highest emigration rates in the world, and for many years, the exodus of its highly skilled labor force has been seen as a loss, a "brain drain." When the Caribbean is compared to other small states, it is evident that the region has a high level of integration to the global economy through international migration. Five Caribbean island states are in the top 10 emigration countries (as a percentage of population) among small states, with emigration rates of 40% or higher of the locally born population (see Table 3.4). The proportions are even larger in subnational island jurisdictions that maintain links with metropolitan powers, such as Aruba, the former Netherlands Antilles, Cayman, Turks and Caicos, the Virgin Islands, Martinique, Guadeloupe and Montserrat. The latter's entire island population was forced to relocate when the Soufriere Hills volcano began erupting in 1995, and about a half of these citizens never returned when the threat abated (Pattullo, 2000).

Several Caribbean island states also appear on the "top 10" list in terms of emigration rates for the tertiary educated (see Table 3.5). Indeed,

Table 3.4 Top Emigrant Countries by Percentage of Native-Born Population Now Living Abroad (2010)

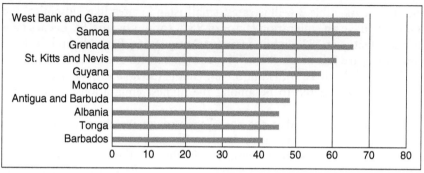

Source: Ratha and Silwal (2012)

Table 3.5 Top 10 Countries by Percentage of Emigration of Tertiary-Educated Population (2000)

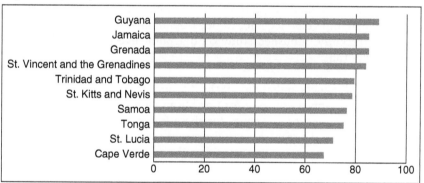

Source: Ratha and Silwal (2012)

Caribbean countries hold the top six positions. Guyana heads the list, with a brain drain rate of 90% of its tertiary educated. The other top countries are small islands like Jamaica, Grenada, St. Vincent and the Grenadines, Trinidad and Tobago and St. Kitts and Nevis. St. Lucia follows after Samoa and Tonga but ahead of Cape Verde. The data in this table reinforce the view that small island states are heavily impacted by international migration and are particularly exposed to the diasporic economy.

The impact of brain drain is particularly heavy in key sectors like health, education and science and technology, which have been negatively impacted by the quantum of highly trained labor that has emigrated. The emigration factor of physicians from developing-country regions to the United States, Canada, the UK and Australia is such that the Caribbean, at 8.5%, is placed third overall after sub-Saharan Africa (14%) and the

Indian subcontinent (11%; Mullan, 2005). However, the emigration factor for small Caribbean islands is at a much higher rate with the exception of Barbados. As Table 3.6 illustrates, small island states like Dominica and Grenada have an emigration factor of 98% for physicians. St. Lucia's emigration factor is 78%, while rates for Antigua and Barbuda and St. Kitts and Nevis are just below 40%. This compares with countries like Jamaica and Ireland (both 41%), Haiti (35%), Ghana (30%) and Sri Lanka (27%), which are considered to be among the highest emigration countries for physicians.

It is on this basis that the social investment in education and other losses due to skilled migration is often deemed to outweigh the benefits from remittances in small economies, like those in the Caribbean (Mishra, 2006; *also* Nurse & Jones, 2010). In contrast, it is argued that many countries lack the absorptive capacity to employ a large share of the tertiary educated, and as such, it is worthwhile for such countries to explore how migrants can contribute to economic development back home and how diaspora-centered policies could utilize the human capital in the diaspora, thereby facilitating brain circulation, diasporic investment and entrepreneurship (Baldacchino, 2006; *Canadian Foreign Policy Journal*, 2011). A recently published study on diaspora investment in the Caribbean argues that

> [T]he willingness and ability of the diaspora to engage represents a significant untapped potential for Caribbean nations . . . while the money is out there, creating avenues for these funds to flow back home and ensuring that the regulatory environment for businesses is conducive to receiving such investments remains a challenge.
>
> (Dhanani, 2013, n.p.)

Table 3.6   Emigration Rates of Physicians in Selected Caribbean Countries (2010)

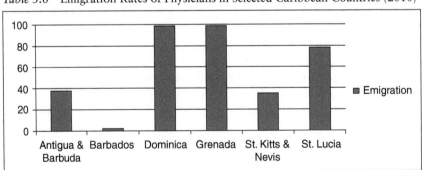

Source: Ratha and Silwal (2012)

Return Migration and Entrepreneurship

Many small island jurisdictions do not have a sizable local industrial or commercial class, and so the main means by which they are able to tap into the diasporic economy is through brain circulation and the transfer of skills. In the literature on brain circulation in the Caribbean, the focus has mainly been on return migration, particularly of retirees. The return of younger persons and the highly skilled has been underrepresented in the literature. Also, most of the focus has been on sociocultural issues—such as identity and social integration—and less on economic issues, like employment, investment and business creation. What often shows up in the literature are issues in relation to the cost of reintegration like employment opportunities, cost of living, cost of housing and land, cost of vehicles and the expense of shipping material possessions.

Social and cultural factors also influence the decision to return. Within Caribbean culture, after a long period abroad, migrants are expected to be wealthy. Therefore, a migrant's potential to produce material evidence of monetary gain, such the construction of a large home, has proved to be a limiting factor in return migration. Social networks and kinship have also impacted the decision to return. Those migrants who had kept closer relations with friends and family in their home country tended to be more inclined to return.

The case of Barbados and return migration is illustrative. From 2000 to 2007, the majority of returning migrants hailed from the United States (43%), the UK (40%), and Canada (10%; Nurse & Jones, 2010). These returning nationals were processed by the Barbados Facilitation Unit for Returning Foreign Nationals (FURN), renamed since 2010 the Barbados Networkers. The decision to rebrand the returning nationals process is in keeping with government's policy of engaging members of the Barbadian diaspora by facilitating their resettlement as a means of encouraging them to invest in the island economy and transfer their skills and expertise (Gill, 2014). The three key objectives of the Networkers Program are specified under the original Charter for Returning and Overseas Nationals (Government of Barbados, 2014): (a) to create the appropriate conditions that would facilitate Networkers in reintegrating into Barbadian society as easily as possible; (b) to increase the potential human and other resources available to the country, directly through the Networkers themselves and indirectly through the creation of a more conducive environment for services and investment by nationals remaining abroad; and (c) to facilitate the development of a retirement industry in Barbados.

The policy initiatives of the Barbados government to tap into the diaspora are passive when compared with the efforts being undertaken in other countries, in part because of the relatively low impact of the diasporic economy on the national economy. Consistent with this line of argument are the findings of Gmelch (2006), who postulated that Barbadian returnees often spend their repatriated savings on consumption to elevate their social status rather than investing in a business. He attributed this to insufficient capital rather than investment priorities. He also notes that "Barbados is a conservative society where people are slow to accept change, especially foreign ideas brought back by their own countrymen" (Gmelch, 2006, p. 66). He argues further that the opportunities for migrants to apply their skills and knowledge are greater within the private sector than the public sector. This is predominantly so because there is less flexibility and less room for innovation in government, as the Barbadian civil service is modeled on the British system and as such is "rigid and hierarchical" (Gmelch, ibid). In contrast, the island's private business community is confronted by competition and is forced to be at least minimally open to change and new ideas. However, it is important to note that there tend to be opportunities to modernize the systems and procedures in the public sector where there is critical mass, for example in the health sector, where there is a significant share of return migrants, as is the case with the nursing profession (Gmelch, ibid.; also Adams et al., this volume).

The Caribbean Diaspora Entrepreneur

Through their various economic activities, migrants and diasporas create markets for a whole range of goods (nostalgic, ethnic, niche and specialty), services (tourism, financial services, telecoms, travel and freight) and intellectual property (copyright, patents, geographic indications). For example, it has been noted that "diaspora populations can play a unique and important role in opening markets for new tourism destinations as well as markets for goods produced in and associated with the cultures of their countries of origin" (Aguinas & Newland, 2012, p. 215).

The concept of the diaspora entrepreneur is often associated with the immigrant entrepreneur who is able to tap into the market potential of the diasporic market and or the markets of the home economies. Diasporic entrepreneurs are also viewed as "opportunity entrepreneurs" because they often operate in emerging and high-demand sectors where a level of quality, expertise and skill are required to be competitive. They are also more likely to invest in innovation than the entrenched local elite businesses in the home countries (Kuznetsov, 2006). These entrepreneurs may also use the diasporic market as a stepping stone or bridgehead into wider international markets. Diasporic markets often start within immigrant and ethnic market spaces and, once successful, allow for crossover into mainstream markets (Nurse, 2011). These observations illustrate that diasporic entrepreneurship is not monolithic but multidimensional. Kuznetsov (quoted in Newland & Tanaka, 2010, p. 19) suggests that diasporic entrepreneurship can be categorized along the following six behavioral models: (a) top executive;

(b) mentoring/venture capital; (c) diaspora members as investors; (d) setting new strategic directions and identifying new opportunities; (e) return of talent; and (f) basic outsourcing.

In the following section, two entrepreneur profiles are highlighted to illustrate the impact of diasporic entrepreneurship on two sectors that are dominant in the diasporic market and critical for the export diversification of the Caribbean small island economy. The first profile is of what can be described as a "returnee model" entrepreneur in the specialty foods sector; the second profile is of a "top executive model" entrepreneur in the creative industries.

CECILE DE LA GRENADE, MANAGING DIRECTOR, DE LA GRENADE INDUSTRIES, GRENADA

Cecile De La Grenade, appointed as governor general of Grenada in May 2013, is a U.S.–trained food technologist credited with transitioning De La Grenade Industries from a cottage industry to a commercial operation with strong export capabilities. De La Grenade returned from the United States, where she studied and worked, to take over from her mother, Sybil, the founder of the company, who started operations in the late 1960s and eventually registered the company in 1984. Before her death in 1991, Sybil had achieved international recognition with a Gold Medal in Monde Selection in 1990 for La Grenade Liqueur and a Grand Gold Medal for Morne Délice Nutmeg Syrup (De la Grande Industries, 2014). After taking over the business, daughter Cecile expanded the product range to include more traditional beverages such as seamoss, mauby and ginger drinks, as well as hot pepper sauce and pepper jelly, that are targeted at the Caribbean diaspora market, particularly in the United States and the UK. The company has also targeted the wider specialty foods market with its range of high-quality products.

> As the cool breezes and rain showers of autumn begin to take hold, it is always good to have the occasional culinary reminder of hot sultry afternoons spent relaxing in the sun. This herbal marinade from De La Grenade is one way to evoke the spirit of hotter climes: specifically the Caribbean.
>
> (Borough Market, 2013, n.p.)

De La Grenade Industries utilizes the nutmeg pericarp (fruit) to manufacture a unique exotic and tasty line of products (jams, jellies and syrups) under the brand name Morne Délice. In 1966, De La Grenade Industries began as a cottage industry, producing these top-quality nutmeg products as well as La Grenade Liqueur, using a 200-year-old secret family formula. In 1990, the Morne Délice Nutmeg Syrup and La Grenade Liqueur were honored by

"Monde Selection, International Institute for Quality Selections" (Grenada History, 1994). In 1992, the De La Grenade and Morne Délice products graduated out of the "cottage industry" category when a modern food processing plant was commissioned (Uncommon Caribbean, 2012).

Grenada is known as the Spice Isle; in spite of its small size, it is responsible for one fifth of the world's total production of nutmeg and mace. The principal import markets are the EU, the United States, Japan and India, with Singapore and the Netherlands as major re-exporters. The spices are often used for baking, confections, syrups (including soft drinks), meat and sausage preparation and vegetable seasoning. Approximately 90% of the spices are used for industrial food production, especially meat flavoring, whereas over-the-counter grocery sales are a small share of the market (FAO, 2014).

The byproducts of nutmeg are traded worldwide as inputs for products such as cosmetics, food preparation, medicinal products and pharmaceuticals. Nutmeg is largely exported in its primary form as a commodity. Consequently, the country does not capture potential revenue from the export of value-added products such as nutmeg oil and other byproducts. Traditionally, the production of nutmeg jelly, syrup and other preservatives was done on a small scale and for the local market. However, since the early 1990s, these value-added products have been taken to another level with the growth of the locally owned firm, De La Grenade Industries. In short, the company has, through its expansion, been able to make a contribution to the further diversification and branding of the Grenadian economy.

FREDERICK MORTON, CEO, TEMPO NETWORKS, HEADQUARTERED IN NEWARK, NEW JERSEY, USA

TEMPO was launched on November 30, 2005, under the ownership of MTV Networks and corporate parent company Viacom based on the vision of founder Frederick Morton, Jr., then deputy general counsel of business and legal affairs at MTV. Morton was born and raised in St. Croix, U.S. Virgin Islands (USVI), to parents who had migrated from Nevis, which is the sister isle of St. Kitts. Morton did his law and management degrees in the United States before joining MTV Networks.

In 2007, Morton bought out MTV and assumed full ownership of TEMPO. The deal came at a time when MTV was engaged in internal restructuring of its cable group to enhance international profitability. According to one business analyst, "by selling its venture in TEMPO to local investors, MTVN lowers its risk with the channel by passing on advertising-sales responsibility to the local buyer but continuing to license its programming to the network" (Becker, 2007).

TEMPO became the first pan-Caribbean music video channel, offering music content from multiple Caribbean genres such as reggae, soca, dancehall, ska, calypso, reggaeton and punta rock. The channel, which also broadcasts news, events, concerts, dramas, documentaries and tourism programming, is viewed in 27 Caribbean territories through local television stations and cable channels with an estimated audience of 3.5 million viewers. Cable and Wireless, the largest telecoms operator in the English-speaking Caribbean, was the charter sponsor (ibid.).

TEMPO broadcasts on Cablevision on Channel 1105 in the New York metropolitan area, which is the most populous urban agglomeration in the United States and home to approximately one third of the Caribbean diaspora population in the United States (McCabe, 2011). TEMPO also broadcasts to other major U.S. cities where there are significant Caribbean diasporic communities like Atlanta, Boston, Washington, D.C., Baltimore, Philadelphia, Miami and Los Angeles. TEMPO offers Caribbean content on multiple social media platforms (e.g., on-air, online, on-mobile). While TEMPO caters mainly to Caribbean audiences and the diaspora, a key target market is "friends of the Caribbean." In effect, TEMPO has aided in deepening and widening the visibility and accessibility of Caribbean music in a context in which marketing and distribution are the key challenges to economic sustainability and commercial success (Nurse, 2006).

In addition, TEMPO has worked with various tourism boards throughout the region to promote Caribbean destinations such as Antigua and Barbuda, Barbados, Grenada, Trinidad and Tobago, Turks and Caicos and USVI. TEMPO also has an online store where consumers can purchase paraphernalia associated with the company and the Caribbean experience.

In line with its notion of social responsibility and diasporic engagement, TEMPO also engages in social initiatives in the Caribbean. An example of the links that Morton maintains with the region and with his parents' homeland is the partnership between TEMPO and the Department of Agriculture in Nevis to showcase agriculture on Nevis through "Agriculture in Style," a television program that has been aired on TEMPO since mid-2014 (Nevis Pages, 2014). Examples of other social initiatives include

- Badness Outta Style, a school tour aimed at combating rising rates of violence in the Caribbean region by creating awareness among youth of the value of Caribbean life.
- One Love/Haiti, an initiative to unite Caribbean people to assist Haiti after the earthquake. The company partnered with the Royal Bank of Canada, Royal Bank of Trinidad and Tobago, the International Federation of Red Cross and the Red Crescent Societies to raise relief efforts to assist the Haitian people.
- TEMPO Water, a campaign targeting Caribbean adolescents to promote good health and well-being by promoting health education to combat hyperactivity, depression, obesity and diabetes.

CONCLUSION

The diasporic economy involves multiple economic activities that create a complex web of transactions among various stakeholders. The rise of the diasporic economy is exemplified by the growth of the remittance economy and the brain drain and returnee phenomenon, which have proven to be strategic resources especially for small island states and territories. The diasporic economy operates as an extension of the home and regional markets as well as a basis for deepening professional and business networking. The case studies of diasporic entrepreneurs show that these firms are tapping into regional and diasporic markets and thus are able to transcend the limitations of small market size, which is a structural constraint to the small island economies of the Caribbean. Second, the diasporic market offers a bridge into mainstream markets and global cities, thereby allowing for market presence and the establishment of firms abroad.

REFERENCES

Aguinas, D. R., & Newland, K. (2012). *Developing a road map for engaging diasporas in development: A handbook for policymakers in host and home countries.* Washington, DC: Migration Policy Institute. Retrieved from www.migrationpolicy.org/pubs/thediasporahandbook-chapt11.pdf

Baldacchino, G. (2006). The brain rotation & brain diffusion strategies of small islanders: Considering "movement" in lieu of "place." *Globalization, Societies and Education, 4*(1), 143–154.

Becker, A. (2007, July 12). MTV Networks sells TEMPO. *Broadcast and Cable.* Retrieved from www.broadcastingcable.com/news/programming/mtv-networks-sells-tempo/28107

Borough Market. (2013, September 23). Product of the week: Herbal marinade. Retrieved from http://boroughmarket.org.uk/product-of-the-week-herbal-marinade

Canadian Foreign Policy Journal. (2011). Strategic opportunities in Caribbean migration: Brain circulation, diasporic tourism and investment, special edition, *17*(2), iii–192.

Dawson, L. R. (2007). *Brain drain, brain circulation, remittances and development: Prospects for the Caribbean.* Caribbean Paper No. 2. Ontario, ON: Centre for International Governance Innovation. Retrieved from www.cigionline.org/sites/default/files/2._brain_drain_brain_circulation_remittances_and_development-_prospects_for_the_caribbean.pdf

De La Grenade Industries. (2014). About De La Grenade. Retrieved from www.delagrenade.com/about.php

Dhanani, Q. (2013, November 12). Channeling Caribbean diaspora dollars back home. World Bank Latin America and Caribbean Blog. Retrieved from http://blogs.worldbank.org/latinamerica/channeling-caribbean-diaspora-dollars-back-home

The Economist. (2011, November 19). The magic of diasporas. Retrieved from www.economist.com/node/21538742

FAO. (2014). Nutmeg and mace overview. Rome: Food and Agricultural Organization. Retrieved from www.fao.org/docrep/v4084e/v4084e0b.htm#1.%20nutmeg%20and%20mace%20%20%20world%20overview

Gallina, A. (2010). *Human mobility report 2011: Migration and human develop-ment in African, Caribbean and Pacific countries.* Brussels: ACP Secretariat.

Global Forum on Migration and Development (GFMD). (2013). *Unlocking the potential of migration for inclusive development.* GFMD 2013-14 Concept paper. April 30, 2013.

Gill, J.-A. (2014, March 18). New vehicle buying provisions for returnees. BGIS-MEDIA. Retrieved from http://gisbarbados.gov.bb/index.php?categoryid=8& p2_articleid=12089

Gmelch, G. (2006). *Returning to the source: The final stage of the Caribbean migra-tion circuit.* Mona, Jamaica: University of the West Indies Press.

Government of Barbados. (2014). Foreign nationals. Bridgetown: Ministry of For-eign Affairs and Foreign Trade. Retrieved from www.foreign.gov.bb

Grenada History. (1994). There is more than that to the nutmeg. Retrieved from www.grenada-history.org/nut_all.htm

Jansen, M., & Piermartini, R. (2009). Temporary migration and bilateral trade flows. *The World Economy, 32*(5), 735–753.

Kapur, D. (2010). *Diaspora, development, and democracy: The domestic impact of international migration from India.* Princeton, NJ: Princeton University Press.

Kenwood, A. G., & Lougheed, A. L. (1992). *The growth of the international econ-omy, 1820–1990: An introductory text.* London: Routledge.

Kuznetsov, Y. (Ed.). (2006). *Diaspora networks and the international migration of skills: How countries can draw on their talent abroad.* Washington, DC: The Inter-national Bank for Reconstruction and Development/World Bank Publications. Retrieved from http://siteresources.worldbank.org/KFDLP/Resources/461197–1122319506554/DiasporaIntro.pdf

Levitt, P. (1998). Social remittances: Migration driven local-level forms of cultural diffusion. *International Migration Review, 32*(4), 926–948.

Maldonado, R., & Hayem, M. (2013). *Differing behavior across sub-regions: Remit-tances to Latin America and the Caribbean in 2012.* Washington, DC: Multilat-eral Investment Fund, Inter-American Development Bank.

McCabe, K. (2011, April 7). *Caribbean immigrants in the United States.* Migration Policy Institute. Retrieved from www.migrationpolicy.org/article/caribbean-immigrants-united-states#6

Mishra, P. (2006). *Emigration and brain drain: Evidence from the Caribbean.* IMF Working Paper 06/25. Washington, DC: International Monetary Fund. Retrieved from www.imf.org/external/pubs/ft/wp/2006/wp0625.pdf

Mohapatra, S., & Ratha, D. (2010). Impact of the global financial crisis on migra-tion and remittances. *Economic Premise,* February, 2. Retrieved from http://site resources.worldbank.org/INTPREMNET/Resources/EP2.pdf

Mullan, F. (2005). The metrics of the physician brain drain. *New England Journal of Medicine, 353*(17), 1810–1818. Retrieved from www.nejm.org/doi/pdf/10.1056/ NEJMsa050004

Mundra, K. (2005). Immigration and international trade: A semi-parametric empiri-cal investigation. *Journal of International Trade and Economic Development, 14*(1), 65–91.

Nevis Pages. (2014, April 3). Partnership between NIA and TEMPO to showcase agriculture on Nevis. Retrieved from www.nevispages.com/partnership-between-nia-and-tempo-to-showcase-agriculture-on-nevis/

Newland, K., & Tanaka, H. (2010). *Mobilizing diaspora entrepreneurship for development.* Washington, DC: Migration Policy Institute. Retrieved from www. migrationpolicy.org/pubs/diasporas-entrepreneurship.pdf

Nurse, K. (2004a). Migration, diaspora and development in Latin America and the Caribbean. *International Politics and Society, 2*(1), 107–126.

Nurse, K. (2004b). Migration and development in the Caribbean. Special Edition on Migration of FOCAL Policy Paper 04–6, June. Retrieved from: www.focal.ca/fpoint/special_edition_migration.pdf

Nurse, K. (2006). *The cultural industries in CARICOM: Trade and development challenges.* St. John, Antigua and Barbuda: EU PROINVEST and Caribbean Regional Negotiating Machinery.

Nurse, K. (2011) Diasporic tourism and investment in Suriname. *Canadian Foreign Policy Journal, 17*(2), 142–154.

Nurse, K., & Jones, J. (2010). *Brain drain and Caribbean–EU labor mobility.* Paper commissioned by Observatorio de las Relaciones Unión Europea—América Latina (OBREAL) for the BRIDGES-LAC project. Retrieved from www.sknweb.com/wp-content/uploads/2011/10/6.2-Brain-Drain-and-Caribbean-EU-Mobility-UWI.pdf

O'Rourke, K.H. (2004). *The era of migration: Lessons for today.* London: Centre for Economic Policy Research. Retrieved from www.cepr.org/active/publications/discussion_papers/dp.php?dpno=4498

OECD. (2014). Key statistics on migration in OECD countries. Retrieved from www.oecd.org/els/mig/keystat.htm

Orozco, M., Lowell, B.L., Bump, M., & Fedewa, R. (2005). *Transnational engagement, remittances and their relationship to development in Latin America and the Caribbean.* Washington, DC: Institute for the Study of International Migration, Georgetown University.

Pattullo, P. (2000). *Fire from the mountain: The tragedy of Montserrat and the betrayal of its people.* London: Constable.

Ratha, D., & Plaza, S. (2011). Harnessing diasporas: Africa can tap some of its millions of emigrants to help development efforts. *Finance & Development,* September, 48–51. Retrieved from www.imf.org/external/pubs/ft/fandd/2011/09/pdf/ratha.pdf

Ratha, D., & Silwal, A. (2012). *Remittance flows in 2011: An update.* Washington, DC: World Bank Publications.

Stahl, C.W. (1982). Labor emigration and economic development. *International Migration Review, 16*(4), 869–899.

Stalker, P (2003). The impact of migration in countries of origin. In *The link between migration, globalization and development* (pp. 62–78). Novib Expert Meeting report. Noordwijk A/D Zee, the Netherlands: Novib Expert Meeting Report.

Swanson, J. (1979). *Emigration and economic development: The case of the Yemen Arab Republic.* Boulder, CO: Westview Press.

Terrazas, A. (2010). *Diaspora investment in emerging markets: Patterns and prospects.* Washington, DC: Diasporas and Development Policy Project, Migration Policy Institute, August. Retrieved from www.migrationpolicy.org

Uncommon Caribbean. (2012). Taste of the Caribbean: Morne Délice Nutmeg Jam. Retrieved from www.uncommoncaribbean.com/2011/08/22/taste-of-the-caribbean-morne-delice-nutmeg-jam/

World Bank. (2012). *World development indicators 2012.* Washington, DC: World Bank Publications.

World Bank. (2013). Migration and remittance flows: Recent trends and outlook, 2013–2016. *Migration and Development Brief, 21.* Retrieved from http://sitere sources.worldbank.org/INTPROSPECTS/Resources/334934–1288990760745/MigrationandDevelopmentBrief21.pdf

4 Pathways to Successful Entrepreneurship in Small Island Economies

The Case of Åland

Katarina Fellman, Jouko Kinnunen,
Bjarne Lindström, and Richard Palmer

STATISTICS AND RESEARCH ÅLAND

INTRODUCTION

The challenges of economic development for small islands are considerable. Much has been written expounding the very real, perhaps structural handicaps to growth that bedevil places that command no economic heft, have small populations, have a limited range and stock of material and financial resources and are subject to the isolationist effects of the sea. And yet one cannot help noting that there are various examples of successful small island economies and of successful firms within such small island units. This chapter serves as a case study of one such island jurisdiction, the Åland Islands, and of some of its successful companies. While useful as a case study unto itself, the chapter dwells also on the potential of extrapolating the experience of this very specific example to other islands.

ÅLAND ISLANDS: POLITICAL BACKGROUND

The Åland Islands is a home-ruled, European archipelago with about 6,800 islands and 29,000 inhabitants, located in the Northern-Central part of the Baltic Sea. Following its separation from Sweden in conjunction with the Russian conquest of Finland in 1809, the archipelago was demilitarized by the middle of the 19th century. In connection with the peace negotiations after the First World War, the Ålanders demanded reunification with Sweden, appealing to the principle of people's right to self-determination. A referendum was suggested by the Ålanders, supported by Sweden, but Finland refused. The "Åland Question" (Barros, 1968) was finally submitted to the League of Nations, which solved the conflict by offering Finland formal sovereignty over the islands, while the Ålanders were granted political autonomy, including special safeguards for their Swedish language and culture (Brown, 1921; Padeldorf & Andersson, 1939). Today, the home rule exercises legislative control over such policy matters as health services, internal communications, education and culture, the police force, postal service, radio/television and local administration.

A MODERN SHIPPING AND SERVICE ECONOMY

Åland has developed into a modern service economy with a high standard of living, low unemployment and growing population. The gross national product (GDP) is around 1.2 billion euros. This implies a GDP per capita of close to US$40,000 (PPP), one of the highest such figures in the world, about 16% higher than the Finnish national average and some 7% higher than the corresponding Swedish figure (ÅSUB, 2014). The population growth is fuelled by a significant influx of migrants, mainly from Finland and Sweden, but also—in growing numbers—from Eastern Europe and the rest of the world (ÅSUB, 2013).

Due to its archipelagic nature, small labor force and limited domestic market, manufacturing is relatively insignificant in the Åland economy. It accounts for only 7% of the value added in the private sector and approximately 5% of the island's GDP. The cornerstone and principal driving force of the economy is international shipping, which accounts for about one fifth of the island's GDP and almost 30% of the value added produced in the private sector (ÅSUB, 2014). As a matter of fact, Åland's economy is more dependent on shipping than most other nations and regions that host various kinds of shipping clusters around the world (Kinnunen & Lindström, 2010). Furthermore, the passenger shipping industry in Åland is heavily dependent on operations with on-board tax-free sales of alcohol, tobacco and cosmetics (Kinnunen, 2005). Mariehamn, the capital city of Åland, is the geographical and commercial center of the international ferry and cruise shipping industry using the busy shipping lanes between Sweden, Åland, Finland and Estonia (Lindström & Palmer, 2011).

Until the end of the 20th century, the transport industry's share of Åland's GDP, with shipping as the main mover, was around 35% to 40% of the total value added in the private sector. However, since the turn of the millennium, the development of Åland's international shipping industry has stalled, and its share of value added has been shrinking. The declining relative weight of the shipping business is compensated by a steady growth in the land-based business-to-business sector, including economic, juridical and logistic support to the shipping industry.

THREE PATHWAYS TO ECONOMIC PROSPERITY IN A SMALL ISLAND ECONOMY

If an island jurisdiction does not happen to be endowed with natural, historical-cultural or other exploitable, preexisting resources, the alternative is to try to induce commercial expansion by exporting high-value-added goods or, more commonly, services to external customers. Most small island economies need to increase external demand in order to induce business growth. Access to a wider market base is essential for the growth of businesses based in sparsely populated, geographically secluded areas.

In modern societies, where basic material conditions are met and the necessary political and social institutions are in place, there is a fair chance for innovation and individual entrepreneurship to emerge and flourish. Thus, despite being an insular, small-scale economy, Åland has managed to pursue three pathways to entrepreneurial success. Two of these avenues to economic development are—at least, in principle—open to all reasonably well-developed island economies. One of them, however, presupposes some kind of political or administrative autonomy (home rule) for the island in question.

We start with a closer look at the first two, "nonpolitical" keys to island prosperity. The first and probably most important is *the ability to transform the geophysical condition of being an island into an economic opportunity.* One often-used option here is to take advantage of the attraction of the water-encircled location—the condition and lure of islandness—in order to develop a successful island tourism industry, whether in warm-water or cold-water locations (e.g., Baldacchino, 2006). Another possibility is to transform the weakest link of most island economies—the dependency on expensive and sparse sea-borne or airborne transportation—into a thriving business. This condition applies particularly well to the case of Åland.

The second principal avenue to small island prosperity is to *focus on niche markets* instead of economies of scale *in the production of island-branded, high-quality goods and services.* This is an opportunity that has gradually become more important in a globalized economy increasingly characterized by niche products, emphasizing customer flexibility and novel service solutions. This option for developing successful small island businesses has also been deployed in the case of Åland, especially during the last two decades.

A third pillar of successful economic development is *to make creative use of the islands' special political and institutional status.* This option is not open to all islands since it presupposes independence (statehood, sovereignty), or at least some sort of special political status (autonomy, home rule). Classical examples of this option focus on the financial sector but also on the shipping and aviation industries, where the use of favorable regulatory frameworks has generated prosperity and economic success in a number of microstates and home-ruled island territories. Surprisingly, this option has not been extensively pursued by Åland business. This is mainly due to a rather weak home rule in the sphere of business and economics, since most of the economic decision making rests with Helsinki, not Mariehamn, and Helsinki is not very keen to part with these powers. However, in some important cases, this has not prevented the Ålanders from making creative use of their institutional peculiarity as a subnational island jurisdiction to enhance their island's economy.

THE EMERGENCE OF A "NATIONAL CHAMPION" IN THE FERRY INDUSTRY

For islands, geographical seclusion from the rest of the world by water is often seen as a hindrance to the efficient access to markets and therefore to economic development. The development of the Åland ferry industry provides a good example of the transformation of the basic conditions of geographical isolation and dependency on sea-borne transportation into a profitable island business venture. Strangely enough, the initial conditions of relative seclusion prompted what is now Åland's largest and most important company to emerge and develop.

Viking Line, the long-standing ferry company of the Åland Islands, is clear testimony of how isolating circumstances can foster successful, indigenously owned and controlled, large-scale businesses. The company was founded in 1959 and has ever since played a key role in the economic development of the Åland Islands. Today, more than half a century after the founding of the company, the prosperity of the small island jurisdiction still largely depends on the performance of this specific company, although that excessive dependence has been shrinking.

Specific disadvantages do arise from small size; but sometimes smallness can be beneficial and turned into a competitive advantage. What makes the Viking Line company especially interesting in this context is that the financial, knowledge and human capital inputs at the time of founding of the company were all derived from domestic sources. One important advantageous feature is that both ownership and executive leadership continue to be firmly embedded in the local community. The company is indigenously owned and heavily export dependent, which is the only way to go if one wishes to expand and still retain local control over one's business.

The emergence of the Åland ferry industry depended on a confluence of favorable conditions including physical, historical, cultural, institutional, political and commercial circumstances. Among these, four key preconditions underlie the founding and long-standing expansion of the Åland ferry industry:

1. Geography: Åland is strategically located in the middle of the Northern Baltic between the economic growth areas of, on the one hand, the Finnish capital city of Helsinki and the Finnish city of Turku and, on the other hand, the Swedish capital city of Stockholm.
2. Culture and history: A rich and multigenerational seafaring tradition and a socially embedded entrepreneurship
3. Institutions: free inter-Nordic travelling (1954), deregulated financial controls and specific jurisdiction allowed for the institutionalization of tax-free sales on board.
4. Markets: Potential large-scale external demand. Rapidly increasing transportation needs between Finland and Sweden from the 1960s onward

The *geographical and cultural-historical preconditions* for the Åland Islands to develop small-scale local and interregional maritime transport have been favorable. By small but incremental steps, shipping has developed from subsistence fishing to interregional trade within the Northern Baltic (between Stockholm and Helsinki), with locally constructed wooden sailing vessels to cross-continental voyages with large sailing ships during the inter-war and immediate postwar years (Kåhre & Kåhre, 1988).

During the post–Second World War years, Åland developed a motor-ized merchant fleet, and ship owners successfully accumulated capital and know-how. Hence, the maritime business on the islands evolved in steps, expanding in size and scope, gradually building up a solid foundation of international shipping competence.

Then there are political-institutional preconditions. We know from previ-ous studies that islands that have obtained distinct juridical personalities can successfully deploy this specific jurisdictional capacity and turn it into an economic resource and advantage (Baldacchino & Milne, 2000). Åland has managed to successfully deploy and transform its juridical/political auton-omy into the specific status of a tax-free zone. Since the early1960s, tax-free sales have been of crucial importance for ferry operations on the routes between Sweden, Åland and Finland.

Åland is one of the few territories in the EU where tax-free sales on board ships travelling to and from the rest of the Union are allowed. This is due to a permanent exemption from the European VAT-rules in Åland's accession protocol to the EU in 1995. Today, tax-free sales on board provide almost 70% of the ferry companies' income, based on sales from duty-free shops and consumption on board (Lindström & Palmer, 2011).

And, finally, there are commercial/market preconditions. Successful eco-nomic growth of small economic entities usually requires large-scale exter-nal demand. Whereas the founders of the Viking Line company did foresee an increasing demand of cruise passengers and car drivers using ferries for transportation and leisure purposes, they could hardly foresee the rapid expansion of the market that occurred in the 1980s and early 1990s.

In the mid-1950s, regular marine transport to and from the Åland Islands was sparse. Many islanders, including a local entrepreneur and sea captain, Mr. Gunnar Eklund, personally experienced these inconveniences of isola-tion. Inspired by the car ferries crossing the English Channel and by the emergence of passenger and car ferry traffic in Danish waters, he foresaw the prospects of developing a new branch of the Åland shipping business. He subsequently managed to attract other local entrepreneurial founders-owners to his idea of providing fast, frequent and reliable ferry transport for the Ålanders.

Apart from the necessity of efficient transport for locals, the founders of Viking Line recognized the increasing transport needs of Finnish expatriate workers living in Sweden. Moreover, car ownership was on the increase, and so was a new form of tourism, which combined the service of transport with a variety of on-board services aimed at satisfying an expanding customer experience.

The founders of Viking Line managed to obtain adequate and reliable funding from local shipping companies. Capital investments by local businesses in the ferry fleet were essential. Local businesses and entrepreneurs ensured that sufficient capital and retained earnings were available to gradually revitalize the fleet.

The Viking Line has succeeded in applying both a strategy of "economics of scale" by gradually expanding its fleet as well as developing a strategy of "economics of scope" by being innovative in offering a suite of experiences tailored to the increasing and widening demand of travelers. The experiences include casino slot and gaming machines, a variety of food and drink, music artists and entertainment, shopping, spa, sauna and relaxing facilities.

These strategies still remain two of the main parameters on the income side in sustaining the Åland ferry industry. First, it is essential to try and increase the transport volume and market share and, second, it is crucial to appeal to the growing and varying demands of discerning customers and to maximize on-board expenditure by consumers through widening and varying the output of on-board accommodation, tax-free sales, food and dining, sauna, night clubs, entertainment and so forth. The main parameter on the expense side is optimizing the cost of bunker fuel. Ever since the sharp rise in fuel prices during the first oil crises in 1973, this has remained a first priority of the Viking Line.

The company has developed into a "national champion" and so far has managed to maintain profitable routes in a highly competitive environment. In so doing, it still is the largest private employer and income provider for the inhabitants of Åland. The company employs approximately 3,100 people and has around 700 staff living in Åland. The rest of the employees live outside Åland, mainly in mainland Finland. Although there has been a gradual development toward economic diversification during the last decade and a half, the company remains the cornerstone of the economy of the Åland Islands.

ISLAND BRANDING OF HIGH-QUALITY "SLOW BEER"

Published research has already identified that a microbrewery could be a small island's largest locally owned manufacturing company. Servicing the domestic market, assuaging the thirst of visiting tourists and exporting initially to the island's overseas diaspora, a brewery with a good product range can thrive by positioning itself carefully as a local product (Baldacchino, 2010).

Stallhagen is a microbrewery selling craft beer, founded in 2004. Its yearly production volume surpassed half a million liters for the first time in 2013. The brewery produces a large number of beer varieties, of which only a few are produced during the whole calendar year. Currently the company employs nine persons. The few so-called standard beers that are produced during the whole year are sold mainly through supermarket chains in Åland and continental Finland and on board some of the passenger ferries trafficking in the Baltic Sea. In addition, its produce is available in about 70 restaurants and cafés around Åland.

Stallhagen also conducts a special Premier Pub program for mainland Finland aimed at convincing pubs to start selling the company's beer on tap. A smaller share of production is also sold to Sweden. Stallhagen has participated in several beer festivals and competitions, where its products have gained many awards and favorable independent evaluations. Similar to the case of Viking Line, the financing of the company was genuinely local and done by mobilizing domestic support and capital. To date, the company has around 1,600 shareholders, the great majority of whom are local residents and companies. Ålands Utvecklings Ab, a venture capital company owned by the Åland government, was engaged early on in the development of the brewery, providing a 20% share of equity input during the first year in operation. In addition, it holds a seat in the company board.

Stallhagen is an illuminating example of place-based marketing and branding. Through marketing and branding, the company aims at evoking emotions and creating attachment to the company's products while tying the image of its product to the place where it is produced. Building an attractive image for a place is important in various different contexts, including tourism and domestic and export sales of agro-food products (Dawson, Fountain, & Cohen, 2011). Stallhagen is active in telling the history of beer making and the colorful story of the real estate on which the brewery stands. The Swedish kings used to have stables and paddocks on the estate, which is the origin of the name of the company: *stall* (stable) and *hagen* (paddock).

Tourists line up to participate in the guided tours around the brewery, which can be combined with a high-quality meal and beer tasting. Visitors can also buy the brewery's products from the minimarket store placed under the same roof and carry them home (at their expense). By hosting tourists, the company enables valuable interactions with prospective new loyal consumers and cleverly combines manufacturing and service provisions under the same roof, enhancing business synergies (e.g., Baldacchino, 2002). In effect, Stallhagen is being marketed in a fashion that very much resembles the way wine is being sold directly from small-scale wineries of wine-producing regions. Since this small company has no big marketing muscles to flex, it actively uses social media applications for visibility.

Customers are made aware of the difference in the production process of Stallhagen and large-scale beer: "The fermenting process is completely natural, without the use of chemical additives. Stallhagen allows its beer to mature for the four to eight weeks required for the completion of the natural production process" (Stallhagen, 2014). Actually, inspired by the slow food movement's ideas of local production, environmental concerns and high quality coupled with the increasingly sophisticated "taste education" of customers, Stallhagen has coined a new concept: slow beer, which it has now been printing on its bottle caps.

In short, Stallhagen makes active use of *product, process* and *place* qualities in its marketing strategy, thus covering all the components of the PPP concept that underlies different food labeling campaigns around Europe and in the United States aimed at tackling the generic McDonaldization of the agro-food industry (Ilbery et al., 2005).

Stallhagen got a head start before the boom of microbreweries in the Nordic countries, especially in Finland, but currently the only segment of beer market that is growing is exactly that of craft beer. The originators of the company were two local beer enthusiasts who were convinced that Åland needed a brewery of its own. The founders were amateurs in beer making, and the company has been lucky surviving the years that passed learning the tricks of the trade.

During its first year, the company started producing Pale Lager, a high-end beer with very low production volume. In the beginning, the local connection and contents of the beer were low, and the brewed beer was transported to the mainland to be bottled. However, this solution turned out to be very costly, and new capital was invested in bottling facilities on the island.

In 2006, the company's market orientation was adjusted. Instead of only producing high-end craft beer different from the large-scale lager beers, Stallhagen started offering two standard beers of its own: Stallhagen III and Dark Lager. They soon found many new local customers, but the financial results were not sufficiently positive. As a consequence, the company sought to acquire fresh working capital several times.

Given the local patriotic sentiments behind the company, it was understandable that the Åland origin was initially actively used in marketing the beer in mainland Finland. However, the outcome was rather disappointing. Every now and then, the autonomous Åland government has been at odds with the central power of the Finnish state. This creates a commercial risk for a product of being associated with the political sphere of Åland. Thus, the use of place in marketing of the products was reoriented to the physical real estate where the brewery is located, whereas the association with Åland has been deliberately downplayed.

In 2010, the then executive director decided to accept another work offer. Injection of new capital and ideas were again necessary, as the working capital was dwindling. The company board soon found a new executive director who was also willing to invest into the company himself, together with the existing owners, in order to recapitalize the company. A new course for the company was set up.

The new strategy was to dramatically increase the number of products introduced each year while at the same time keeping the standard beers in assortment and to raise prices by 20%. The more exotic beers would be sold mostly on tap, with their main markets outside the home region.

The members of the company board were also replaced to better represent owner interests.

The new board with its fresh executive director decided to make this "leap of faith" that would either make or break the company. Luckily, the new strategy seems to work. Production and sales are soaring, and the company has had the pleasant problem of temporarily having sold out its production. New investments were made in the beginning of 2014 to increase the production capacity to 800,000 liters.

There are various lessons to be learned from the Stallhagen story. Among these, the case confirms that external markets are extremely important. All means of escaping the geographic limitations of islandness should be applied to reach the markets outside one's own domestic location: via exports, site sales to tourists and using the Internet for visibility and brand recognition. However, the same marketing arguments do not apply in the home market, where one does not need to preach to the converted. Second, using place as part of a marketing strategy has to be weighed against any risk that the place may bear unfavorable connotations in specific external markets and over which the company has no control. Third, local history may contain stories that enchant the customers and can engage them emotionally with the products. Fourth, the way to success is often found through trial and error, and patient owners are necessary.

CREATIVE USE OF INSTITUTIONAL AND JURISDICTIONAL CONDITIONS

There are a few examples of companies that have utilized the options that the Åland autonomy provides to develop successful businesses. Although the Åland autonomy does not cover business taxation and most business regulations, Åland's legislative powers include fundamental areas such as education, the promotion of industry and labor market policy as well as areas like health care, environment and planning, which have proven to be important for business development and for attracting competence.

One of these successful companies is Paf (Ålands Penningautomatförening ~ Åland Gambling Machine Association), which has been offering gaming to the public since 1966. Paf is governed by public law and operates as a gaming company under an Åland government license. The business objective of the Paf Group is also to generate funds for nonprofit humanitarian causes and social welfare in Åland. Therefore, all business activities that Paf is involved in are strictly regulated and formalized.

Since 1967, Paf has run a gaming business aboard passenger ferries and cruise ships registered in Åland. The company offers gaming solutions, such as slot machines, lotteries and casino games, to the shipping companies, none of which could have been established without the autonomy of the Åland Islands.

Åland's internationally oriented shipping industry opens up important networks of contacts and export opportunities. In Åland, many growing businesses have started off as suppliers to or spin-offs from the shipping companies, for example, in the areas of finance, computing and in diverse areas of technology.

However, during the 1990s, the passenger ferry business suffered a series of economic mishaps. The tragic sinking of the ferry *Estonia* in 1994 claimed 852 lives; alcohol taxation in neighboring countries was lowered, there was heightened ferry competition in the Baltic Sea, and a trend in favor of the registration of ships under foreign flags was introduced. More than 90% of the income of the Paf Company was generated from passenger traffic at that time. There was also uncertainty about what effects membership in the European Union (since 1995) would have. Since Paf operates within the area of government-licensed lotteries, the parent company is only allowed to offer games exclusively in Åland and on board Åland-registered ships. These challenges and the surrounding uncertainty forced Paf to create new business activities—to think outside the proverbial box.

In 1995, Paf came up with the idea to offer some of its gaming products through a new channel and market: the Internet. The company's intention was to crossbreed traditional gaming activities in Åland and at sea with digital interactive gaming. Gradually, business opportunities developed from local and regional activities to global opportunities (Dahlström & Hedin, 2010).

The support of the Åland government was needed to realize the plans. As the company did not require any financial support at the time, it received approval from the government, the Legislature and its own board of directors. Over the years, the company has gained a substantial level of public trust, which was crucial for securing political support. However, politicians demanded that Paf keep the riskier parts of the business activities outside the parent company.

Hence, the company took advantage of the autonomy of Åland in its business progress. Another advantage was that the distances to the decision makers were short: people were well known, and key decisions could be taken expeditiously. The connection to the gaming activities on board the ships was a prerequisite for the substantial investments in the new technology; the firm had the resources thanks to that business.

Already in 1996, Paf was testing digital gaming on a local website. The test revealed that market conditions were favorable for developing e-gaming solutions: there was the fast development of the Internet, the expansion in the usage of credit cards and the presence of a new generation of online players. The Internet initiative then took off with the launching of betting in December 1999. A couple of months later, a version of the blackjack game was introduced, and since then the business has expanded considerably (Fellman, 2009).

During these first tests, the company learned the necessity of acquiring engineering- and science-based knowledge. From the start, the ambition had been to purchase technical "turnkey" solutions to minimize the risks, in accordance with policy guidelines. But several problems in finding a technical supplier contributed to a situation in which Paf had to step down in the production chain. It was simply not able to find a contractor of the complex system it needed at that time. The founding of a partly owned subsidiary implied a "purchaser-provider" business model aimed at minimizing the risk of Paf in this phase. Paf was just the purchaser and holder of the license (Dahlström & Hedin, 2010).

In this phase, Åland Utvecklings Ab, the government-owned venture capital company, contributed with external capital, since Paf had to invest quite aggressively in the technical development and was not allowed to bear the full risk itself. Thus, once more the business development of the company took advantage of the institutional conditions of Åland (Fellman, 2009).

Internet games today include slot machines, betting, lottery, bingo, poker and casino and skill games. The parent company Paf operates gaming activities on Åland, on board Åland and Finnish ships and on the Internet. The fully owned subsidiary Paf Consulting Ab, its subsidiary and associated companies, manage the international gaming operations, including those in international waters.

Over the last 15 years, Paf has developed from being primarily a monopoly to a group operating in an international environment. From that perspective, the experience of competing within the shipping sector has been valuable; the majority of the returns are nowadays generated outside the monopoly.

When online gaming was introduced in 1999, the turnover of the group in total was €34.9 million. From these, Paf distributed €5.1 m in grants and loans to humanitarian welfare activities in Åland (Fellman, 2009). In 2013, the total turnover had increased to €108.2 m; €20 m was available for distribution to a broad spectrum of charitable causes (Paf Annual Report, 2013). During the same period, the number of employees in the group more than doubled: today there are more than 300 persons employed by the group. Thus, the development of the business has been considerable after Internet gaming was launched; the gaming license was a precondition for this expansion.

The online gaming environment is complex and requires skilled professionals to keep the process at the forefront in terms of product development and technology. In order to attract a skilled workforce to migrate to Åland, productive networking between different actors in the region is essential. There are various examples of fruitful collaboration where labor market authorities, child and health care and educational institutions have been involved.

Another strategy to recruit has been to establish subsidiaries and branches outside Åland. These qualified development units within the company are located in larger labor market areas such as in Helsinki, Stockholm, Tallinn and Madrid. This strategy means that the company keeps key competence in house. Accordingly, the international business networks of Paf today comprise export channels, markets and technology as well as knowledge interactions, for the benefit of the Åland society.

To conclude, the specific jurisdictional status of Åland was a necessary condition for the development of Paf. However, the autonomy alone was not a sufficient condition for the business expansion; three other prerequisites had to be in place. First, the Internet opened up totally new markets and opportunities for e-commerce. Second, the long tradition of on-board gaming and entertainment honed the specific skills and a significant part of the resources that were required for the investments. Third, the crisis in the core business sector forced the firm to come up with new ideas and look at other possibilities for growth. This simultaneous concoction of circumstances, together with hard work and some luck, made the success story possible.

LESSONS LEARNED

In this chapter, we have presented three examples of contemporary successful business strategies from the Åland Islands: one drawn from the shipping industry, one from the beverage industry and one from Web-based gaming. Common to these three success stories is that they *combine a strong island rootedness with successful expansion in much larger national, regional and international markets.*

However, some success factors are of special importance. The first one is efficient use of key local resources. Primary maritime expertise, traditions and close professional contacts across different sectors of society were vital in the Åland case. Thus, a successful commercial utilization of multigenerational nautical know-how, plus a tight relationship between political and economic elites, has probably been critical to the evolution of the island's merchant fleet, from local sea-borne transportation to a competitive modern shipping industry.

A second important factor is to be timely: to be at the leading edge of a fast-growing new market niche or a technology that provides scope for innovation and new entrants. This is a success factor that has been especially important in two of the Åland cases. Beer brewery Stallhagen has thus ridden on a wave of rapidly growing interest among beer drinkers in local microbreweries producing "hand-made," quality beer for the high-end market, and Åland's successful gaming company Paf has been able to make creative use of the new Internet technology that made the introduction of Internet gambling possible.

A third potential success factor is the possibility to exploit the openings for entrepreneurship and new revenue sources offered by the special political or administrative status of many small island communities throughout the world. The gaming company Paf is a good case in point. Without Åland's home rule and legislative control of the gaming industry, Paf would never have been established and consequently would also have failed to develop into the successful player on the international gaming market that the company is today.

And yet, none of these success factors is unique to Åland. Almost all islands around the world are endowed with some sort of exploitable resources, and every island has the opportunity to establish and develop specialized commercial activities based on island-branded niche products. The special political status as an economic success factor is, however, not an option open to all islands. But it is certainly not unique to the Åland Islands. On the contrary, there are many islands around the world with equal or even more political autonomy than Åland, which also—albeit in other market areas—have been able to economically exploit this potential success factor.

Thus, most of the world's small-scale economies, not just the islands, have the possibility to take advantage of any of these economic success factors. However, each community has its own economic history, capital resources, enterprise culture, tax regime, social conditions and specific geopolitical context. Every successful island economy must therefore be built around its own partly unique set of success factors. Ideally, these should also interact and create positive synergies in the economy as a whole instead of giving rise to only a few isolated business successes.

The three Åland cases presented in this chapter also underline the importance of utilizing the right combination of success factors. There is a significant synergy between the island's political status, Paf's expansion in the gaming market, the marketing of a new quality beer and the shipping companies' strong position in the international passenger ferry business. Without Åland's own gaming legislation, Paf would not exist, and without the Åland-owned passenger fleet accepting on-board gaming, Paf would never have obtained the financial resources necessary for its entry into the huge Web-based gaming market that emerged after the turn of the millennium. Furthermore, it is the archipelago's position as an autonomous territory outside the EU's VAT-area that has made it possible for the shipping companies to maintain the crucially important duty-free sales on board passenger ships *en route* to and from Åland. The corresponding connections are less clear in the Stallhagen case. However, the extensive Åland passenger ferry operations have had a positive effect in terms of marketing and offering a platform for on-board sales to a wider customer base.

CONCLUSION

The world's many different island communities would do well to become better informed about each other's business success stories and not just share tragic narratives about their island condition. A strong and durable small island economy *is* possible; it implies utilizing the island's own specific prerequisites and creating a winning combination of relevant success factors.

Furthermore, in order to embark upon a path of sustained economic growth, a small island territory may also need a fair bit of luck, which usually equates to favorable external conditions existing at the right point in time. Of course, luck may and does run out; and many businesses fail, on islands as much as elsewhere. Critical decisions taken at important moments may be found to have been the wrong ones after the passage of time. This is the reality of the world of business. But islanders instinctively know of these risks: their islands' economic history, just like Åland's, would have various examples of these failures, too. In any case, in such situations, actual and potential island entrepreneurs need to be on the lookout for the next business opportunity and the next niche market opening.

REFERENCES

ÅSUB. (2013). *Befolkningen 2012.* Statistikrapport 2013:6. Mariehamn: Statistics and Research Åland.

ÅSUB. (2014). *Nationalräkenskapsdata 2011.* Statistikmeddelande 2014:1 Mariehamn: Statistics and Research Åland.

Baldacchino, G. (2002). A taste of small-island success: A case from Prince Edward Island. *Journal of Small Business Management, 40*(3), 254–259.

Baldacchino, G. (2006). *Extreme tourism: Lessons from the world's cold water islands.* Amsterdam: Elsevier.

Baldacchino, G. (2010). Islands and beers: Toasting a discriminatory approach to small island manufacturing. *Asia Pacific Viewpoint, 51*(1), 61–72.

Baldacchino, G., & Milne, D. (2000). *Lessons from the political economy of small islands.* London: Palgrave Macmillan.

Barros, J. (1968). *The Åland Island question: Its settlement by the league of nations.* New Haven, CT: Yale University Press.

Brown, P.M. (1921). The Åland Island question. *The American Journal of International Law, 15*(2), 268–272.

Dahlström, M., & Hedin, S. (Ed.). (2010). *Regional trajectories to the knowledge economy: Nordic–European comparisons.* Oslo: Nordic Innovation Centre.

Dawson, D., Fountain, J., & Cohen, D. (2011). *Place-based marketing and wine tourism: Creating a point of difference and economic sustainability for small wineries.* Paper presented at the 6th AWBR International Conference, France: Bordeaux Management School, June 9–10.

Fellman, K. (2009). *Crossbreeding entertainment at sea and the digital gaming world—the case of licensed gaming operators.* Unpublished Working Paper. Mariehamn: Statistics and Research Åland.

Ilbery, B., Morris, C., Buller, H., Maye, D., & Kneafsey, M. (2005). Product, process and place—an examination of food marketing and labelling schemes in Europe and North America. *European Urban and Regional Studies, 12*(2), 116–132.

Kåhre, G., & Kåhre K. (1988). *Den åländska segelsjöfartens historia.* Mariehamn: Ålands Tidnings-Tryckeri AB.

Kinnunen, J. (2005). *Migration, imperfect competition and structural adjustment: Essays on the economy of the Åland Islands.* Helsinki: Helsinki School of Economics. Acta Universitatis Oeconomicae Helsingiensis. A-258. Helsinki HeSE print.

Kinnunen, J., & Lindström, B. (2010). *Den ålandsbaserade sjöfartens ekonomiska betydelse. En studie av klustereffekter och framtidsscenarier.* Rapport 2010:6. Mariehamn: Statistics and research Åland.

Lindström, B., & Palmer, R. (2011). *The significance of duty-free sales on board ferries to the transnational transport system in the Baltic Sea Region*. Report 2011:8. Mariehamn: Statistics and Research Åland.

Padeldorf, N. J., & Andersson, G. A. (1939). The Åland question. *The American Journal of International Law, 33*(3), 465–487.

Paf Annual Report. (2013). Retrieved from www.paf.com/static/content/docs/about/20140416-Annual-Report-Paf-2013_en.pdf

Stallhagen. (2014). Brewing philosophy. Retrieved from www.stallhagen.com/en/bryggeriet-2/filosofi

Part 2
Niche Natural Products and Manufacturing

5 Knitting and More from Fair Isle, Scotland

Small-Island Tradition and Microentrepreneurship

Richard W. Butler

INTRODUCTION

The modern academic concept of the entrepreneur owes much to the writing of Schumpeter (1950), who proposed that the core ingredients of entrepreneurship were creativity, innovation and change. A creative entrepreneur brought about innovation in response to changes in situations (Hartwell & Lane, 1991). Schumpeter went on to propose five categories of innovation: production of new goods, new methods of production, new markets, new sources of supplies and new types of organization (Cauthorn, 1989). In the examples discussed in what follows, there is clear evidence of the presence of three of the five categories, those relating to goods, markets and organization. The literature on entrepreneurship contains few references to its role in tourism, despite the importance of key individuals in introducing significant innovations into tourism and hospitality (Butler & Russell, 2010). In the particular context of Fair Isle, the innovations discussed are not related directly to tourism but rather to the responses of key individuals (entrepreneurs) to changes in the nature of life on the island, many of which were brought about by changes in tourism, as noted elsewhere (e.g., Shaw & Williams, 1998). As such, these entrepreneurs have reacted to changes rather than being major agents of change themselves and certainly are not characterized by destructive energy or activities, creative or otherwise, as suggested by Schumpeter (1950). All of the individuals discussed can be described as organic, serendipitous and revitalizing entrepreneurs (Butler & Russell, 2012), developing existing opportunities, moving into new directions and taking advantage of changes in circumstances as they have occurred. That these innovations have taken place among a very small population is not in itself surprising. As Wright (1951, p. 134) has noted:

> I believe that in every generation of every culture there will be found at the least a few people who speculate about possibilities of doing things; both technologically and socially and who are not content to rest at mere speculation.

One might argue that in small isolated communities, such as the one being discussed here, the need to innovate and explore new approaches and to maintain contact with other communities becomes of considerable importance.

CONTEXT

The setting of this chapter is Fair Isle, the most remote of the inhabited British Isles, lying midway between the archipelagos of Orkney and Shetland to the north of the British Mainland. Fair Isle lies almost 60 degrees north and is in a highly exposed maritime location at the junction of the Atlantic Ocean and the North Sea. It is known internationally for two attributes: it is the foremost location in the British Isles for viewing rare and vagrant bird species, mostly during spring and autumn migrations and, of more relevance here, it has given its name to a particular style of knitting. The geometrical cultured patterns which characterize Fair Isle patterns have been in existence for several centuries and have been adopted in many forms in a large number of countries. On Fair Isle, they have been responsible for providing an important source of income to the island community for the past 150 years. Their retailing represents an interesting, if somewhat depressing and not unfamiliar, example of small-scale entrepreneurship that has struggled to survive because it has suffered considerably from much larger external competitors who have paid no regard to product authenticity or traditional rights (Brouder & Eriksson, 2013). Fair Isle illustrates the way in which small island communities (65 residents in this case) often produce entrepreneurs and innovators, partly out of sheer necessity for survival and partly because of unique attributes and differing ways of resolving problems. As well as entrepreneurs in knitting goods, the island has witnessed the creation of a construction company and enterprises in boat building, chair making, spinning wheel construction and art (painting and photography) production. As will be discussed, all these activities reflect local needs and talents and have found a ready market, locally and to visitors, both in person and in electronic form.

The Shetland Isles, of which Fair Isle is one, have been exposed to external influences for many centuries. While relatively remote in terms of distance, they have had much contact with outsiders, and this is reflected in the outlook and attitudes of their residents. Maritime activities have dominated the lives and lifestyle of Shetlanders for at least a thousand years, when the islands' settlement by Vikings began. They have been the base for voyages of exploration and colonization in the North Atlantic, for fishing (the traditional major occupation on the islands), whaling and, most recently, the development of oil and gas reserves in the North Sea and Atlantic. These activities have resulted in widespread travel by Shetlanders and extensive contact with travellers who have visited the islands for conquest, exploitation of resources and trade. The inhabitants have a long history of trading with visitors, a tradition that has continued with modern-day tourists. Fair Isle's exposed location resulted in a limited number of vessels calling there for trade, particularly in the days of sail, and islanders would venture out to passing boats and trade items such as fish for items not found on the Shetland archipelago. Among the items from Fair Isle that were bartered along with fish were knitted goods, in particular hats, setting the pattern that continues today. Such trading occurred throughout the Shetlands, one of the reasons being the fine wool that was available from the local sheep and that was highly prized in knitted form. The once-unique patterns and designs from Fair Isle began to appear throughout Shetland and further afield, and purchasing such items locally at source began to disappear. Only in the last half century has there been a resurgence in sales, reflecting local entrepreneurial attitudes and actions, as discussed in what follows.

FAIR ISLE KNITTING

Fair Isle knitting today is practiced on a commercial basis by five island residents, with two more learning the art. Before the significance of the knitting in island life and the importance of the entrepreneurial activities of the knitters can be appreciated, it is necessary to provide some context and background with respect to the history of knitting on the island and the origins of the distinctive patterns.

The origin of the knitting patterns to which Fair Isle has given its name is lost in history. One oft-quoted but entirely unverified and almost certainly incorrect suggestion is that the patterns date from the 16th century, when the *El Gran Grifon*, a ship of the Spanish Armada, was wrecked on Fair Isle in 1588 and most of its crew was stranded on the island for several weeks. Such were their numbers (300) that they and the island population came close to starvation before their removal to the Shetland mainland, and it has been argued that during this period, the sailors passed on patterns to the island knitters, the conjecture being that the patterns resembled Moorish designs hitherto unknown in Shetland (Brower, 2014). A more likely origin is that the patterns originate from trade with the many Baltic-based ships from an earlier period—Shetland had considerable trade with Hanseatic League ports in the 15th and 16th centuries—as the patterns resemble those found in Scandinavia and the northern Baltic (Exclusively Fair Isle, 2014). O'Dell (1939, p. 180) notes:

> Whatever their ultimate origin, the Fair Isle patterns are due to Scandinavian or at least Central European influence . . . the patterns probably came from Central Asia and the route may have been via the Moors and Spain, or via the traders of Northern Europe.

Given the similarity to patterns in the Faroes, Norway and Spain and the fact that those areas were all visited by the Vikings from the 10th to the 13th centuries, O'Dell's conclusions seem reasonable. Certainly by the middle of the 19th century, patterned knitted items were being traded from Fair Isle, and the patterns and garments have evolved since then. In the 1920s, the patterns were limited to Fair Isle; but, by the end of the 1930s, they were widespread throughout Shetland (Butler, 1963).

Traditional Fair Isle knitting is made with a double strand of very fine wool, using double-pointed needles and a knitting belt, each needle knitting a different color or shade of wool. The speed with which island knitters knitted was remarkable, and when they were filmed in the mid-20th century, the film was slowed down for viewing because it was felt it would not be seen as realistic because of that speed (personal survey Butler, 1963). The colors used as late as the mid-20th century were created using local dyes from plants such as heather and berries found on the island, producing reds, blues and yellows. Moreover, the natural colors of the wool itself—moorit (brown), shaela (grey), eesit (fawn) and natural white—were used and became increasingly popular. Because it was extremely soft and easily detached, the wool was traditionally pulled from sheep rather than being sheared off. In the mid-20th century, the wool was sent away to a mill in Brora in Sutherland, on the Scottish mainland, to be spun into yarn. The knitting in the 1960s was overseen by a Knitters Committee that examined every article and awarded the trademark "Fair Isle, made in Fair Isle" to distinguish such hosiery from items knitted elsewhere that might have the mark "Fair Isle, made in Shetland." As discussed in what follows, the ability of nonislanders to use the term "Fair Isle" has proven to be a major problem in the second half of the 20th century. The Knitters Committee also oversaw and limited the use of the traditionally dyed colored wool, but gradually the use of indigenous plant dyes disappeared, and all colored wool is now dyed chemically.

The knitting had a very limited market until the late 1920s, as visitors were few and only one formal outlet (in London) existed for the produce. The situation changed dramatically from 1921 when the then Prince of Wales (later King Edward VIII) wore a Fair Isle patterned vest when he ceremoniously drove off the first tee on the Old Course in St. Andrews in that year. He had been made Captain of the Royal and Ancient Golf Club, a position that involved a well-publicized drive off to waiting caddies, the lucky one who retrieved the ball being rewarded with a gold sovereign. Pictures of the prince in his Fair Isle garment were widely disseminated in the media of the day, and the style became instantly popular with the well-to-do and the aristocracy in subsequent years. Visitors to the Fair Isle Bird Observatory began to replace this market from the 1950s, and island visitors in general now make up the majority of the purchasers of the genuine article.

Despite the speed of the knitters, making a complete Fair Isle patterned sweater or cardigan takes many hours, around 100 for completely hand-knitted garments. In order to speed up the process and to reduce the time involved, Shetlanders in general started to introduce garments that were mostly of plain, unpatterned wool knitted on a machine, with a Fair Isle patterned yoke knitted by hand. This arrangement is the most common form found today in Shetland; but on Fair Isle, the practice now is to produce a fully patterned garment on a hand machine, with the final stitching up being done by hand in such a way that no seams are visible. The result is very impressive and externally hard to distinguish from the traditional completely hand-knitted item. The cost of a sleeved garment done on a machine and hand finished is around £300 (about US$520) each, depending on size and pattern, while those that are done entirely on a machine in Shetland cost around £200 (US$340) each. The traditional fully hand-knitted garments are now only produced for family members except on rare occasions and, if sold, cost in the region of £900 (US$1,560) each.

Not surprisingly, hats, scarves, gloves, headbands and similar smaller items are much more popular today, especially as souvenirs, retailing on the island from £15 to £40 (US$26 to US$68). Many of the patterns are traditional, but new ones have been added, and color combinations can be requested by purchasers. The current knitters each have websites (e.g., Coull, 2014; Exclusively Fair Isle, 2014; Fair Isle, 2014; Fair Isle Yarns, 2014; Ventrillon, 2014) illustrating patterns and garments and take orders online as well as in person. At the time of writing (2014), the bulk of the annual production is purchased by cruise passengers and visitors to the Bird Observatory, and little remains toward the end of the each year when tourist visitation ends. The output barely keeps pace with demand at present, and the income generated is an important element in several household budgets. Before the recent popularization of Fair Isle knitting from the 1960s onward, knitters were paid a very low rate, and in 1938, the average income from knitting for each croft was in the region of £0.5 per year (about $0.85). By 1963, it was £500 (US$850) a year or more, reflecting a much more realistic price being paid to the knitters themselves, with orders being sent directly to customers as far away as Australia (Butler, 1963). At the present time, the average income of knitters is several thousand pounds a year, a considerable amount when one considers the very limited alternative sources of income on the island and the low rents paid to the National Trust for Scotland (NTS).

The knitting has always remained a female prerogative, with women and girls being the producers. Traditional life on islands such as Fair Isle involved the men being engaged primarily in fishing, cutting peat (with women carrying the sods home) and some agriculture, particularly related to sheep, with the women planting and caring for most of the crops, especially the vegetables, and engaging in preparing fish (gutting, salting and drying) and in making and repairing clothing. Knitting in Shetland has been a traditional local craft for centuries. As noted, by the 19th century, the produce, along with fish, was traded with passing ships for tools, foreign foodstuffs and beverages and other items not available on the islands. A significant advantage to such bartering was the avoidance of customs and excise taxes that would have been due if such items had been sold and bought in a store. Casual visitors to Fair Isle, such as tourists, were rare until after the Second World War; thus, most knitting produce was sold through an agent to the London market. The knitters were not paid anything remotely resembling a fair wage for the hours of work involved, but there was no perception of an alternative market beyond the opportunities to trade with passing ships whose numbers were declining: with the disappearance of sailing ships, few boats needed to call in to Fair Isle or similar locations and instead made Lerwick their only port of call in Shetland (if at all).

The popularity of Fair Isle knitwear with increasing numbers of visitors to the island in the 20th century made the local residents realize that there was a considerable potential market for their product. Initially this was in the form of military personnel, as armed forces were stationed on Fair Isle during the Second World War. After hostilities ended, the market for knitwear was limited to staff and visitors at the Fair Isle Bird Observatory (FIBO), established in 1948, but as cruise ships began to call at the island from 1958 onward, demand increased noticeably (FIBO, 1959). The regular arrival of cruise ships to Fair Isle has been viewed as positive for the island from the first visit of the National Trust for Scotland cruise ship *Meteor* in April 1958. The FIBO Annual Report of that year noted that the cruise ship passengers "provided an entirely new outlet for the knitwear and woven goods produced by the islanders; and quite apart from the economic benefit it proved a major social occasion" (FIBO, 1959, p. 6). Cruise ship visits resulted in passengers (generally 150 to 200 at a time) being taken on tours of the island and hosted to a tea in the community hall. At such events, local knitwear and other crafts were displayed and available for purchase. This pattern of activities continues to the present day, with up to 10 cruise ships calling in an average year. Demand from the start was such that it outstripped production even in the 1960s and 1970s because of limited production, reflecting the time required to hand knit the garments. Moreover, orders were taken from visitors who could not purchase an item while on the island, resulting in goods being sent worldwide. At the same time, in Shetland and elsewhere, the use of hand frames for knitting was drastically reducing the time taken to knit a sweater or cardigan, and in many cases a "Fair Isle" yoke was added to allow the garment to be sold as "Fair Isle," despite the absence of any direct link to the island. While Fair Island knitters still do not produce such garments, remaining loyal to "all-over" Fair Isle patterned products, it was realized that hand frames could be used to produce the Fair Isle patterns for complete garments.

Demand pressure continued to increase as more visitors began to arrive each year, and as a result, the knitters decided that the use of hand frames would resolve the problem of excessive demand compared to limited supply. Given the proven reliability of the visitor market, a group of island women decided to work together and form a worker's cooperative. This was founded in 1980 as Fair Isle Crafts Ltd. This innovation represented the three elements of entrepreneurship noted earlier: a new market (tourists), a new method of production (hand frames) and a new approach to organization (the cooperative). The hand frames were an immediate success and allowed the knitters on the island to continue to produce the traditional patterned garments in a much shorter time and at a much lower price than would have had to be charged for patterned garments knitted entirely by hand. While this innovation meant that they were able to meet the then existing demand, the shorter waiting time and lower price resulted in further increased demand. The numbers of visitors coming to the Bird Observatory increased markedly, reflecting the rebuilding of the observatory in the 1980s and then a new building constructed again in 2012, with its capacity enlarged overall from 12 to 48. Occupancy rates also increased as bird watching became more popular (FIBO Annual Reports). With an air service commencing in 1968, many more short-term tourists as well as committed longer-stay bird watchers began to appear. Apart from the increase in cruise ships already noted, there was a significant rise in the number of pleasure yachts and other boats coming to the island. For example:

In July 2011, several hand-knitters on Fair Isle revived the tradition of bartering by making and bartering Fair Isle Fisherman's keeps for items offered by the crew of the passing Tall Ship *Sorlandet* from Norway, with remaining keeps auctioned to raise funds for an extension to the island's George Waterston Memorial Centre and Museum (www.exclusivelyfairisle.co.uk/).

Instead of perhaps 200 tourists being present in an average year in the 1960s, by the 1980s, there were in excess of 2,000 tourists a year visiting Fair Isle.

One major problem faced by the cooperative was the inability to trademark the Fair Isle style of knitting, and thus it was unable to limit the use of the term "Fair Isle" to goods produced on the island. The major stumbling block to gaining trademark rights was the traditional widespread use of the term over many years in many different places, including throughout Shetland and other locations in Scotland. This meant that anyone anywhere could produce knitted goods with similar patterns and style them "Fair Isle." While the absence of a trademark meant that prices for genuine Fair Isle goods could not be raised to an optimum level reflecting their rarity and the time involved in their production, the market and the demand have remained sufficiently high to permit several knitters to remain active on the island. The issue of low prices being paid for traditional knitted garments has been highlighted in the media in recent years with the renewed popularity of Fair Isle patterns among the fashion cognoscenti. Both *The Economist* (2010) and *The Independent* (Mesure, 2010) have focused on this problem. The luxury goods outlet Thistle and Broom has instituted a specific project—the Fair Isle Knitting Project—relating to Shetland (albeit not Fair Isle) knitted garments in effort to ensure their continued traditional production by native Shetlanders (Bowie et al., 2014). The Thistle and Broom website contains a lengthy rationale for the company's involvement in purchasing and reselling Shetland knitwear. An illuminating excerpt is copied below:

> As a newlywed in the 1970s, the young groom found himself standing in the Made in UK gallery of the veritable London luxury goods purveyor Harrods as he described "sight-seeing." He and his bride subsequently discovered a Fair Isle jumper bearing a price tag of £175.00 along with the label of their local knitting cooperative. Once back on Unst (current population about 700) he tracked down his knitting neighbour, only to discover that she had been paid a mere £15.00 for nearly a month's worth of knitting and the cost of her yarns. A Shetland woman (or man) applying more than sixty years of expertise and spending more than 110 hours hand-knitting a full size jumper and 12 hours on a pair of gloves still earns about £65 for the pullover and £11 for the gloves on the islands when their garment sells. Yet, walk into Harvey Nichols (Scotland's flagship luxury goods purveyor) and a machine-made, in Italy, merino wool Fair Isle inspired pullover (i.e. knock off) under Alexander McQueen's label sells for upwards of £240! What's equally important is that the purchase of Mr. McQueen's, or any other label, of "Fair Isle style" fails to provide any economic benefit to Shetland. Both circumstances are equally abhorrent. As a result of the endemic poor compensation, the native population undervaluing their most globally recognised product and upscale clothing designers being inspired but not ethically compelled to source locally, instead of hundreds of legacy knitters of multiple generations continuing this iconic art form perhaps two hundred remain.
>
> (Bowie et al., 2014)

The label "Fair Isle, made in Fair Isle" on garments in the 1950 and 1960s to distinguish them as being produced on Fair Isle has disappeared, and some current garments produced in Fair Isle have the Fair Isle star to distinguish them from items produced elsewhere (Fair Isle Star Motif, 2014).

The original fully hand-knitted garments take more than a hundred hours to produce, and few are made for sale at the present time because of the price that would have to be charged (around £900 for a sweater or cardigan). Those that are produced are mostly knitted as gifts to family and friends and are nearly all made by a very few now elderly original Fair Islanders. One of the current knitters notes:

> These skilled and talented ladies included Annie Thomson, Edith and Aggie Stout, all born on Fair Isle in the early 1900s and who, along with their sisters and cousins, had been taught to hand-knit by their

mothers and grandmothers at the tender age of 3 or 4 years old in order to help supplement their families' income. The tradition of Fair Isle hand-knitting is still practiced and passed on by mothers, grandmothers and great-grandmothers to their daughters on Fair Isle today, although nowadays this is mostly for the pleasure of knitting for family members and friends.

(Exclusively Fair Isle, 2014)

The Fair Isle cooperative ended in March 2011, having lasted for more than three decades, and its long-term existence demonstrated the location-specific knowledge and routines and skills identified by Brouder and Eriksson (2013) as important in microfirm survival. Its termination reflected a decline in numbers of active knitters, as elderly members did not wish to continue on a commercial basis. The demise of the cooperative came about because of the reduced number of knitters engaged in commercial activity and the loss of any economies of scale. Moreover, the advent of the World Wide Web allowed individuals to promote and market their work cheaply and efficiently; and so the benefits of being a member of a cooperative declined accordingly. Five women currently knit on a commercial basis on Fair Isle and two children are being taught the craft. Around 30 sweaters, 200 hats and 30 scarves, along with gloves and headbands, are made in the average year at present. An island woman is also teaching textile and design courses (Coull, 2014). Thus, while the organizational innovation that was the cooperative has ended, the element of new markets has continued to be developed, with all of the knitters having websites and engaging in online promotion and selling via the World Wide Web (e.g., Exclusively Fair Isle, 2014; Fair Isle, 2014). No progress has been made on trademarking "Fair Isle," but Fair Isle–produced goods can now use the recently established Scottish Crofting Produce Mark. This can be used on foodstuffs (meat, vegetables, fruit, dairy produce and preserves) and wool produce (knitting and tweed that comes from a crofter [or similar small agricultural producer] who is a member of the Scottish Crofting Foundation and meets standards of quality, hygiene, animal care and traceability of origin; Scottish Crofting Federation, 2014; www.kathycoull.com).

OTHER FAIR ISLE ENTREPRENEURS

The adage that "necessity is the mother of invention" (or innovation, and hence entrepreneurship) has been proven correct in other ways on Fair Isle. While knitting probably remains the major source of income on the island in terms of exports, individuals with other talents have taken advantage of the new market in the form of tourists to create and promote their products. Five individual products have emerged, three of which can be seen as traditional and two reflecting more recent ventures.

The best established of these is the production of *spinning wheels*, items that have been vital to the production of the yarn for knitting on Shetland. One individual, Stewart Thomson, continues to manufacture spinning wheels on Fair Isle, and he has now crafted well over a hundred wheels, some of which are still in use on the island and others that have been bought by visitors over the years. Given the absence of trees on Shetland generally and Fair Isle in particular, many of the wheels have been made from wood salvaged from shipwrecks and that found on the shore. This source of supply has diminished over the years (Thomson, personal communication, 2012), and wood from a variety of sources has been used recently. The production of the spinning wheels is a great fascination to tourists, and demonstrations of their use often take place at the Bird Observatory, where visitors are encouraged to try spinning yarn. Thomson came to Fair Isle in 1942 and only began making spinning wheels late in life (he was born in 1924) primarily as a hobby, and as with the knitting, demand for his work outstrips his ability to produce the supply. But he has been producing wheels on a regular basis; in 2010, he noted "two are on the bench" (Thomason, 2010, n.p.). He also then donated his 106th wheel for auction to the FIBO fundraising campaign for the new observatory (Thomason, 2010). That wheel was made from local materials and included parts from the original bird observatory (naval huts from the 1940s). A wheel takes about 200 hours to complete and sells for more than £300.

A somewhat similar craft in terms of being a traditional island artifact is the Fair Isle *straw-backed chair* (Fair Isle Straw Crafts, 2014). Of a type also known as "Orkney chair," the Fair Isle model differs slightly in that the back of the chair is stitched in a manner unique to Fair Isle. The straw used in the chairs is from Shetland oats and a small crop is produced on Fair Isle, both for the chairs and to encourage migrating birds to stay longer on the island. Oats are the traditional cereal crop of the Scottish Islands but are no longer grown on Fair Isle for human consumption.

> The straw is Shetland Oats, which produce a fine, long stemmed straw, ideal for working and which grows very well on Fair Isle. Because it has almost disappeared in Shetland, I have to thrash enough seed from my own crop to plant the following year.
>
> (Thomson, 2012, n.p.)

The continued production is further evidence of the integration of traditional activities with the modern economic activity of tourism. The wood in the chairs, as in the case of the spinning wheels, comes mostly from salvaged timbers and also now from commercial sources. The base is paneled and generally fitted with twin drawers, all fastened with wooden trenails. The chairs are more than a meter high, the back providing shelter from drafts, and have been made on the island for more than a century. They have been exported for almost two decades, each one being unique, depending on the nature and origin of the wood being used.

The third traditional craft developed into an export industry on Fair Isle is *boat building*. Boats have been crucial for survival of Shetland communities, and Fair Isle is no exception. The maintenance of the ferry boat on the island manned by islanders has been critical to the survival of the community. The traditional Fair Isle small fishing boat resembles a scaled-down Viking long ship and, when used for fishing in the 19th century and earlier, had a single central sail. The boats normally would have a crew of four or six and featured high prows and sterns. On Fair Isle, they were kept at the South Harbour and hauled out of the water into "stalls" cut out of the turf. Ian Best, the current boat maker, gained qualifications and experience in boat building in Norway over 3 years before returning to Fair Isle, where he runs a croft as well as the boat-building business. One of his boats has been on exhibition at the National Museum of Scotland and, in recent years, the revival of the Shetland tradition of rowing races has increased interest in the traditional "yoals" he constructs. The market for these boats has widened from Shetland to Europe, and the boats are used for rowing and also traditional fishing. The yoal is clinker built from Scottish larch and is light, manageable, flexible and well suited to the often rough water surrounding the Shetlands. It can be powered by oar, sail or outboard motor (Best, 2014).

Two other entrepreneurs work on Fair Isle, both incomers to the island. One, Tommy Hyndman, is an artist and also in the hospitality business, offering accommodation at the Haa—the house of the old factor, the local estate manager (Auld Haa Guest House, 2014)—and runs a blog (Auld Haa Blog, 2014). The other, David Wheeler, also operates a website in the form of the Fair Isle News (Fair Isle, 2014) and offers high-quality photographic images.

Almost all of the individuals discussed, like most adults on Fair Isle, also have more formal occupations, all part time. Multiplicity of employment is a key factor in most Scottish Islands, especially the small islands such as Fair Isle. It is not unknown for individuals to hold six or more part-time positions, many with the local authority, in order to earn a reasonable income. Positions on Fair Isle include airport manager, fire brigade member, road worker, harbor master, janitor, cook and computer and music support staff, as well as teacher at the local school, nurse, shopkeeper and post office manager, meteorologist, ferry boat crew member, construction worker, cleaner at the bird observatory and more. Other positions become available as the need arises, such as working on the communications mast, at the lighthouses or on harbor repairs. For a number of years, there was a formal construction company on Fair Isle, the Norsemen, and the shareholders were involved in house reconstruction and modification and also in finishing the construction of the latest Bird Observatory in 2012 when the company undertaking the job went bankrupt (FIBO, 2013).

CONCLUSION

Visiting Fair Isle a half century after my first visit has provided an opportunity to discover how the small community has adapted to significant changes in its situation. The outlook in 2014 is much more positive than it was in 1962/3. While agricultural production has declined in importance, the economic activities described in this chapter have proved remarkably successful. Knitting has become of greater importance to the island economy than it was 50 years ago and is much better integrated with tourism and the external market. The other activities have all started operation on a commercial basis since my first visit and seem economically viable, although the ages of some of the producers may suggest that at least the spinning wheel and chair production may not continue for many more years.

Not surprisingly, not all entrepreneurial efforts on Fair Isle have been successful. When the South Light was automated, the previous living quarters of the staff were acquired by the National Trust for Scotland; a workshop established for a silversmith to produce jewelry on the island and a café were planned to open there. But neither of these enterprises has been successful, and others will no doubt fail in the future. An attempt to produce Fair Isle tweed was made in the 1960s but did not last long, and weaving is no longer continued. Given the modern penchant for the exotic and rare, especially in fashion, and the resurgence in demand for Harris tweed—another sought-after clothing product whose brand is intimately connected to the island of provenance, and with its own ups and downs (Harper & McDougall, 2012)—it might well be opportune to restart tweed production on Fair Isle, although the number of part-time opportunities for work noted earlier would not allow much time for this at present.

It is perhaps significant that those entrepreneurial activities that have been most successful on Fair Isle have all been related to the traditional crafts of the island. Knitting, wood product manufacturing and boat building continue being practiced largely by "native" Fair Islanders. To some extent, there has been limited evidence of a bidirectional split in production as noted by Markwick (2001), with the products having different meanings and forms for tourists and for locals. But, in general, the goods produced on Fair Isle have stayed very close to their traditional designs and functions, despite the massive changes in the market and promotion of the products, as well as the change in production method in the case of knitting. Undoubtedly, the cachet of the Fair Isle name, internationally known for its knitting and for its remoteness, has helped the establishment and maintenance of the market for the items produced and given them an element of uniqueness and rarity that is much in demand in the present day. The fortunate combination of a steadily growing tourism (and market) presence, a supportive landlord (NTS) and the islanders' penchant for innovation has resulted in the island being a successful base for a surprising number of individual entrepreneurs using traditional skills in producing marketable goods.

ACKNOWLEDGMENTS

I am most grateful to the Leverhulme Foundation for the award of an Emeritus Professorship, which provided the funding for the study on which this chapter is based, and to the residents of Fair Isle for being so helpful with advice and information.

REFERENCES

Auld Haa Blog. (2014). Retrieved from http://fair-isle.blogspot.co.uk/p/b-b.html

Auld Haa Guest House. (2014). Retrieved from www.go-bedandbreakfast.co.uk/auldhaaguesthousefairisle/

Bowie, A., Simpson, M., Halcrow, R., Irvine, J., Sutherland, E., & Williamson, M. (2014). Fair Isle knitwear. *Thistle and Broom*. Retrieved from www.thistleandbroom.com/scotland/fair-isle-knitwear.htm

Brouder, P., & Eriksson, R.H. (2013). Staying power: what influences micro-firm survival in tourism? *Tourism Geographies, 15*(1), 125–144.

Brower, D. (2014). Of Spaniards, shipwrecks and sheep. *Twist Collective*. Retrieved from www.twistcollective.com/collection/component/content/article/35-features/1090-of-spaniards-shipwrecks-and-sheep

Butler, R.W. (1963). *Fair Isle: A geographical study of the development of an isolated island community*. Unpublished B.A. dissertation. Nottingham: University of Nottingham.

Butler, R.W., & Russell, R. (2010). *Giants of tourism*. Wallingford: CABI.

Butler, R.W., & Russell, R. (2012). The role of individuals in the development and popularization of tourist destinations. In C.H.C. Hsu & W.C. Gartner (Eds.), *The Routledge handbook of tourism research* (pp. 132–144). Abingdon: Routledge.

Cauthorn, R.C. (1989). *Contribution to a theory of entrepreneurship*. New York, NY: Garland Publishing.

Coull, K. (2014). The Fair Isle textile workshop. Retrieved from www.kathycoull.com

The Economist. (2010, 25 November). Dropped stitches: Imitation and demography threaten a traditional Scottish brand. Retrieved from www.economist.com/node/17581676

Exclusively Fair Isle. (2014). Genuine Fair Isle knitwear designed & handcrafted on Fair Isle: The home of Fair Isle knitting. Elizabeth Riddiford. Retrieved from www.exclusivelyfairisle.co.uk/

Fair Isle. (2014). Fair Isle. Retrieved from www.fairisle.org.uk/

Fair Isle Bird Observatory (FIBO). (1959). *Annual report*. Ipswich: Healeys Printers.

Fair Isle Bird Observatory (FIBO). (2013). *Annual report*. Ipswich: Healeys Printers.

Fair Isle Star Motif. (2014). The history of Fair Isle knitwear. Retrieved from www.exclusivelyfairisle.co.uk/history-of-fair-isle-knitting.php

Fair Isle Straw Crafts. (2014). Proprietor Stewart Thomson. Retrieved from www.fairisle.org.uk/Crafts/straw_crafts.htm

Fair Isle Yarns. (2014). Fair Isle yarns. Retrieved from www.spanglefish.com/FairIsleYarns/

Harper, C., & McDougall, K. (2012). The very recent fall and rise of Harris tweed. *Textile: The Journal of Cloth and Culture, 10*(1), 78–99.

Hartwell, M., & Lane, J. (1991). *Champions of enterprise: Australian entrepreneurship 1788–1990*. Double Bay, NSW: Focus Books.

Ian Best. (2014). Ian Best, boat builder. Retrieved from www.fairisle.org.uk/ianbest boatbuilder/

Markwick, M. C. (2001). Tourism and the development of handicraft production in the Maltese Islands. *Tourism Geographies, 3*(1), 29–51.

Mesure, S. (2010). Fair Isle boom leaves islanders out in the cold. *The Independent (UK)* 12 December. Retrieved from www.independent.co.uk/life-style/fashion/news/fair-isle-boom-leaves-islanders-out-in-the-cold-2158110.html

O'Dell, A. C. (1939). *Historical geography of the Shetland Islands.* Lerwick, Shetland: T. & J. Mason.

Schumpeter, J. A. (1950). *Capitalism, socialism and democracy.* New York, NY: Harper-Collins.

Scottish Crofting Federation. (2014). Scottish crofting produce. Retrieved from www.crofting.org/index.php/scpbrand

Shaw, G., & Williams, A. M. (1998). Entrepreneurship, small business culture and tourism development. In D. Ioannides & K. G. Debbage (Eds.), *The economic geography of the tourist industry: A supply-side analysis* (pp. 235–255). London: Routledge.

Thomason, L. (2010). Special spinning wheel auctioned. *Shetland Times.* 19 March. Retrieved from www.shetlandtimes.co.uk/2010/03/19/special-spinning-wheel-auctioned/

Ventrillon, M. (2014). Fair Isle knitwear. Mati Ventrillon. Retrieved from www.fairisleknitwear.co.uk

Wright, D. M. (1951). Schumpeter's political philosophy. In S. E. Harris (Ed.), *Schumpeter: Social scientist* (pp. 152–157). Cambridge, MA: Harvard University Press.

6 Entrepreneurs in Aquaculture

A Case Study from the Faroes

Gestur Hovgaard

INTRODUCTION

This study is located and contextualized in the Faroe Islands, an autonomous country within the Danish Realm, with home rule since 1948. The country is responsible for the conservation and management of living marine resources within its 320-km (200-mile) exclusive economic zone, the protection of the marine environment, subsurface resources (including oil and gas deposits), trade, fiscal policy and industrial relations, transport, communications, culture, education and research. The 18-island archipelago is located between Scotland and Iceland in the North Atlantic Ocean and has a resident population of around 48,000. The name translates as the island of sheep (*Føroyar* may reflect the Old Norse word *fær*, for sheep), suggesting correctly that mutton is a staple food. However, the Faroese people have depended mainly on traditional fishing for their economic survival. Today, Faroese fisheries and aquaculture are the basis for the production and export of high-quality Faroese fish products, representing 95% of merchandise exports and around one third of total Faroese GDP over the last 10 years.

Over less than two decades, saltwater aquaculture in the Faroes has grown into a true global business, making the islands the fifth-largest producer of Atlantic salmon in the world. Annual production of fish farming has increased from 15,000 tons in 2006 up to 63,000 tons in 2012 (Faroe Fish Farmers Association, 2013), accounts for 3.5% of Faroese wage earners (Statistics Faroe Islands, n.d.) and is responsible for about one third of the country's total export revenues (Búskaparráðið, 2013).

This chapter provides explanations for this small island industrial success. It will outline the main threads of its evolution from an entrepreneurial perspective. Entrepreneurial roles will be explained by means of intersections and interactions within a specific historical and socio-institutional context. In particular, it will be argued that a small island entrepreneur is heavily dependent on a combination of specific ties, including local family, national institutions and regional networks, which are very often personal and personalized. Business success is strongly shaped and driven by embedded historical trajectories, where smallness presents its advantages as well as its disadvantages.

ENTREPRENEURSHIP: A CONTEXTUAL APPROACH

Although one should not underestimate the intrinsic psychological importance of the creative urge (Amabile, 1996), innovation can be seen as a final stage in a much longer creative process that involves various individuals and groups across various sectors. It is not inspired only by individuals. Innovation requires diversity as well as collectivity, and the balance between these dimensions is a crucial aspect of innovative activities (Fuglsang, 2008).

Social science theory did not pay much attention to the role and function of entrepreneurship until the 1980s, though with some important exceptions (e.g., Hagen, 1962; Kirzner, 1973; McClelland, 1967). The entrepreneur was until then seen mainly as a glorified individual and passionate profit-driven founder; but since then, perspectives have shifted towards an understanding of entrepreneurship as something that happens in a social context, in and with collectives, networks and organizations and in the direction of a strategic imperative (Sundbo, 1995, 1998. There is thus a tendency in entrepreneurship studies to locate the entrepreneur as an actor who navigates under the influence of external factors (Gartner, 1995).

Entrepreneurship is a multifaceted phenomenon; it has no unified understanding, and several subdomains can be detected (Gedeon, 2010). An important conceptual distinction is between so-called Schumpeter I and Schumpeter II entrepreneurial types (Freeman, 1974; Phillips, 1971). The former type is the classical one, referred to as the *extrapreneur*, the one that creates a new business, from scratch. The second type is the one that operates typically in a team within a corporation, known as the *intrapreneur*, deploying creative ideas but within a given organizational structure rather than one that s/he creates. An additional, third type refers to the one who breaks down barriers among disciplines, professions and cultures. This is the *interpreneur*, a form of entrepreneurship that has increased much in importance (Chesbrough, 2003; Lundvall, 2011). Fuglsang (2008) equates the interpreneur with a Schumpeter III type:

> ... where new mechanisms of creativity and diffusion of innovation are becoming important, and where market mechanisms and social mechanisms are blended in new ways. . . . new strategic arenas of innovation are being formed to which many types of actors are linked, such as universities, companies, government institutions and user groups. Furthermore, employees and consumers are interlinked in new ways at the systemic rather than only the individual level.
>
> (Fuglsang, 2008, p. 12)

Numerous studies are showing that specific geographical environments create specific entrepreneurial cultures or spirits, often illustrated by positive cases of community commitment, support and development. But the rules of entrepreneurship may change over time (Baumol, 1990), and different entrepreneurial roles can be brought into play in one and the same time, something that Schumpeter may have overlooked (Fuglsang, 2008). Furthermore, the entrepreneur is not necessarily driven by profits only; s/he serves a social function in changing economic structures or developing new products and services. Other motivations could be a sense of idealism, a desire for specific problem solving or a devotion to communities or localities.

This approach invites a praxis-oriented and contextualized view of entrepreneurship and innovation. Understanding the context is key to appreciating when, how and why entrepreneurship happens, and qualitative or combined methods help to capture the diversity and richness of the context (Hovgaard, 2001; Welter, 2011). This chapter refers to context in three interconnected fields: social, institutional and spatial embedding of entrepreneurial activities.

The most common perspective in entrepreneurial research is the network of interpersonal relations (Granovetter, 1985, 1992). In this approach, trust and transactions are dependent upon the mechanisms of coupling and decoupling out of social networks. These networks may be professional, but they may also include family, household and "old boy" networks, a field that has gained a following in entrepreneurial research (Fineman & Gabriel, 1996).

The institutional context refers to Karl Polanyi's substantive understanding of the role of the economy in society, which links individual action in networks with systemic conditions in a dynamic and relational perspective (Hovgaard, 2001; Olofsson, 1995). Institutions are the embodiment of human meaning and purpose (Polanyi, 1957, p. 254). These embodiments comprise the formal as well as informal rules, routines and habits of society. Institutions extend as well as restrict individual and collective action, and by their changing nature over time, history plays a crucial role in enabling and guiding entrepreneurial activity. Here, institutional theorizing often uses the concept of *path dependency*, which, in a Schumpetarian business cycle perspective, would mean that learning and new discoveries are developing out of known bundles of production elements: organizations, technologies, networks. Entrepreneurial decisions in the past shape the present and, in small environments, the influence of single individuals may be even stronger to create collective knowledge and experiences, making the past a stronger influence on future paths.

THE EARLY DAYS

Modern Faroese aquaculture begins in 1947 when a relatively new voluntary organization, the Faroese Trout Fishers Organization (FTO) was established. *Føroya Sílaveiðufelag* began to put out salmon fry in Faroese streams, where none had previously existed. This idea was developed with the help of experts in Denmark and Iceland and was launched with fry from Iceland. The fisheries committee of the Faroese parliament supported the initiative, because they saw the opportunity to make an income from recreational anglers. The hobbyist fishing organization, with some breaks, continued its activities to put out fry, and in the early 1960s, the salmon started to reappear in small numbers, and it was proven that it had developed into its own stock (Jacobsen, 2011, p. 20). The next step was to take roe from the Faroese stock and start breeding locally. For this purpose, a breeding station was constructed in 1963 (Jacobsen, 2011, p. 20).

The early work of the FTO was important because it laid the foundations for local knowledge about hatching and breeding, which later became vital to the fledgling aquaculture industry (Jacobsen, 2011, p. 19). The first important experiences in how salmon reacts to the Faroese natural environment, its feeding preferences and habits were also developed at this stage.

Meanwhile, two entrepreneurs, Elith Gotfred (1915–1958) and Menning Geyti (1912–1988), were trying to transform fish farming into a proper business. Both were inspired by the Danish system, with freshwater fish farms in onshore ponds. At that time, Denmark was considered to be the regional leader in aquaculture, production having increased from 400 tons in 1945 to 8,200 tons in 1964 (Jacobsen, 2011, p. 39). Both entrepreneurs tried over several years to develop their fish farms into a running business. They faced challenges with breeding, water quality and water supply, feed composition and feeding patterns, and both also faced serious financial problems. They were also exposed to direct sabotage; Geyti once and Gotfred twice had to witness the destruction of the fish stock by hostile acts—however, without the causes known (Jacobsen, 2011, p. 29 ff). In the late 1950s and early 1960s, there was hardly any institutional support for innovative entrepreneurial action. Only two persons were involved in fisheries-related research, and aquaculture was not part of this. But one of these, Andrias Reinert, a devoted member of FTO, became interested in this potential business opportunity, and it became his lifelong interest. He travelled to Denmark and Norway to obtain his first experiences with this business, and in 1965, he produced the first basic report on the potential of Faroese aquaculture (Jacobsen, 2011, p. 38). This report inspired the third important pioneering entrepreneur to finally decide to enter this business. This was a successful fisher and skipper, Júst í Túni (1919–1995). His engagement exemplifies vital entrepreneurial linkages between traditional fisheries and aquaculture. Through his fishing activity, í Túni had experienced and been fascinated by the first Norwegian sea-based aquaculture farms in the Sunnmøre region.

The first start-ups in the 1950s had failed because the Danish system with onshore freshwater ponds could not be adapted to the Faroese situation: the inflow of water is often too low and too cold, especially during winter. The Norwegians had detected, some say by chance (Jacobsen, 2011, p. 56), that salmon grows much better in salt water than in fresh water but needed to gain a certain size (around 100g, or 3.5 oz.) before they could survive at sea.

When í Túni started his first season in 1966, he wanted to grow his trout in seawater. One of the new technical innovations coming from Norway was sea-based fish cages. The Norwegian who successfully pioneered aquaculture was Erling Osland (Jacobsen 2011, 67 f). í Túni visited Osland in Norway, and he was thus inspired to construct a caged fish farm site at a beach nearby the village of Oyrarbakki on the island of Eysturoy. í Túni was also supported in his work by Reinert, who represented the public authorities and also had an excellent network outside the Faroes, in Norway in particular.

í Túni experienced his own share of technological difficulties and fatal mistakes. Only a few broods survived the first year, but the lessons learned were invaluable. The trout he was using was the same that the Faroese Fisheries Research Station was using to experiment successfully with their growth potential in Faroese waters (Jacobsen 2011, 59). The year after, in 1967, roe was purchased in Denmark and Iceland; this became the pedigree for all later trout production in the Faroes. This was done through a systematic breeding program started at that same time in cooperation between the Faroese authorities and the entrepreneur. By 1969, the harvested stock was expected to weigh about 30 tons, but only 16 tons were secured.

In 1970, í Tuni was looking for new ways to secure his business. A new public/private company, P/F Fiskaling, was set up, with í Túni as managing director (Jacobsen, 2011, p. 91). New processes in production and marketing and various technological refinements were made. Through experiments with different types of cages and nets and different types of feeders, the basis for future breeding protocols was laid. The experimentation with nets was important, because nets are mobile, while ponds are not. One of the interesting local inventions was the then well-known problem with water supply, especially for the hatching of roes and development of juveniles. An elderly local gentleman told í Túni that he knew about a local spring with warmer water. A search process started, and multiple warm-water sources were located around the central areas of the Faroes (Eysturoy and Streymoy Islands). A particularly good source near the place known as Við Áir thus became the center for the development of Faroese aquaculture (Jacobsen, 2011, p. 96). For years, marketing had become a difficulty, and it was only in 1971, after a long lull, that the first farmed fish were sold again. The product was produced by the sales company Faroe Seafood, as a trial, sent to a restaurant trader in New York with a stunning reception. The label Arctic Rainbow became for a short period a well-known label in the high-end restaurant business in New York (Jacobsen, 2011, pp. 79, 92). The market slowly opened up, and a sales agreement with the Danish supermarket chain Irma in 1974 was another milestone (Jacobsen, 2011,p. 103). Reinert has claimed that the Faroese, at this particular point of time, were even ahead of the Norwegians in producing high-quality trout (Jacobsen, 2011, p. 105).

With a functioning production process and an opening market, a shift from "exploration" to "exploitation" was imminent, and this switch typically demands increased focus toward the organizational and financial side of the business. í Túni had realized that a steady production with regular (rather than seasonal) slaughtering during the year was a precondition for business viability. Setting up Fiskaling was one step in this direction; but í Túni was frustrated by how Faroese politicians remained hesitant in making investments in large-scale aquaculture production. Public funding was a necessity, because the private capital simply was not there.

Instead, í Túni managed to get Danish big business interested in making investments to start up large-scale production, a project that included a research station (Jacobsen, 2011, p. 111). But the political apparatus intervened once more, and the negotiations between Danish capital and the Faroese government broke down because of disagreement on the organizational form that the venture should take. Disappointed, í Túni left Fiskaling in 1974 (Jacobsen, 2011, pp. 111, 115).

With the withdrawal of í Túni and the failed project with the Danes, Fiskaling had become a pure public company, now with Mr. Reinert as managing director, but also the only player in the business. One positive outcome was that the political system started to realize the potential of aquaculture, and public financial allocation to Fiskaling increased, at least temporarily (Jacobsen, 2011, p. 113).

EXPANSION AND COLLAPSE

Norwegians were the first to realize, in 1971, that Atlantic salmon was a better species for industrial aquaculture production than trout. í Túni had learned this while being in Norway, and in 1973, he started to experiment with breeding Atlantic salmon in the Faroes. One important factor that made this first experimentation possible was the warmer water from the hot springs and the fact that spawning salmon had been discovered in some Faroese lakes some years earlier. He took roe and semen from two wild salmon and, with the help of the Public Road Authorities (Landsverkfrøðingurin), he obtained the use of a shed on a parking spot near the hot spring where he could breed the first stock. This first experiment with salmon breeding was successful and was thereafter taken over by Fiskaling.

The first salmon smolt was put in nets in May 1975. Apart from problems with the feed that contained too little fat, it was also realized that the salmon matured too quickly, and a scientific breeding program was needed. However, as things turned out, this whole process could be skipped. How the Faroese managed to get their breeding stock of salmon, which shortly hereafter became the basis for full-scale industrial production, is quite an extraordinary story.[1]

In 1973, Reinert led a delegation to Norway to try to find out how the Norwegians had managed to turn salmon fish farm production into a profitable venture. Another person, Hjalti í Jákupsstovu, had been doing his study in Norway, and via his network there, Reinert got in touch with Bjørn Myrseth, a producer and soon to become a leading figure in Norwegian salmon production. Myrseth showed his smolt station to the Faroese team and explained its operation. The Norwegian Sea Research Institute (NSRI; Havforskningsinstituttet) was also visited, and here Reinert attended a seminar on salmon breeding at the research station in Sunndalsøra. At the following dinner, Reinert had the opportunity to sit together with Arne Kittelsen, NSRI director, and its chief scientist, Trygve Gjedrem. Gjedrem had a cousin who was married in the Faroes and knew other people there, too. To have such things in common paved the way to a congenial conversation, as Reinert fondly remembers; he took the opportunity to request the purchase of cultivated Norwegian salmon roe. Although strictly against all rules, Reinert managed to get his Norwegian roe, and these stocks became the foundation for the upcoming Faroese salmon production. Scientific cooperation between Fiskaling and the research station in Sunndalsøra, Norway, continued over several years; mainly to the advantage of the Faroese (Jacobsen, 2011, p. 133 ff; 180 ff).

At the beginning of the 1980s, the expansion that could have been set into motion some years earlier finally did take off. That year, six entrepreneurs started production, and they all had their education and experiences from stays in Norway. Among these starters was the company Bakkafrost, which today is the largest farmed fish producer in the Faroes (Bakkafrost, n.d.). Two public funding instruments (Ídnaðargrunnurin and Menningargrunnurin) were the only financial providers in these years, since the private financial market considered this new industry too high an investment risk (Jacobsen, 2011).

During the early1980s, farmed salmon had become a relatively safe business, not the least because prices skyrocketed, especially in 1983 to 1985. Exploitation replaced exploration, and many new companies entered the business. In 1985, 50 companies now had licenses to produce trout and salmon, and 10 smolt stations were operating (Jacobsen, 2011, p. 253). Now, even finance capital started showing an interest, and local banks, international feed producers and Faroe Seafood (FS), the large Faroese fish export company at that time, started to invest in aquaculture operations (Jacobsen, 2011, p. 259 f, 253). At that time, there were also 270 aspiring entrepreneurs, as the government had 197 applications for breeding operators and 73 applications for smolt operators (Jacobsen, 2011, p. 248); 63 breeding operators actually came into operation (Reinert, 1997).

In these years, a Klondike gold rush–like atmosphere prevailed in Faroese aquaculture, and the idea that entrepreneurs had to have solid competence in the industry was lost behind other ambitions. Aquaculture naturally became high politics, and the policy was that it should be a key component of rural development and for supporting small-scale operations. Indeed, local villagers, fishers or farmers were considered deserving of priority in the supply of licenses for grow-out sites and hatcheries (Jacobsen, 2011, p. 242 ff; Reinert, 1997). The many new entrepreneurs saw their options for creating personal wealth; others saw just an alternative or supplementary way of living.

The growth in Faroese aquaculture was not distinctive; rather, the growth in international production was tremendous, and already in early 1986, there were declining market prices and signs of overproduction, a problem that increased in the years to come.

Neither were diseases distinctive, a problem the Norwegians faced earlier than the Faroese. A ban on importing the eyed salmon ova from Sunndalsøra in 1985 was an attempt to avoid the onset of disease (Reinert, 1997, p. 61). But the avoidance was short lived. As from 1986, the Faroese fish farms were hit with infectious pancreatic necrosis (IPN), Hitra disease, furunculosis, costiasis, and later on, bacterial kidney disease (BKD). Problems with algae (such as Alexandrium tamarense; Chan et al., 2012) and ectoparasitic sea lice (such as *Lepeophtheirus salmonis*) also showed up (Finstad et al., 2011).

Despite obvious problems of overexploitation, the political system continued to hand out new licenses at the same time as it increased the capacity of existing ones. The logic was that increased production might prevent the impending collapse, something that created a destructive competitive logic in which unprofitable businesses were kept artificially alive, and conflicts on regulatory issues were prominent, especially on the regulation and distribution of smolt. Although new legislation was passed to address the problems in 1987 to 1988, the institutional system turned out to be too weak to manage these issues properly (Apostle, Høgnesen, & Reinert, 2002), quite comparable to what happened in the commercial fishery at that same time (Mørkøre, 1993).

RESTRUCTURING AND CONTINUING CONCENTRATION

Behind the environmental realities at sea and the international markets during the 1980s, there were immense institutional tensions between different stakeholders, precipitating a major reorganization of the industry in the 1990s. The many entrepreneurs had back in 1980 organized into a powerful interest group (Havbúnaðarfelagið, or HF); the financial system suddenly had enormous resources at stake; so did the FS and the feed industry also, with Havsbrún, a locally owned feed manufacturer, and the internationals EWOS and Skretting as the major players. An especially serious outbreak of furunculosis in several smolt sites in 1991 was decisive. But the problems of the industry were further strengthened by the fact that the whole Faroese economy, including the banking system, basically collapsed in the early 1990s (Apostle, Holm, Hovgaard, Høgnesen, & Mortensen, 2002).

The first bankruptcies turned by in 1990, and the government realised there were more to come and encouraged mergers and consolidation (Løgtingstíðindi, 1990, p. Vol. I, 16). By 1995, only 20 out of 63 operators were still in business; annual production had decreased from a peak of 19,000 tons to 8,000 tons (Jacobsen, 2011, p. 273; Reinert, 1997, pp. 67, 64).

A more or less secret committee close to the minister was in 1991 given the task to outline a new direction for the industry (Jacobsen, 2011, p. 319 ff).

The direction was that the survivors needed more space in the fiords, ideally only one operator in each fiord, for fallowing and to keep different year-classes separate. Besides that, there was also a need to increase economies of scale. One main problem was that companies that went bankrupt or those who had never started up still had a legal right to retain their concession. The committee assumed the right to withdraw licenses from companies that could not meet their obligations.

Although the whole industry was on its knees, it was also a fact that some companies had managed better than others, financial management as one prime example. In practice, the decision on who was to survive or not was made by the banks in close cooperation with the remaining companies. Limited operational support from the government to keep remaining business alive was followed by tough requirements upon financial and other operational conditions.

A new local context slowly emerged in which a reorganized industry could start to look ahead again. A main problem was finance, which basically was made possible by combined arrangements between the banks and the feed companies. This was the situation around 1994 and 1995, when a group of Danish entrepreneurs purchased majority shares in one of the running businesses. Government attitudes in many respects were the opposite of what they earlier had been. Foreign capital was more welcomed, and the rules of local ownership were interpreted more broadly. But the situation changed when Norwegian capital entered massively into the business, and the danger of a whole industry going into foreign hands became immense. Although legislation put limits on foreign ownership, creativity in organisational forms meant that in practice, a great part of Faroese aquaculture was actually taken over by these global players. In particular, the then new giant Pan Fish was aggressive. Moreover, legislative changes were also met by counteraction from local actors: the attempted and failed takeover of the locally owned fish-meal factory and feed producer Havsbrún in 2001 serves as the key example.

Together with the outbreak of a new round of diseases, the infectious salmon anemia (ISA) from 2000, and new global players, Chile in particular, pushed the industry into still another stage of crisis, with the bottom reached in late 2003 early 2004. Although new legislation opened the doors widely for external investments, the interest was not there, and restructuration was basically internal. The global industry was in a stage of crisis, and the Pan Fish empire collapsed in 2002 because of its high-risk investment in the pelagic fisheries complex and falling market prices (Berge, 2005). Through the HF, it was the local industry that pushed new regulations to meet environmental and production demands. It was not a restructuration free of conflict, but it was driven in a relatively open dialogue on fundamental issues between the industry and the institutional system. One of the important issues was the access conditions of foreign capital already mentioned; another was the allowance of the banks to get a mortgage in breeding licenses, something that was conducted in 2004. What Reinert and others had proclaimed about the need for responsible environmental management years ago was now pursued closely.

Although the latest crisis-ridden restructuration was locally managed, the context was clearly global, with the EU setting the stage. Minimum prices, tariff walls and antidumping provisions became part of daily life from the early 1990s. Faroese producers felt the squeeze by the market and the environment (Jacobsen, 2011, pp. 305, 375). ISA was successfully eradicated by a vaccination program approved and facilitated by the EU in late 2004 (Jacobsen, 2011, p. 389). Equally important, a fundamental change in EU food policy from security to safety became new regulatory mechanisms that Faroese producers also had to relate to (Phyne, Apostle, & Hovgaard, 2006).

In 2004, only two companies managed to rear and sell farmed fish: Bakkafrost and Luna. Bakkafrost is today the dominant producer of about 80% of total production. It is basically a family-owned company but also one of the absolute success stories at the Oslo stock market over the last few years. It is strongly vertically integrated, most lately by purchasing the Faroese fish meal producer Havsbrún. Luna has been a gourmet, locally owned family business since 1929, which has operated under the brand name Hiddenfjord since 2011. The remainder of Pan Fish merged with Marine Harvest in 2005, today the world's largest producer of Atlantic salmon. This company is also present in the current Faroese aquaculture system. Together, these three companies constitute the present industry, which since the 2003/2004 crisis has been able to grow and secure its position as a major industrial player based on what today in popularized form is called the "the world's best farming system" (Jacobsen, 2011, p. 395).

MODES OF AQUACULTURE ENTREPRENEURSHIP

This chapter has covered the main historical threads in the development of Faroese aquaculture from an entrepreneurial and contextualized field of action. The judicious blend of exploration strategies (in a context of uncertainty and risk) and exploitation strategies (in a more stable and secure market environment) is vital here (March, 1991). Any entrepreneur or company needs to balance these two features, and this balance depends upon product maturity, prevailing conditions in its external environment and its institutional context, including how norms, routines, rules and practices are reflexively derived and structured (Hovgaard, 2008, p. 117).

Three periods of development have been outlined, and each period was dominated by a certain entrepreneurial mode.

The first period is an exploratory phase, driven by extrapreneurs, single individuals with an idea they attempted to transform into a viable business proposition. Via processes of trial and error, Gotfred, Geyti and in particular í Túni explored the opportunities based on available knowledge and technologies but gained no entrepreneurial profit. Their motives were first of all idealistic, and although failing in creating successful businesses, they clearly paved the way for this business sector to finally succeed, which points to the path-dependent nature of business evolution.

The year normally associated with the beginning of a profitable period in Faroese aquaculture is 1980. The six starters that year and their followers were entrepreneurs clearly facing a different challenge: that of exploitation. These kinds of challenges concern the organization of the company, financial management, feed optimization, disease prevention and so forth. The mode of entrepreneurship in this period changes toward intrapreneurship. The motive is also more clearly oriented toward profit making but still rooted in family, locality and/or community values. In this period, the challenges of exploration of course still are there, but they are externalized from the individual to the institutional level. Diseases, the distribution of licenses, the stable supply of smolts and international regulatory regimes are features that exist outside the reach of the single person or company. Although those who survived the first large round of concentration were somehow "chosen" by the political and financial systems, they were mainly those companies that had done well from the process of exploitation.

The political system wanted to govern the direction of the industry toward a small-scale territorial alternative they were not able to manage, and the necessary competence building did not follow. In the third period, starting from the 1990s, large-scale production outperforms its small-scale alternative. Now Faroese aquaculture increasingly becomes part of a global food system, which from the entrepreneurial perspective was most evidently reflected in the massive appearance of international (mainly Norwegian) players in the 1990s. In this period, we see a fusion of local and extralocal actors and local-local actors in a mode of interpreneurship in which strategic positioning plays the vital difference between success and failure. The public–private divide is more clearly segregated, with the important institution Fiskaling going into the direction of being a research center only, and now with the private sector pushing the public authorities to follow suit in managing environmental demands.

The three remaining companies in Faroese aquaculture represent diverse organizational outcomes of the historical path. Marine Harvest is a highly globalized nonlocal company, which in the 1990s entered the local scene and secured a foothold there. Bakkafrost is a local family company from the 1960s, which becomes a large vertically integrated corporation that now has "gone global." Finally, there is the family company Luna/Hiddenfjord, which maintains its strong local foothold and has adopted a deliberate niche strategy.

A SMALL ISLAND DIMENSION?

In this final section, I return to the importance of the context—that is the social, institutional and spatial embedding of entrepreneurial activities— and will particularly relate these to the issues of islandness and smallness.

While the structural disadvantages of small island development are well known, much less has been said about their advantages.

Faroese aquaculture is an alternative to the traditional fisheries that buffers a highly fisheries-dependent economy from the huge risks associated with one single industrial activity.

We must acknowledge the ideal natural conditions that exist in the waters around the Faroe Islands for this type of industry. A near-pristine natural environment with plentiful and regular supply of fresh water and sheltered bays, along with near-steady sea and air temperatures all the year round, makes for ideal breeding conditions. "The abundance of nature and the cool and steady sea temperature of the North Atlantic Current surround the Faroe Islands, providing perfect conditions for salmon" (Bakkafrost, 2014). This creates a net advantageous situation for the development of this industry in the Faroes and provides a convenient niche few competitors can emulate.

Small size, of course, also has its constraints and challenges. For example, there is now a fish farm in practically every suitable bay and fjord in the Islands (Vinnuhúsið, 2014). With the industry getting close to saturation point, huge incentives exist to branch out into more lucrative and higher-value-added operations. One of these is ethical fish farming, which deploys technology and other practices to minimise waste and environmental strain while developing less-stressed and better-tasting fish. Hiddenfjord seems to follow such a business strategy and has been noticed by top chefs in London (Prince, 2011).

The importance of civil society in business development for rural and small island settings is legendary (Baldacchino, 2005a, 2005b; Hovgaard, 2001). It applies to the development of the aquaculture industry as well. Especially in its pioneer phase, Faroese aquaculture was heavily dependent upon local support, cooperation and exchange of experiences. The establishment of the FTO and its role in laying the foundation for a Faroese breeding stock serves as another example of this. Of course, receiving (or exchanging) information is a vital though not sufficient way to get things to work, so there is also a locality effect, with an entrepreneurial elite dominated by idealism and civil society offering vital support functions.

One interesting issue from a small island perspective, though, is how Faroese aquaculture develops in an extraordinary relationship with the outside world via personal networks based on what could be termed "cultural heritage" and "bridging social capital" (Bærenholdt, 2007; Woolcock & Narayan, 2000). The founders of the first groundbreaking companies gleaned vital experiences, knowledge and networks from the outside world, and so did those few people who represented the institutional system (the public sector). The cultural heritage and social capital dimension is perhaps best reflected in the story in which the Faroese managed to get their hands on Norwegian breeding stock. Although asymmetric in quality, such a critical transfer is based on Nordic relations of reciprocity and solidarity, today also applied formally within the common Nordic research system, for instance.

The development of the aquaculture sector as a combination of entrepreneurial, civil society and public institutional (including science) drivers is not unusual. A trait of smallness here would be the vital role that the network of a very few individuals plays in this development, including the flexibility between entrepreneurial and institutional representatives, again, especially in the developmental phase of the business but not uncommon in its mature phase, either. These individuals strategically and artfully combined local resources and extralocal impulses. More than anyone else, Reinert was the key intermediary between the exploration and exploitation phases, dedicated to regular updating of knowledge and skills, something that on the environmental side was not well recognized until around the year 2000. Unfortunately, it seems to be a trait of the Faroese institutional system to greatly underestimate the importance of this entrepreneurial role in innovation. Nor has there been much acknowledgement of the equally vital role and importance of the public sector, especially as financial supporter in the higher-risk early stages of development, as bridge to extralocal contacts, research and development facility, industry regulator, health guarantor and license provider.

CONCLUSION

This chapter has shown that Faroese aquaculture provides evidence of a small island industry, which is basically constructed "from within" but still manages to cope with global economic restructuring. This is done within a market-based context without ruling out the importance of a differentiated and open institutional system, including civil society and public-sector traits with a vital path-shaped accumulation of knowledge. This may not be a particularly small island characteristic, but when it is allowed to work within a small island context, it makes a clear positive difference. Moreover, a few individuals (including entrepreneurs but also public servants) may play a critical role in small jurisdictions, especially as knowledge bearers. A tight and complex relationship among firms, cultural mediation and institutional dynamics creates a strong regional system of innovation, but relatively similar contexts create different outcomes, even in aquaculture (Doloreux, Isaksen, Aslesen, & Melançon, 2009). The Faroese aquaculture industry is a clear success, and the traces of derivative entrepreneurial options are visible. One may here see the workings of a small island innovation system.

NOTE

1. Trout continued to be a species in production, but mainly as a replacement when there were not enough salmon smolt or for some special markets. No trout is today cultivated in Faroese aquacultural production.

REFERENCES

Amabile, T. M. (1996). *Creativity in context: Update to the social psychology of creativity.* Boulder, CO: Westview Press.

Apostle, R., Høgnesen, Ó. W., & Reinert, A. (2002). Aquaculture as a diversification strategy in the Faroes. In R. Apostle, D. Holm, G. Hovgaard, Ó. W. Høgnesen, & B. Mortesen (Eds.), *The restructuring of the Faroese economy* (pp. 123–154). Frederiksberg: Samfundslitteratur.

Apostle, R., Holm, D., Hovgaard, G., Høgnesen, Ó. W., & Mortensen, B. (2002). *The restructuring of the Faroese economy. The significnace of the inner periphery.* Frederiksberg: Samfundslitteratur.

Bærenholdt, J. O. (2007). *Coping with distances. Producing Nordic Atlantic societies.* New York, NY: Berghahn Books.

Bakkafrost. (2014). The history of Bakkafrost. Retrieved August 22, 2014, from www.bakkafrost.fo/default.asp?menu=232

Baldacchino, G. (2005a). Island entrepreneurs : Insights from exceptionally successful knowledge-driven SMEs from five European island territories. *Journal of Enterprising Cultures, 13*(2), 1–32.

Baldacchino, G. (2005b). Successful small-scale manufacturing from small islands: Comparing firms benefiting from locally available raw material input. *Journal of Small Business & Entrepreneurship, 18*(1), 21–37. doi:10.1080/08276331.2005. 10593330

Baumol, W. J. (1990). Entrepreneurship: productive, unproductive and destructive. *Journal of Political Economy, 98*(3), 893–921.

Berge, A. (2005). *Salmon fever. The history of pan fish.* Bergen, Norway: Octavian Publishing.

Búskaparráðið. (2013). *Búskaparáðsfrágreiðing.* Retrieved from http://setur.fo/fil eadmin/user_upload/SSS/PDF-filur/Buskaparadid/Buskaparadsfragreiding_sept_2013.pdf

Chan, C. X., Soares, M. B., Bonaldo, M. F., Wisecaver, J. H., Hackett, J. D., Anderson, D. M., & Bhattacharya, D. (2012). Analysis of *Alexandrium tamarense (Dinophyceae)* genes reveals the complex evolutionary history of a microbial eukaryote. *Journal of Phycology, 48*(5), 1130–1142.

Chesbrough, H. W. (2003). *Open innovation: The new imperative for creating and profiting from technology.* Boston, MA: Harvard Business School Publishing.

Doloreux, D., Isaksen, A., Aslesen, H. W., & Melançon, Y. (2009). A comparative study of the aquaculture innovation systems in Quebec's coastal region and Norway. *European Planning Studies, 17*(7), 963–981.

Faroe Fish Farmers Association. (2013). Salmon production hits record high in 2012. Retrieved August 21, 2014, from http://salmon-from-the-faroe-islands. com/news-salmon+faroe+islands+record.htm

Fineman, S., & Gabriel, Y. (1996). *Networks and empires: Experiencing organisations.* London: Sage.

Finstad, B., Bjørn, P. A., Todd, C. D., Whoriskey, F., Gargan, P. G., Forde, G., & Revie, C. W. (2011). The effect of sea lice on Atlantic salmon and other salmonid species. *Atlantic Salmon Ecology*, 253–276.

Freeman, C. (1974). *The economics of industrial innovation.* Harmondsworth: Penguin.

Fuglsang, L. (2008). Innovation with care: What it means. In L. Fuglsang (Ed.), *Innovation and the creative process: Towards innovation with care.* Cheltenham, UK: Edward Elgar.

Gartner, W. B. (1995). Aspects of organizational emergence. In I. Bull, H. Thomas, & G. Willard (Eds.), *Entrepreneurship: Perspectives on theory building* (pp. 67–86). Oxford: Pergamon.

Gedeon, S. (2010). What is entrepreneurship? *Entrepreneurial Practice Review, 1*(3), 16–35.

Granovetter, M. (1985). Economic action and social structure: The problem of embeddedness. *American Journal of Sociology, 93*(3), 481–510.

Granovetter, M. (1992). Economic institutions as social constructions: A framework for analysis. *Acta Sociologica, 35*, 3–11.

Hagen, E. E. (1962). *On the theory of social change: How economic growth begins*. Homewood, IL: Dorsey Press.

Hovgaard, G. (2001). *Globalisation, embeddedness and local coping strategies— a comparative and qualitative study of local dynamics in contemporary social change*. Roskilde: Roskilde University.

Hovgaard, G. (2008). Getting waste to become taste: From the planning of innovation to innovation planning. In L. Fuglsang (Ed.), *Innovation and the creative process. Towards innovation with care* (pp. 112–130). Cheltenham, UK, and Northampton, MA: Edward Elgar.

Jacobsen, H. (2011). *Ringar á sjónum*. Torshavn, Faroe Islands: Havbúnaðarfelagið.

Kirzner, I. M. (1973). *Competition and entrepreneurship*. Chicago, IL: University of Chicago Press.

Løgtingstíðindi. (1990). Løgtingstíðindi. *Volume I, 16*, p. 16. Løgtingstíðindi. Retrieved from http://logting.elektron.fo/lgt/FrameYvirlit.asp?ar=1990

Lundvall, B.-Å. (2011). Økonomisk innovationsteori: Fra iværksættere til innovationssystemer. In E. Sørensen & J. Torfing (Eds.), *Samarbejdsdrevet innovation i den offentlige sektor* (pp. 41–58). København: Jurist og Økonomforbundets Forlag.

March, J. G. (1991). Exploration and exploitation. *Organizational Learning, 2*(1), 71–87.

McClelland, D. C. (1967). *The achieving society*. New York, NY: Free Press.

Mørkøre, J. (1993). Interessegrupper og strategier inden for det færøske fiskerierhverv— økonomiske og politiske implikationer. In S. T. F. Johansen, R. F. Johansen, & G. Hovgaard (Eds.), *Krisen på Færøerne. Problemstillinger og perspektiver* (pp. 63–90). Roskilde: Publikationer fra Institut for Geografi, Samfundsanalyse og Datalogi.

Olofsson, G. (1995). Embeddedness and integration: An essay on Karl Polanyi's "The Great Transformation." In N. Mortensen (Ed.), *Social integration and marginalisation* (pp. 72–113). Copenhagen: Samfundslitteratur.

Phillips, A. (1971). *Technology and market structure: A study of the aircraft industry*. Lexington, MA: Lexington Books.

Phyne, J., Apostle, R., & Hovgaard, G. (2006). Food safety and farmed salmon. Some implications of the European Union's food policy for coastal communities. In D. L. VanderZwaag & G. Chao (Eds.), *Aquaculture law and policy. Towards principled access and operations* (pp. 385–420). New York: Routledge.

Polanyi, K. (1957). *The great transformation: The political and economic origins of our time*. Boston, MA: Beacon Press.

Prince, R. (2011). Wild salmon from the Faroe Islands. Retrieved from www.telegraph.co.uk/foodanddrink/recipes/8691401/Wild-salmon-from-the-Faroe-Islands.html

Reinert, A. (1997). Aquaculture: Fish farming on the Faroe Islands. In L. Lyck (Ed.), *The Faroese economy in strategic perspective* (pp. 60–77). Stockholm: NordREFO.

Statistics Faroe Islands. (n.d.). Statbank. Retrieved from www.hagstova.fo/en

Sundbo, J. (1995). *Innovationsteori—tre paradigmer*. Jurist- og Økonomforbundets Forlag.

Sundbo, J. (1998). *The Theory of innovation: Entrepreneurs, technology and strategy*. Cheltenham, UK: Edward Elgar.

Vinnuhúsið. (2014). The fish farming industry on the Faroe Islands. House of Industry. www.industry.fo/Default.aspx?ID=3782

Welter, F. (2011). Contextualizing entrepreneurship-conceptual challenges and ways forward. *Entrepreneurship Theory and Practice, 35*(1), 165–184. doi:10.1111/J.1540-6520.2010.00427.x

Woolcock, M., & Narayan, D. (2000). Social capital: Implications for development theory, research, and policy. *The World Bank Research Observer, 15*(2), 225–249.

7 Biosciences and BioVectra on Prince Edward Island, Canada

James E. Randall

INTRODUCTION

To much of the world, the stereotype of Prince Edward Island (PEI) as "the Gentle Island" on the east coast of Canada is one characterized by potatoes, lobster and tourism. However, a new economic driver has recently appeared on this idyllic and bucolic landscape. Biosciences production, something more commonly associated with large metropolitan centers, has risen in prominence in island employment, exports and public policy. This chapter will describe and explain the rise of this sector in the context of the literature on small island entrepreneurship and biosciences clusters. In particular, it will present a case study of one company that has been a formative actor in this knowledge-intensive set of economic activities: BioVectra Limited and its predecessor, Diagnostic Chemicals Limited (DCL).

In addition to developing a better understanding of this island setting through a description of the company and sector, this research is guided by the question: what factors are most important in explaining the emergence of this company and this sector on a small island otherwise dominated by seasonal economic activities? It addresses this question through a case study approach, including a thematic analysis of public and company documents, interviews with individuals and groups associated with the company, government and industry, and quantitative data. In the next section, the scholarship on island entrepreneurship is reviewed, focusing on work associated with subnational island jurisdictions and the economic geography of biosciences "clusters." A description of the PEI economy and the methods used in the research is then provided. The analysis and interpretation section summarizes the themes that emerged in reviewing the variety of primary and secondary data, linking back to the factors that the literature suggests are supposed to be prominent in explaining the emergence of these kinds of activities.

BACKGROUND

PEI is the smallest of 10 Canadian provinces and the only wholly enisled province (albeit connected by a 13-km bridge to continental Canada since

1997). Its resident population is around 150,000. It is an example of a subnational island jurisdiction (SNIJ; Baldacchino, 2006; Baldacchino & Milne, 2006, 2009; Grydehøj, 2011). The economies of many SNIJs and small island developing states (SIDSs) have historically been dismissed as motley leftovers of empires, despite the fact that many of these places had enviable levels of prosperity, at least as measured on a per-capita basis (Baldacchino & Milne, 2009). The language used to describe small islands is one replete with terms such as "vulnerable," "fragile" and "remote" (Briguglio, 1995; Guillaumont, 2010; McGillivray, Naudé, & Santos-Paulino, 2010). Yet a steady corpus of research suggests that some of these small sovereign and nonsovereign islands have developed considerable economic and political capacities (Baldacchino, 2006a; 2006b; Dunn, 2011; McElroy & Mahoney, 2000), including preferred trade deals, opportunities for labor mobility, access to domestic and/or foreign capital and assistance in times of natural disasters. The variation in the ability of islands to exercise these powers is a function of their jurisdictional clout, their articulation of a local identity, their ability to defend the identity of minorities and their level of paradiplomacy—that is, the degree to which they represent themselves politically to other external jurisdictions and entities (Baldacchino, 2006a; Bartmann, 2006).

From this conceptual description, there are certain features of these islands that resonate and may help us understand the growth of both the biosciences sector and lead firms within this sector on PEI. The first is that governments in small island jurisdictions are disproportionately large and more personalized, and decision makers are more accessible (Baker, 1992). Grydehøj (2011) refers to this as a high degree of *de facto* internal jurisdictional capacity compared to other jurisdictions with similar *de jure* distributions. Although often portrayed as a disadvantage (Armstrong & Read 2000), in some small island jurisdictions, this can serve as an advantage for locally based companies. Since small island governments tend to be larger and more visible, entrepreneurs are able to cut through the layers of administration and bureaucracy to reach decision makers more easily (Baldacchino, 2006, p. 862). Combined with this enhanced public-sector presence are the influence, impact and otherwise "towering role" of key individuals (Baldacchino, 2006).

The scale of small islands has contributed, indirectly, to economies that are more specialized and export oriented and less reliant on the relatively sparse supply of natural resources (Baum et al., 2000; Hudson, 2000). As such, companies must be highly competitive to succeed in the global marketplace. At the same time, a relative absence of internal competition means that governments are more likely to shape public policy to provide a competitive advantage to locally based companies; and businesses may be more likely to exercise cooperation or collaboration with other island businesses in the broader sector, even to the extent of taking on a mentorship role (Baldacchino, 2011).

"Biosciences" is a convenient but sometimes confusing label that encompasses a set of economic activities drawn from various industrial sectors. Feldman (2000) defined the biosciences as "Any activity that substantially involves research, development, or manufacture of (1) biologically active molecules, (2) devices that employ or affect biological processes, or (3) devices and software for production or management of biological information" (p. 359). She defines biotechnology more narrowly as "The use of recombinant DNA methods or broadly defined as anything related to life sciences" (ibid.). The "life sciences" can be considered an even larger collection of activities and has been defined as "[t]hose firms that apply the possibilities of organisms, cell cultures, parts of cells or parts of organisms, in an innovative way for the purpose of industrial production. They may also supply related services, and hardware and software" (BioPartner, 2005, p. 188). Despite the often interchangeable use of these terms in the literature, "biosciences" will be used here, since it is commonly used to describe the activities of this grouping of companies on PEI, including that of DCL and BioVectra. This label includes firms engaged in aquaculture, the manufacture of pharmaceuticals, bioscience-related equipment and medical devices, research and development and other professional services (Jupia Consultants Inc., 2014).

Much of the scholarly work on the emergence of clusters in the biosciences has focused on the large, global, metropolitan-centered regions such as Boston, San Diego, Washington, DC, and San Francisco (USA) and Cambridge (UK; Cooke, 2004a, 2004b, 2005; Feldman & Francis, 2004; Walcott, 2002). In Canada, with few exceptions (Economic Development Winnipeg, Inc., 2013; Robin, 2013), the literature has concentrated on the growth and evolution of biosciences clusters in the three largest urban centers of Toronto, Montreal and Vancouver (Lowe & Gertler, 2008; Niose & Bas, 2001). There are invariably commonalities in the factors that precipitated the development of these clusters. These include a well-established research infrastructure, often associated with the presence of large, research-intensive universities and government laboratories, local investment capital from both private (e.g., venture) and public sources and an ample supply of highly skilled research scientists/entrepreneurs and related service specialists (Gertler & Vinodrai, 2009).

The conventional literature on entrepreneurial clusters suggests that large anchor companies and their supply chains are important nuclei to the establishment of the cluster by generating highly trained staff who spin off new companies, providing opportunities for new locally based companies that provide goods and services to the anchor company and to other vendors (Nelson, 2005). Nelson's research suggests that this has not happened in the case of the biotechnology cluster in Massachusetts and the regions where large pharmaceutical companies are located (e.g., New Jersey and Chicago). In these locations, the presence of large pharmaceutical companies was unimportant to the development of the cluster. Instead, a different type of supply chain exists: one characterized by the presence of investment capital, executive talent and trained scientists, service professionals that are experienced in bioscience commercialization (e.g., lawyers, accountants, real estate managers), access to good airports and communities that provide a high-quality of life for highly trained personnel and their families. Clusters in this model are less about firms that transact goods and more about the interchange of knowledge and wisdom that is embedded and shared by the founders, scientists and other professional service providers.

Research by Gertler and Vinodrai (2009) suggests that the conditions required to establish and maintain geographic clusters of firms in the life sciences or biotechnology may be more heterogeneous than previously thought. In addition to studying the formation of life sciences clusters at Toronto, Montreal and Vancouver, they examined these sectors at the second-tier Canadian urban centers of Halifax, Ottawa and Saskatoon. Their analysis shows that the presence of the life sciences in these centers is linked to factors that include federal funding for public research institutions and highly productive university researchers, provincial policies that favor some sectors over others and a historical legacy. They also point to the role of lead or anchor firms, industry associations and civic entrepreneurship, the structure of local venture capital, the state of human capital and the ability to attract and retain highly skilled personnel.

Although not specific to the biosciences, Doloreux and Dionne's (2008) case study of the transportation equipment manufacturing firm Bombardier in the rural region of La Pocatière, Quebec, has relevance to this research because of locational similarities. They found that innovation in this rural, peripheral region occurred because of the presence of local teaching institutions with an emphasis on applied research and technology transfer in agriculture and agronomy, the presence of community entrepreneurs or visionaries and informal knowledge exchange and cooperation. The entrepreneurs were defined as "[o]rganized actors who envision new institutions as a means of advancing interests which they value highly for the development of their community" (ibid., p. 274). Much of the knowledge transfer and collaboration took place across public institutions—the local college, public research centers—rather than between the parent company and any spin-off firms. Doloreux and Dionne (2008) did not think of this group of companies as a cluster in the conventional sense because almost all of the production from Bombardier was exported, and support companies were not spun off from Bombardier.

This review of the literature suggests that entrepreneurship in small island jurisdictions is conditioned very much by the political, economic and geographic context of the place, with some features, such as the influence of visionary leaders, role of educational institutions and governments, small scale, peripherality and export orientation, being broadly applicable across different knowledge-based industrial sectors.

THE ECONOMY AND BIOSCIENCES ON PRINCE EDWARD ISLAND

Many SIDSs and SNIJs have experienced stronger, albeit more volatile, economic success relative to comparable mainland jurisdictions (Armstrong, et al., 1998; McElroy & Pearce, 2006). Such is not the case for PEI, where the standard of living and economic performance has been consistently weak in comparison to the rest of Canada: the mean PEI household income has consistently been less than 85% of the Canadian average; the provincial GDP per capita has rarely risen above 75% of the Canadian average; and the province has consistently ranked as having one of the highest unemployment rates in Canada (Prince Edward Island Statistics Bureau, 2014). Despite these features, there are signs that the biosciences sector as a whole is becoming a more prominent part of the provincial economy. In 2012, biosciences firms on PEI generated more than $188 million (Cdn) in sales, resulting in $116.4 million in direct and indirect production on the island and a further $23.5 million in provincial induced effects (Jupia Consultants Inc., 2014). This constituted 2.7% of the provincial GDP. These combined direct and indirect impacts contributed more to the economy than the fishing and seafood preparation and packaging sectors combined. Although total employment in the biosciences was still estimated to be less than 1,000 employees in 2012, the overall impact on total labor income is relatively greater than the numbers of employees because of relatively higher salaries. In 2012, the average annual employment income for employees in the biosciences was just over $54,000 Cdn compared to the total industry average of $38,589 (Jupia Consultants Inc., 2014).

The biosciences sector has been one of the fastest growing on the island, with revenue increasing by a mean of 33% annually between 2006 and 2012. In comparison, accommodation and food services, a surrogate indicator for the tourism sector, increased by only 2.4% annually over the same period. In 2004, the biosciences sector on PEI constituted approximately 4% of the total merchandise exports from PEI. By 2013, this had increased to 7.1% of the $926 million in total international exports. This represents a 147% increase in biosciences product exports compared to a 39% increase in exports from all sectors of the provincial economy (Jupia Consultants Inc., 2014). The number of biosciences firms on PEI has increased from 12 in 2002 to 26 in 2012. While private-sector employment has remained relatively stable since 2006 at between 400 and 600 employees, sales revenue had more than doubled by 2012 (*Guardian*, Charlottetown, 2014; Magner, 2014; PEI BioAlliance, 2012).

METHODS

The objective of this research is to develop a better understanding of PEI–based island entrepreneurship through a description and analysis of a leading biosciences company and sector. A case-study design was used to address the research objectives. This allows the researcher to explore an issue by using a variety of lenses so as to reveal and better understand multiple aspects of the phenomenon (Baxter & Jack, 2008). According to Yin (2003), case studies are especially useful when the focus of the study is on answering "how" and "why" questions, when you cannot manipulate the behavior of those involved in the study and when the researcher believes that the contextual conditions are relevant and/or where the boundaries between the phenomenon and the context are not clear. All of these are applicable in the study of the role of biosciences on PEI. The primary interest here is to develop a better understanding of how DCL and its successor, BioVectra, emerged and evolved on a small island setting.

Case studies use information from a variety of sources, including interviews with key informants, archival records, company reports and publications, academic papers, newspapers and magazine articles and statistical databases, brought together or triangulated to add strength to the findings (Hancock & Algozzine, 2006; Stake, 2000). The gathered qualitative and quantitative information is assessed in light of the research questions, and tentative answers are organized into broader themes.

For this study, more than 50 items from local and regional newspapers, journals and trade magazines were gathered and reviewed by looking for the key phrases "Diagnostic Chemicals Limited," "BioVectra" and "biosciences." Company reports, reports from the industry-led BioAlliance organization and provincial government reports were also assessed. Face-to-face interviews using a semistructured format were conducted with four individuals and one three-person focus group associated with the companies, government and industry associations. As the founder of DCL/BioVectra, Dr. Regis Duffy was a key respondent. Although the questions varied depending on the background of the interviewee, a consistent theme of the questions was to explore (1) the relationships and roles of the companies on PEI, with a focus on its biosciences sector, and (2) decision making regarding the location of company operations on PEI, or "Why PEI?" The interviews were audio recorded, transcribed and reviewed for underlying themes.

ORIGINS AND GROWTH OF BIOSCIENCES AND DIAGNOSTIC CHEMICALS/BIOVECTRA

Before the 1970s, the biosciences were virtually nonexistent on PEI. As the result of an attempt to find summer employment for a group of students at the University of Prince Edward Island (UPEI), the then dean of science, Dr. Regis Duffy, posted a 1969 advertisement in the *Chemical Engineering News* seeking contract funding for pesticide analysis. The one response from a New Jersey company required him to produce a chemical compound that could be used in blood testing to detect cardiac arrests. From this modest start, and with the seasonal assistance of Dr. Douglas Hennessy, his former mentor and professor at his alma mater Fordham University in the United States, the newly formed company Diagnostic Chemicals Limited (DCL) started producing medical chemical compounds and medical diagnostic testing kits for hospitals and laboratories across North America. Duffy has been described in various articles and magazines as "the son of a potato farmer," "the eldest of a dozen children," "a hefty, bespectacled, genial entrepreneur" and "an upbeat, positive, almost irrationally happy man" (Bruce, 1991; Lynch, 1996). Perhaps more germane, Horne (1992) described him as "A good example of the right man at the right time," where his knowledge and interest in chemistry and his entrepreneurial instincts came together to seize an opportunity. Lynch (1996) suggests that, when he investigated the market for chemical compounds in the health care industry, "An entrepreneurial light lit up Duffy's academic mind."

Until 1976, production of the chemical compounds and medical diagnostic kits took place in a modest Charlottetown "garage" rented for $60 Cdn./month. By 1992, DCL had become "Canada's largest producer of chemical reagents (used to test patients' blood sugar, cholesterol, calcium and other levels) and Canada's first packager of diagnostic kits" (Spence, 1992, 40). In 2001, the biochemical division of the company began operating under the name BioVectra, and in 2007, the diagnostic division was split off and sold to the multinational biotechnology company Genzyme Corporation, which in turn was purchased in 2011 by the Japanese chemical company Sekisui and renamed Sekisui Diagnostics PEI. In 2013, BioVectra was sold to Questcor Pharmaceuticals of California, a long-time BioVectra customer, and in August of 2014, Questcor itself was purchased by Ireland-based Mallinckrodt Pharmaceuticals.

By 2007 (the year of the split), revenues in DCL had increased from Can$23.3 million (2002) to almost Can$38 million, in constant dollars, while employment increased from 134 to 195. After the sale of the diagnostic division to Sekisui Chemicals, BioVectra's sales climbed from just over $14 million to around $68 million in 2014. Industry Canada (2013) estimated that current employment at Sekisui Diagnostics PEI was 110 and sales were in the $25 to $50 million range. Taking the most conservative estimate, total employment in both BioVectra and the former diagnostic division of BioVectra was around 360 and $93 million, respectively, in mid-2014.

ANALYSIS

A review of the documents and interviews suggests the following themes are important in describing and understanding the emergence of the biosciences and DCL/BioVectra on PEI: (1) the pivotal role of individual actors; (2) the dichotomy of conservatism and entrepreneurship; (3) strategic business decisions; (4) biosciences as a cluster on PEI; (5) the role of DCL/BioVectra as anchor firms within that cluster; (6) government, governance and the private sector; (7) accessibility, isolation and location; and (8) human capital and the labor market. These themes are now reviewed in turn.

Pivotal Role of Individuals

As noted earlier, Dr. Regis Duffy played a pivotal role in the creation and nurturing of DCL/BioVectra and the biosciences sector on PEI. Duffy's multiple, long-term roles in the community—as an elected City of Charlottetown councilor, as the first chair of the BioAlliance organization, as an Islander and as the owner of DCL—gave him the credibility in the community that benefited the company and encouraged a positive government attitude toward the biosciences sector. As one interviewee stated, "He was instrumental in attracting other players to the sector; very few conceived here; a lot of people came from somewhere else . . . It's been a lesson in entrepreneurship and commitment to the community and leadership."

As is often the case with locally based entrepreneurs who become leaders within an anchor firm or sector, the rationale for remaining in a community is as much about a sense of civic responsibility as it is economic. For example, Duffy (2005) noted that he was driven by the need to reverse the trend of educated college and university graduates migrating to other parts of the country, raise the Atlantic region's gross domestic production per person to something closer to the national average and attract venture capital to support businesses in Atlantic Canada. Despite growth in the company, the split of DCL and BioVectra and subsequent multiple sales to outside companies, in his business dealings, Duffy would insist that production stay on PEI.

Conservatism Versus Entrepreneurship

One of the prevailing themes in the material and the interviews was a dichotomy between conservatism and entrepreneurship at the level of individuals, institutions and island society in general. Duffy epitomized these seeming contradictions. He was described as the son of a potato farmer who served as a priest before earning his doctorate in chemistry (Day, 2006). At the same time, he is quoted as saying,

> I've always been interested in the commercial aspect of business, getting out and selling something . . . The background of most people here [PEI] is fishing and farming. If you are a farmer, fixing things is a big part of your day; a lot of farmers are pretty entrepreneurial, they haven't got a choice.
>
> (Lynch, 1996, p. 138)

Meanwhile, island government and business were characterized as conservative and risk averse in their approach to economic development. One interviewee described the provincial government lending practices as follows:

> They are built on low risk loans to low risk people you know are going to get paid back and a percentage of the loans to high risk that you

know aren't going to be paid back. Call them investments but they're all shaped as loans.

Nevertheless, PEI was consistently described as having a beauty that inspired business potential. Duffy is quoted as saying, "This place [PEI] seems to encourage innovation, creativity . . . we all appreciate living and working in this beautiful, unspoiled atmosphere" (MacIntyre, 1994, p. 84).

The perception of the existence of an entrepreneurial island culture in spite of the low-risk attitudes may be linked to the hardships faced by islanders and their obligations to somehow make ends meet even in difficult or unforeseen circumstances. In Duffy's words, "Any fool can make money in Toronto . . . but you have to be smart to make money in Prince Edward Island" (Bruce, 1991, p. 13).

Strategic Business Decisions

As is the case with many small islands, the export of natural resources is not a new phenomenon on PEI. Just under $1 billion (Cdn.) in products and services were exported from PEI to other countries in 2013, of which less than $60 million was from the pharmaceutical/medicines and other basic organic chemicals sectors (Prince Edward Island Statistics Bureau, 2014). Almost all of the production of both BioVectra and the former diagnostics division now owned by Sekisui is exported, and the proportion sold outside Canada has been increasing over the life of the companies. BioVectra is currently sending about 85% of production to the United States, 10% to Japan, and 5% to Europe (personal communication with company representative). Although the medical diagnostic kits and the chemical reagents are both exported, the distribution of the markets is quite different. Sales of the chemicals are primarily to a small number of large American pharmaceutical companies, while sales of the diagnostic kits are distributed widely to many hospitals and laboratories throughout the United States.

Part of the companies' export orientation is linked to the small scale of PEI and even the Canadian domestic market. "Trade with foreign nations is the only viable option for small Canadian companies . . . the problem is that Canada is a big country with a small population" (Duffy 2005, p. A7). Effectively, the small size of the island market has forced companies like BioVectra and DCL to become more attuned to the needs of the regional and international markets. As discussed in what follows, the province's small size is also linked to ease of access to government decision makers and other companies in the sector. As Rory Francis, the executive director of the BioAlliance, stated, "From Day 1, we've used our small size to our advantage by using the relationships we have to work together in an economic development role. . ." (Moreira, 2014, p. B6).

In addition to the smaller size of the PEI and Canadian markets, Duffy's greater knowledge of the American market and perception of differences in business climate were important factors in explaining the export orientation. Lynch (1996, p. 139) quotes Duffy as saying, "The American market is very open, it's innovative, it's entrepreneurial. The Canadian market place is very institutionalized." According to Duffy, one of the most significant business decisions by DCL was setting up a branch of the company in Oxford, Connecticut, in 1983 to market and distribute diagnostic kits in the United States. This eased regulatory approval for products sold in the American market. The implementation of the North American Free Trade Agreement (NAFTA) also benefited the company by reducing tariffs and duties on imported supplies and exported finished products to and from the United States (Lynch, 1996).

Horne quotes a Diagnostic Chemicals employee as saying, "We're trying to elevate chemistry to a fine art" (Horne 1992, p. 52). This quote reflects the importance of quality, customer service and market knowledge to DCL and BioVectra. Several of the interviewees and the background articles stressed the importance of quality control as a key consideration in the success of the company. This was important in a niche manufacturing sector dominated by a few large firms that already had established relationships with hospitals and labs. In 1997, Duffy stated, "We succeeded because we decided to focus on the US market . . . offering 30% price discounts . . . worked well in the 1980s; but in the 1990s it's customer service that counts" (cited in Yarr, 1997, p. 25). Issues of quality are really part of several larger trends, including adapting or innovating constantly, increased contracting out by large American corporations to smaller companies like DCL and BioVectra to reduce capital costs and a shift back to North American suppliers and away from Asian manufacturers to avoid quality issues, something especially important in the health products market. In a sector that is increasingly regulated, the large American customers are looking for reliable suppliers to undertake the quality control tasks for them (Lynch, 1996). Although many small companies may find it difficult to gain knowledge of the market, Duffy notes that the small size of his company was an advantage, allowing it to be more mobile and nimble and incur lower product development costs (Lynch, 1996).

Biosciences as a Cluster on Prince Edward Island

The scale of the biosciences sector on PEI is much smaller than one would find in the larger mega-centers in the United States and is small even by Canadian standards. In 2012, the BioAlliance estimated that there were 36 companies and approximately 1,100 employees in both the public and private sectors of the biosciences, with half of this total being employed in universities and government and a further 360 being employees at BioVectra and DCL/Sekisui. Perhaps as a result of this size and the relative youthfulness of many companies in the sector, the relationships across the sector were described by several interviewees as cooperative rather than competitive.

Although the group of companies is described as a cluster by governments and the BioAlliance, it is not a cluster as defined by the transactions among local companies. In fact, as discussed in the previous section, almost all of the suppliers and customers for these two companies are outside Canada. Several interviewees specifically made the point that the PEI "cluster" is not like those described by Porter (1998, p. 90), where the close proximity of companies, customers and suppliers amplifies all of the pressures to innovate and upgrade. As one interviewee associated with BioVectra stated,

> Clusters are not a valuable tool for us. In larger areas where there are multiple needs it can generate activity. After the fact we can see that as a natural process these clusters have developed but that's just part of the natural process; they are there because the market is there or because the HR people are there or the technology is available. I don't think it's that critical.

However, when researchers probed about the use of the term "cluster" in this context, a richer interpretation emerged. One interviewee suggested that companies in the trades sector, including pipefitters, electricians, mechanical engineers and "instrument guys," have increased their knowledge and capacity as a result of the needs of the lead companies. Another described the cluster as "About bringing together the set of relationships around the strategy and maintaining that for the long term."

A theme in the current literature on biosciences clusters is the link to nearby research-intensive universities, both for the research infrastructure and the presence of the highly skilled scientist entrepreneurs. The only university in the province and (to a lesser extent) the only vocational college have contributed to the growth of the biosciences on PEI. The former UPEI president, Wade MacLauchlan, was reported by several interviewees to have been instrumental politically in convincing the federal government to locate the National Research Council (NRC) labs at the UPEI campus in Charlottetown. There are several celebrated examples of faculty members with cross-appointments at UPEI, lab facilities at the NRC and private-sector companies (*Guardian*, Charlottetown, 2011; Magner, 2014), reflecting the economies of scope so prevalent in small island societies. Several interviewees noted the importance of the graduates from the bioscience technology program at Holland College, and Duffy stated, "We use all the technicians coming out of UPEI with BSc degrees. We probably have forty to fifty of them out there [BioVectra facilities]."

Diagnostic Chemicals and BioVectra as Anchor Firms

Both DCL/Sekisui and BioVectra have played dominant roles in PEI's biosciences sector. Prior to the purchase of DCL by Sekisui Chemicals in 2007, approximately half the employment and revenue generation in the sector was attributable to DCL/BioVectra. Since then, the combined employment and sales of Sekisui and BioVectra are at least half of the sector total on PEI.

One interviewee described BioVectra/DCL as playing a "cornerstone" role, while several others described it as being a mentor to other companies. A government interviewee described DCL and BioVectra as playing "a leadership role, a human resources role and a revenue anchoring role." One way this has emerged is the willingness of these lead companies to share knowledge with other companies in the sector. One interviewee stated that

> Earlier stage companies struggle with how they move their product (like simple logistics at borders), regulatory strategy, just being able to access some of the folks who have been there, done that . . . willing to share that knowledge with earlier stage companies . . . that aspect of being the anchor or the grandfather in the room is vitally important.

Another stated that technicians and scientists from these companies regularly meet their counterparts from other companies and provide operational and planning advice. Further exchange of information and cooperation by BioVectra for the sector as a whole takes place through the meetings of the industry-led BioAlliance organization.

The term most often used by the interviewees to express DCL and BioVectra's leadership role in the local economy was "credibility." From one perspective, it was suggested that the success of these companies encouraged other companies in the biosciences to consider relocating to PEI. As one interviewee stated,

> The fact that we have BioVectra, Sekisui, Novartis, give PEI external credibility. They are the three companies that underpin, that are the foundation . . . there are other companies that are becoming core elements of the foundation . . . but in terms of brand value, locally, nationally and internationally, it just makes PEI credible as a place to do business if you are in the biosector.

Perhaps more important than external credibility was the civic community role undertaken by the company and senior management. Several interviewees pointed to the fact that DCL and then BioVectra have repeatedly shown themselves to be good corporate citizens. One interviewee stated that

> People didn't have a clue about what was happening in the company, but DCL has a strong community brand as a good company . . . good local leadership . . . good employment . . . without that . . . that conditioning of the environment was absolutely crucial.

This community credibility has been instrumental in accessing capital from provincial and federal sources and shaping economic development policy to benefit the company and the sector. As one interviewee noted, "[We] can point to a company that has been successful based on science and technology. Without that local experience, it would have been very difficult to orient the public policy pieces on the board to support this cluster development." One interviewee described it as creating an enabling mindset for current and prospective companies and public policy. This abstract leadership role is perhaps best described by Holloway (2004, p. 67) as "If PEI's bioscience community has a commercial heart, BioVectra is it."

Government, Governance and the Private Sector

The federal government and provincial governments in Atlantic Canada have long-standing traditions, often highly criticized, of intervening directly in the region's economic development (Coffey & Polèse 1987; Savoie 1997, 2003). One interviewee recalled some of these direct interventions as

> The early days, back in the 1970s, a lot of companies would come here government sponsored: ski manufacturer, aluminum wheel manufacturer, eyeglass manufacturer; there isn't one firm in the industrial park from that era that is left. I call it the economic messiah approach to economic development. Salvation comes from the outside.

In contrast, DCL/BioVectra is a local startup, working its way to growth from a local position and with some commitment to the region.

The role of government in supporting both DCL/BioVectra and the biosciences sector was a consistent theme in the documents and interviews. Early on in the life of the companies, provincial and federal government departments provided DCL with loan guarantees for the mortgages on their facilities and equipment, as well as research and development (R&D) money to bring new chemical compounds to market. This assistance, in programs that included funding to support R&D, support to attend trade fairs, labor subsidies and tax concessions, has continued to support the sector (Magner, 2014). As the largest company in the sector, BioVectra continues to benefit from this assistance, for example, through a provincial loan of $14.8 million to expand one of its manufacturing facilities (*Chronicle Herald* Halifax, 2010, p. C5) and almost $3 million to develop two generic drugs employing sustained-release delivery technology (*Guardian* Charlottetown, 2013, p. A3). Despite these examples, several interviewees noted that the scale of research and development at BioVectra is increasingly outstripping the investment ability of governments. As Duffy stated,

> Initially, when companies are small, the access to capital is critical. For BioVectra today, access to capital is not as critical. It is a much more profitable company. It's got $68 million in sales and shouldn't have to depend on government.

The ability of lead companies like DCL and BioVectra to shape public policy was mentioned consistently as an advantage to operating on PEI. As a company interviewee stated,

> If we have a request, there's absolutely no problem within a few days of having all the people we need at the same table and there isn't any, well, "this is my jurisdiction" or "this is your jurisdiction," there's a bit of that and there's a bit of, well, "we're not sure we can do that because of our rules and regulations, but maybe *you* could do it" [i.e., another player represented at the table] so there's a real spirit of cooperation and I think you get that in a smaller jurisdiction.

This characteristic accessibility to government has also been touted by government as an advantage for biosciences companies. In a speech given to business leaders in Toronto, Robert Ghiz, then premier of PEI, stated,

> If you are going to Ontario or B.C. [British Columbia], you're not going to sit down with those people [high-ranking provincial, federal and university officials]. You're going to hire a lobbyist and they're going to go around and do the dog and pony show . . . In PEI, we can make things happen a lot more quickly.
>
> (cited in Dobby, 2012)

This access and relationship has produced an environment that is conducive to the biosciences in general and BioVectra and DCL in particular. As one interviewee stated, "We have great tax policy, good employee strategies, a whole host of things that successive governments have employed to try to make this as friendly an environment as possible and we just couldn't get that in another jurisdiction."

As the previous quote suggests, government support for the biosciences and for DCL/BioVectra has transcended partisan politics. Over the past 15 years, both Conservative and Liberal governments have been in power provincially, and both governments have supported the growth of the biosciences. According to one interviewee,

> [The sector has received] tremendous political support . . . not just government programs; subsequent premiers (like Pat Binns and Robert Ghiz) and federal ministers, regardless of political stripe, and have oriented programs in areas to ensure it was beneficial to this sector.

Moreover, there is a unique convergence of characteristics associated with governance on Prince Edward Island that is difficult to replicate in other settings. As one interviewee stated,

> You have a small jurisdiction that is a province, a magnified federal presence, and seat of provincial government in this urban area. Those things

don't exist in very many places, whether an island or not that have that combination; it's an intangible and it's not an intangible; partly it's scale but partly it's the other things that go along with it . . . and because the resources are there and they're more easily accessible at our scale, you're down to a smaller number of relationship complexities to make it work. In a small jurisdiction where you have closer relationships, it's often very bad or very good . . . you can't hide.

Several interviewees touched on the economic and political relationship between the biosciences and the more traditional primary sectors that have historically dominated the economic fortunes of the province. Companies in the aquaculture and fish health areas of bioscience can be seen by government and the public to be linked, thereby justifying public policy decisions and investments that favor all bioscience firms.

Accessibility, Isolation and Location

Duffy and other early innovators in the sector recognized that the geographic isolation of the island and the dependence on primary production set limits on the kinds of economic activities that might be competitive globally. Rory Francis, executive director of the BioAlliance, is quoted as saying, "We all recognize the limits of our natural resource base to further expand our economy. We're an Island, after all" (*Guardian* Charlottetown, 2005, p. B8). Early in the life of DCL, Duffy noted that the future of PEI depends on the development of high-value-added industry, "The days are gone when you could haul steel in here, fabricate it and sell it . . . Forget it, freight rates are too high" (Mahon, 1982, p. 63).

The diagnostic kits and chemical compounds being manufactured at DCL and BioVectra did not require the transportation of heavy supplies to the island or heavy finished products to their off-island customers. From 1984, Duffy stated, "Because of the light weight of the product we can afford to ship everything by air and still be competitive" (cited in Foster, 1984, p. 67).

When asked about why the company remained in Prince Edward Island, Duffy noted that most of the 10 to 12 customers for their products are located in the northeastern United States. "We are closer to Boston than to Toronto" (cited in Foster, 1984, p. 68). Issues associated with isolation and inaccessibility appear to be more closely associated with the travel of company and customer management than the products themselves. One interviewee noted, "You can get here. But connections, timing, pricing, convenience to get back to your home offices [can still be a problem]."

A company interviewee noted that it is a challenge for customers from the south and west of the United States to get to PEI, "But it hasn't held us back." Quoting the president of Questcor regarding the rationale for purchasing a company like BioVectra on PEI, Mullin (2013) reports, "The point is that we don't really need access . . . When Warren Buffett buys a business, he doesn't mess with it. He leaves it alone. We'll keep in touch."

Human Capital and the Labor Market

Issues surrounding the characteristics of the local labor market and the qualities of human capital were complex and ambiguous. In several places, the interviewees and the documents suggest that there is an ample supply of highly qualified employees for DCL and BioVectra. For example, in 1982, Duffy argued,

> We've tried to lead the way so no one can ever say again that we haven't, in Atlantic Canada, the expertise to do the job. Above all, we are proving that we have as much talent as any other area on the North American continent.
>
> (cited in Department of Regional Economic
> Expansion, 1982, p. 26)

In 1991, Duffy stated, "We have an amazing supply of talent . . . eighty percent of the chemists and technicians are from PEI" (cited in Bruce, 1991, p. 17). In reference to having most of the company staff come from Atlantic Canada, Duffy noted, "We try to hire the right people; do a lot of our own training; pay them as well as we can; and then give them responsibility" (cited in Horne, 1992, p. 51).

In the interview with Duffy, he noted,

> In Canada, the human resources supply chain is incredibly good. We have had no problems getting people. We use all the technicians coming out of UPEI with BSc degrees; we probably have forty to fifty out there; we have ten to fifteen people who get their PhDs in chemistry from off-Island. We have a good source of people and, combined with lifestyle, you have a good combination to attract people. Workforce is stable. At BioVectra we are turning over [staff] less than five percent per year.

At the same time, ability to continue to attract highly qualified researchers to a relatively unknown region was mentioned several times as a problem that continues to plague the sector and its firms. One company official expressed the concern that

> The disadvantage is to try to get people with expertise to join us. We don't have a big pool to draw from in the local area. By local area I don't mean PEI; it means Atlantic Canada and perhaps even wider than that.

Reference is also made to the importance of a stable workforce to the operations of the companies. In 1984, Duffy stated, "The stability of the island's labor force makes this an ideal location for industries such as ours" (cited in Foster 1984, p. 66). One company representative stated that one of the advantages of this location is employee retention and commitment,

> In Chicago, you would see people moving quickly among the big four [biopharm companies] all within about twenty miles of each other to get

a higher salary or get promoted. In PEI, there is an employee loyalty that I've seen that is a lot more than anywhere else I've worked.

The occasional movement of highly qualified personnel between companies was seen as a sign of a growing maturity within the PEI biosciences sector and a reflection that the next stage of development might reflect the situation at larger biosciences clusters. At the same time, the collaborative nature of the sector suggests that innovation might be occurring without the movement of people to new or competitor companies. As one company interviewee stated, "We're still a very small cluster so there's not a great deal of movement; but there is a lot of cooperation amongst the firms; if there's a problem, another company may assist in correcting that problem."

DISCUSSION

Employment and sales in the biosciences sector and the case study companies is still small compared to the overall PEI economy. However, it is exceptional in so many ways that it deserves attention as an island entrepreneurial activity. This exceptionality includes recent growth relative to the traditional sectors of the economy, strong export orientation, reliance on a highly paid and highly skilled labor force and international corporate acquisition activity. While exporting PEI potatoes and crustaceans is and remains a feature of the island economy, exporting diagnostic kits or biopharmaceuticals has the good fortune of not being dependent on the vagaries of the weather or a natural resource but on the ability to attract highly skilled scientists and investment capital and the vagaries of the global market for these chemical products.

The growth of the biosciences and especially the niche manufacturing associated with BioVectra and DCL/Sekisui cannot be attributed to many of the factors associated with the development of biosciences clusters elsewhere in North America. An existing research infrastructure was not considered to be especially critical in creating and expanding DCL and BioVectra. Moreover, although the research capacity of UPEI has increased significantly in recent years, it is nowhere close to that of those universities associated with biotechnology clusters in Toronto, Boston or San Francisco. Other than the university affiliation of key entrepreneurs such as Regis Duffy and the ability of the educational institutions to provide a ready source of competent technicians, at this time, the role of the educational institutions appears to be largely incidental to the continued growth of these companies.

PEI also cannot be considered an especially advantageous setting for bioscience companies that need to acquire long-term investment capital. Although various government programs have been able to provide small amounts of project-based capital for new firms, and collaborative government support was an important feature in the early growth of DCL and BioVectra, the amount and length of funding required to support research and development for these larger firms is beyond the political and financial capability of most government programs. What has sustained research and development has been capital acquired and reinvested as a result of the purchase of the locally based companies by multinational corporations such as Genzyme and Sekisui.

Nor do BioVectra and DCL/Sekisui have strong local supply-chain linkages. This might be understandable given the small scale of the island and the adopted business model. Also, PEI lacks an alternative supply chain characterized by a ready source of investment capital, access to executive talent, trained scientists, service professionals and international accessibility. The only feature in common between PEI and university towns in larger centers is a perceived high quality of life for the personnel and their families. Nevertheless, larger firms like DCL and BioVectra have played a significant collaborative role in mentoring other bioscience companies, in enabling and shaping public policy and in raising the capacity of educational institutions and other service providers.

As a subnational island jurisdiction, and unlike the province of Québec, PEI does not have a clearly defined minority population; nor does it have a propensity to engage in paradiplomacy. The island has a local identity defined by agricultural production, seasonal tourism and the strongest ethnic homogeneity and highest relative poverty and unemployment in Canada. None of these features have contributed to the rise of the biosciences sector. Political rhetoric implies that the aquaculture, fish and animal health companies of the island's biosciences are a natural knowledge-based extension of the prevailing primary activities; but the production of medical diagnostic kits and biopharmaceutical chemicals has little functional connection to these activities. Research on subnational island jurisdictions suggests that these places are able to use their jurisdictional clout to economic advantage. At face value, PEI has little formal jurisdictional clout in Canadian federal politics: less than 2% (4 of 308) of the seats in the Canadian House of Commons are allocated to PEI and, as of 2014, only one of those seats was held by a member of the majority Conservative federal party in power. At the same time, the impact of the federal and provincial government presence on the island and especially in the capital of Charlottetown is greater than what the mere numbers of elected officials might suggest. Not only is access to government decision makers touted as a locational advantage for companies, but interaction across the very personalized network of politicians, entrepreneurs and bureaucrats takes place quickly via formal meetings of the BioAlliance. Informally, BioVectra assumes a strong civic responsibility for island economic development and mentorship of smaller biosciences companies.

CONCLUSION

Whether on a remote small island or in a peripheral mainland region, the presence and credibility of key entrepreneurs has been one distinguishing feature in Prince Edward Island's biosciences. Regis Duffy brought research skills and an entrepreneurial approach that were extremely rare at universities in the 1970s. The fact that he was born and raised on the island generated community and political credibility for himself, his company and, by extension, the biosciences sector.

One of the challenges for this nascent biosciences sector in the future is the perceived uncertainty regarding local employment and investment by large, international corporations as decision making shifts to nonlocal boardrooms. The mergers and acquisitions associated with Diagnostic Chemicals and BioVectra may be signs of the business success of those firms, sources of private capital investment and indications of maturity in the sector. However, this trend may also be viewed with some trepidation. If credibility in the community as a result of "island ownership" was crucial in their formative years, an increased level of nonisland control of BioVectra and DCL/Sekisui also places them increasingly at the whim of global, neoliberal forces. Perhaps at the root of this concern regarding nonlocal corporate decision making is the history of ownership within the traditional island agricultural sectors by multinational corporations such as McCain Foods and J.D. Irving Limited and the fear that this longstanding feature of the island's political economy is increasingly becoming a feature of this knowledge-based sector.

ACKNOWLEDGMENT

This research would not have been possible without the contributions of Dr. Regis Duffy, founder of BioVectra and former Dean of the Faculty of Science, University of Prince Edward Island, Canada. The usual disclaimers apply.

REFERENCES

Armstrong, H. W., De Kervenoael, R. J., Li, X., & Read, R. (1998). A comparison of the economic performance of different micro-states, and between micro-states and larger countries. *World Development, 26*(4), 639–656.
Armstrong, H. W., & Read, R. (2000). Comparing the economic performance of dependent territories and sovereign microstates. *Economic Development and Cultural Change, 48*(2), 285–306.
Baker, R. (Ed.). (1992). *Public administration in small and island states.* West Hartford: Kumarian Press Library of Management for Development.
Baldacchino, G. (2006a). Innovative development strategies from non-sovereign island jurisdictions: A global review of economic policy and governance practices. *World Development, 34*(5), 852–867.
Baldacchino, G. (2006b). Small islands versus big cities: Lessons in the political economy of regional development from the world's small islands. *Journal of Technology Transfer, 31*(1), 91–100.

Baldacchino, G. (2011). Surfers of the ocean waves: Change management, intersectoral migration and the economic development of small island states. *Asia Pacific Viewpoint, 52*(3), 236–246.

Baldacchino, G., & Milne, D. (2006). Exploring sub-national island jurisdictions: An editorial introduction. *The Round Table, 95*(386), 487–502.

Baldacchino, G., & Milne, D. (Eds.). (2009). *The case for non-sovereignty: Lessons from sub-national island jurisdictions*. London: Routledge.

Bartmann, B. (2006). In or out: Sub-national island jurisdictions and the antechamber of para-diplomacy. *The Round Table: Commonwealth Journal of International Affairs, 95*(386), 541–559.

Baum, T. G., Hagen-Grant, L., Jolliffe, L., Lambert, S., & Sigurjonsson, B. (2000). Tourism and cold water islands in the North Atlantic. In G. Baldacchino & D. Milne (Eds.), *Lessons from the political economy of small islands: The resourcefulness of jurisdiction* (pp. 214–229). Prince Edward Island: St. Martin's Press & Macmillan Press in association with the Institute of Island Studies.

Baxter, P., & Jack, S. (2008). Qualitative case study methodology: Study design and implementation for novice researchers. *The Qualitative Report, 13*(4), 544–559.

BioPartner. (2005). *The Netherlands life sciences sector report 2005: New challenges ahead*. Ede, the Netherlands: BioPartner Network.

Briguglio, L. (1995). Small island developing states and their economic vulnerabilities. *World Development, 23*(9), 1615–1632.

Bruce, H. (1991, December). Very fine chemistry. *Commercial News, 70*(12), 12–17.

Chronicle-Herald (Halifax). (2010, August 24). P.E.I. firm gets $14.8m loan., p. C5.

Coffey, W. J., & Polèse, M. (Eds.). (1987). *Still living together: Recent trends and future directions in Canadian regional development*. Montreal: The Institute for Research on Public Policy.

Cooke, P. (2004a). Regional knowledge capabilities, embeddedness of firms and industry organisation: Bioscience megacentres and economic geography. *European Planning Studies, 12*(5), 625–641.

Cooke, P. (2004b). Life sciences clusters and regional science policy. *Urban Studies, 41*(5–6), 1113–1131.

Cooke, P. (2005). Rational drug design, the knowledge value chain and bioscience megacentres. *Cambridge Journal of Economics, 29*(3), 325–341.

Day, J. (2006, November 25). Good chemistry. *Guardian* (Charlottetown), p. A1.

Dobby, C. (2012, May 22). Prince Edward Island focuses on attracting biosciences innovation companies to cut deficit. Financial Post. Retrieved from http://business.financialpost

Doloreux, D., & Dionne, S. (2008). Is regional innovation system development possible in peripheral regions? Some evidence from the case of La Pocatière, Canada. *Entrepreneurship and Regional Development, 20*(3), 259–283.

Duffy, R. (2005, December 28). Offering Atlantic Canada new economic life. *Guardian* (Charlottetown), A7.

Dunn, L. (2011). The impact of political dependence on small island jurisdictions. *World Development, 39*(12), 2132–2146.

Economic Development Winnipeg Inc. (2013). *Winnipeg life sciences growing stronger—health and biotech*. www.economicdevelopmentwinnipeg.com/uploads/files/00210_Life%20Sciences%20Profile%20SS%281%29.pdf

Department of Regional Economic Expansion. (1982). Add blood and shake. *Evolution, 1*(2), 26–27.

Feldman, M. P. (2000). Where science comes to life: University bioscience, commercial spin-offs, and regional economic development. *Journal of Comparative Policy Analysis: Research and Practice, 2*(3), 345–361.

Feldman, M. P., & Francis, J. L. (2004). Homegrown solutions: Fostering cluster formation. *Economic Development Quarterly, 18*(2), 127–137.

Foster, C. (1984). Diagnostic kits spell success for PEI firm. *Atlantic Insight, 6*(5), 65–68.

Gertler, M. S., & Vinodrai, T. (2009). Life sciences and regional innovation: One path or many? *European Planning Studies, 17*(2), 235–261.

Grydehøj, A. (2011). Making the most of smallness: Economic policy in microstates and sub-national island jurisdictions. *Space and Polity, 15*(3), 183–196.

Guardian (Charlottetown). (2005, June 11). Coming together, next generation of P.E.I.'s economy taking shape, BioAlliance looks to build economy through bioscience products, services, p. B8.

Guardian (Charlottetown). (2011, April 6). Bioscience industry on P.E.I. marks commercial successes, p. B11.

Guardian (Charlottetown). (2013, May 15). Harper announces $7.7 million in funding for three island companies, p. A3.

Guardian (Charlottetown). (2014, May 3). P.E.I. bioscience sector coming of age, p. B9.

Guillaumont, P. (2010). Assessing the economic vulnerability of small island developing states and the least developed countries. *Journal of Development Studies, 46*(5), 828–854.

Hancock, D., & Algozzine, B. (2006). *Doing case study research: A practical guide for beginning researchers.* New York, NY: Teachers College Press.

Holloway, A. (2004). Island of dreams. *Canadian Business, 77*(19), 66–68.

Horne, S. (1992). Diagnostic Chemicals Ltd. in PEI. *Atlantic Lifestyle Business, 3*(2), 50–52.

Hudson, A. (2000). Offshoreness, globalization and sovereignty: A postmodern geopolitical sovereignty? *Transactions of the Institute of British Geographers, N.S., 25*(3), 269–283.

Industry Canada. (2013). Complete profile—Sekisui Diagnostics PEI Inc. Retrieved from www.ic.gc.ca

Jupia Consultants Inc. (2014). *The Prince Edward Island bioscience cluster economic impact audit.* Charlottetown: BioAlliance. Retrieved from www.peibioalliance.com

Lowe, N. J., & Gertler, M. S. (2008). Building on diversity: Institutional foundations of hybrid strategies in Toronto's life sciences complex. *Regional Studies, 42*(9), 1–15.

Lynch, A. (1996). Sweat equity: Atlantic Canada's new entrepreneurs. *Nimbus,* 135–143.

MacIntyre, W. (1994). Diagnostic Chemicals Ltd. In W. MacIntyre (Editor), *17 Doors to Prince Edward Island and a window on Cathay* (pp. 83–84). Charlottetown, Canada: Friends of St. Andrew Press.

Magner, M. (2014). *Turning size to competitive advantage: Prince Edward Island bioscience cluster case study.* Charlottetown, Canada: Prince Edward Island BioAlliance.

Mahon, A. (1982). There are all kinds of things we could do here. *Atlantic Business.* (January/February), 63.

McElroy, J. L., & Mahoney, M. (2000). The propensity for political dependence in island microstates. *INSULA: International Journal of Island Affairs, 9*(1), 32–35.

McElroy, J. L., & Pearce, K. B. (2006). The advantages of political affiliation: Dependent and independent small-island profiles. *The Round Table: Commonwealth Journal of International Affairs, 95*(386), 529–539.

McGillivray, M., Naudé, W., & Santos-Paulino, A. (2010). Vulnerability, trade, financial flows and state failure in small island developing states. *The Journal of Development Studies, 46*(5), 815–827.

Moreira, C. (2014, May 16). Life science sector jolts P.E.I. economy. *The Chronicle Herald* (Halifax), p. B6.

Mullin, R. (2013, January 21). An unusual deal. *Chemical and Engineering News Online*, p. 18. Retrieved from www.cen-online.org

Nelson, L. (2005). The role of research institutions in the formation of the biotech cluster in Massachusetts: The MIT experience. *Journal of Commercial Biotechnology, 11*(4), 330–336.

Niosi, J., & Bas, T. G. (2001). The competencies of regions: Canada's clusters in biotechnology. *Small Business Economics, 17*(1–2), 31–42.

Porter, M. (1998). Clusters and the new economics of competition. *Harvard Business Review*. (November/December), 77–90.

Prince Edward Island BioAlliance. (2012). Next generation prosperity: Strategy for Prince Edward Island bioscience cluster development 2012–2015. Retrieved from www.peibioalliance.com

Prince Edward Island Statistics Bureau. (2014). *40th annual statistical review 2013*. Charlottetown, PEI: Department of Finance, Energy and Municipal Affairs. Retrieved from www.gov.pe.ca

Robin, J. (2013). Saskatchewan biosciences: Building public, policy, and industry support. *Industrial Biotechnology, 9*(6), 311–313.

Savoie, D. J. (1997). *Rethinking Canada's regional development policy: An Atlantic perspective*. Moncton, Canada: Canadian Institute for Research on Regional Development.

Savoie, D. J. (2003). Royal commission on renewing and strengthening our place in Canada: Reviewing Canada's regional development efforts. Retrieved from http://gov.nl.ca

Spence, R. (1992). Closer to the customer. *Profit*. (September), 40.

Stake, R. (2000). Case studies. In N. Denzin & Y. Lincoln (Eds.), *Handbook of qualitative research* (2nd ed., pp. 435–454). Thousand Oaks, CA: Sage.

Walcott, S. M. (2002). Analyzing an innovative environment: San Diego as a bioscience beachhead. *Economic Development Quarterly, 16*(2), 99–114.

Yarr, K. (1997). The right chemistry. *Atlantic Progress, 4*(3), 24–26.

Yin, R. K. (2003). *Case study research: Design and methods* (3rd ed.). Thousand Oaks, CA: Sage.

8 Entrepreneurial Traits, Niche Strategy, and International Expansion of a Small Firm on a Small Island Territory

Ligne St. Barth in St. Barthélemy, France

Karen L. Orengo Serra and Sopheap Theng

INTRODUCTION

The prosperity of small island economies also depends on the capacity of their (mostly small) local firms to become actively involved in international business activities (Williams, 2011). The small island populations and their limited access to resources produce small local markets, which force these companies to operate by either restricting themselves to satisfying local demand or else branching out quickly into exports. In this way, some small and medium enterprises (SMEs) from small island states and territories do manage to become national, regional or international leaders in niche markets soon after their establishment, even without engaging their domestic market. This phenomenon differs from the traditional pattern of firm international-ization, in which a firm gradually and incrementally acquires knowledge of foreign markets, with the size and age of the firm being important elements in this process (Johanson & Vahlne, 1977; Johanson & Wiedersheim-Paul, 1975).

In contrast, international new ventures (INVs), or born-global firms, explore international markets and their opportunities from their outset. Such INVs come with two main characteristics: they are created by dynamic entrepre-neurs who bring to the firm a strong international network and who pay great attention to customer relationship building; and they emerge from an innovative exercise involving fairly unique products, processes, marketing and/or distribution not easily replicated (Cabrol & Niemvo, 2009; Oviatt & McDougall, 1994). Applying a successful niche market strategy requires firms from small island jurisdictions to develop differentiated assets allowing them to both identify and retain customers, as well as to position themselves as competitive firms in nondomestic markets. Gaining and keeping a sustain-able competitive advantage in the national, regional or international arena is greatly facilitated by locating a product or service clearly within a local tradition and tapping into the tropes and characteristics associated with a particular location: in our case, an island brand riding on the cachet, good standing and success of the island as a brand unto itself (Baldacchino, 2010).

This chapter focuses on the Franco-Caribbean firm Ligne St. Barth as a case study and on the island of St. Barthélemy (or St. Barth), where the firm originated and where it continues to be based. The study looks at the niche strategy approach by identifying the entrepreneurial elements in the strategic actions of the firm's management and its links to the process of internationalization. A qualitative approach involving content analysis is applied to the case study. Using qualitative coding, a model of the entrepreneurial management elements under review is created; this model includes the conditions under which the firm operates and the activities that describe or are related to its international exposure.

This chapter is divided into four basic sections. After a broad literature review, the chapter introduces the island of St. Barth and its emergence as a contemporary exclusive and up-market destination. Then follows an overview of Ligne St. Barth, itself an up-market operation based on smart use of local products for discerning customers only. The methodology and research design applied in this study are then described. The ensuing analysis positions the niche strategy approach of the firm in the context of observed entrepreneurial traits. Finally, some emerging issues and challenges are discussed in the conclusion.

REVIEW OF THE LITERATURE

In our globalizing world, pursuing a niche strategy is a powerful marketing tool for small and medium-sized enterprises hoping to compete. A niche strategy seems to be the appropriate strategy to survive, grow and be profitable: market size remains small and manageable, but high added value and effective, place-based branding and marketing secure high profit margins, eliminate effective competition and secure the potential for sustained (niche) market share. These are the opportunities available to even a new-start-up firm to exercise and test its superior competence (Dalgic & Leeuw, 1994). Pursuing a niche strategy is an application that has implications for competitiveness and relationship marketing (Toften & Hammervoll, 2012); it is a continuous process based on strong, long-term relationships developed between the firm and its stakeholders, allowing the firm to anticipate and fulfill customer expectations in a competitive and sustainable way while creating subtle but real entry barriers to competitors through accumulated customer goodwill (Dalgic et al., 1994; Shani & Chalasani, 1992; Toften et al., 2012).

Firms that focus on niche markets exhibit a strong entrepreneurially oriented strategy that allows managers to develop durable and long-term relationships with various members across the value chain (suppliers, financiers, agents, customers). Entrepreneurially oriented firms are willing to accept risk and be competitively aggressive, paving the way to "the processes, practices, and decision-making activities that lead to new entry" (Lumpkin & Dess, 1996, p. 136). Innovation, creativity and proactiveness are some of the key dimensions of entrepreneurial orientation (EO; Wiklund & Shepherd, 2003). Innovation is a firm's attitude toward new ideas in which entrepreneurs translate opportunities into marketable concepts and thus produce change (Kuratko & Hodgetts, 2004). Creativity, EO and commitment unleash good ideas through the development stages of the innovation diffusion process (Kotler & Keller, 2006; Kuratko et al., 2004). Such a firm's strategy is strongly linked to the entrepreneurial traits of the managers and/ or owners of the firm, their commitment to the market and their ability to deal with it.

Even for SMEs hailing from small island states and territories, a niche strategy represents an interaction of the firm's resources, competences and abilities to create a favorable environment for growth at the international level (Zucchella & Palamara, 2007; Zucchella et al., 2007). By definition, niches are often waiting to be identified, and they may exhibit no traditional barriers. Barriers emerge later, in seeking to survive and build competitive advantage. A niche market is characterized by nonprice competition. Quality, innovation and adaptation to customers' needs then become critical factors; they could unwittingly become the significant obstacles to the firm's growth and very survival.

International SMEs applying a niche market approach share some fundamental similarities: they possess unique assets, focus on a narrow global market segment and are strongly customer oriented. In small, open island economies, local firms face constraints accessing resources, dealing with the narrow local market and facing their limited capacity to supply a mass market. Even when they consider exports, they often must import and export raw materials and use oligopolistic supply mechanisms, adding to production costs. Ligne St. Barth, from the island of St. Barthélemy, is a born-global firm that continues to succeed in the international arena and has cleverly built its reputation alongside the powerful image and reputation of its island home and regionally available local products. These factors also explain why small island entrepreneurs consider INVs and why their staff develop international skills right from the beginning by orienting ventures mainly or completely toward satisfying off-island, often foreign markets (Williams, 2011).

The INVs' perspective emphasizes this off-island disposition on an individual level rather than on a firm level (Cabrol et al., 2009). The firm's strategic know-how often resides in a key individual and his/her know-how in new ventures, networks and markets, especially because INVs often start operations without any formal organizational structure. This is one of the characteristics of global start-ups: the dynamism of the new venture is seen through the entrepreneur's skill set and personality instead of the firm's own vantage point (McDougall, Shane, & Oviatt, 1994). With an internationally oriented mind-set and knowledge (including international experience, education, employment, internships and foreign social relationships), such a well-equipped entrepreneur has a greater awareness and appreciation of internationalization even before the inception of the new venture. This would explain his/her ability to establish international networks soon after the establishment of the firm and to learn by actively seeking knowledge about international markets, potential customers and competitors and the operational environment overseas (Oviatt & McDougall, 1994, 1995). The accelerated internationalization process of an INV can therefore be explained by the entrepreneur's personal knowledge about the foreign market and about the internationalization process itself learned by prior experience and network development; this knowledge base reduces the ambiguity and complexity (and associated risks and costs) in pursuing international market strategies, often even before the actual foundation of the firm. Internationalization does not result from the gradual and incremental accumulation of experience in foreign markets, as traditional models of small firms development might suggest. Small island states and territories do not come with that kind of economic buffer.

DEALING WITH LUXURY

Dealing with the luxury market is a niche unto itself. Luxury is first grasped as a deviation from the norm in a particular society at any given time. The current luxury commodity within hypermaterialist Western societies is no longer the same as that of two centuries ago. But what remains constant is that, by definition, luxury is the privilege of wealthy elites as opposed to the reach of the masses. It could be referred to as elegance, refinement and beauty; but it is mostly about exclusivity, a restricted access to highly coveted, rare objects, services, treatments and properties. Veblen (1899) was already discussing how the demonstrative display of wealth translates into ostentatious consumption, beyond need and utility. The one who can dedicate his/her time freely to unproductive tasks exudes high status: it is here that the foundations of luxury and luxurious leisure started to be laid down. Bourdieu (1979) insists on this principle of distinction, with its provocative dimension that displays its waste of time and money, wealth and power. Lipovetsky and Roux (2003) consider that distinction also has a narcissistic dimension that is just as important as its social dimension. They insist on the rationale to privately enjoy those goods that make one dream, without any necessary public demonstration. Moreover, an upscale market should be distinguished from luxury. It is part of the extension of luxury: these are products and consumption patterns for followers. Upmarket products cater to individuals who benefit from a rise in their standard of living. The *nouveau riche* enjoy the abundance of goods in hyperconsumerist societies and can lay claim to more sophisticated goods, well above the standard; but they have some way to go: they do not reach the dizzy heights of exclusivity associated with the luxury level.

But, beyond the business organization *per se* and the nature of the very particular luxury industry, contextual factors can matter significantly. In our selected case, context provides a readily available platform and springboard for going up-market. Hence, the specific, geographical and socioeconomic context in which this firm was established and remains embedded and wedded—as evidenced also by its name—invite us to a more detailed analysis of the island of St. Barthélemy.

HISTORY OF ST. BARTH: AN EXCEPTIONAL LOCATION

Luxury Applied to Tourism

With the discourse of ostentatious consumption, challenging distinction, self-fulfillment, the valorization of a singularity, the operationalization of luxury is easily transferred to the realm of tourism. This gives rise to a specific tourist mode of consumption, seeking an adequate territorial landscaping and planning, according to rigidly exclusive selection criteria. Luxury tourism is thus based on the production of specific services intended for customers who stand out from the others by their financial power and/or by virtue of belonging to a certain social class.

The issue of accessibility is specific to the case of luxury tourism. Luxury tourism destinations need to be easily accessible to wealthy clients. This does not typically require costly construction and massive infrastructures, such as those that target jumbo jets and cruise ships loaded with many thousands of passengers. In the case of luxury tourism, the client organizes his/her route by combining flights on regular routes (first class, of course) with those on secondary routes (such as by helicopter, personal executive jet or superyacht) that lead him/her directly to his/her tourist accommodation. The quality of the physical support and its immediate environment is a major and nonnegotiable prerequisite: luxury tourism is compulsorily set within an attractive surrounding recognized for its singularity and its character.

At the heart of economic and political capital, luxury focuses on lavish palaces, mansions and other large luxury hotels located in privileged islets (Forbes.com, 2011). It is set within lovingly maintained or restored heritage properties or modern buildings with futuristic designs and hedonistic appeal. They are the meeting places of local oligarchies, discreet business rendezvous and/or a nexus for well-heeled international visitors. Within urban areas, luxury establishments gather within the most famous worldwide historic districts (as in Venice, Bruges, Upper Manhattan or Quebec City). Finally, the concentration of these establishments prevails within internationally renowned destinations where luxury has emerged as the primary focus of interest within an attractive and comfortable setting in a suitably preserved environment. St. Barthélemy is one such place.

A Small, Long-Neglected Island

St. Barthélemy (better known as St. Barth) lies 2,500 km from New York, 180 km from Puerto Rico and 6,500 km from Paris. It is located close to St. Martin (the main regional air hub) and several islands with diverse political status: Anguilla, St. Kitts, Nevis, St. Eustatius and Saba. The island's land area is just 21 km². Until the 1970s, its residents faced harsh living conditions. This flat and dry island, commonly known as the "barren rock," has sparse and largely thorny vegetation. Its maritime tropical climate oscillates between "lent," a dry season (December to May), and "wintering," a rainy season (July to October), when it faces the risk of cyclones. Temperatures vary through the year due to the presence of the trade winds; but the territory enjoys regularly mild temperatures and constant ventilation. The island records a low mean annual precipitation: having a supply of drinking water has been a regular challenge.

Officially discovered by Columbus in 1493, St. Barthélemy was occupied by France in 1649 and became a French colony in 1659. The island was not the object of any specific strategic considerations that bedeviled colonial interests in the region; it continued to serve as a hideout for the last Caribbean Indians and a few privateers. Too rocky and too dry, this island did not produce any economic wealth (such as bananas or sugar cane); it was deemed surplus and useless to France. Its development started in 1784 when France ceded the island to Sweden in exchange for French vessels' free port storage rights in the Swedish port city of Gothenburg. Sweden, only a small colonial power, opened a free port in St. Barth where ships of all nationalities could anchor and store their goods. The island thus enjoyed a period of relative prosperity thanks to the status of its port—called Gustavia, after Gustav III, King of Sweden—and associated exemptions from customs and tax payments. This economic boom was interrupted in 1877, when Sweden ceded the island back to France. St. Barth suddenly became a double periphery: one in relation to the French colonial empire and a second in relation to the French Antilles. In 1946, it was administratively linked to the Guadeloupe archipelago, located 230 km further south, when the latter was incorporated as a French *département* (same as Martinique and French Guyana). Throughout this period, the small but resilient community of St. Barth continued to be marked by poverty and neglect.

A Judicious Statutory Evolution

Therefore, the history of St. Barth unfolded within a context of a colonial administrative deficiency; this power vacuum has favored the development of a pragmatic and democratic culture within local island governance that integrates local customary rules and imported practices from nearby colonial islands. This territory, long affected by a double insularity within the exclusive logic of French centralist public policy, has wisely evolved within a decade. St. Barth rose from the status of a simple district of Guadeloupe to that of an overseas collectivity (*Collectivité d'Outre Mer*, or COM), with the election of its own Territorial Assembly in 2007, as part of a referendum approved by 95.5% of voters.

Further developments were imminent. On January 1, 2012, St. Barth ceased being an outermost region and left the European Union (EU). It was only the second territory to ever do so in the EU's history, along with Greenland. The change was made to facilitate trade with countries outside the EU, notably the United States. The change in St. Barth's status was made possible by a provision of the Lisbon Treaty, which allows the European Council to change the EU status of a Danish, Dutch or French territory on the initiative of the member state concerned.

The evolution of St. Barth's local governance is significant for a better understanding of how luxury tourism took off and matured within the territory. The evolution of the legal status of the island, largely supported by the local community, is critical for the island locals to be able to maintain control over and shape the future of their island beyond tourism and to enjoy the wealth now circulating in the island's economy.

Setting Up Luxury Tourism in St. Barth

The construction of St. Barth as an upscale tourism destination took three decades. From the beginning, with the arrival of the first business and show-business visitors from North America, tourist activity was already associated with luxury.

The origins of tourism in St. Barth can be traced to the landing of the first plane, belonging to Rémy De Haenen, in 1945 on the St. John plain, which would subsequently became the island's airport (Theismann, n.d.). The arrival of this aircraft was going to break the centuries-old isolation of the territory. Previously, access to and from St. Barth was limited to a few exchanges by sea with neighboring islands. But with the arrival of the airline, St. Barth got closer to the United States, along with the territories that have strong economic ties with the United States, such as Puerto Rico (with its air hub in San Juan) and the archipelago of the Bahamas (with the hub in Nassau), from which tourists may decide to pursue their journey farther south. The first visitors arriving in St. Barthélemy were aviation fans in search of the last, pristine, still-ignored small island. Air accessibility revealed a territory that until then was perceived in terms of secluded poverty. These amateur pilots were joined mostly by North American sailors. By then, it was already the authentic, rustic and preserved aspects of this small, forgotten island that appealed to well-heeled North American visitors such as David Rockefeller.

The history of tourism in St. Barth is not built on territorial planning. The island community was unaware of the process of bourgeoning tourism development. The place was selected by the first international visitors, who laid the foundation of the tourism industry and its focus on luxury tourism. Thus, in 1957, David Rockefeller is one of the illustrious precursors of tourism in St. Barth. Seduced by this island, discovered by chance, he dropped the Bahamas archipelago, which, he felt, had become too accessible and was losing its elitist character. The geographical position of St. Barth is quite interesting: the island is slightly withdrawn in the north of the Caribbean arc, but it is nevertheless close to the United States. The businessman fell under the charm of this small island and its tropical and rustic, out-of-time character. He decided to invest and bought land overlooking the sea at its northern end. The Rothschild family built an estate in a coconut grove next door to what later became the Hôtel Guanahani & Spa. From then on, a trendy phenomenon would grow within the wealthy circles of the United States. At first, guests would join the tycoon in his villa: politicians, businesspersons, Hollywood stars. And each year, among these guests, the first proper tourists to St. Barth, some decided to invest in the island, buying land and real estate. At that time, St. Barth was a small, rural island with no demographic pressure, where land had no productive value and so was still relatively cheap. Gradually, St. Barth has become a discrete destination for a handful of elites from the eastern coast of the United States (Cousin & Chauvin, 2013).

Construction of the Destination

Thus, since the 1960s, the tourist process started to unfold, starting with the construction of comfortable and luxurious private villas, arranged around Saint-Jean Bay and across the northern coast of the island, less exposed to the winds. A few hotels followed. Among the first top open and perhaps most renowned facilities is the Eden Rock St. Barths, a hotel built by the adventurous pilot Rémy De Haenen. Since its opening, generations of movie stars have paraded there. A few have been tracked: Baron de Rothschild, David Rockefeller (*Architectural Digest*, 1983), Brigitte Bardot, Robert Mitchum, Howard Hughes, Steve Martin (Willett, 2013), Greta Garbo and Sharon Stone.

Clearly, tourism development in St. Barth is driven by external demand and supported by the arrival of financial capital and international investors. The tourist economy specializes in catering to a prosperous and highly targeted clientele. To do so, it has learned how to use the strengths of the destination smartly: the scarcity of space and selective accessibility. On this small island, the amount of coveted space available is reduced, so that its financial value is in constant increase. Thus, there is simply no place for those who cannot afford it, knowing that daily living costs are also high.

Yet the economy is not regulated only by price and scarcity of land. Accessibility remains a discriminatory criterion and is a function of an intriguing infrastructural bottleneck: the only runway on the island is just 650 meters long. It cannot welcome large planes: thus, flights into St. Barth do not bring in more than 20 passengers each. This bottleneck helps maintain the exclusivity of the island (e.g., Doumenge, 1988). Accessibility is reserved both by of its cost and by the low number of seats available: the airline market is also controlled essentially by two small local companies, and flights are often operated as taxi rides on demand.

The stage was thus set: here is a subnational island jurisdiction, located in the Caribbean (known for its salubrious climate, vibrant cultures and exotic biota) under the purview of France (synonymous with the fashion industry) that had been discovered and transformed into a retreat for the few and privileged. The short runway and the high cost of everything ensure that it should remain so. St. Barth exudes quality, exceptionality and luxury.

HISTORY OF LIGNE ST. BARTH: AN EXCEPTIONAL PRODUCT AND SERVICE

The ultimate shopper finds Nirvana in St Barth. Check out the section below in the delights of Gustavia and St Jean's, where designer boutiques line the *rues* and luxury reigns. The duty free shopping is also good, where you will find a lot of locally made clothing and accessories, as well as the wonderful *Ligne St Barth* body care and spa products.
(Nash, 2012, pp. 13–14)

Ligne St. Barth is a small, family-owned manufacturing business focused on highly specialized professional beauty products. Ligne St. Barth is quite unique in its class, mainly because it is based and set in an extremely open island economy with a small population and very limited natural resources. Ligne St. Barth also departed from most small island state and territory INVs, which focus on service provision, by (first) becoming a manufacturing niche microfirm with a global reach within a few years of its inception.

The firm was established in 1983 on St. Barth by Hervé Brin, a chemical engineer, and his wife Birgit Brin, a hotel and hospitality specialist. The history of this microenterprise is linked to an intimate knowledge of native Caribbean tropical plants by Hervé's great-great-grandmother (Beauty San, 2013). The background of the founders' profile explains the achievement of the firm, combining inherited knowledge and education with modern technology in the low-scale manufacturing of unique and high-quality beauty products. Hervé and Birgit started with a sun lotion based on red seeds from the rare roucou tree (*Bixa orellana*). The firm was the first to develop roucou sun-care products commercially, and this remains a unique international product. The positioning of roucou sun-care products, along with the firm's other cosmetic lines, is also a function of how this entrepreneurial duo continues to control the entire production process from plantation through to harvesting and processing and finally manufacturing and distribution. In the case of roucou seeds, the firm engaged in an agreement with the last remaining Indian community in the Caribbean to guarantee the supply of this raw material.

EXPORT STRATEGY: ENTRY INTO INTERNATIONAL MARKETS

Riding on this initial success, in 1988, Ligne St. Barth increased the range of its products, facilitating the international expansion of the firm. Celebrities, international top models, showbiz artists and businesspeople were approached to serve as the marketing communication tools for the firm's foreign expansion and demonstration. These people indirectly advertise the Ligne St. Barth brand as brand ambassadors. From this same year, the firm formally began its internationalization through the establishment of an export branch in United States.

SUBSIDIARIES AND STRATEGIC ALLIANCES: DRIVERS FOR INTERNATIONAL EXPANSION

With the increasing demand in Europe for Ligne St. Barth products, subsidiaries were opened in Munich, Germany, in 1993 and two more, in Switzerland and Austria, in 1995. The firm has a staff complement of 12 in Munich and 20 in St. Barth.

As part of its performance and growth strategy, the firm added a new component to its business portfolio in 1998: St. Barth Treatments by Ligne St. Barth is a new concept of consulting services developing partnerships with luxury villas and exclusive hotels. St. Barth Treatments includes the creation of the concept and planning of a spa, participation in its project management and implementation, driving the marketing strategy, facilitating recruitment and training and providing ongoing support and advice. Using this strategy, the firm has grown its brand recognition without lowering its price range, plus venturing into the knowledge and service sectors. The first strategic partnership was secured with Lacure Inc., a worldwide luxury villa rental specialist firm, which challenged Ligne St. Barth to develop a spa in a luxurious residence, Roaring Pavilion in Jamaica, a first-class location on a private estate with its own beach, with Céline Dion, Jack Nicholson and Don Johnson among its first clients. The venture was a success: from the following year, the firm continued positioning itself internationally as a luxury brand in the niche market of beauty products and services. The core strategy was focused on making their exotic, high-quality products and services available in luxury hotels.

MARKETING BUSINESS NETWORKS AND STRATEGIC ALLIANCES FOR INTERNATIONAL POSITIONING

In 2001, the firm opened its third extension to its production unit. To reach the male market, the firm developed an additional range of products exclusively for men, again expanding its product portfolio. This strategy permitted the firm to penetrate the luxury market of notorious brands targeted to the masculine upper class. This explains the presence of Ligne St. Barth in the marketing events of luxury brands such as Jaguar, Porsche and Mont Blanc. Only in 2003 did the firm open its first and only store in Gustavia, St. Barthélemy, tapping into the visitor and tourist market there.

From 2005 to 2007, the firm experienced a fast product portfolio expansion, including perfumes, beach clothes and accessories for spa treatments. Product distribution is restricted to only the most exclusive five-star hotels and resorts. Promotion is driven by invitation to luxury events (such as WIMCO, Die Bilderwerkstatt, Atelier Voyage) from prominent luxury organizations. In 2007, the firm entered the media industry, launching *Spa & Travel by Ligne St. Barth*, a magazine dedicated to worldwide destinations for beauty and well-being.

After 2007, the firm became immersed in the research and development (R&D) of innovative active natural ingredients, while it started receiving international acclaim from luxury firms (partners) and the media. The high quality and uniqueness of Ligne St. Barth products and services are now well recognized around the world. In 2012, Ligne St. Barth launched Deep Sea, a high-quality face cream, unique in its active ingredients, formulation and invariable luxury packaging and cost (Deep Sea, 2014). With Deep Sea, Ligne St. Barth consolidates its presence in the international luxury beauty niche market. The autonomy of management and strong network relationships with prestigious partners and high-profile customers worldwide drive and sustain the foreign expansion of the firm. It is hard to believe that such a global player is based on a small and peripheral island like St. Barth, and yet this is the firm's crucial and natural competitive advantage.

METHODOLOGY AND RESEARCH DESIGN

This research makes use of a qualitative case study approach, using the qualitative coding of content analysis, to explore the niche strategy approach adopted by Ligne St. Barth in order to identify entrepreneurial elements and their contribution to the firm's internationalization. Case study methodology recommends using only one case when it is a critical case that tests the theory; such a case can then be used to confirm, challenge or extend a theoretical approach (Yin, 2009).

Qualitative coding allows all segments of the information collected to be reviewed. From this, one can then produce initial categories of meaning, based on frequent comparisons (Hernandez, Fernandez, & Baptista, 2006). Content analysis refers to a systematic interpretation of textual, visual or audio material, such as newspaper editorials, television news, advertisements, public speeches and other units of analysis. Through the development of analytical constructs or categories, content analysis allows the researcher to get to know the context and, specifically, the network of correlations that are assumed to explain how available texts inform any hypotheses and the conditions under which these correlations could change. Analytical constructs also ensure that an analysis of given texts aligns with the texts' context of use (Krippendorff, 2004).

In the process of gathering and classification of the data related to Ligne St. Barth, we classified the gathered data under two headings. External data were drawn from magazine articles, newspapers, blogs, web pages, videos and university databases (Wiley, EBSCOhost, Proquest). Internal data were provided exclusively through the company webpage and YouTube videos about the business. The coding process suggested three main categories (Creativity & Innovation, Knowledge Acquisition and Caribbean Traditions) and three subcategories (High-Quality Products & Processes, Network Relationships and Internationalization). The categories and subcategories emerged from specific codes that emerged from an analysis of data drawn from 37 external and 51 internal documents. For validation, we asked a group of international business graduate students to interpret the data and come up with their own analytic categories. Two additional categories were suggested: Luxury and Lifestyle Experience; both were subsumed and consolidated as part of the Caribbean Traditions category.

LIGNE ST. BARTH, CARIBBEAN LUXURY AND LIFESTYLE AT INTERNATIONAL LEVEL

The interesting issue in this firm is that its niche market approach is driven by the entrepreneurially oriented strategy of the owners, who capitalize on St. Barth as a luxury French Caribbean location with its own established brand in order to reach its own international markets. For that, entrepreneurs were obliged, from day one, to develop highly sophisticated products and services. Location and place association is at the core of the firm's growth strategy.

The Caribbean Traditions category orients the positioning of Ligne St. Barth in its international niche market. Externally and internally, Caribbean Traditions is the platform that positions the brand as representative of that particular lifestyle. For the purposes of this study, Caribbean Traditions includes the glamorous and refined Caribbean lifestyle, the use of Caribbean plants as raw material for therapeutic treatments and luxury—the idea that well-being is more important than price. The location of the firm on the island of St. Barthélemy is an important driver for the firm's penetration of foreign niche markets with unique, refined and high-quality products. The entrepreneurial propensity of the firm's business owners can be seen in their creativity and innovation in combining technology with Caribbean traditions in a unique and efficient manner. The main features of the products are their composition (organic—no preservatives, artificial colors or perfumes), formulation and purification processes.

The Creativity & Innovation category is a feature of the firm that reinforces its internationalization process. Creativity leads to innovation, an attitude that drives the company toward new ideas, through which entrepreneurs convert opportunities into marketable concepts generating change and exports (Kuratko & Hodgetts, 2004). Innovation and exports are complementary strategies for the growth of SMEs (Golovko & Valentini, 2011). Participation in export markets can promote organizational learning and, thus, strengthen firm performance in innovation and quality (Golovko et al., 2011). Firms that habitually generate high levels of entrepreneurial innovation are able to acquire an external knowledge base (Kreiser, 2011).

Creativity & Innovation was manifested from the firm's inception. This category involves positioning the core brand as representative of the island's particular lifestyle. The island is known as the new St. Tropez of France in the Caribbean, and St. Barth's residents and visitors include artists, entrepreneurs, millionaires and business tycoons (MacDonogh, 1999). The brand appeals to the luxury tourism traditions of France and the Caribbean; visitors expect to find high-quality, limited-edition, handmade products that are unique to that geographical area. The brand appeals to the service associated with the product, in a specific, Caribbean setting. The Caribbean island dimension gives tourism products an important specificity that allows these economies to establish marketing strategies based on the differentiation and diversification of health-related tourism and hydrotherapy products. The advantage of being located on a *Caribbean* island allows them to overcome the natural barriers of single-island isolation and appeal to a regional brand that enjoys enormous recognition (Crusol & Vellas, 1996). Creativity & Innovation is also reflected in the firm's ability to transform its resources (raw materials, knowledge, social networks, family heritage, international brand of Caribbean tourism and experience in related sectors) into business-oriented assets.

Innovation positively affects another analytic category, Knowledge Acquisition, by strengthening the firm's commitment to open-mindedness and its receptivity to any resulting new information (Wang, 2008). The creativity of the owners of Ligne St. Barth enables the development of a highly sophisticated and differentiated offer that requires the same sector as a tool of international success. Thus, this industry (professional beauty) is highly globalized. This propensity for knowledge development is consistent with the strong presence of intellectual capital in island states and territories (Henry & Watkins, 2013). Human capital constantly develops intellectual capital to compensate for deficiencies that exist due to a lack of resources or organizational assets in the businesses in these countries (Henry et al., 2013); others have called this the island resilience that emerges in response to a perceived state of economic vulnerability (Briguglio et al., 2004).

The High-Quality Products & Processes subcategory reinforces international expansion, as the products and processes fully comply with the international quality standards of this niche market.

Establishing Network Relationships (such as by acquiring partners, ambassadors and customers and maintaining their loyalty and commitment to the firm and its brands) drives the internationalization of Ligne St. Barth. Network relationships favor the development of new skills and the acquisition and exploitation of new knowledge that can be transformed into opportunities to develop market-specific knowledge (Chetty & Campbell-Hunt, 2003; Coviello, 2006; Coviello & Munro, 1995, 1997). Networking helps SMEs gain knowledge about foreign institutions so that they are aware of current rules and regulations, customs and practices so that they can integrate their products with similar global brands at minimal cost and error while gaining in familiarity with the global business environment (Senik, Scott-Ladd, Entrekin, & Adham, 2011). Similarly, social networks can become business networks, helping the firm to locate and source those resources necessary for its internationalization (Ellis & Pecotich, 2001) and to find and seize opportunities offered by international trade, strategic alliances and the generation of knowledge, trust, and solidarity (BarNir & Smith, 2002; Ellis, 2011; Zhou, Wu, & Luo, 2007). These two subcategories contextualize the firm's ability to exploit opportunities and networks to expand its product portfolio and diversify its forms of internationalization (e.g., direct export to joint ventures and wholly owned subsidiaries).

The codes identified in the process of creating categories and subcategories show an entrepreneurial type of management dynamics. The firm's founders have shown a strong entrepreneurial orientation, allowing the firm to offer a product with intrinsic characteristics that make it unique in its kind, form and use. The place-derived uniqueness of the product explains the linking of the firm to affluent partners and prestigious networks, which, in turn, helps ensure its successful internationalization. From the very beginning, the business, commercial and product features of the operation were part of the Caribbean tradition. Thus, Ligne St. Barth is linked to and embedded in a specific cultural heritage, which guarantees its authenticity and helps explain why it is considered today to be an icon of the island jurisdiction it represents.

In the process of validating and contextualizing the case study, a new category called Luxury Brand emerged from the firm's internationalization process. This category confirms Ligne St. Barth as an international luxury brand, positioned at the same level as such other luxury brands as Jaguar, Mont Blanc or Porsche.

Caribbean Traditions (35%) and Internationalization of the Firm (21%) emerged as the categories most frequently identified in the data analysis. Since the firm's foundation, Caribbean Traditions has been the quintessential signature of its international expansion in niche markets. This characteristic promotes and is promoted by Creativity and Innovation (15%) and High-Quality Products and Processes (12%) as basic elements that reinforce the internationalization of Ligne St. Barth. In terms of external and internal data, Network Relationships (9%) emerges as an entrepreneurial element that works intrinsically with High-Quality Products & Processes (11%), strengthening the firm's international activity.

CONCLUDING REMARKS AND EMERGING ISSUES

Since its inception in 1983, Ligne St. Barth has maintained control and autonomy over its product and strategy, emboldened by the very unique context in which the small firm was set up and the specific insider experience and knowledge of the founding owners. Throughout the firm's first 10 years, the owners developed skills at the management level (e.g., acquisition, knowledge management and transfer, processing), which allowed them to capitalize on their business operations. The subsidiary formation, initiated in 1993, was part of the firm's international expansion strategy.

Ligne St. Barth has taken advantage of the international juncture between the luxury market, the health and beauty industry and tourism, namely, the importance of the physical and emotional health of consumers belonging to a professional and highly mobile class with purchasing power for discretionary spending on goods and services. This focus coincided serendipitously with the mid- to late-1990s boom and worldwide expansion of trade in many industries and was strengthened by the liberalization of barriers in telecommunications and the development of e-commerce. This communication revolution allowed small businesses to secure access to knowledge, products or markets that previously would have been impossible to obtain. SMEs forthcoming from small island states and territories have been enormously advantaged by the opportunities presented by the World Wide Web in advertising their very existence, their location and their products and services. Business does not follow automatically, of course. Ligne St. Barth is a clear example of the need for strong networks; but it has had positive start.

In 1998, the company formed a partnership with the five-star hotel La Cure and introduced a new business concept (consulting): St. Barth Treatments by Ligne St. Barth. In 2001, the company, supported by the already positioned brand, safely executed a new approach through the expansion of its portfolio of business activities (products and services) with the introduction of perfumes, the launch of *Spa & Travel* and the customization of St. Barth Treatments. This trend, especially throughout the 2000s, can be explained by the results of Knowledge Acquisition and management (High-Quality Products & Processes and Network Relationships). Indeed, for Ligne St. Barth, the 2000s represent a transformative evolution of the firm from a microenterprise with an internationally distributed magazine to a consulting small firm with a Munich-based European subsidiary for marketing and distribution.

Sales for the U.S. market are organized from the headquarters in Gustavia, St. Barthélemy. The company appears to have pursued a growth strategy of vertical and horizontal integration, always focusing on international markets. Ligne St. Barth is assumed to be very conscious in maintaining a structure of operation and distribution exclusive for the European market, even if there are exclusive distributors in the United States. Ligne St. Barth has opened its niche market through e-commerce to expand the experience obtained through visiting the spa to living it in your home (the most recent video clips from the company show this trend). The company is aware of the behavior of the modern consumer and the fact that Internet purchasing has flourished, taking advantage of the lifestyle of consumers who make their purchases online. During the expansion period, the owners displayed a high level of entrepreneurship. They were able to maximize their knowledge and relationships while also identifying skilled human resources to enhance creativity and innovation assertively. The best example was the recent launch in 2012 of its Deep Sea product, a small-scale artistic luxury product devised after years of research. Deep Sea advertising again evokes the firm's country-brand marketing communication tool for positioning in the luxury niche market of natural beauty products in which high quality and innovations are still competitive drivers for small firms in niche markets. Then maintaining positioning in niche markets depends on how the firm is able to differentiate its product and provide value added to customers, such as, in Ligne St. Barth case, high quality, good customer perception, reliable information and company image. In niche strategy, the firm focuses on the customer and provide the customer with the products they need now and in the future (Dalgic et al., 1994). That means that the firm must be proactive or entrepreneurial. The firm has to forecast future customer needs. Niche market firms can involve their customers in the design of the product; the firms are halfway there (Dalgic et al., 1994).

Highly entrepreneurial firms are characterized by constant innovations and the ability to capitalize in those niche markets better than multinational firms (MNFs). Long-term relationships with partners and customers are necessary to succeed with a niche market strategy. Through relationship marketing, entrepreneurially oriented firms are then better positioned to develop and manage strong network relationships and customer relationships than are large firms because these relations constitute intangible assets for competitiveness, particularly for small firms and also for INVs (Dalgic et al., 1994; Shani et al., 1992). "Successful niche marketing appears to require the use of specialization, relationship marketing, developing internal dynamic capabilities and building protective barriers" (Toften et al., 2012). In the case study, we found that the success of Ligne St. Barth as an INV can be explained because of the competences of the owners in know-how to acquire resources to capitalize in the uniqueness of their product portfolio and the marketing strategies focus on specialization and quality to develop and position Ligne St. Barth as a luxury brand in international niche markets. In fact, there is a positive relation between niche strategy and internationalization of SMEs. Niche strategy frequently characterizes INVs as well as the ones that internationalize quickly and intensely (Zucchella & Palamara, 2007). Strongly performing small firms in niche markets belong to the business-to-business market, where direct contact with global industrial customers supports customer orientation and problem solving and strengthens client relationships without the need for large investments in marketing and promotion (Zucchella & Palamara,

2007). The adoption of a niche strategy is not just a defensive move of firms looking for protected market spaces, but it entails being entrepreneurially proactive and innovative in shaping market niches and not just discovering them (Zucchella & Palamara, 2007), as Ligne St. Barth has shown. Likewise, the global competition and the behaviors of large MNFs, which confirmed their ability to enter both small market niches and mass markets, impose a dynamic strategic approach on small firms in their niches. Constant innovation and creativity constitute, among other things, important management assets for Ligne St. Barth to survive in this highly competitive sector.

REFERENCES

Architectural Digest. (1983). Gentle geometry: Mr. & Mrs. David Rockefeller's house in St. Barth. October, pp. 120–125.

Baldacchino, G. (2010). Island brands and "the island" as a brand: Insights from immigrant entrepreneurs on Prince Edward Island. *International Journal of Entrepreneurship & Small Business, 9*(4), 379–393.

BarNir, A., & Smith, K. (2002). Interfirm alliances in the small business: The role of social networks. *Journal of Small Business Management, 40*(3), 219–232.

Beauty San. (2013). *Ligne St. Barth.* Retrieved from www.beautysanspa.com/ligne-st-barth-en

Bourdieu, P. (1979). *La distinction: Critique social du jugement.* Paris: Editions de Minuit.

Briguglio, L., & Kisanga, E. J. (Eds.). (2004). *Economic vulnerability and resilience of small states.* Malta: Formatek.

Cabrol, M., & Niemvo, F. (2009). The internationalization of French new ventures: The case of the Rhone-Alps region. *European Management Journal, 27*(4), 255–267.

Chetty, S., & Campbell-Hunt, C. (2003). Explosive international growth and problems of success amongst small and medium-sized firms. *International Small Business Journal, 21*(1), 5–27.

Cousin, B., & Chauvin, S. (2013). Islanders, immigrants and millionaires: The dynamics of upper-class segregation on St. Barths, French West Indies. In I. Hay (Ed.), *Geographies of the super-rich* (pp. 186–200). Cheltenham: Edward Elgar.

Coviello, N. E. (2006). The network dynamics of international new ventures. *Journal of International Business Studies, 37*(5), 713–731.

Coviello, N. E., & Munro, H. J. (1995). Growing the entrepreneurial firm: Networking for international market development. *European Journal of Marketing, 29*(1), 49–61.

Coviello, N. E., & Munro, H. J. (1997). Network relationships and the internationalization process of small software firms. *International Business Review, 6*(4), 361–386.

Crusol, J., & Vellas, F. (1996). *Le tourisme et la Caraïbe.* Paris: Harmattan.

Dalgic, T., & Leeuw, M. (1994). Niche marketing revisited: Concept, applications and some European cases. *European Journal of Marketing, 28*(4), 39–55.

Deep Sea. (2014). Deep sea dream: Ligne St. Barth. Retrieved from www.youtube.com/watch?v=IwojQoUsWF8

Doumenge, F. (1988). Considerations for small island development today. In G. Baldacchino & R. Greenwood (Eds.), *Competing strategies for socio-economic development of small islands* (pp. 337–347). Charlottetown, Canada: Institute of Island Studies, University of Prince Edward Island.

Ellis, P. (2011). Social ties and international entrepreneurship: Opportunities and constraints affecting firm internationalization. *Journal of International Business Studies, 42*(1), 99–127.

Ellis, P., & Pecotich, A. (2001). Social factors influencing export initiation in small and medium-sized enterprises. *Journal of Marketing Research, 38*(1), 119–130.

Forbes.com. (2011). *Dialed in Saint Barth.* Retrieved from www.sbhonline.com/forums/threads/67233-Forbes-com-Dialed-In-Saint-Barth

Golovko, E., & Valentini, G. (2011). Exploring the complementarity between innovation and export for SMEs growth. *Journal of International Business Studies, 42*(3), 362–380.

Henry, L., & Watkins, D. (2013). *Intellectual capital in developing micro-states: The case of Caribbean SMEs.* 5th European Conference on Intellectual Capital 2013, 11–12 April 2013, Bilbao, Spain: 204–212. United Kingdom: Academic Conferences Ltd.

Hernández, R., Fernández, C., & Baptista, P. (2006). *Metodología de la Investigación.* México: McGraw-Hill/Interamericana de México.

Johanson, J., & Vahlne, J. (1977). The internationalization process of the firm—a model of knowledge development and increasing foreign market commitments. *Journal of International Business Studies, 8*(1), 23–32.

Johanson, J., & Wiedersheim, F. (1975). The internationalization of the firm: Four Swedish cases. *Journal of Management Studies, 12*(3), 305–323.

Kotler, P., & Keller, K. L. (2006). *Marketing management,* 13th edition. New York, NY: Pearson.

Kreiser, P. M. (2011). Entrepreneurial orientation and organizational learning: The impact of network range and network closure. *Entrepreneurship Theory and Practice, 35*(5), 1025–1050.

Krippendorff, K. (2004). *Content analysis: An introduction to its methodology.* Thousand Oaks, CA: Sage.

Kuratko, D. F., & Hodgetts, R. M. (2004). *Entrepreneurship: Theory, process and practice.* Mason, OH: Thomson/South-Western.

Lipovetsky, G., & Roux, E. (2003). *Le luxe éternel: De l'âge du sacré au temps des marques.* Paris: Gallimard.

Lumpkin, G. T., & Dess, G. G. (1996). Clarifying the entrepreneurial orientation construct and linking it to performance. *The Academy of Management Review, 21*(1), 135–172.

Macdonogh, G. (1999, 19 April). Small, but perfectly prosperous. *New Statesman.* Retrieved from www.newstatesman.com/node/134575

McDougall, P. P., Shane, S., & Oviatt, B. M. (1994). Explaining the formation of international new ventures: The limits of theories from international business research. *Journal of Business Venturing, 9*(6), 469–487.

Nash, K. C. (2012). *St. Barts travel adventures.* New York, NY: Hunter Publishing.

Oviatt, B. M., & McDougall, P. P. (1994). Toward a theory of international new ventures. *Journal of International Business Studies, 25*(1), 45–64.

Oviatt, B. M., & McDougall, P. P. (1995). Global start-ups: Entrepreneurs on a worldwide stage. *Academy of Management Executives, 9*(2), 30–43.

Senik, C., Scott-Ladd, B., Entrekin, L., & Adham, K. A. (2011). Networking and internationalization of SMEs in emerging economies. *Journal of International Entrepreneurship, 9*(4), 259–281.

Shani, D., & Chalasani, S. (1992). Exploiting niches using relationship marketing. *The Journal of Services Marketing, 6*(4), 43–52.

Theismann, V. (n.d.). *The lost paradise of Remy de Haenen.* Retrieved from www.edenrockhotel.com/pdf/RemyDeHaenen.pdf

Toften, K., & Hammervoll, T. (2012). Niche marketing research: Status and challenges. *Marketing Intelligence and Planning, 31*(3), 272–285.

Veblen, T. (1899/1970). *The theory of the leisure class: An economic study of institutions*. London: Unwin.

Wang, K. (2008). Entrepreneurial orientation, learning orientation, and firm performance. *Entrepreneurship Theory and Practice, 32*(4), 635–657.

Wiklund, J., & Shepherd, D. (2003). Knowledge-based resources, entrepreneurial orientation, and the performance of small and medium-sized businesses. *Strategic Management Journal, 24*(13), 1307–1314.

Willett, M. (2013). House of the day: Steve Martin is selling his spectacular St. Barts villa for $11.4 Million. *Seattle PI*, June 3. Retrieved from www.seattlepi.com/technology/businessinsider/article/HOUSE-OF-THE-DAY-Steve-Martin-Is-Selling-His-4573078.php

Williams, D. A. (2011). Impact of firm size and age on the export behavior of small locally owned firms: Fresh insights. *Journal of International Entrepreneurship, 9*(2), 152–174.

Yin, R. (2009). *Case study research: Design and methods (applied social research methods)*. Thousand Oaks, CA: Sage.

Zhou, L., Wu, W., & Lou, X. (2007). Internationalization and the performance of born-global SMEs: The mediating role of social networks. *Journal of International Business Studies, 38*(4), 673–690.

Zucchella, A., & Palamara. (2007). Niche strategy and export performance. *Advances in International Marketing, 17*(1), 63–87.

9 LYSI in Iceland

Purifying the Gold of the Sea

Gylfi Dalmann Aðalsteinsson and
Runólfur Smári Steinþórsson

INTRODUCTION

Iceland, a small island state located in the North Atlantic, is the home country and base of LYSI Ltd, a local company with a global reach that has sought to be and remains at the forefront of knowledge on the production of marine lipids, which are omega-3 fatty acids. LYSI was established in 1938, and the basis of its foundation was that of serving as a key provider of vitamins and nutrition to both people and livestock.

In this chapter, we review the sociopolitical and economic contexts that led to the emergence and growth of LYSI. We also briefly chart the now 70-plus-year journey of this company, identifying highlights and key strategic decisions along the way. We also comment on the powerful corporate reputation of this firm and how it aligns nicely with the Icelandic brand. This review summarizes the challenges involved in LYSI's development; they will hopefully serve as critical learning points in comparison to and reflections on similar stories by small businesses based in other small island jurisdictions.

Up in the North Atlantic, Iceland was quite a remote and isolated country in the early 20th century. At that time, transportation, the important lifeline to and from the country, was limited; a few shipping routes were served on a regular basis mainly by the Icelandic Steamship Company, established in 1914, and the Danish shipping company DFDS. Iceland was then a very poor country but on the brink of modernization. It had a population of around 80,000 and a GDP per capita that was 50% of that in Denmark, with as much as 70% of the population working in fisheries and agriculture (Hannibalsson, 2009). Fishing and related industries still employed 12% of the labor force in 2002 (Baldacchino & Vella Bonnici, 2006, p. 8).

Today, a century later, Iceland is a prosperous and modern country, well connected both by sea and by air. The population now is around 325,000 inhabitants, and the GDP per capita is similar to that of other Scandinavian countries. However, with a land mass of 103,000 km², Iceland is not a geographically small country and is roughly the same size as South Korea. Moreover, if one adds the Exclusive Economic Zone (EEZ) of Iceland, it has quite a large area under its administrative control (Central Bank of Iceland, 2012).

A small population inevitably means that the local economy is dependent on foreign trade, as there are limits to both the scope and scale of production for the restricted local market. Economic activity is also often concentrated when it comes to production of goods and services. Iceland is highly dependent on the importation of inputs, raw material and goods that are not produced in the country. Economic activity in Iceland is clustered around a few sectors: mainly fisheries, energy-intensive industries and tourism when it comes to foreign trade (export revenues). Iceland's industrial specialization is, to a great extent, path dependent: a large EEZ, abundant and partly cheap (water, geothermal and wind) energy supplies and pristine nature play a pivotal role in the Icelandic economy (Central Bank of Iceland, 2012).

Small states are often economically vulnerable and politically flexible, as was epitomized in Iceland in the 2008 financial crisis: Iceland was one of its first dramatic casualties (Danielsson & Zoega, 2009). But Iceland has also recovered rather fast because of its political and economic flexibility (Aðalsteinsson & Haraldsdottir, 2013). As Baldacchino (2005, p. 34) has pointed out, small jurisdictions need to be "able to respond quickly and flexibly to exogenous changes and shocks"; and social capital might be a key explanatory variable for explaining small island resilience in the face of structural vulnerabilities.

At the turn of the 19th century, Iceland was one of the most backward and least developed countries in Europe. Iceland's modernization and economic development were triggered and then fueled by industrialization in the fisheries sector. Iceland's economic development started late in the 19th century, but it gained serious momentum after the first trawler came to Iceland in 1905. The Second World War marked an important milestone; unlike most countries, the effect of the war greatly enriched Iceland. The country had declared "perpetual neutrality" when it became a sovereign nation in 1918, but Britain unilaterally decided to occupy Iceland in 1940. This action was then followed by an even more substantial American military presence from 1941, with more than 50,000 Allied soldiers. The presence of so many military personnel greatly increased domestic demand: the price of fish rose sharply, and there was practically full employment (Whitehead, 1998).

The American military presence ensured there were no shortages in Iceland, unlike elsewhere in Europe; imports from the United States, which represented less than 2% of Icelandic imports before the Second World War broke out, rose rapidly to 65% by 1944 (Ingimundarson, 1996, p. 21). Far better access to the U.S. market had a positive effect on the export of fish oil and related products. The price of fish products quadrupled during the war, and their value peaked during the last stages of the war. At that time, they represented almost one tenth of Iceland's total exports (Johnson & Jónsdóttir, 2008).

Iceland today enjoys the 16th highest GDP per capita in the world. Its wealth still remains inextricably linked to the economic activity of fishing and related industries. Iceland's full independence in 1944 would have been harder to sustain from an economic perspective without this economic pillar. Just as for many other islanders, the sea has been and oddly remains Iceland's key resource (Baldacchino, 2004; Dolman, 1988). Iceland was badly hit by the 2008 financial crisis; a bold vision that this small country up north in the Atlantic Ocean could be the home of a financial center on a European or Western scale was blown to pieces. But the economy was practically saved by the increased production of exports from the traditional sectors, fisheries and ocean-related activities being some of the lingering core elements of the Icelandic economy.

HISTORY OF ICELANDIC FISH OIL: THE GOLD OF THE SEA

The history of fish oil in Iceland can be traced back almost as long as the country has been inhabited. The first settlers in the late 900s brought the knowledge of producing fish oil with them from Norway. The name of fish oil in Icelandic, *lýsi*, is drawn from the word "light"; and, as the name implies, it was an important source of light for centuries. In the Nordic countries, the oil made from the blubber of marine animals (seal, shark, walrus and whale) was primarily used, a role taken up by vegetable fat in Southern Europe (Johnson & Jónsdóttir, 2008). Lamps that used fish oil as their primary source of fuel were not replaced by kerosene lamps until the late 1800s.

The first documentation of fish oil is from 1096 AD in an ancient law that stated that each man was required to pay the church where he was to be buried a tax in the form of fish oil (Johnsen, 1958, p. 121); thus, the oil served as a form of currency. In the early 1300s, fish oil and stockfish became Iceland's most valuable export commodities, surpassing Icelandic-made cloth. The oldest written document of trade with fish oil and its value is a ruling from Niðarós (modern-day Trondheim) in 1340. Norwegians who had sailed to Iceland for trading purposes were required to pay tolls with fish oil and stockfish even though they preferred to pay with cloth, something that was not accepted by the Icelanders because stockfish and fish oil were considered to be far more valuable goods (Jóhannesson, 1958).

There were important developments in northern Europe that did increase the demand for Icelandic fish oil in the Middle Ages. Cities were growing, and some of the streets were lit with oil lamps; but in some of these urbanizing spaces, it was fish oil that was used as the light source. Merchants bought a great deal of fish oil in the 14th and 15th centuries, but later most of production was exported to the growing city of Copenhagen. Fish oil was thus a valuable commodity, and its price remained stable, unlike price variations of stockfish and cloth. In the year 1630, Iceland exported 1,445 barrels of fish oil; in 1880, this had risen to 9,000 barrels (Johnson & Jónsdóttir, 2008).

During this time, fish oil was also used to clear sulfur that was processed from mines, some of which were located in Iceland, and used to produce gunpowder for the Royal Danish Army. King Fridrik II of Denmark decreed in 1562 that he would purchase all the fish oil produced in Icelandic towns, and a year later, he proclaimed his ownership of the sulfur mines in the Myvatn area in northeast Iceland (Johnson & Jónsdóttir, 2008).

In Iceland, fish oil was also used as a supplement to animal feeds and as an application against some animal diseases. It was also consumed by people during times of hardship, used for cooking and to soften the often hard and rough clothing produced from animal skins. Its healing powers were also praised, but how it worked exactly or why was unknown for a long time. Cod liver oil was considered to possess healing powers against sicknesses that were common among children. In Britain in the 1850s, fish oil was used against tuberculosis, malnutrition and other preventable diseases caused by poverty (Johnson & Jónsdóttir, 2008, p. 17).

The healing power of lysi was well known, even though the exact reasons were not discovered until the early 20th century. It was Sir Edward Mellanby (1918), a British doctor, who allegedly confirmed that cod liver oil contained essential micronutrients (Mohr, 2008; Semba, 2012). The American researcher Elmer McCollum was one among several researchers that were also studying the health benefits of cod liver oil in the early 20th century. His studies led to the identification of an active nutritional compound that could clarify the benefits, named vitamin A. Further studies by McCollum and colleagues (1922) on modified cod liver oil resulted in the identification of another active compound, this time vitamin D (Mohr, 2008).

This was the context to and the basis of knowledge of the qualities of fish oil. In Iceland, fish oil had been an important product for many reasons and purposes. Economically, the marine lipids had already proved valuable, and the new knowledge about the vitamins in cod liver oil further strengthened the production of cod liver oil as a business opportunity. LYSI Ltd. could exploit this tradition while now taking it further into an export direction as international demand picked up.

THE EVENTS LEADING TO THE ESTABLISHMENT OF LYSI

The background to the establishment of LYSI can be traced back to the year 1918, when Tryggvi Ólafsson, after graduation from the Commercial College in Iceland, got to know about the production of fish oil through his first job in Siglufjörður (Aðalsteinsson, Kjaran, & Gislason, 2006). A few years later as a businessman operating a coal store, owner of fishing vessels and exporter of fish oil, in company with his brother Þórður Ólafsson, and as an entrepreneur in Iceland, he further pursued the idea that there was much more to be known about the qualities of fish oil, which was looked upon by many as a raw commodity having no potential for processing and value added. Based on this interest and belief, he set up a small research laboratory at his own home and started testing fish oil and the different ion), a US$50,000 prepayment for the goods and a US$7,500 loan that made it possible for the brothers to build the production plant needed to produce the volume of fish oil required to fulfill the contract (Aðalsteinsson et al., 2006; Johnson & Jónsdóttir, 2008: 54).

THE ESTABLISHMENT OF LYSI

LYSI Ltd. was thus established in January 1938, with Tryggvi Ólafsson as the largest shareholder, holding almost 75% of the stock; his brother Þórður Ólafsson had most of the remaining 25%, and three other individuals held minor shares (Johnson & Jónsdóttir, 2008, p. 51). At first, LYSI purchased fish oil that was produced locally in various fishing towns throughout the country, but, after building its new factory, it had the equipment necessary to produce the fish oil on site. Soon, LYSI was collecting all the discarded fish liver from the fish that were being landed in Reykjavik. The first fully equipped factory was built in 1937, and during the first 20 years in business, LYSI sold its product almost exclusively to Upjohn. However, in the late 1950s, Upjohn lost interest in Icelandic cod liver oil. Faced with a dramatically changed market situation, LYSI needed to react and adapt quickly to the new business environment. This resulted in a change in scope and sophistication, from being a bulk supplier to being a more direct producer of consumer products.

In 1959, LYSI began producing winterized medicinal cod liver oil in consumer packaging. A year later, the company built a well-equipped laboratory, and its regular research into cod liver oil started supporting further development of LYSI products.

In the mid-1970s, a series of scientific papers based on research among Greenland's Inuit concluded that consumption of fish lipids, derived largely from whale, seal and fish, reduced the risk of coronary disease in humans (e.g., Dyerberg, Bang, & Hjorne, 1975). This information had a huge impact on consumer behavior, and consequently, cod liver oil was given a new lease on life (Sigurðsson, 1988). This information further supported LYSI's efforts in research and development, with the result that LYSI has built up a reputation of being one of the leading knowledge depositories in the field of omega-3 fatty acids and their utilization.

The company's quality policy has for a long time been based on continuous training, the production of defect-free products, research and constant improvements. A strong quality department has been backed up by an expert in-house laboratory. All employees are involved in ensuring the implementation of the quality system. The "Quality Manual" and "Operations Manual" ensure that information pertaining to the quality system is accessible, received and implemented by all concerned. Every employee is introduced to and instructed on the quality system through documentation and training courses. Ongoing training and increased competence of personnel has been a top priority (Aðalsteinsson et al., 2006).

The late 1990s charted a new era in LYSI's history as a direct manufacturer; sales rapidly expanded, and research and new product development were stronger than ever. The company received both ISO 9001 and ISO 22000 food safety certification during this time. In 2005, LYSI inaugurated its new processing plant, which was uniquely equipped for the production of marine lipids, utilizing state-of-the-art technology at all stages of processing. Three years later, a production unit for fish oil concentrates was added. In 2007, the factory was approved by the Icelandic Medicines Control Agency (IMCA) to be fully qualified as Good Manufacturing Practice for Active Pharmaceutical Ingredients, or GMP (API) compliant. The GMP (API) license for LYSI's packing department meant that the firm became the world's first cod liver oil manufacturer to be so certified. The company's sales and marketing efforts over past decades were recognized in 2007 when LYSI won the President of Iceland's Export Achievement Award for its "unique achievement in the sales and marketing of marine lipid products and for the vision the company demonstrates in product development and for the build up of knowledge and expertise in its field" (Shop Icelandic, 2014). One of the latest expansions of the company has been its fish oil refinery, completed in 2012, which doubled the company's output for fish oils, from 6,500 to 13,000 tons annually (www.lysi.is, n.d.).

Although the early financial arrangement with Upjohn helped the Ólafsson brothers establish LYSI, the initial financing for their company was entirely raised by them. The Icelandic government also provided the company with some institutional support, for example, by including them in state support programs for small enterprises. However, it is difficult to evaluate precisely the extent to which LYSI has benefitted directly from these programs. The Icelandic state has also been supportive of LYSI's export drive by including the company's managers among overseas business delegations and trade missions led by Icelandic diplomats (Aðalsteinsson et al., 2006).

LYSI has now developed a brand reputation as a company associated with producing and marketing a wide range of health products with some very unique features. These include cod liver oil, halibut liver oil, shark liver oil and other fish oils suitable for human consumption. All these products are rich in vitamins and omega-3 polyunsaturated fatty acids, which are now known to be likely contributors to the reduction of cholesterol levels in human blood and to somewhat improve the condition of the heart (Aðalsteinsson et al., 2006).

These products, all sold under the brand name LYSI, are marketed as health products with very unique features. The company promotes the brand via its distributors, via the Internet and by direct and online advertising. Moreover, a unique production process based on steam, first introduced by the Ólafsson duo in the 1940s, guarantees the quality of the products (www.lysi.is, n.d.).

LYSI remained a family business until 1998, when Icelandic investors bought shares in the company. When this happened, LYSI became a joint stock company. Today, Ólafsson's granddaughter Katrín Petursdóttir manages the company and its 115 employees. Petursdóttir has a business diploma from the Technical University of Iceland and managerial experience in the marine industry. The company's production team now requires especially skilled workers, such as biochemists, nutritionists, quality managers and marine specialists (www.lysi.is, 2014).

LYSI is first and foremost an exporting company with sales to almost 100 countries worldwide, 30 to 40 of which are regular clients. These include the United States, Canada, the U.K., France, Finland, Denmark, Poland, Japan and China. LYSI has also developed an important home market in Iceland. The company has a market share of more than 50% of the Icelandic health food market. For LYSI, the domestic market plays an essential role as a benchmark, a testing ground and a research site (Aðalsteinsson et al., 2006).

Today, LYSI offers a wide range of marine lipids with variable levels of omega-3 EPA/DHA fatty acids. Products can be tailor made according to customer requirements by blending different oils and/or adding vitamins, antioxidants and flavor (Natural Fish Oils, Bulk and Consumer Products, n.d.). LYSI produces consumer goods but also delivers bulk products in variable package sizes: 22 kg (buckets), 190 kg (drums), 900 kg (intermediate bulk containers), 21,000 kg (tank containers) and in flexi-tanks. Batch sizes normally range from 2 to 65 metric tons; however, standard products can be made available in smaller batches if and when required. The exported products are the same as those sold on the domestic market, although the design of the packaging may be different, in accordance with consumer culture, tastes and nuances (Aðalsteinsson et al., 2006).

LYSI has grown considerably in the latest decade. It registered a turnover of US$15m and employed 45 employees in 2002; 10 years later, its turnover had grown to US$90m, with a staff complement of 115 employees. It weathered the 2008 financial crisis well. On average, exports represent 80% to 85% of the company's output by volume. LYSI has more than 50% of domestic market share when it comes to health products consumed in Iceland (*Frjáls Verslun* 300 stærstu, 2002–2012).

DISCUSSION

LYSI has developed into a leading company when it comes to research, product development and sales of marine lipids. Its location in Iceland allows the company to associate itself with that country's widespread reputation for pureness and high health standards while maintaining access to raw material—indeed, one of the few locally available sources of raw material in Iceland that is otherwise a waste from its fishing industry. LYSI has no problem associating itself explicitly with its country of origin. Its slogan, *It's Pure, It's Clean, It's Icelandic*, makes a clear statement of identity and association.

For decades, LYSI has recognized the importance of research and development (R&D), a factor that has led to the development of new products targeted toward specific markets. The continuing success of the company's R&D enables enhanced product and analytical-method development, production support, close cooperation with developers of medical products and research cooperation with different academic institutions like University of Iceland and Matís, the Icelandic Food and Biotech R&D.

LYSI's advanced refinery is specially designed for flexibility and customized solutions. Independent processing steps provide the opportunity to work on different types of oil simultaneously, allowing LYSI to maintain the shortest lead times possible. LYSI uses the latest technology to help ensure compliance with strict regulations and meet customer requirements for low contaminant levels in the final product.

LYSI has an in-house quality control and R&D laboratory that is well equipped and fully accredited to ISO 9001 and ISO 22000 standards, as well as good manufacturing practice standards (GMP), led by a chemist approved by the American Oil Chemists' Society (AOCS). Moreover, LYSI has extended the scope of these standards by incorporating special requirements for sanitary measures, work surroundings and premises, which is a prerequisite for obtaining authorization for pharmaceutical production and packaging.

Today, LYSI maintains a leadership position in its field, fuelled by expertise in manufacturing high-demand fish oil products from both Icelandic fish stock and imported crude fish oils from other parts of the world. Getting the most out of its extensive equipment and accumulated know-how, LYSI offers its customers a broad range of natural health products. LYSI has been building a relationship with its suppliers and customers for decades, which is central to its solid business model. LYSI works with its suppliers to source raw materials in accordance with quality standards to ensure that customers receive the wholesome products they expect and deserve. LYSI has been able to build a good reputation among its clients based on its accomplishments and quality products. This reputation is shared and consolidated by other stakeholders such as suppliers and local banks. This is due to its long association with the traditional fishing industry and because of the knowledge that resides within the company. LYSI's primary goal is to continue as a reliable producer of marine products geared to the improvement of health and quality of life. The link between leadership in research and development on one hand and marketing and sales on the other is also obvious to the management and owners of LYSI. Building on more than 70 years of operational experience, LYSI remains among the foremost of all firms engaged in research and product development in the field of marine lipids. Not bad at all for an Icelandic company.

Iceland may not have any gold left to mine beneath the earth, but it has lots of liquid gold left to harvest in the sea. While LYSI's evolution and development are somewhat unique, this is also one other powerful example of a locally owned company from a small island state that has developed a strong brand identity crafted around a dependable, mainly locally available and high-value-added product that is associated with Iceland's enduring flagship- and resource-based industry.

REFERENCES

Aðalsteinsson, G.D., & Haraldsdottir, H.V. (2013). Human resource managers in Iceland: Different duties after the economic collapse. *European Journal of Management, 13*(3), 137–146.

Aðalsteinsson, G.D., Kjaran, J.I., & Gislason, B. (2006). *Nissos manual, Icelandic version.* Reykjavik: Viðskiptafræðistofnun. Network of Islands for Small Scale Organizational Success (NISSOS) Project supported by the European Commission's Leonardo da Vinci Program.

Baldacchino, G. (2004). The coming of age of island studies. *Tijdschrift voor Economische en Sociale Geografie, 95*(3), 272–283.

Baldacchino, G. (2005). The contribution of "social capital" to economic growth: Lessons from island jurisdictions. *The Round Table: Commonwealth Journal of International Affairs, 94*(1), 31–46.

Baldacchino, G., & Vella Bonnici, J. (2006). *Successful small business from small islands.* Mimeo. Retrieved from: www.islandscholar.ca/download_ds/ir%3Air-batch6–5739/OBJ/ir_ir-batch6–5739.pdf

Central Bank of Iceland. (2012). *Economy of Iceland.* Retrieved from www.cb.is/library/Skr%C3%A1arsafn---EN/Economy-of-Iceland/2012/EOI_2012.pdf

Danielsson, J., & Zoega, G. (2009). *The collapse of a country.* March 12. Retrieved from www.hi.is/files/skjol/felagsvisindasvid/GZ_og_JDeng-published-3-jdgz-final.pdf

Dolman, A. J. (1988). Book review. *Development & Change, 19,* 173–176.

Dyerberg, J., Bang, H. O., & Hjorne, N. (1975). Fatty acid composition of the plasma lipids in Greenland Eskimos. *American Journal of Clinical Nutrition, 28*(9), 958–966.

Frjáls verslun. (2002–2012). Reykjavík: Heimur.

Hannibalsson, I. (2009). What do companies in Iceland need to do in order to succeed following the collapse of the economy of that small country? In L. Robinson (Ed.), *Developments in marketing science. Proceedings of the Annual Conference of the Academy of Marketing Sciences, 23* (pp. 71–75). Baltimore, MD: Omnipress.

Ingimundarson, V. (1996). *Í Eldlínu Kaldastríðsins: Samskipti Íslands og Bandaríkjanna 1945–1960.* Reykjavík: Vaka-Helgafell.

Johnson, H. G., & Jónsdóttir, S. (2008). *Gull hafsins. Saga Lýsis hf.* Reykjavík: Lýsi hf.

Jóhannesson, J. (1958). *Íslendingasaga II.* Reykjavík: Almenna bókafélagið.

Johnsen, B. (1958). *Heilbrigði úr hafdjúpum.* Prentsmiðja Guðmundar Jóhannssonar: Reykjavík.

McCollum, E., Simmons, N., Becker, J., & Shipley, P. (1922). Studies on experimental rickets. XXI. An experimental demonstration of the existence of a vitamin which promotes calcium deposition. *J. Biol. Chem., 53,* 293–312.

Mellanby, E. (1918). The part played by an "accessory factor" in the production of experimental rickets. *Journal of Physiology (Lond.), 52,* 11–14.

Mohr, S. B. (2008). A brief history of vitamin D and cancer prevention. *Annals of Epidemiology, 19*(2), 79–83.

Semba, R. (2012). The discovery of the vitamins. *International Journal of Vitamin and Nutrition Research, 82*(5), 310–315.

Shop Icelandic. (2014). LYSI. Retrieved from http://shopicelandic.com/store/food/lysi-fish-oil

Sigurðsson, Ó. (1988, November 29). Fæðast þyngstu born í heimi í Færeyjum? *Morgunblaðið.* p. 22. Retrieved from http://timarit.is/view_page_init.jsp?issId=122196&pageId=1693696&lang=is&q=Dyerberg

Whitehead, T. (1998). *The ally who came in from the cold: A survey of Icelandic foreign policy 1946–1956.* Reykjavík: Centre for International Studies and University of Iceland Press.

www.lysi.is. (2014). Lysi. Retrieved from http://www.lysi.is

10 Coconut Power
Biofuel from Coconuts in the Solomon Islands

Carola Betzold

INTRODUCTION

Coconuts are everywhere in the South Pacific. Indeed, the coconut tree is the "tree of life" (Adkins et al., 2006), "a vital component of island ecosystems, a staple food and often the only local source of income," particularly in rural areas (Leplus, 2003, p. 1). Producing copra, the white flesh of the coconut, is a labor-intensive process, and high labor cost combined with a generally low and volatile copra price have made coconuts less attractive to farmers. Across Pacific small island states, the coconut industry has thus declined (e.g., Woodruff, 2007, p. 61).

At the same time, electricity prices on small islands are extremely high. There are serious diseconomies of scale, with wholesale power plants needing to be established on island communities that lie off the main grid. Moreover, electricity comes almost exclusively from expensive imported fossil fuel. This reliance on fossil fuel import not only strains national budgets—up to one third of all imports are petroleum imports (Woodruff, 2007, p. 15)—but make small islands also vulnerable to price shocks. Not surprisingly, then, renewable energy has recently received a lot of attention. Many small island states have expressed their interest in developing renewable energy, with some even ambitiously seeking to be fueled 100% by renewable energy in the near future. But the move toward renewable energy has also attracted the interest of private individuals who see potential economic benefits from renewable energy; indeed, renewable energy provides important business and employment opportunities for island entrepreneurs, at least in certain niches of the sector (e.g., Stuart, 2006, p. 142). One such niche is biofuel from coconut oil. Coconut fuel not only has the potential to significantly reduce the reliance on expensive fossil fuel imports; it also contributes to the revival of the coconut industry. A number of mainly private initiatives have therefore experimented with using coconut oil for transport as well as for power generation.

In the Solomon Islands, Solomon Tropical Products Ltd. (STP) ventured into the biofuel sector in the mid-2000s. By now, it is not only the largest coconut oil producer and processor in the country but also the only company with a license to feed its surplus electricity onto the grid. How did STP get there? How did the business idea emerge, and what contributed to its success? This chapter reviews STP's development of coconut biofuel with a view to "island success factors" that have been shown to be important for businesses on small islands elsewhere.

SUCCESS FACTORS FOR ISLAND BUSINESSES

Small island economies are alleged to suffer from a number of structural handicaps because of their small size, remoteness and insularity. These factors are problematic since they are associated with a range of disadvantages, including a small domestic market, limited natural and human resources, expensive transport costs, difficulties in exploiting economies of scale, vulnerability to external shocks, and dependence on a narrow range of products (Armstrong & Read, 2003; Briguglio, 1995; Guillaumont, 2010). Such challenging conditions do not bode well for island business, yet recent research has refuted the pessimistic picture by focusing instead on success stories of small enterprises on small islands.

A recent project, titled NISSOS, has analyzed small firms in five European island states and territories: Åland (Finland), Iceland, Malta, Saaremaa (Estonia), and the Scottish isles of Skye and Shetland. The project looked at two successful, small-scale enterprises per island state or territory: one in manufacturing based on local materials, one IT intensive and technology driven (Baldacchino, 2008). The cases were selected in terms of five variables: local ownership, small size, manufacturing, technology adaptation, and export orientation (Baldacchino, 2005a; 2005b; Baldacchino & Fairbairn, 2006; Keskpaik, 2006).

Other research looks at examples of successful small businesses in Canada. Siemens (2010), for instance, focuses on a sample of 10 very small companies in rural areas of Vancouver Island and other islands in British Columbia. On the other end of the country, Baldacchino (2002) analyzes the strategies of a manufacturer on Prince Edward Island.

Finally, some studies are interested in a very different region of the world, the South Pacific. Baldacchino (1999), for instance, examines the success of a soap manufacturer in Fiji. Fiji is also the focus of Connell (2006), who examines the production of the bottled water of the same name, FIJI. Naidu and Chand (2012) are particularly interested in the financial challenges of small and medium-sized manufacturing enterprises in Tonga and Fiji; Novaczek and Stuart (2006) look at women entrepreneurs in Vanuatu and Fiji; Yusuf (1995) surveys a sample from entrepreneurs across the South Pacific region as to their perceptions of success factors.

Across the different regions, this research has highlighted common challenges, including the small local market, expensive transport, weak infrastructure, lack of access to financial support, and recruiting staff (Siemens,

2010). But beyond these challenges, the research also points to common "success factors" in terms of both the personal characteristics of the entrepreneur and the political, economic, and institutional environment that facilitates the germination and operationalization of the business idea. As they are explained in greater detail elsewhere, I will only briefly list these success factors here. First, the entrepreneurs tend to belong to what Baldacchino (2008) calls a "glocal" elite. They typically have spent long periods of time away from the island for education and/or for work, or they are expatriates that settled on the island, lured by the island quality of life (Baldacchino, 2005a; also Fairbairn, 2006; Siemens, 2010; Yusuf, 1995). Mostly, the entrepreneurs have nurtured their business idea while working for another, often larger company; their firms are thus cases of intrapreneurship (Baldacchino, 2008). Core input to the product is sourced mainly or even exclusively from the island (Baldacchino, 2005a; Novaczek & Stuart, 2006). The companies often identify strongly with the island where they are based and brand their products accordingly, as an exotic, rare niche product that deliberately "romances" the island paradise myth (Baldacchino, 1999; 2005b; Connell, 2006; Sarkar, 2011). The workforce is typically very loyal to the company, as they are paid above-average salaries, and employees are often related to the entrepreneur—family members are very often part of the workforce (Baldacchino 2005a; Keskpaik 2006; Siemens, 2010). Finally, public policy can make a difference; government can support local enterprises by, for instance, providing training opportunities (Siemens, 2010) or financial and regulatory incentives to set up businesses (Baldacchino, 2006; Yusuf, 1995).

How do these factors come into play in the Solomon Islands? Here, I turn to Solomon Tropical Products Ltd., a medium-sized family business established by Australian emigrants. Using interviews and media reports as well as reports and other gray literature, I will discuss success factors with regard to the company's core product, biofuel from coconut oil, which STP independently developed and uses for power generation.

SOLOMON TROPICAL PRODUCTS AND ITS COCONUT FUEL

Solomon Tropical Products is a small, family-owned company based in Honiara, the Solomon Island capital. John Vollrath, an Australia-born emigrant, came to the Solomon Islands as a volunteer through his church. In order to further fund the church's work there, he established STP in 1995 and started exporting timber. His wife, Betty Vollrath, continued her work as a seamstress under the same company (Bevan Vollrath, personal communication, June 16, 2014). The company has since grown to about 120 employees overall; while clothing remains one division, the company is today mainly producing and processing coconut oil (Bevan Vollrath, personal communication, November 20, 2013). Until recently, STP was the largest producer and exporter of coconut oil in the Solomon Islands (*Solomon Star*, 2010a) and remains the only company in the country to sell electricity as an independent power producer (Bevan Vollrath, personal communication, May 28, 2014).

STP started to buy copra—from which it extracts coconut oil—in 2002, when the government deregulated the copra market (McGregor, 2006; *Solomon Star*, 2010b). A family friend back in Australia was at the time using vegetable oil in diesel engines and thus inspired STP's development of coconut oil (Bevan Vollrath, personal communication, November 20, 2013). At first, STP tried mixing coconut oil with kerosene or regular diesel, akin to what other entrepreneurs across the South Pacific have done, most notably Tony Deamer in Vanuatu (Deamer et al., 2005). In 2006, after several years of trial and error, and having successfully run its own engines on coconut oil or coconut oil blends, STP was ready to launch its first coconut biofuel commercially. Called Cocolene, the fuel was technically a "B20 mix," a mixture containing 80% filtered coconut oil and 20% kerosene (Mamu, 2006; Rikimae, 2006).

As the diesel price increased and with it the electricity price, however, STP looked into replacing diesel entirely with coconut oil (King & Mackay, 2012). As John Vollrath explains, "[D]iesel prices were so high that we were running out of it [i.e., diesel fuel], and I needed to run my engines and my truck on coconut oil" (cited in Beaumont, 2013, n.p.). Accordingly, the company experimented with different procedures to extract and purify coconut oil to turn it into fuel suitable for engines as well as diesel generators. In March 2010, the research and development paid off, and STP launched its coconut biodiesel, a biodiesel based 100% on coconut oil, that is, a "B100." This coconut diesel, obtained through a process called trans-esterification, whereby free fatty acids are removed from the coconut oil, is actual diesel and does not, as opposed to the previous blended fuel, require any engine modifications (*Solomon Star*, 2010a).[1]

Before STP could start full-scale production, however, the diesel price fell due to the global financial crisis, making coconut oil no longer competitive; as a result, the company took its biodiesel from the market and have not been able to get back to it since (King & Mackay, 2012; also, Bevan Vollrath, personal communications, November 20, 2013, and April 29, 2014). STP remained very much interested in coconut fuel, however. Yet with the relatively low diesel price, as well as technical issues with some vehicle engines, selling fuel for transport is currently not tenable; what was and remains profitable, however, is using coconut oil, blended with regular diesel, for power production. Electricity tariffs are high enough to justify the higher production cost of coconut oil, while coconut oil competes directly with bulk diesel prices in the transportation sector (Bevan Vollrath, personal communication, June 16, 2014). Power generation, indeed, was from the beginning a second pillar of the coconut fuel business, and as soon as STP was confident that coconut oil could successfully be used as a fuel, it approached the government to get a policy on independent power production and a license for feeding electricity onto the grid. STP's talks with the government were successful: since 2009, STP has produced and sold electricity to the state-owned Solomon Islands Electricity Authority (SIEA). Today, STP is the only company in the country to have a license for feeding electricity onto the main grid; together with the government, it plans to significantly expand its power production over the next years (Bevan Vollrath, personal communication, November 20, 2013, and April 29, 2014).

SOLOMON TROPICAL PRODUCTS' SUCCESS FACTORS

How does the STP story compare to the success factors identified earlier? To recap, the success factors are the entrepreneur's glocal background; intrapreneurship; locally sourced input; strong island identification and island branding; a loyal workforce, often with family ties to the entrepreneur; and supportive government policies.

International Connections

STP conforms to the first success factor, the international connections of successful island entrepreneurs, who form part of a glocal elite (Baldacchino, 2008). The Vollraths, the directors of STP, are from Australia. Founder John Vollrath and his wife emigrated in the early 1990s; their son, Bevan Vollrath, followed in the mid-2000s. Personal connections to Australia remain, and they are important for business. It was a family friend from Perth who initially started STP onto coconut oil. Through him, the Vollraths learned about the possibility of using vegetable oil, including coconut oil, as a fuel. When STP started to experiment with coconut-based fuel, scientific advice and technical input also came from abroad. Another family friend, a scientist from New Zealand, helped with the technical background. And STP obtained information on the chemical background from an Australian company working on biodiesel. Additionally, Bevan Vollrath emphasizes, the entrepreneurs simply researched and read as much information as they could find on the Internet and experimented with the little equipment and material available, learning from trial and error (Bevan Vollrath, personal communication, November 20, 2013, and May 28, 2014).

For these online searches as well as contacts abroad, the English language is also a benefit, as is the cultural Western background. Classes in the Solomon Islands are in pidgin language rather than English, and business education is not part of the curriculum: "[T]he way that other countries go about their trade and contractual requirements is not taught, [which] can at times be a disadvantage to some islanders wanting to trade" (Bevan Vollrath, personal communication, June 1, 2014, and November 20, 2013). As opposed to the West, the Solomon culture is more collectivist and puts less emphasis on fiscal prudence, competition, and (individual) achievement (Saffu, 2003).

"We [Australians] go get it. If we're not happy with what we got, we demand it. If we can't achieve in a quick time, then we go and see and investigate and find out why we're not getting service. Here in the Solomons the local people operate quite a bit differently. There is no urgency about today. If it happens today, that's good. But if it happens tomorrow, well, okay. Whereas the white man's European way is, we must have it today!" (Bevan Vollrath, personal communication, November 20, 2013)

While the international network certainly is an advantage, expatriates also face some challenges. The Solomon culture is rather collectivist, with much emphasis on the larger family, the *wantok*. Business is often carried out within the *wantok* rather than with foreigners, which can make business life difficult for foreigners. Overall, Bevan Vollrath thus concludes that being an expatriate "can be an advantage one day, and the next day, a disadvantage" (Bevan Vollrath, personal communication, November 20, 2013).

Locally Sourced Material

If international connections are important, so is the local connection. A central dimension of this local connection is locally sourced material, in this case the coconut oil. The main ingredient for coconut fuel is, of course, coconuts. In the Solomon Islands, as in the other South Pacific islands, coconut trees are ubiquitous. As Bevan Vollrath remarks, "The majority of those islands [in the Solomon Islands] are inhabited, and all the islands have coconut trees" (Bevan Vollrath, personal communication, November 20, 2013). It was the very abundance of coconuts across the Solomons that made STP venture into coconut fuel, as STP founder John Vollrath recalls: "There were all these coconuts not being utilized; no coconuts were being picked up at all. [. . .] They were just going to rot under the tree. And then I heard about coconut oil. So I decided to buy a small coconut mill" (John Vollrath, as cited in the *Sydney Morning Herald*, 2007).

Indeed, a considerable number of coconuts remain unharvested. Although there are no reliable data on coconut production in the Solomon Islands, one estimate puts the total annual number of coconuts at more than 370 million, of which 200 million are processed and exported and 65 million consumed fresh, the remainder going unharvested (Solomon Islands Coconut Sector, n.d., p. 15). Bevan Vollrath estimates that half of all coconuts are not being collected, which translates into "[. . .] 25-thousand tonnes in the islands, rotting under the tree that you could turn into real money" (John Vollrath, as cited in To'abaita Authority for Research & Development [TARD], 2006; also in the *Sydney Morning Herald*, 2007).

Why are so many coconuts not harvested and not "turned into real money"? To some extent, geography is to blame: parts of the Solomons are sparsely populated, remote, and difficult to access (Solomon Islands Coconut Sector, n.d., p. 4). Another important reason, however, has to do with costs. Producing copra, the dried flesh of the coconut, is a very labor-intensive process, and it is only profitable at a certain price. The coconut price, however, like other commodity prices, fluctuates strongly and has, over the past years, declined overall, though less so in the Solomon Islands. With low and volatile prices, copra production declined, too, as many farmers turned to other cash crops, and, importantly, stopped replanting coconut trees (McGregor, 2006; Raturi, 2006; Woodruff, 2007; Young & Pelomo, 2014).

Copra production per se is thus not necessarily economically attractive; for a reasonable return on labor, value needs to be added to the copra—for instance, by processing it into coconut oil. The price of coconut oil needs to be high enough to make copra production viable to local farmers, including in rural areas and outer islands, where transportation costs are even higher and hence not only make imports more expensive but also reduce the price farmers obtain for their copra. At the same time, for coconut fuel to be competitive, the price of coconut oil needs to be low enough for coconut fuel to be cheaper than imported fossil fuel, even after processing the oil into diesel (McGregor, 2006; Woodruff, 2007, p. 69; Young & Pelomo, 2014). The Vollraths are aware of this trade-off and the limited room for maneuver between these two price constraints. On the one hand, John Vollrath underlines the importance of high enough copra prices, in particular for people living in remote outer provinces, where the additional transport costs make copra production even less profitable: "We need to service you people and the outer provinces [. . .] and make sure you got the right price for producing copra" (as cited in TARD, 2006). On the other hand, Bevan Vollrath explains the importance of high enough diesel prices: the process of making biofuel "can only be profitable if the [price of regular] diesel fuel sold is higher than the cost of copra, the white flesh of the coconut, the cost of manufacturing that into an oil, and then manufacturing that oil into biodiesel" (Bevan Vollrath, personal communication, April 29, 2014).

In 2006, when Cocolene, the blended coconut fuel, came on the market, diesel prices were rather high; STP even calculated a price difference of up to 100% between coconut fuel and imported fossil fuel (Rikimae, 2006). The actual difference at the time was smaller, if still considerable: In 2006, one liter of coconut fuel cost SB$5.50 (US$0.78), compared to regular diesel at SB$7.00 (US$0.92) per liter (Mamu, 2006). Given the price advantage, a number of "adventurous motorists" have switched to coconut fuel (Cloin 2007a, p. 124; also Rikimae, 2006). In 2010, coconut biodiesel was still cheaper than regular diesel. While imported diesel sold, in early 2010, at about SB$11 (US$1.50) per liter in Honiara (and considerably more in the more remote provinces), one liter of coconut diesel cost about SB$6.20 (US$0.85), even less than what the B20 coconut blend cost (SB$8.30 or

US$1.00), according to *Solomon Star* (2010a). Due to the financial crisis, however, diesel prices fell, while coconut oil prices remained comparatively high. Yet for biodiesel to be competitive, the price difference between coconut oil and regular diesel needs to be at least SB$3.50 (US$0.50), which corresponds to the cost of processing coconut oil into biofuel. Hence, STP had to take its coconut biodiesel off the market, although it still uses coconut oil blended with regular diesel to produce power (Bevan Vollrath, personal communication, April 29, 2014; June 1, 2014; June 16, 2014).

Island Identity

The second dimension of STP's local connection is STP's island identity and island branding. Island branding, the conscious romanticizing of the exotic island, is of particular importance for export products (Connell, 2006). Although STP produces its coconut fuel explicitly for domestic use, this success factor is nonetheless quite important. STP emphasizes the company's Solomon identity—despite its Australian-born directors—and its marketing focuses on the benefits to the Solomon Islands: economically, politically, and environmentally.

STP is proud to be "wholly Solomon Islands" (Bevan Vollrath, personal communication, November 20, 2013) and to benefit the country with its biofuel. Indeed, these benefits are reportedly what motivates its directors: they want "the Solomon Islands to be a better place," John Vollrath has said (quoted in Rikimae, 2006). And coconut fuel does so in three ways, as STP underlines: it improves rural lifestyles by providing income, employment, and electrification; reduces the country's dependence on expensive fuel imports; and, last but not least, emits significantly fewer pollutants (*Solomon Star*, 2010a). Coconut fuel adds value to the copra and thus brings higher prices to farmers, especially in rural areas, where the coconut fuel additionally can be used directly in generators for power production and thus contributes to rural electrification. "We want to encourage local products," says John Vollrath. STP's former head scientist Francis Kapini similarly stresses that "local people will directly benefit and price will be affordable" (both cited in Palmer, 2010a, n.p.; also Beaumont, 2013; *Solomon Star*, 2010c; Bevan Vollrath, personal communication, November 20, 2013).

By switching from imported fossil fuel to domestically produced coconut fuel, the Solomon Islands could significantly reduce its energy dependence and import bill: "This coconut biodiesel project is about the potential of the country to be self-reliant and to be energy independent to some degree. Not a single cent will be leaving this country" (*Solomon Star*, 2010a). And so biofuel could "save the country thousands of dollars," John Vollrath points out (as cited in Rikimae, 2006, n.p.).

Finally, biofuel has environmental benefits, reducing air pollution and greenhouse gas emissions, again a motivation for STP to develop biofuel (Bevan Vollrath, personal communication, November 20, 2013; *Solomon*

Star, 2010c; *Sydney Morning Herald*, 2007). Francis Kapini stresses that their product is "made locally, [is] environmentally clean and safer than imported diesel" (as cited in Palmer, 2010b; *Solomon Star*, 2010c, n.p.).

STP's marketing focus on countrywide benefits seems to work. The public as well as politicians express their support for coconut fuel because of its benefits to the Solomons, especially its potential for rural development. A local truck owner is thus cited: "This [interest among vehicle owners] is because, it is not only clean, but it will help local copra farmers"; and hence, "the country will vastly benefit" (as cited in Palmer, 2010a, n.p.; also Kay, 2010; *Solomon Star*, 2010c). The government similarly emphasizes the reduction in import dependency and potential for rural development. The government representative who officially launched STP's biofuel in 2006, for instance, is cited as saying, "I'm pleased to see this thing come into reality and it's in line with the government's policy. It shows that we can sustain fuel using our natural resources" (as cited in Mamu, 2006; also Palmer, 2010a, n.p.).

Supportive Government

Indeed, the government's support is yet another success factor for STP. The government has stressed its interest in renewable energy and wants to actively promote biofuel alongside solar and hydro, with a view to reviving the coconut industry (Mamu, 2010). While implementation is sometimes lacking, and more could be done (King & Mackay, 2012), Bevan Vollrath emphasizes that the government has a clear interest in biofuel and that STP has enjoyed "the [government's] support all the way through" (Bevan Vollrath, personal communication, November 20, 2013, and April 29, 2014).

Government support is of particular importance for power generation. Electricity is only available in parts of the country; where it is available, it is available through the state-owned Solomon Island Electricity Authority (SIEA). The private sector has, to date, not played a significant role, although some businesses, particularly hotels and resorts, produce their own electricity (King & Mackay 2012, p. 9; Bevan Vollrath, personal communication, May 28, 2014), mainly with diesel generators. Businesses, however, were unable to sell their excess electricity for lack of a policy allowing independent power producers (IPPs) to do so. STP therefore recognized early on the importance of bringing the government on board. Having had a good relationship with the Solomon Islands government and being involved in many government meetings on trade and aid, STP approached SIEA, which is part of the Mines and Energy Ministry, and lobbied for an IPP policy. In 2007, the Solomon government passed such legislation, which, importantly, includes renewable energy: the policy mandates that electricity from diesel generators must have some biofuel content (Bevan Vollrath, personal communication, November 20, 2013; April 29, 2014; June 16, 2014; see also, e.g., Mamu, 2006; *Solomon Star*, 2010a).

With the policy in place, all STP needed was a license from SIEA. In September 2009, STP and SIEA signed an agreement that would allow STP to feed its surplus electricity onto the main grid at a cheaper rate, which would "assist SIEA reduce its heavy reliance on imported diesel fuel and at the same time [provide] a source of revenue for STP" (Mamu, 2010). Although the agreement was suspended on procedural grounds shortly after, STP went back onto the grid in April 2010 and "have been back on the grid ever since, and we haven't had a problem with the authorities" (Bevan Vollrath, personal communication, April 29, 2014; also Mamu, 2010). Quite to the contrary; SIEA and the government want to expand STP's power production capacity. Already, capacity has grown from 200 kW to 400 kW, with a "mini-powerhouse" of 2 MW that started operations in 2014. Further capacity increases are planned, including as part of a 10-year plan, supported by the World Bank, to expand and improve electricity access and renewable energy in the Solomon Islands (Bevan Vollrath, personal communication, April 29, 2014).

Improving electricity access is a central concern, as only a minority of the Solomons is connected to the grid. The Solomon Islands has the lowest electrification rate in the region, with fewer than 20% of households having access to electricity and much fewer in rural areas (King & Mackay 2012, p. 54). The potential for using coconut fuel for electrification, particularly in the outer islands, is thus considerable, and STP campaigns for government and donor support in this context (Mamu, 2006). Donor support would bring in needed capital to scale up coconut fuel production: "If the aid donors get behind it, we could be producing 10 tons a day of eco-friendly coconut, or coco bio-diesel, which is 100% green," said John Vollrath in 2007 (*Sydney Morning Herald*, 2007). Yet, as Bevan Vollrath explains, applying and reporting to donors is a rather complicated bureaucratic procedure beyond the scope of a small family business. Nonetheless, STP's efforts were recently rewarded when it obtained funds through the Secretariat of the Pacific Community and its European Union–funded Increasing Agricultural Commodity Trade (IACT) project, which "has boosted our rural income business development greatly" (Bevan Vollrath, personal communication, November 20, 2013). The funds allowed STP to pursue a scheme for rural electrification in which STP sells a diesel generator, to be run on coconut oil, together with a crushing mill to villages and guarantees to buy back coconut oil from the village. Thus, the village has, through the generator, electricity, with which it can power the crushing mill. The coconut oil thus obtained will in turn fuel the generator but also provide cash income. But the electricity from the generator can also be used for lighting or refrigeration, with households paying through the provision of copra to the mill operators, thus using barter payment (Bevan Vollrath, personal communication, May 28, 2014). In other words, the "business of making coconut oil pays for the generator" (Bevan Vollrath, personal communication, November 20, 2013) and thus ensures the sustainability of the electrification scheme (King & Mackay, 2012, p. 36). The villagers already add value to the raw product, the copra, before sale, and hence substantially increase the income for the community, while STP can buy the oil rather than the copra from the villages, which allows it to trade higher volumes—a "win-win situation" (Bevan Vollrath, personal communication, November 20, 2013; also Mofor et al., 2013, p. 32).

Finally, the government provides an additional incentive for renewable energy by not taxing coconut fuel (Bevan Vollrath, personal communication, November 20, 2013). While this is a clear benefit to STP, it is not necessarily a long-term interest of the government. Across Oceania, a large part of state revenue comes from import duties; if coconut fuel is substituted for imported fossil fuels, revenue from import duties would decrease. Similarly, using coconut oil domestically would decrease export earnings. If, additionally, coconut and other biofuel are exempted from taxation, the overall impact on government finance could be negative (Cloin, 2007a, 2007b, p. 37). Bevan Vollrath hence cautions that the government may reconsider its taxation of biofuel once STP produces enough coconut fuel to impact the amount of diesel imports coming into the country: "Once we start [. . .] to have quite an impact on the volumes of diesel fuel coming into our country, then they [that is, the government] may look at this and close it" (Bevan Vollrath, personal communication, November 20, 2013).

Other Factors

In other contexts, factors that were identified as important include intrapreneurship as well as a loyal workforce that often includes family members. Intrapreneurship in this case does not play a role; John Vollrath did not come up with the idea to develop biofuel from coconut oil while working in another company. However, STP already existed when the idea of biofuel came up, and this helped cover start-up costs and especially costs related to research and development. Bevan Vollrath estimates that STP invested about SB$300,000 (ca. US$40,000) in equipment before being able to deliver electricity to the grid (Bevan Vollrath, personal communication, November 20, 2013). This money came largely from other parts of the company. This is an important advantage, given the well-known difficulty of securing capital on islands with a typically only poorly developed financial sector (Naidu & Chand, 2012). The reliance on several income sources has been remarked elsewhere, too, but with a view to individual islanders: Baldacchino and Fairbairn (2006, p. 336) speak about "strategic opportunism," which, for them, refers to occupational multiplicity, including "waged and non-waged labor, petty commodity production, subsistence fishing or agriculture and home working." Such a strategic opportunism applies to island companies, too, as the STP case indicates, although here, one might better speak of "income multiplicity" rather than "occupational multiplicity." When John Vollrath established STP in

1995, he originally worked in saw milling, while his wife, Betty Vollrath, became active in clothing manufacturing, also under the umbrella of STP. Over time, the company's portfolio has diversified and today has several divisions. Clothing manufacturing remains one area of activity, but STP also works in coconut oil processing, soap and detergents, biodiesel production, and power generation; additionally, STP operates its own trading vessels to buy copra directly from farmers (Bevan Vollrath, personal communication, November 20, 2013). Such a diversification allows STP to venture into new areas, as it did with biofuel, but also to respond flexibly to changing conditions, as in times of low diesel prices, when it took the biodiesel off the market, while at the same time increasing coconut oil exports as well as soap production (Bevan Vollrath, personal communication, May 28, 2014, and April 29, 2014).

Flexibility is also important with regard to the workforce. Here, STP differs from many previously studied island enterprises, which rely on qualified employees, often with university education and off-island experience or training, and pay above-average salaries to retain their workforce (Baldacchino, 2005a). STP, in contrast, does not require any specially skilled or trained workers. Employees have not been trained off island and typically have no secondary education. Rather, STP recruits villagers, mostly men, and trains them on site, a practice common in small businesses (Baldacchino, 2005b). As Bevan Vollrath explains, with only one third of the Solomon working-age population being employed, there is always a sufficient labor supply. And, with little regulation, STP can flexibly respond to increases or decreases in sales volumes by hiring and laying off staff as needed (Bevan Vollrath, personal communication, April 29, 2014). STP is, however, a typical island business in being a family enterprise that remains controlled by the founder, John Vollrath, and his family—his wife and his son (Baldacchino, 2005b). Having family members on board also increases flexibility; as Bevan Vollrath explains,

"with family members [. . .] you can accommodate for the losses on a different month, and you get the profits from another month. It doesn't impact on the product line of the company so much. So having family members has its direct advantages." (Bevan Vollrath, personal communication, April 29, 2014)

Family members additionally bring their personal commitment to the enterprise: former STP scientist Francis Kapini thus comments, "When you work in an environment where 90% of the work ethic is passion and 10% is wages and salary, anything is possible" (as cited in *Solomon Star*, 2010a, n.p.). Bevan Vollrath similarly highlights their commitment and passion. One success factor, for him, is "never giving up. One failure is one step closer to your success. Just keep resetting your goals to achieve" (Bevan Vollrath, personal communication, May 28, 2014).

CONCLUSION

Overall, STP, as the largest coconut oil producer and processor in the Solomon Islands, can be seen as a success, an evaluation that Bevan Vollrath shares (Bevan Vollrath, personal communication, November 20, 2013). The different factors that contribute to that success are very similar to the factors identified in other small island contexts: international connections, locally sourced material, island identity and branding, and government support. But STP also knows the challenges typical of small island businesses: high transportation costs, large distances to major Asian and European markets, small profit margins, and vulnerability to external price shocks, as when the global diesel price fell as a result of the global financial crisis (Bevan Vollrath, personal communication, April 29, 2014).

While there is little to be done about structural disadvantages, there is nonetheless considerable potential for small island entrepreneurs in the biofuel sector. Indeed, biofuel is an important element of the move toward renewable energy, and STP's is only one of several initiatives to use coconuts for transportation and power generation (Cloin, 2007b; Leplus, 2003; Mofor et al., 2013). Almost all island countries and territories in the South Pacific have experimented with or looked into coconut fuel. Coconut fuel has many advantages, economic and environmental, and almost all tropical islands have some biofuel potential, although this is not always economically viable (Mofor et al., 2013). State support is thus critical, in this case allowing biofuel to "take off" while, in other cases, fiscal incentives, public–private partnerships, and standardization are other possible policy measures (Biopact, 2006; Cloin, 2007b, p. 126). With such state support, there is considerable potential for coconut fuel to contribute to the transition toward renewable energy in the Solomon Islands and beyond.

NOTE

1. When coconut and other vegetable oil is not processed into biodiesel but used directly (pure or as a blend) in engines and generators, these require modification and/or more maintenance (Cloin, 2007b).

REFERENCES

Adkins, S., Foale, M., & Samosir, Y. (Eds.). (2006). *Coconut revival: New possibilities for the "Tree of Life,"* Canberra. Proceedings of the International Coconut Forum held in Cairns, Australia, 22–24 November 2005, Australian Centre for International Agricultural Research.

Armstrong, H. W., & Read, R. (2003). The determinants of economic growth in small states. *The Round Table: Commonwealth Journal of International Affairs, 92*(368), 99–124.

Baldacchino, G. (1999). Small business in small islands: A case study from Fiji. *Journal of Small Business Management, 37*(4), 80–84.

Baldacchino, G. (2002). A taste of small-island success: A case from Prince Edward Island. *Journal of Small Business Management, 40*(3), 254–259.

Baldacchino, G. (2005a). Island entrepreneurs: Insights from exceptionally successful knowledge-driven SMEs from 5 European island territories. *Journal of Enterprising Culture, 13*(2), 145–170.

Baldacchino, G. (2005b). Successful small-scale manufacturing from small islands: Comparing firms benefitting from locally available raw material input. *Journal of Small Business and Entrepreneurship, 18*(1), 21–38.

Baldacchino, G. (2006). Innovative development strategies from non-sovereign island jurisdictions? A global review of economic policy and governance practices. *World Development, 34*(5), 852–867.

Baldacchino, G. (2008). Entrepreneurship in smaller jurisdictions: Appraising a glocal elite. *Comparative Education, 44*(2), 187–201.

Baldacchino, G., & Fairbairn, T.I.J. (2006). Editorial: Entrepreneurship and small business development in small islands. *Journal of Small Business and Entrepreneurship, 19*(4), 331–340.

Beaumont, M. (2013, 19 November). Solomon Islands "Coconut Power." BBC Queen's baton relay. Retrieved from www.bbc.com/news/world-24991742

Biopact. (2006). An overview of biofuels in the Pacific. Biopact: Towards a green energy pact between Europe and Africa. Retrieved from http://news.mongabay.com/bioenergy/2006/12/overview-of-biofuels-in-paci fic_06.html

Briguglio, L. (1995). Small island developing states and their economic vulnerabilities. *World Development, 23*(9), 1615–1632.

Cloin, J. (2007a). Coconut oil as a fuel in the Pacific Islands. *Natural Resources Forum, 31*, 119–127.

Cloin, J. (2007b). *Liquid biofuels in Pacific Island countries*. Technical report. Miscellaneous Report 628, Suva, Fiji: Secretariat of the Pacific Community Applied Geoscience and Technology Division (SOPAC).

Connell, J. (2006). "The taste of paradise": Selling Fiji and FIJI water. *Asia Pacific Viewpoint, 47*(3), 342–350.

Deamer, T., Newell, R., Deamer, Z., Deamer, E., & White, J. (2005). Issues in using coconut oil as a fuel in Vanuatu. Secretariat of the Pacific Community Applied Geoscience and Technology Division (SOPAC). Retrieved from http://ict.sopac.org/compendium-documents/CLR_201001977_Issues%20in%20using%20Coconut%20Oil%20as%20a%20Fuel%20in%20Vanuatu.pdf

Fairbairn, T.I.J. (2006). Entrepreneurship and small business development: A Pacific perspective. *Journal of Small Business and Entrepreneurship, 19*(4), 355–366.

Guillaumont, P. (2010). Assessing the economic vulnerability of small island developing states and the least developed countries. *The Journal of Development Studies, 46*(5), 828–854.

Kay, J. (2010, June 24). Coconut magic: Bio-diesel. *Solomon Star*. Retrieved from www.solomonstarnews.com/viewpoint/letters-to-the-editor/6543-coconut-magic—bio-diesel

Keskpaik, A. (2006). Manufacturing on the Estonian Islands: Trends and prospects. *Journal of Small Business and Entrepreneurship, 19*(4), 409–418.

King, S., & Mackay, T. (2012). *Facilitating private sector participation in the promotion of energy security in Papua New Guinea, Solomon Islands and Vanuatu: Solomon Islands country review*. Technical report. Noumea, New Caledonia: Secretariat of the Pacific Community.

Leplus, A. (2003). *Biofuel energy from coconut in the Pacific Islands: The Lory Cooperative Pilot Project*. Master's thesis. Wageningen, The Netherlands: Wageningen University.

Mamu, M. (2006, September 20). Coconut biodiesel debuts in Solomons. *Solomon Star*. Retrieved from http://archives.pireport.org/archive/2006/September /09–21–12.htm

Mamu, M. (2010, April 26). STP back on SIEA grid. *Solomon Star*. Retrieved from www.solomonstarnews.com/news/business/5156-stp-back-on-siea-grid

McGregor, A. (2006). *Solomon Islands smallholder agriculture study. Volume 3: Markets and marketing issues*. Technical report, Australian Government. Canberra: Australian Overseas Aid Program.

Mofor, L., Isaka, M., Wade, H., & Soakai, A. (2013). *Pacific lighthouses: Renewable energy road mapping for islands*. Technical report. Abu Dhabi: International Renewable Energy Agency.

Naidu, S., & Chand, A. (2012). A comparative study of the financial problems faced by micro, small and medium enterprises in the manufacturing sector of Fiji and Tonga. *International Journal of Emerging Markets, 7*(3), 245–262.

Novaczek, I., & Stuart, E.K. (2006). The contribution of women entrepreneurs to the local economy in small islands: Seaplant-based micro-enterprise in Fiji and Vanuatu. *Journal of Small Business and Entrepreneurship, 19*(4), 367–380.

Palmer, E. (2010a, March 11). Breakthrough for local company. *Solomon Star*. Retrieved from www.solomonstarnews.com/news/national/3787-breakthrough-for-local-company

Palmer, E. (2010b, March 12). More show interest in coconut bio fuel. *Solomon Star*. Retrieved from www.solomonstarnews.com/news/national/ 3819-more-show-interest-in-coconut-bio-fuel

Raturi, A.K. (2006). *Status of and potential for utilizing coconut oil (CNO) in power generation and industrial use in Pacific island countries*. Washington, DC: World Bank Report.

Rikimae, J.A. (2006, April 5). Solomons project tests coconut oil for "bio-diesel." *Solomon Star*. Retrieved from http://pidp.org/archive/2006/April/04–06–15.htm

Saffu, K. (2003). The role and impact of culture on South Pacific Island entrepreneurs. *International Journal of Entrepreneurial Behavior & Research, 9*(2), 55–73.

Sarkar, A. (2011). Romancing with a brand: A conceptual analysis of romantic consumer–brand relationship. *Management & Marketing, 6*(1), 79–94.

Siemens, L. (2010). Challenges, responses and available resources: Success in rural small businesses. *Journal of Small Business and Entrepreneurship, 23*(1), 65–80.

Solomon Islands Coconut Sector. (2010). *Coconut sector strategy: Solomon Islands*. The International Trade Centre Document EC-10–174.E. Geneva, Switzerland: International Trade Centre.

Solomon Star. (2010a, February 27). Fuel for the nation: Solomon Tropical Products goes into biodiesel. Retrieved from www.solomonstarnews.com/news/business/ 3359-fuel-for-the-nation-solomon-tropical-products-goes-into-biodiesel-

Solomon Star. (2010b, March 12). Yes, we can make our own diesel. Retrieved from www.solomonstarnews.com/viewpoint/editorial/3810-yes-we-can-make-our-own-diesel

Solomon Star. (2010c, May 1). Know the value of coconut. Retrieved from www. solomonstarnews.com/news/business/5369-know-the-value-of-coconut

Stuart, E.K. (2006). Energizing the island community: A review of policy standpoints for energy in small island states and territories. *Sustainable Development, 14*(1), 139–147.

Sydney Morning Herald. (2007, May 7). Aussie producing oil from coconuts. Retrieved from www.smh.com.au/news/World/Aussie-producing-oil-from-cocon uts/2007/05/07/1178390212839.html

To'abaita Authority for Research & Development (TARD). (2006, September 25). Solomon tropical products company plans to buy copra from villages. Retrieved from http://toabaita-authority.blogspot.ca/2006/09/solomon-tropical-products-company.html

Woodruff, A. (2007). *An economic assessment of renewable energy options for rural electrification in Pacific Island countries.* Technical report. Suva, Fiji: Pacific Islands Applied Geoscience Commission (SOPAC).

Young, D., & Pelomo, M. (2014). *Solomon Islands coconut value chain analysis.* Technical report. Washington, DC, and Canberra, Australia: World Bank, Australian Department of Foreign Affairs and Trade, International Fund for Agricultural Development.

Yusuf, A. (1995). Critical success factors for small business: Perceptions of South Pacific entrepreneurs. *Journal of Small Business Management, 33*(2), 68–73.

Part 3
Tourism Segments

11 Visiting Guam or *Guahan*? The Colonial Context and Cultural Decolonization of an Island's Tourism Industry

Michael Lujan Bevacqua and Hermon Farahi

INTRODUCTION

On the western Pacific island of Guam (or *Guahan* in Chamorro), the village of Tumon stands in contrast to many of the others. Set near a golden-blue bay fished for millennia atop flat land farmed for centuries, Tumon today is not filled with fishers or farmers but with hotels and shops. Its main thoroughfare is now named for the Spanish Jesuit priest who brought colonization to Guam in 1668: Pale' San Vitores. San Vitores Road passes by Matå'pang Beach, named for the *maga'låhi* (chief) who killed San Vitores and resisted European colonization. To drive down San Vitores Road now is to drive through a featureless concrete canyon of duty-free shopping, Las Vegas entertainment centers, strip clubs, and Hilton, Hyatt, Ohana, and other franchise hotels. Throughout the day and into the night, San Vitores Road mills with foreign tourists.

About 60% of Guam's government revenues derive from tourism, and Tumon is the industry's crown jewel (Schumann, 2006, p. 19). Each year, 1.3 million tourists visit Guam, primarily from Japan. This demographic dominance is seen in the many signs in Tumon translated into Japanese, with restaurants and stores all featuring menus in Japanese and staff fluent in the language. Annually, 1 out of every 18 Japanese overseas travelers visits Guam. However, Russian, Korean, and Chinese travelers are also on the rise as the Guam tourism industry seeks to diversify following the bursting of Japan's "Bubble Economy" (Iyoda, 2010, p. 12).

For these tourists, Tumon forms the basis for their impressions of Guam, although in the hotels, the Polynesian-themed dance shows, and the supermarket shelves, there is little to represent the actual island, its ancient culture, and its indigenous Chamorro people. Instead, Tumon offers a pastiche of tourism models inundated with a generic Americana.

Tumon represents the successes and difficulties of recent Chamorro history. Guam has been transformed from a "backwater colony" of the United States to a multibillion-dollar economy, but this was accomplished at the expense of the visibility and recognition of indigenous culture under sometimes-constricting political conditions.

This chapter focuses on the historical background to and the emergence of indigenous entrepreneurship in Guam's tourism industry. Guam's colonial status has both stimulated and inhibited tourism and economic growth. It has restrained the visibility of Chamorro culture in the tourist imaginary, as seen in the example of Tumon. Nevertheless, burgeoning cultural revitalization movements, in conjunction with indigenous entrepreneurial efforts, are leading to indigenous cultural tourism and a localization of the tourism industry. This dynamic is also essential to the long-term sustainability of the island's tourist economy.

TOURISM, ENTREPRENEURSHIP, AND DEVELOPMENT IN HISTORICAL CONTEXT

Beyond the established Schumpeterian concepts of entrepreneurship, scholars such as Rochelle Cote (2013), Dennis Foley (2012), Ronald D. Camp II, Robert B. Anderson, and Robert Giberson (2005) have recently begun to articulate the concept of *indigenous entrepreneurship*. Definitions that involve indigenous communities in economic activities (i.e., as recipients of aid and/or loans) are common in international development circles that focus on economic motivations and indicators (presuming an orientation toward a capitalist market system), with their own internal system of values focused on profit maximization. Other scholars posit that indigenous entrepreneurism is more than economic in motive; it includes collective, community, and kinship-based values, organizational models, and goals specific to indigenous peoples (Cahn, 2008; Peredo & Anderson, 2006). Tourism offers an effective space for indigenous entrepreneurial activity, often earmarking the very products, performances, and places that indigenous people value culturally for commodification.

Tourism is closely related to development, as observed in its many ancillary or niche-specific forms (such as ecotourism, cultural tourism, heritage tourism, experiential tourism, and creative tourism). It is often prescribed as a panacea for economic growth in the developing world and among marginalized populations. This relationship is even more pronounced in the case of small islands, whose distinctive natural and cultural assets can provide the basis for an easy transition into a tourist economy (Conlin & Baum, 1995; Lockhart & Drakakis-Smith, 1997). But historical circumstances and political-economic contexts can limit and present obstacles to the development of a cultural tourism industry predicated on the desires of a local people while restricting the ability of local agents to effectively engage in entrepreneurial activity, as is the case in Guam.

Furthermore, scholars and practitioners who employ the prefix "indigenous" in conjunction with entrepreneurship and cultural tourism may assume relatively homogenous and easily identifiable "peoples" with intact cultural practices to draw upon. This is hardly ever the case in practice.

As this chapter argues, the history of colonization and the contemporary political status of the island of Guam have obfuscated the identity of the Chamorro people, further challenging the ability to express a unified entrepreneurial or tourism modality.

As a result of colonialism, Chamorro performing arts have been historically repressed and rendered almost nonexistent. However, since the 1980s, as part of an indigenous renaissance amongst Chamorros, members of the community have begun recreating dance, music, and chant traditions based on regional, cross-cultural, and creative reinterpretations (Flores, 2002; Rabon, 2001). This process of cultural revitalization continues to this day. However, when a cultural product may be perceived as "questionable" in its "authenticity" (Flores, 2002), it presents challenges not only in creating internal cohesion around what is an accepted "tradition" but also external complexities as to its representation.

Notwithstanding the colonial context and structural political-economic factors, burgeoning indigenous revitalization movements in the region now provide some impetus to develop a more representative cultural tourism industry and entrepreneurial capacity. However, historical analysis is needed to understand how these factors have impacted and continue to limit the growth of the tourism industry in Guam.

WHERE AMERICAN COLONIALISM CONTINUES

The ABC Store, a common marker of tourist destinations in the Pacific, has several locations in Tumon. Inside these stores, one can always find a section of materials representing Guam. Almost all materials sold there, such as T-shirts, bags, and chocolate candies, are made in foreign factories with no meaningful ties to the island, though they often imply such ties. One phrase in particular appears prominently: "Guam: Where America's Day Begins."

That phrase exemplifies the colonial contradictions of Guam as a U.S. colony. Guam is 3,800 miles west of Hawai'i and 6,000 miles west of California, and its time zone is indeed ahead of the rest of the United States. "Where America's Day Begins" was a slogan developed in the late 1960s and popularized in the 1970s as a means of representing Guam in a tourist context. Even this popularization of the Westernized "Guam" has come at the cost of the obscuring of the Chamorro "*Guåhan*."

Guam remains one of 17 "non-self-governing" territories, almost all islands, recognized by the United Nations Decolonization Committee (U.N., 2014). It has no formal representation in the U.S. federal government that controls its laws. Residents of Guam are U.S. citizens, eligible to serve in the U.S. military, but they cannot vote in elections for U.S. president. Every 2 years, Guam elects a "nonvoting delegate" to the U.S. Congress, who serves on committees but cannot vote on the passage of laws (Burnett & Marshall, 2001).

Many in the United States might not even know about Guam. Most of those who do know Guam primarily as a U.S. military base, to which 39% of the island's land area is already dedicated, and nothing more (Lutz, 2010). If anything, Guam's military role is set to expand even more as U.S. troops get relocated from Okinawa, Japan. As a colony, Guam's relationship to the United States is a morass of inclusions and exclusions.

As a territory, the benefits that Guam receives, whether legal protections through the U.S. constitution, the right to local self-government, or even the ability to participate in federal aid programs, are not rights but tenuous privileges (Limtiaco, 2014). These privileges can be rescinded at will by Congress or changes in U.S. federal policy. References to Guam as "American" or "Where America's Day Begins" are a façade, not guaranteed by federal laws or U.S. legal decisions.

COLONIAL GAINS

With most of the remaining formal colonies in the world being small islands, some scholars have questioned whether the label "colony" or "colonies" is appropriate, since dependency may simply be a lingering and fundamental aspect of their reality (Aldrich & Connell, 1998, pp. 3–4). Some form of colonialism may be necessary to sustain livelihoods, given the remoteness and small size of many of these islands.

World history suggests that colonial experience can also be beneficial, bringing in new ideas, new technologies, and new connections (Baldacchino & Royle, 2010). Indeed, some of the world's richest island territories are also those that have been colonized the longest (Feyrer & Sacerdote, 2009). For small island polities such as Guam, colonialism is often portrayed as a safety net without which they would have nothing and be nothing (Bevacqua, 2007). However, as Aimé Césaire (1972, p. 33) notes, this line of reasoning fails to address significant aspects of colonialism: "[O]f all the ways of establishing contact, was [colonization] the best? I answer no." Regardless of subsequent benefits, colonialism is a nondemocratic system specifically designed to empower a few and disenfranchise many others, including the majority of the colonized peoples.

While being a U.S. colony has materially benefited Guam, it is important to recognize the problems with such a relationship. As Leon Guerrero (1996, p. 84) argues:

> Contrary to what many people believe, most of Guam's economic development has been for the benefit of outsiders who came to colonize the island. Whether they were the Spanish many years ago, the Americans who have controlled Guam since the turn of the century, or the Japanese who occupied the island during World War II and occupy our beaches today, these outsiders came to Guam for their own benefit. Each group

used Guam for their own purposes without the consent of the Chamorro people of Guam . . . Although economic development associated with colonization did benefit the people of Guam, this was a side effect, and not the principal intent of the colonizers.

Colonialism often distorts or prevents internal economic growth in a colonized space, especially if such would conflict with the colonizer's geo-strategic interests. Colonial status has helped to bring Guam to a certain point, but further steps will require placing more economic and political control completely in the hands of a local government and also an increased emphasis on genuine Chamorro cultural offerings rather than sensationalized Polynesian and American tropes.

As small island polities such as Guam consider their economic and political future, it is essential that they be able to soberly and critically consider the economic constrictions of colonialism and the potential economic and political benefits of alternative governance models.

War and Land Loss

Prior to World War II, the majority of Chamorros lived subsistence agrarian lifestyles and relied primarily on a barter economy (Rogers, 1999, p. 158). World War II destroyed much of the island's infrastructure. American intentions of turning Guam and Micronesia into "Fortress Pacific" led to the majority of the island's lands being taken by force to be transformed into military bases. Thousands of Chamorro families were displaced and unable to resume their livelihoods as farmers or fishers. Chamorros seeking means of sustaining themselves and their families joined the U.S. military or began to work for the newly established government of Guam (Leon Guerrero, 1996, p. 86).

With much of traditional Chamorro life lost, the postwar years become a period of intense Americanization. Chamorro families began to voluntarily Americanize themselves and adopted many of the trappings of the idealized American life. American fashion, food, cars, culture, music . . . all came to Guam and replaced older Chamorro cultural forms. Perhaps the most notable way in which this Americanization took place is through the loss of the Chamorro language. In 1950, 100% of Chamorros in Guam spoke the language, but today only 20% do, 85% of whom are over the age of 60 (Pa'a Taotao Tåno', 2010).

To Hawai'i or Not to Hawai'i

In the postwar era, official U.S. government documents indicate a need to keep Guam firmly within the U.S. orbit, since its proximity to Asia might offer enticing political alternatives to its alliance with the United States (Friedman, 2001). The island had to be developed but also isolated, so the requirement of a naval security clearance was imposed on all personnel entering or leaving the island. As Chamorros sought to rebuild and find new means of developing the island, this security clearance requirement became a severe impediment. It applied to everyone: U.S. citizens, Chamorros, and foreign nationals. It made the development of tourism, along with attracting any type of investment, next to impossible (Leon Guerrero, 1996, p. 86).

The security clearance was rescinded in 1962, but not to help the Chamorro economy. As the new governor of Guam, Bill Daniels was irritated to be subjected to screening by the Navy. He complained to U.S. President Kennedy, and the restriction was lifted (Tolentino, 2014).

With the end of the security clearance, Guam was now better prepared to take advantage of its proximity to Asia, although immigration control was still firmly in U.S. hands. From 1962, citizens of the United States and its close allies could freely visit Guam, making a tourist economy feasible. Although Guam was politically aligned with the United States, the geographic distance prohibited most tourist travel. Japan offered relatively short and cheap flights, and, by 1964, its travel industry had been liberalized, leading to a drop in airfares, and Guam's tourist economy was born (Schumann, 2006, p. 8).

The island became engaged in a conversation over its tourist image. Guam was undertaking a shift in meaning at the regional and global levels. No longer was it to be a dot on the map or a single link in a chain of U.S. military bases. Guam could now represent itself, to attract the gaze and the spending dollars of markets throughout Asia.

The prevailing representation was mired in colonial feelings of inferiority (Fanon, 1965), driven by the idea that no one would want to visit Guam for itself. In order to develop a lucrative visitor industry, Guam would have to take on the trappings of some other place that was richer and more culturally established. Local leaders looked to places such as Hawai'i, Tahiti, Macau, and Las Vegas on which to graft and develop Guam's tourist image.

In the 1960s, a different tourist image was also suggested, primarily through the writings of Antonio Palomo, a Chamorro politician and historian. Through editorials that appeared in his magazine *The Pacific Profile*, he advocated that Guam needed to be true to itself in order to succeed. He argued that mimicking the already-visible Hawai'i or Las Vegas might work in the short term but not in the long run (Palomo, 1965, p. 4).

Palomo's position was lost in the discussion, however. Guam represented itself as "America in Asia" and a Polynesian paradise, weighing its viability as a tourist site on its ability to market itself as the poor man's Hawai'i, offering an exotic Polynesian experience, American culture and consumerism, and a significantly cheaper flight for Japanese tourists.

Colonial ideology privileged the American, not Chamorro, presence on Guam. Furthermore, much of the Western imperial gaze of the Pacific and Pacific Islander cultures derived from an amalgamation of sensationalized Polynesian concepts, although Chamorro culture differs significantly from

Polynesian. On this island, newly christened "Guam: Where America's Day Begins," Japanese tourists consumed Americanized food and products overlaid with a generic, depoliticized Polynesian culture (Schumann, 2006, p. 300).

Nevertheless, the development of the tourism industry coincided with a Chamorro cultural renaissance and "brown power" political movement. Chamorros were losing their language and other aspects of their culture, facing marginalization due to the influx of foreign workers and foreign tourists (Bettis, 1993, p. 287); these trends offered a rude wake-up call. A key part of this cultural resurgence was the development of dances meant to reflect ancient Chamorro heritage (Rabon, 2001).

Shop and Don't Stop

In the 1980s, as Japan's economy boomed, so did Guam's, with more than a million Japanese tourists visiting annually in the 1990s, with Tumon as the hub. In the aftermath of the Second World War, U.S. military had evicted long-time Chamorro owners and residents and confiscated their property to repurpose the Tumon area as a recreational spot instead of the productive agricultural and rich historical area it had been for centuries (Hattori, 1996). Although the military would later return most of the land to the local government, few properties were returned to their original owners. Instead, the land was sold to Japanese companies and investors in the tourist industry. Small hotels appeared in the 1960s; the first major hotel, the Hilton, was built in 1971, and numerous other franchises followed in the 1980s.

The more Japanese visitors arrived, however, the more disconnected Tumon became from the rest of the island. From the airport, Japanese tourists would be bussed to their hotels in the expanding concrete jungle of Tumon. They would visit high-end shopping stores such as Fendi and Louis Vuitton, eat at American-inspired restaurant chains such as Planet Hollywood or TGIF, and watch Polynesian cultural shows. Signage in Tumon was Japanese only in some areas, flouting a 1974 law requiring that all signs be printed in English and Chamorro, the two official languages of Guam (Rogers, 1999, p. 225). Tourists remained in Tumon for the majority of their stay, only leaving for bus tours around the rural southern half of the island or for organized water sports.

Although Guam's economy reached global proportions, this was also a time of disenchantment and confusion on the part of Chamorros. The majority of hotels were owned by off-island companies; not a single locally owned hotel was owned by Chamorros, but by Filipinos or Caucasians. All of this was accompanied by a continued lack of recognition for indigenous Chamorro culture. The local tourist industry clung to its Polynesian façade, erasing and omitting culturally Chamorro elements from the marketing lexicon.

The colonial relationship between Guam and the United States had brought Guam some benefits as a polity in the Pacific, with a multibillion-dollar economy and a far greater global presence and visibility than any of its Micronesian neighbors. As the new millennium began, however, the colonial realities of Guam would play more of an economically constricting role.

The Colonial Ceiling

The Japanese market cooled by the year 2000; combined with Typhoon Pongsana, 9/11, SARS, and the Afghanistan–Iraq conflict, this decline "practically brought the island's economy to a standstill" (Schumann, 2006, p. 38). Guam's tourist industry had to seek out new markets to survive. Russia and China were the largest potential markets in the region; however, it was difficult to pursue them as options due to U.S. political antagonism. Guam grew tourism markets steadily in Taiwan and South Korea, but they paled in comparison to the existing Japanese market and also offered far less potential than those of Russia and, in particular, mainland China (Hart, 2011). In 2005, Guam ranked seventh among U.S. states and territories visited by overseas travelers, but its growth potential would be even larger were it not hampered by its colonial status and obvious ties to the United States (Schumann, 2006, p. 40).

Outreach to Russian and Chinese markets was constrained by the amount of time (4 to 12 months) it usually took for citizens of these countries to be awarded U.S. tourist visas (Alvarez, 2013). This political bottleneck resulted in huge economic losses for Guam, as people from these nations would instead save and plan for more expensive trips to other destinations in the United States. Many commentators have noted China's economic rise as central to Guam's economic future, but this conflicts with current U.S. foreign policy.

In 2012, U.S. Homeland Security allowed a Guam-only visa waiver for Russian citizens. The Guam Hotel and Restaurant Authority estimates that 15,000 Russian tourists would visit Guam during 2014, far above the pre-waiver average of 600 a year (Daleno, 2014). The Russian market is more affluent and high-spending than the current Japanese market (White, 2013). However, this exception made for Russian tourists in Guam can be rescinded unilaterally by the U.S. government should any diplomatic conflict arise (as with the application of sanctions). Thus, the opening of the Russian market does not signify a reliable benefit for Guam's economic development and the future of its tourist industry.

The Russian market will probably not develop into a primary economic engine for Guam, but China does hold the potential to revolutionize Guam's tourist industry and economy. As an editorial from the *Pacific Daily News* noted, "China had about 102 million outbound travelers from April 2013 to March 2014. Capturing even a small fraction of that would mean a huge boost to our visitor industry" (Deliver, 2014).

Encouraged by the exception made by U.S. Homeland Security for Russian tourists, there has been renewed hope that a Guam-only visa waiver may be possible for Chinese tourists. In both 2013 and 2014, Government of Guam delegations travelled to Washington, DC, to meet with federal officials on a number of topics, the most critical of which was the China Guam-Only Visa Waiver proposition. These recent efforts have so far yielded nothing. The United States–Guam relationship currently prohibits Guam's further economic development.

THE CULTURAL TURN

In the 1980s, the average tourist to Guam was fairly affluent and high spending in the glitzy, high-end, high-rise-hotel tourist paradise that Tumon had become. As Japan's economy went into recession, the Japanese demographic market shifted. The spending power of the average Japanese tourist decreased, and the designer stores and overpriced restaurants in Tumon were no longer preferred (Daleno, 2013).

With this shift in demographics, tourists were now looking to get more for their money and seek new, less expensive ways of enjoying the island. The Tumon-based tourist experience was based primarily on shopping, but, as Tony Lamorena, former director of the Guam Visitors Bureau recalled, this was not to Guam's advantage:

> As Mr. Shinmachi, President of the Japan Association of Travel Agents (JATA) said, "Don't build any more shopping centers. Don't build any more buildings. Start improving in your natural beauty. People go to Guam not because they want to go shopping. They go to Guam because they want to enjoy the environment, the history of Guam."
>
> (qtd. in Schumann, 2006, p. 240)

Tourists became less oriented toward American consumerism and more toward seeking a meaningful and noncommodified cultural experience (Guam Visitors Bureau, 2014). Faux-Polynesian tourist experiences had brought Guam to a certain level, but, at the start of the 2000s, it became clear that Guam's tourism industry would have to change in order to sustain itself, let alone grow.

The Guam Visitors Bureau organized conferences bringing together government officials, tourist industry representatives and cultural leaders to discuss incorporating more Chamorro elements into tourism, especially language, culture, and food. Individual hotels had already begun to localize their product in response to visitor demand and marketing needs. Many incorporated local foods, along with Chamorro names for restaurants and multipurpose meeting rooms. Beyond that, however, many hotels had no incorporation of culture or language (Schumann, 2006, p. 302). Even with evident Japanese tourist interest in a more authentically local cultural experience, industry still showed resistance. Hotels particularly continued excluding Chamorro dance performances. At present, out of the 15 major hotels in Tumon, only 1, the Sheraton, regularly features such performances (Rabon, 2014).

DECOLONIZING GUAM'S TOURISM INDUSTRY

Despite industry reticence, the Guam Visitors Bureau (GVB) has attempted to "decolonize" the image of Guam to meet tourist demand but also to be more representative of what actually exists in Guam culturally. Superficial changes were implemented, such as the creation of new logos and the printing of new Chamorro-themed Hawaiian-print shirts. More far-reaching reforms dealt with expanding the tourism industry beyond Tumon, establishing a village ambassador program in 2009 (*The Marianas Variety*, 2009a). Each of Guam's 19 villages selected a cultural representative, whether a musician, weaver, blacksmith, carver, farmer, or traditional healer, who could be used as a point of contact among tour groups, the visitor industry, and the wider community. The GVB offered villages a series of grants in order to create community tourism partnerships or projects, known as "fiesta grants," in reference to Guam's village or neighborhood parties often featuring cock-fighting, carnivals, gambling, and dance and music performance in addition to feasts (*The Marianas Variety*, 2009b). Arrangements were made for buses filled with Japanese tourists to attend fiestas in two villages, with some seed funding to organize activities and food for the guests.

These interventions, while well meaning, were unsuccessful. Most villages didn't have the infrastructure to provide a telling experience for visitors. Historic sites were not well identified, and the village ambassadors did not have facilities adequate for hosting tourists. The village fiesta program ended at the pilot stage, with no industry exploration into addressing its limitations as well as possible solutions.

Third-Space Guahan

Local entrepreneurs are working now to carve out their "third space" (Bhabha, 1994) outside the limits of the existing commercial tourist industry. They are blending entrepreneurial foresight with community organizing approaches and indigenous cultural principles, including non–market-based principles. Chamorros in particular are simultaneously reclaiming indigeneity while producing cultural commodities in the private and public sectors, albeit on a smaller scale than the foreign-controlled commercial tourism industry. Recent efforts by both community groups and corporations reveal the way efforts are being made to cater to the demands of the tourist industry while also no longer obscuring the Chamorro culture or people but celebrating and promoting these and their heritage. These efforts have met mixed success.

The opening of the Lina'la Cultural Village and Eco Park in 2011 represented the first large-scale corporate attempt to take advantage of changing visitor demands in Guam (Lina'la Beach & Culture Park, 2014; Visit Guam, 2014). This cultural tourism park was created by entrepreneur Mark Baldyga of the Baldya Group, a tourist company that runs the largest Las Vegas entertainment center in Guam, the SandCastle, and has been the Mariana Islands' largest entertainment and tour attraction operator since 1990 (Guam SandCastle, 2014). Baldyga hoped corporate sponsors would fund local school trips, while the park also made money from tourist entertainments. In contrast to the magicians, showgirls, and white tigers of their existing attractions, the Lina'la Cultural Village is meant to provide a historical reenactment of the life of ancient Chamorros. The park included a small museum, a reconstruction of an ancient settlement, a petting zoo, and a nature walk surrounded by native plants. Employees in the cultural village were required to speak the Chamorro language and also wear loincloths and traditional jewelry while working (Sachs, 2013). While being lauded at its opening for offering a uniquely Chamorro experience, the Lina'la Cultural Village has not been an economic success. Employees at the park have noted that very little money is spent on advertising, which is critical, as the area is hidden away in the jungles at the north end of Tumon. Moreover, the general tourism industry, still based significantly on packaged group tours, has yet to embrace the cultural village (Guelu, 2013).

Local batik artist, educator, and entrepreneur Judy Flores spearheaded the creation of the Gefpå'go cultural village in 1992 in the southern village of Inarajan (Inetnon Gefpago, 2014) to preserve her husband's ancestral Chamorro culture. The southern half of Guam remains largely rural with little to no economic development compared to the central and northern areas. Gefpå'go Cultural Village was built in the heart of the village, along the bay, with numerous historic sites within walking distance to help bring jobs and cultural awareness to the area. In the cultural village itself, Chamorro elders were hired to demonstrate traditional activities such as rope making, roof thatching, salt making, and weaving (Martinez, 2014). Gefpå'go hosts annual arts and dance festivals and recently added a restaurant, one of the few in the southern half of the island. Taking a drive through the less developed southern portion of Guam has now become a significant part of the Guam tourist experience; thus, Gefpå'go has become a major stop for tourists travelling on their own or with group tours (Cruz, 2013).

In partial response to the rejection of Chamorro dance by the tourism industry, the organization Pa'a Taotao Tano' (The Way of Life of the People of the Land) was created in 2001 by former Speaker of the Guam Legislature Carlos P. Taitano and Master of Chamorro Dance Frank Rabon (Pa'a Taotao Tano', 2013). Its mission is to perpetuate Chamorro culture and artistry, and it has become one of the most visible entities in terms of representation of Chamorro culture. Pa'a Taotao Tano' has more than 1,000 members and at least 16 cultural performing groups, with dance collectives not only in Guam, but also in

Japan and the United States. The motivation for creating this formal organization was the hope that it would help Chamorros have a greater impact on the
representation of their island. Pa'a Taotao Tano' offers dance performances,
dance classes, Chamorro language lessons, cultural demonstrations, teacher
training, and AmeriCorps internships (Onedera-Salas, 2011). By forming this
organization, the group has slowly been able to integrate itself into Guam's
tourism industry. Members of Pa'a Taotao Tano' are periodically hired to conduct blessing ceremonies, to sing for events, and also to demonstrate weaving
and other cultural activities at the poolside of hotels. While kitsch Polynesian
cultural forms still permeate Tumon, Pa'a has been successful in proving the
viability of replacing these with Chamorro cultural arts. According to Victor
Lujan, the group's enterprise manager, Pa'a Taotao Tano' made a bet with
the largest package tour operator in Guam several years ago that Chamorro
dance would be just as appealing to Japanese tourists as Polynesian dance. As
part of these package tours, visitors are offered lessons in music or dance. The
tour operator agreed to offer Chamorro dance on a probationary basis. The
Chamorro dance lessons have proved to be as popular as the Polynesia dance
courses. This has led Pa'a Taotao Tano' to begin negotiations with bringing
Chamorro dance into multiple hotels in Tumon by 2015 (Lujan, 2014).

Both Gefpå'go Cultural Village and Pa'a Taotao Tano' represent Chamorro-
focused organizations that have been making inroads into the local visitor
industry. The foundation to their success, however, also identifies a problem with today's entrepreneurial environment. Both of these groups were
initially supported through federal funding, primarily through the Administration of Native Americans (ANA) grants. Both continue to apply for
and receive these federal funds while also relying on grants from the local
government of Guam. The lack of private capital and investment remains
a most difficult issue confronting potential island entrepreneurs who wish
to portray a more authentic image of Guam life and Chamorro culture.

RECOMMENDATIONS

As Chamorro revitalization movements gain more traction, their forms of
cultural expression may see more representation in the tourism sector, con-
stituting an opportunity for mutual engagement between the visibility and
development of an authentic cultural tourism and indigenous entrepreneurial efforts. Although the colonial history and political status of Guam present structural disadvantages to indigenous entrepreneurship and growth in
the tourism sector, trends point to a welcome change in the status quo. Visitors are increasingly seeking "authentic experiences" through alternative
modalities: that is, cultural, creative, eco-, and experiential tourism. Some
of these promising modalities are reviewed in turn below.

  (1) Public–Private Industry Partnerships—The Guam Visitors Bureau
is advocating private–public policies and collaborations that stipulate the

procurement and sourcing of more local products where feasible. This may impress foreign-owned establishments with the needs of local communities and also may stimulate foreign investment, as the costs of local products may be significantly less than imports. Positive marketing and public-relations benefits of working with local communities may help enterprises promote themselves as sustainability and social responsibility minded, in line with the new, more green-conscious, tourist demographic. More attempts are needed to balance the immediate costs of shifting to local procurement with the potential long-term benefits (in terms of both revenue and brand awareness) presented by sustainable local development initiatives.

(2) Ecotourism—In his study, Schumann (2006, pp. 36–37) notes, "Due to the island's natural beauty, Guam has the potential to establish and promote more ecotourism sites and activities for its visitors. There are currently no tours offered to visitors that are specifically designated as ecotourism activities."

He recommends promoting and marketing the existing Marine Preserve Areas and the unique National Park that is the only site in the U.S. National Park System (composed of 385 parks) that honors the bravery and sacrifices of all those who participated in the Pacific Theater of World War II.

However, Schumann also states that "it appears that Guam is not prepared to cater to travelers who are looking for unique experiences" (ibid., p. 130). Indigenous entrepreneurs may seize upon this opportunity, promoting such initiatives as ecotours with indigenous environmental ethics and conservation efforts, including heritage preservation efforts. Indigenous modes of eco- and cultural tourism provide a unique opportunity for local stewardship and management of natural resources (Bunten, 2010, p. 299).

(3) Cultural Patrimony—More can be done to develop tourism programs around locales of cultural significance. Cultural-heritage tourism projects may center around the many archaeological sites on the island, including those featuring the megalithic archaeology of *latte*-stone sites. Special consideration to the cultural sensitivities of ancestral sites, especially burial sites, is called for. Nevertheless, cultural archaeology may be a venue for heritage tourism routes, with which the Chamorro people may highlight their culture in the tourist imaginary. However, access to many sites of cultural significance are restricted due to military land tenure and security concerns, a feature of continuing colonialism.

(4) New Technology and Creative Tourism—New movements in the tourism sector, facilitated by digital technology, emphasize self-designed itineraries via websites or apps like AirBnB or Japan's Rakuten. This new "creative tourism" (Richards, 2011) opens up possibilities for more genuine cultural interactions and increased microeconomic transactions beyond the scope of all-inclusive commercial tourist destinations. Small local entrepreneurs may also thus engage directly with clients in the tourist economy. This new creative tourism is an example of Schumpterian notions of the entrepreneurial exploitation of innovation (Peredo & McClean, 2006).

CONCLUSION: OUR HERITAGE GIVES LIFE TO OUR SPIRIT

In August 2014, the gates to Sagan Kutturan Chamoru opened on a hill overlooking Tumon Bay (Kutturan Chamoru Foundation, 2014). In contrast to that gaudy concrete jungle below, Sagan Kutturan Chamoru is a simple set of eight remodeled buildings, each of which offers the opportunity to learn about a different aspect of traditional Chamorro culture, such as carving, traditional navigation, weaving, and blacksmithing. Apprenticeships in the Chamorro language for these trades began in 2014. The intention is to expand the center's offerings to include education on culinary arts and traditional medicine (Aoki, 2014).

The Sagan Kutturan Chamoru was first incorporated as a nonprofit organization in 2006 by many local artists, including Jill Quichocho Benavente, a master of Chamorro carving, in order to promote indigenous Chamorro art and industry and to provide an economic outlet for their products. However, the 8-year journey until the opening of its doors was a convoluted one. Different hotels and government agencies promised financial support, but, finally, leaders of this artist collective had to take a more grass-roots approach, relying on hard work from volunteer artist-activist entrepreneurs who donated their time and proceeds from sales of their artwork.

The opening of Sagan Kutturan Chamoru is representative of the shift described earlier whereby Chamorros are seeking to decolonize their island's primary industry. Rather than continue to market the island as a fake or entrust its representation to others, this collective is indicative of how more Chamorros are seeking ways to preserve and promote their culture while also providing an engaging tourism experience to visitors. As Ed Benavente, a long-time decolonization activist and a leader in the Sagan Kutturan Chamoru (2014), has noted, *"I irensia, lina'la, i espiritu-ta* (Our heritage gives life to our spirit). So long as we are true to our culture, it will always be there to nourish our spirit and sustain us."

REFERENCES

Aldrich, R., & Connell, J. (1998). *The last colonies.* Cambridge: Cambridge University Press.
Alvarez, E. (2013, August 7). Personal communication.
Aoki, Dance. (2014, August, 14). Center focuses on Chamorro culture. *Pacific Daily News.* Retrieved from www.guampdn.com/article/20140815/NEWS01/308150003/Center-focuses-Chamorro-culture
Baldacchino, G., & Royle, S. A. (2010). Postcolonialism and islands: An introduction. *Space and Culture, 13*(2), 140–143.
Bettis, L. (1993). Colonial immigration on Guam: Displacement of the Chamorro people under US governance. In G. McCall & J. Connell (Eds.), *A world perspective on Pacific Islander migration: Australia, New Zealand and the USA* (pp. 265–296). University of New South Wales, Australia: Center for South Pacific Studies.

Bevacqua, M. L. (2007). *Everything you wanted to know about Guam but were afraid to ask Žižek.* MA thesis. University of California at San Diego.

Bhabha, H. K. (1994). *The location of culture.* London: Routledge.

Bunten, A. C. (2010). More like ourselves: Indigenous capitalism through tourism. *American Indian Quarterly, 34*(3), 285–311.

Burnett, C. D., & Marshall, B. (Eds.). (2001). *Foreign in a domestic sense: Puerto Rico, American expansion, and the Constitution.* Durham, NC: Duke University Press.

Cahn, M. (2008). Indigenous entrepreneurship, culture and micro-enterprise in the Pacific Islands: Case studies from Samoa. *Entrepreneurship & Regional Development, 20*(1), 1–18.

Césaire, A. (1972). *Discourse on colonialism.* Trans. J. Pinkham. New York, NY: Monthly Review Press.

Conlin, M. V., & Baum, T. G. (1995). *Island tourism: Management principles and practice.* New York, NY: John Wiley & Sons.

Cote, R. (2013). *From disadvantage to success? Indigenous entrepreneurship in the urban marketplace: An international comparison.* International Sociological Association: Research Committee on Social Stratification RC28 Conference, St. Lucia, QLD, Australia, July 16–20.

Cruz, Y. (2013). *Networks enhance Inarajan village's sense of place.* MA thesis. University of Illinois, Urbana-Champaign.

Daleno, G. D. (2013, October 26). Guam tourism numbers up, spending per visitor down. *The Pacific Daily News.* Retrieved from http://pidp.org/pireport/2013/October/10–28–05.htm

Daleno, G. D. (2014, September 26). Russian tourist arrivals decrease: Suspension of direct charter flights stems flow. *Pacific Daily News.* Retrieved from www.guampdn.com/article/20140926/NEWS01/309260012/Russian-tourist-arrivals-decrease-Suspension-direct-charter-flights-stems-flow

Deliver. (2014, July 4): Deliver: China visa waiver for Guam is in line with US tourism strategy. *The Pacific Daily News.* Retrieved from www.guampdn.com/article/M0/20140706/OPINION01/307060016/Deliver-China-visa-waiver-Guam-line-US-tourism-strategy

Fanon, F. (1965). *The wretched of the earth.* Trans. C. Farrington. New York, NY: Grove Press.

Feyrer, J., & Sacerdote, B. (2009). Colonialism and modern income: Islands as natural experiments. *The Review of Economics and Statistics, 91*(2), 245–262.

Flores, J. (2002). The re-creation of Chamorro dance as observed through the Festival of Pacific Arts. *Pacific Arts, 25* (December), 47–63. Retrieved from www.jstor.org/stable/23411394

Foley, D. (2012). Teaching entrepreneurship to indigenous and other minorities: Towards a strong sense of self, tangible skills and active participation within society. *Journal of Business Diversity, 12*(2), 59–76.

Friedman, H. M. (2001). *Creating an American lake: United States imperialism and strategic security in the Pacific basin, 1945–1947.* Santa Barbara, CA: Greenwood Publishing.

Guam SandCastle. (2014). SandCastle Dinner Theater and Entertainment. Retrieved from www.guam-sandcastle.com/en

Guam Visitors Bureau. (2014). Guam Tourism 2020 Plan. Retrieved from www.guamvisitorsbureau.com/research-and-reports/reports/guam-tourism-2020-plan

Guelu (Pseudonym). (2013). Personal Communication.

Hart, T. (2011, July 15). Benefits of China visa waiver for Guam touted. *The Marianas Variety.* Retrieved from www.mvguam.com/component/content/article/19011-benefits-of-china-visa-waiver-for-guam-touted.html#.VDFxpBY0_Kk

Hattori, A. P. (1996). Righting civil wrongs: Guam Congress walkout of 1949. In Political Status Education and Coordinating Commission, *Kinalamten pulitikat: Sinenten i Chamorro*. (*Issues in Guam's political development: The Chamorro perspective*; pp. 57–69.) Hagåtña, Guam: Political Status Education and Coordinating Commission.

Inetnon Gefpago. (2014). Cultural arts program. Retrieved from www.inetnongef pago.com/

Iyoda, M. (2010). *Postwar Japanese economy: Lessons of economic growth and the bubble economy*. New York, NY: Springer.

Kutturan Chamoru Foundation. (2014). Fafa'nå'gue. Retrieved from http://kuttur anchamoru.org/about/fafanague/

Leon Guerrero, A. (1996). The economic development of Guam. In Political Status Education and Coordinating Commission, *Kinalamnten pulitikat: Issues in Guam's political development* (pp. 83–101). Hagåtña, Guam: Political Status Education Coordinating Commission.

Limtiaco, S. (2014, April 28). Case for equal rights of territory residents in US Appeals Court. *The Pacific Daily News*. Guam. Retrieved from www.guampdn.com/ article/20140429/NEWS01/304290009/Territory-residents-rights-case-now-fed eral-appeals-court

Lina'la Beach & Culture Park. (2014). Baldyga Group. http://en.guam-bgtours.com/ park/about-linala-beach-and-culture-park

Lockhart, D., & Drakakis-Smith, D. W. (Eds.). (1997). *Island tourism: Trends and prospects*. New York, NY: Thomson Learning.

Lutz, C. (2010). US military bases on Guam in global perspective. *The Asia-Pacific Journal*, July 26. Retrieved from www.japanfocus.org/-catherine-lutz/3389

Lujan, V. (2014). Personal Communication.

Martinez, L. (2014, February 6). Touring the past: Inarajan festival highlights cultural history. *The Pacific Daily News*. Retrieved from www.guampdn.com/ article/ 20140207/LIFESTYLE/302070014/Touring-past-Inarajan-festival-highlights-cultural-history

The Marianas Variety. (2009a, July 30). GVB's village ambassadors selected. Retrieved from http://mvguam.com/component/content/article/7787-gvbs-village-ambassadors-selected-.html

The Marianas Variety. (2009b, October 2). Mayor's family awarded fiesta grant. Retrieved from http://mvguam.com/local/news/8840-mayors-family-awarded-fiesta-money.html

Onedera-Salas, S. (2011, July 6). A celebration of dance. *The Pacific Daily News*. Retrieved from www.guampdn.com/article/20110706/COMMUNITIES/10706 0303/A-celebration-dance

Peredo, M., & Anderson, R. (2006). Indigenous entrepreneurship research: Themes and variations. *International Research in Business Disciplines, 5*, 253–273.

Peredo, A. M., & McLean, M. (2006). Social entrepreneurship: A critical review of the concept. *Journal of World Business, 41*(1), 56–65.

Pa'a Taotao Tåno'. (2010). *Chamorro language assessment survey (CLAS) project*. Administration for Native Americans Grant. Guam: Micronesian Business Association. Retrieved from www.acf.hhs.gov/sites/default/files/ana/guam_0.pdf

Pa'a Taotao Tano'. (2013). Way of life of the people of the land. Retrieved from www.paataotaotano.org/about/

Palomo, A. (1965). "Wanted: Distinctiveness." *Pacific Profile*. Document available in the Micronesia Area Research Center, University of Guam.

Rabon, F. (2001). *Pa'a Taotao Tåno': A way of life, people of the land: Chamorro chants and dances*. Hagåtña, Guam: Irensia Publishing.

Rabon, F. (2014, September 22). Personal Communication.

Richards, G. (2011). Creativity and tourism: The state of the art. *Annals of Tourism Research, 38*(4), 1225–1253.

Rogers, R. (1999). *Destiny's landfall: A history of Guam.* Honolulu, HI: University of Hawaii Press.

Sachs, A. (2013, April 13). An American in Micronesia: Without a passport. *The Washington Post.* Retrieved from www.washingtonpost.com/lifestyle/travel/an-american-in-micronesia—without-a-passport/2013/04/18/0a4773ae-9e1e-11e2-a2db-efc5298a95e1_story.html

Schumann, F. R. (2006). *Private and public sector collaboration in Guam's tourism industry: Is Guam prepared for the future?* PhD thesis. Beppu, Japan: Ritsumeikan Asia Pacific University.

Tolentino, D. (2014). Governor William "Bill" Daniel. *Guampedia.* Retrieved from www.guampedia.com/governor-bill-daniel/

U.N. (2014). Non-self-governing territories. United Nations Committee on Decolonization. Retrieved from www.un.org/en/decolonization/nonselfgovterritories.shtml

Visit Guam. (2014). Lina'La LLC. Retrieved from www.visitguam.com/listings/Lina-La-LLC/342/0/

White, J. (2013, May 13). The Russian tourist: A closer look at Guam's emerging new market. *The Marianas Variety.* Retrieved from http://mvguam.com/local/news/29452-the-russian-tourist.html#.VDFyGRY0_Kk

12 Medical Tourism in Barbados

Negotiating Inherent Tensions

Krystyna Adams, Rebecca Whitmore,
Rory Johnston, and Valorie A. Crooks

INTRODUCTION

This chapter examines the planning for medical tourism taking place in Barbados, a small island state in the Anglophone Caribbean. In addition to a comprehensive overview of medical tourism in Barbados, the chapter highlights the inherent tensions in developing a locally beneficial medical tourism industry. By identifying competing visions put forth by various stakeholders in the Barbadian medical tourism sector, including staffing and ownership formats, regulation and investment incentives, and differing ideas of appropriate developmental scale and scope of services, we provide insights into the important considerations this small island state is facing when seeking to develop this much-hyped but poorly understood sector. This chapter draws on our long term-research program examining medical tourism in Barbados and the wider Anglophone Caribbean. Since 2011, we have undertaken 69 semistructured interviews and three focus groups with a wide range of health system and tourism-sector stakeholders in Barbados, compiled a comprehensive collection of state and media reports discussing medical tourism, and collectively spent more than a year conducting on-site ethnographic fieldwork that has included many informal conversations with users of the Barbadian health system from a wide range of backgrounds. Together, these datasets and experiences provide a rich understanding of the potential considerations and hopes arising from the ongoing discussion about medical tourism development in a small island setting. Exploring these considerations and hopes suggests ways in which Barbados and other small island states seeking to develop their medical tourism sectors can negotiate a structure for medical tourism that can best meet their development goals.

MEDICAL TOURISM

The term "medical tourism" refers to the practice of patients moving across national borders with the intention to access medical care, typically paid for out of pocket (Snyder et al., 2013). Patients have long traveled across borders in pursuit of medical treatments, particularly from low-income countries with poor quality or limited range of healthcare services to better-equipped health systems in higher-income countries. However, recent years have seen the emergence of many new flows of patients, particularly of patients from high-income nations traveling to low- and middle-income countries who are looking to access less costly, faster, alternative, or unproven treatments that are unavailable in their home jurisdictions. Medical facilities seek medical tourists in order to generate income, while governments are interested in developing the sector in order to generate employment, improve health infrastructure, and increase their reserves of foreign exchange (Connell, 2013a; Lunt et al., 2014).

Development of a medical tourism sector is presented as an economic development strategy, particularly for tourism-dependent countries seeking diversification of their tourism product (Smith, 2012). Groups such as the Medical Tourism Association, an American-based group, and the reports of consultancies such as McKinsey and Deloitte, have predominantly informed the existing medical tourism discourse (Labonté, 2013). Media sources reinforce the depiction of the sector as a driver of economic development, highlighting the profitability of medical tourism ventures in places such as Thailand and India (Collinder, 2013; Eden, 2012). This dominant discourse provides a primarily positive frame for the sector, which is in sharp contrast to the ethical concerns about the potential harmful impacts of the practice that are rarely mentioned outside of academic literature (Mainil, 2011). Commonly cited ethical concerns about medical tourism include issues of individual patient safety as well as concerns for equitable distribution of health resources (Snyder et al., 2013; Turner, 2007). These latter concerns have primarily framed medical tourism as both a symptom of and driver of health system inequity, chiefly in its potential to draw public resources toward private medical facilities catering to (relatively) few wealthy locals and foreign tourists (Smith, 2012). As medical tourism centers on private, curative services, it is argued that it serves as a diversion of attention and resources from primary health care and, more generally, services that are most relevant to the public health burden (Snyder et al., 2013). While these concerns are supported by examples of supportive public policies and government involvement to develop medical tourism sectors in established destinations such as India, Thailand, and Malaysia, they often do not concede the constructive intentions that governments have for the medical tourism industry in resource-constrained contexts with regard to both economic development and health system improvement (Ormond, 2011).

As a high-value service industry, medical tourism may be particularly attractive for governments in small island states seeking to diversify their economies (Campling & Rosalie, 2006; Connell, 2013b). The size and geographic characteristics of small island states inform their economic, environmental, and social vulnerability. With a small domestic market, small island states have limited ability to exploit economies of scale. Furthermore, they typically have a limited resource base, including raw materials and manpower to provide services and expertise. As a result, small island states regularly rely on foreign investment and imported goods, resulting in precarious work options for the populations and limited social and economic security. Finally, environmental problems are particularly intense for small islands with relatively large coastlines and fragile ecosystems (Briguglio, 2003). This vulnerability poses significant restrictions upon the economic diversification options of small island states (Campling & Rosalie, 2006).

Many small island states, including those in the Caribbean region, have well-established tourism industries, facilitating the development of industries that utilize this infrastructure and reputation as tourism destinations (Zappino, 2005). Connell (2013b) notes that the Bahamas, Barbados, and Cayman Islands have all indicated interest in developing medical tourism in order to generate employment and investment, as well as to improve provision of care locally. Furthermore, Connell (2013b) highlights the influx of foreign patients to Cuba for medical tourism as providing evidence that islands in this region could attract foreign patients. As a form of tourism diversification, medical tourism may be a particularly appealing export industry for small island states due to their existing familiarity with tourism exports, as well as the attractiveness of using medical tourism activities to improve the quality of and access to health care on the islands (Connell, 2013b). By increasing demand for health care services through an influx of international patients, medical tourism discourse suggests that this could enable health care providers that otherwise lack adequate demand for their services to successfully operate on the island and/or prompt foreign physicians to work on the island, potentially providing otherwise unavailable care to local patients (Horowitz, Rosensweig, & Jones, 2007; Turner, 2007). However, as described by Connell (2013b), medical tourism projects in the Caribbean are driven by business rather than health care rationales and are associated with potential ethical issues. As will be described in more detail later in this chapter, the realization of the touted benefits may only be realized within certain contexts, including the right regulatory framework.

The remainder of this chapter discusses existing medical tourism activities and planning for medical tourism in Barbados to provide a nuanced exploration of medical tourism's potential impacts in small island contexts.

BARBADOS'S ECONOMIC CONTEXT

At 430 km^2 and a population less than 300,000, Barbados is a densely populated small island state. The most easterly country in the Caribbean archipelago, Barbados shares many elements of its colonial history and economic development with neighboring islands. This small country has faced the challenge of developing its economy with limited natural resources and a limited opportunity to generate economies of scale at the time of independence, especially due to the sharp decline in the profitability of the sugar industry that served as the foundation of its economy since colonial times (Worrell et al., 2011). In 1966, Barbados emerged as an independent state while facing an uncertain economic future stemming from its small size and relatively isolated location. The degradation of its agricultural land from long and intensive sugar production and reliance on existing preferential trade agreements remaining from its Commonwealth ties put the country in a weak competitive position in the global market for its established export sectors (Bishop, 2010).

Throughout the 1950s and 1960s, the government of Barbados sought new economic development opportunities that would no longer rely on the declining sugar industry. With a small economy and limited resources, Barbados was particularly focused on development activities related to service export (Downes, 2001). The development of service industries was attractive due to limited export restrictions, opportunities to attract large amounts of foreign investment quickly, and the suitability of Barbados for tourism activities given its warm climate and attractive landscape (Bishop, 2010). Throughout the 1960s and 1970s, investment in the service sector, particularly tourism, resulted in rapid economic development (Downes, 2001). By the late 1970s, tourism contributed to national GDP a share equivalent to the manufacturing sector or the sugar industry (Worrell et al., 2001). In the 1980s, following the international debt crisis, the remaining manufacturing sector collapsed, and the sugar industry continued to decline. As a result, investment in the service sector and especially service export activities like tourism was encouraged via loan and debt-relief stipulations (Downes, 2001). By the mid 1980s, Barbados's service industries were contributing 73% of total GDP, with tourism contributing between 15% and 18% of service sector GDP during this decade (Clarkson & Craigwell, 1997).

The birth of the international business and financial sector in the late 1970s provided a new opportunity for Barbados to expand its service exports (Worrell et al., 2001). While in 2000 tourism accounted for two thirds of all foreign exchange earnings (Erikson & Lawrence, 2008), the international financial sector continues to provide a significant contribution to total GDP. Estimates of the percentage of GDP contribution from the financial export sector are not readily available, likely because offshore activities are excluded from national GDP estimates (Clarkson & Craigwell, 1997). The exclusion of data on offshore activities, including offshore banking, corporate registries, and offshore medical schools, challenges attempts to better understand the contribution this sector makes to the Barbadian economy. However, reports on this sector indicate that Barbados has successfully attracted business from various companies as a result of the country's political stability, confidentiality practices, and low tax rates (Erikson & Lawrence, 2008; Ministry of Finance and Foreign Affairs, 2005). However, this sector is increasingly challenged by global demands for reform, including increased oversight and regulation of subsidiary activities. Pressures to respond to these reformatory demands may be particularly influential for countries like Barbados given the importance of reputation for the success of the tourism sector (Ogawa et al., 2013). These reforms may encourage offshore entities to shop around for a more desirable regulatory environment, limiting the growth of this sector in countries that undergo these reforms (Erikson & Lawrence, 2008).

Overall, the history of Barbados's economic activity from the 1950s to the present day demonstrates that the country has always maintained a relatively liberal economy and that the scope and form of economic activities have responded to global macroeconomic trends, including globalization and neoliberalism (ECLAC, 2000). While these economic approaches have sustained Barbados's impressive economic development over the past 60 years, concerns about the long term-sustainability of these economic development strategies have long been raised.

The work of economists such as St. Lucia's Sir Arthur Lewis (1915–1991) highlights concerns about economic development strategies in the Caribbean that are echoed in current issues arising around planning for medical tourism. Lewis's work presents the idea that export-oriented development in the Caribbean should follow a model of "industrialization by invitation." This strategy sought to recognize and respond to the challenges faced by newly independent small island states like those in the Caribbean, particularly their high levels of unemployment, limited natural resources, small domestic supply of capital, and narrow economic diversification, by pragmatically calling for national governments like Barbados's to open their economies to private foreign investment in manufacturing and services. However, it balanced this call for foreign investment against an expectation that national governments would be careful in only accepting competitive offers that would advance and not exploit countries' current economic positions in viable niches and not liberalize their economies wholesale (Downes, 2004). The long-term goal of Lewis's strategy was to establish and integrate a diverse range of industries in the Caribbean. This was done with the intent of increasing local manufacture of value-added goods for both export and import substitution, simultaneously increasing employment and reducing the Caribbean's deep reliance on expensive imports that had been developed and sustained over centuries of colonial administration (Farrell, 1980). Furthermore, given the small size of each Caribbean country, Lewis envisioned regional economic and institutional cooperation as key components in achieving the largest possible share of these benefits (Downes, 2004).

The development path envisaged by Lewis and other proponents of "industrialization by invitation" has not been realized in Caribbean countries like Barbados that, despite great strides in economic development since the 1960s, continue to be deeply dependent on imported goods and foreign investment, thus maintaining a high level of vulnerability to global economic volatility (Andrian et al., 2013). The sociopolitical and geographical context of Barbados has made the pursuit of the service export industry particularly appealing; however, this pursuit has posed certain challenges to economic development in the global economic climate, as discussed in Lewis's work (Erikson & Lawrence, 2008). In 2008, tourism accounted for 14% of Barbadian national GDP (Worrell et al., 2001). The large contribution that tourism and other service exports make to national GDP informs the necessity of Barbados's competitiveness in exporting its services. While regional commitments to the Caribbean Single Market Economy and Caribbean Community Secretariat facilitate sharing of resources between member states and enhanced bargaining power when negotiating access to the regional market, members like Barbados have also agreed to increasingly liberalize their services (Bishop et al., 2011; ECLAC, 2012). This has further enhanced competition within the region, as many members export the same types of services and seek out investment from the same pool of investors (ECLAC, 2012). Along with challenges to regional coordination, concerns regarding scarce local sources of investment and challenges to import substitution, as discussed by Lewis, continue to be relevant today for countries like Barbados pursuing economic development—such as via a medical tourism sector—in the context of its service-based economy.

Barbados's dependence on international trade activities can be exploited by outside actors such as foreign investors, enabling them to overwhelmingly benefit from these relations while placing the burdens of these activities (including environmental degradation) on the small island state (ECLAC, 2000). As Lewis pointed out in the "industrialization by invitation" model, involvement by outside actors is not necessarily problematic and in fact is likely necessary to some degree in small island states like Barbados with limited supplies of capital for expanding industry (Downes, 2004). However, Caribbean countries must carefully consider their policy structure and regulatory environment to find the right balance between enticing foreign investment and maximizing benefits to local economic development (Griffith, Waithe, & Craigwell, 2008). Striking this balance may prove to be especially challenging given the vulnerability of Caribbean countries like Barbados as a result of their dependence on economic activities that are easily disrupted by global macroeconomic policies and structural reforms (ECLAC, 2000). As a result, many of the economic development strategies presently pursued by Caribbean countries focus on diversifying their expansive, if volatile, service export industries through such means as offshore medical schools, offshore banking, heritage, sports, and medical tourism (Mercer-Blackman et al., 2013; Worrell et al., 2001).

This chapter now focuses on the development of the medical tourism sector in Barbados and provides an overview of the challenges and opportunities Barbados faces in trying to find the right balance in protecting local interests while growing this new industry.

Medical Tourism in Barbados

Barbados's small size, with regard to both population and economy, restricts the ability to provide comprehensive curative health care for all its citizens due to limited health human resources, training opportunities, and insufficient demand for specialists (Campbell et al., 2008). Thus, the Barbadian context demonstrates the potential for medical tourism to expand health care resources on the island to cater also for domestic demand (Gonzales et al., 2001). This context, particularly in terms of Barbados's service-based economy and limited health care resources, has influenced the particular strand of pro–medical tourism discourse by various stakeholders on the island, including the Barbadian government, health care workers, tourism operators, and other individuals and groups positioned to benefit from medical tourism activities. It is thought that these benefits can outweigh concerns cited in the medical tourism literature if properly regulated. However, the existing literature on tourism development demonstrates a need for contextual analyses to understand how these benefits might be realized, who stands to gain from the industry, and who may be unfairly burdened by the industry (Ormond, 2011). Without such considerations there is concern that, at best, medical tourism destinations like Barbados may simply serve as hosts to an industry with limited domestic benefits or, at worst, medical tourism will disrupt long-term development and equity-enhancing processes (Johnston et al., 2013).

The medical tourism sector in Barbados is currently very small, consisting of one fertility clinic that has had success recruiting foreign patients. This facility, the Barbados Fertility Centre (BFC), has been accredited by the most recognizable international hospital accreditation organization, Joint Commission International, and draws the majority of its patients from the United States, the United Kingdom, and Canada. While this facility is the only existing example of medical tourism in Barbados, the success of this steadily growing business demonstrates the potential for other similar types of medical tourism ventures (Connell, 2013b).

Dr. Juliet Skinner, the principal physician at the BFC, founded the clinic in 2002 with co-owner and head nurse Anna Hosford. The clinic was developed soon after Dr. Skinner, a Barbadian national, returned to Barbados after completing her medical training in Ireland (Barbados Fertility Center, 2014). Due to its small population size, Barbados had no fertility specialists practicing on the island prior to the development of the BFC. Recognizing this, the BFC was created with the regional and international market in mind, as they would provide the number of cases necessary for the facility to be feasible in a small island setting (Johnston et al., 2013). Barbados's setting has been leveraged by the clinic in its international marketing, its relaxing, tropical atmosphere represented as an asset for those looking to conceive (Connell, 2013b). Along with regional patients visiting the BFC, Barbados also serves as a medical hub for the Eastern Caribbean, providing care to regional patients through both formal cross-border care referrals and informal, patient-initiated travels to the island (Snyder et al., 2013). This latter flow of regional patients has not been readily framed as medical tourism, which is more closely associated with utilization of medical services by non-Caribbean patients.

Barbados has expressed strong interest in significantly expanding its existing medical tourism sector. In the mid-2000s, the concept of medical tourism emerged in media reports and government press releases as an increasingly viable strategy for simultaneously diversifying Barbados's tourism product and increasing access to high-tech and sophisticated medical treatment. In this period, the Barbadian government initiated a concerted effort to expand the country's medical tourism sector. This effort was spurred in part by a series of regional and local conferences on the topic of health tourism and ongoing planning for the construction of a new private hospital by a group of foreign investors. Interest among public-sector administrators and members of government resulted in the development of an interministerial Health and Wellness Tourism Task Force to oversee the expansion of the sector. This task force oversaw an extension of the existing incentive framework for investment in recreational tourism to include medical tourism facilities and a call for bids to see a long-defunct hospital located on public land get developed privately as a new facility oriented to the international patient market (Johnston et al., 2013).

In 2011, the Barbadian government accepted a bid tendered by the company American World Clinics (AWC) that would see the defunct St. Joseph hospital site redeveloped into a new 85-bed, multispecialty hospital staffed on a time-share basis (Johnston et al., 2013; Nussbaum, 2011). This staffing format would provide hospital space for a rotating roster of foreign (primarily American) specialists visiting for a period of time each year as well as local physicians willing to pay the annual membership fee. In order for the project to be financially and clinically feasible, the majority of patients would need to be medical tourists (Johnston et al., 2013). This project model was reported to be most acceptable to government stakeholders, as it was perceived to pose limited impacts to the existing Barbadian health system, to offer employment for Barbadians as nurses, lab technicians, and other skilled professionals, and to potentially retain local, privately paying patients who would otherwise travel internationally for specialized care. While AWC's Barbadian hospital was originally projected to be operational by 2014, construction of the facility has still not begun at the time of this writing, and no other projects on a similar scale have been initiated. The long-term lack of action suggests that, for the time being, large-scale medical tourism to Barbados will continue to be an idea rather than a reality.

While Barbados's medical tourism sector remains small, ongoing discussions in the media and by various local and industry stakeholders indicate continued interest in its expansion (Kirton, 2013). As we have set out, key questions around health equity and local economic benefits remain unanswered in current discussions of medical tourism development in Barbados. These questions are linked to the scale and style of medical tourism to be developed, particularly as numerous other Caribbean islands have described similar plans for developing their own medical tourism sectors, which could result in regional oversaturation of the industry. Current medical tourism discourse in Barbados is informed by the perceived success of the offshore model in other service sectors, including offshore medical schools and finance centers, and the existing transnational mobility of patients and providers throughout the region (Connell, 2013a). Complex questions of scale and ownership related to medical tourism emerge from this narrative. These are further explored in the Barbadian context by discussing major tensions facing policy makers planning for and developing a medical tourism sector that could help Barbados realize its long-term development goals.

COMPETING VISIONS OF MEDICAL TOURISM SECTOR DEVELOPMENT IN BARBADOS

Attempts to develop a Barbadian medical tourism sector have been characterized by at least four overlapping, multiple tensions in its planning and visioning: large- versus small-scale developments, offshore versus local ownership, staffing by local versus foreign doctors, and appropriate regulation versus onerous red tape. Despite these tensions, which are reviewed in what follows, medical tourism is widely perceived by many local stakeholders as having potential for innovative development of a new tourism market in the Caribbean. In the sections that follow, we address the tensions at play in the development of medical tourism and how they might influence the shape of this sector's development in Barbados.

Health Services Export in a Small Island Setting: A Question of Scale

The popularization of medical tourism as both an identifiable practice and an economic development policy has been deeply informed by the success of a limited number of large, full-scale hospitals in exporting their services internationally. The experiences of private hospitals in Asia that offer a comprehensive range of services, particularly Bumrungrad in Thailand, Raffles in Singapore, and the Apollo chain in India, have been closely associated with contemporary discussions of medical tourism (Chee, 2007). The successes of these hospitals highlight the novelty of health service export from the Global South and have been used to advance the idea of medical tourism as an economic and health system development strategy elsewhere (Ormond, 2011). Large projects such as the Cayman Islands' Health City are arguably emblematic of the contemporary visions associated with the sector's development (Connell, 2013a). However, the dominant focus on large, capital-intensive hospital projects and the export of a comprehensive range of medical services neglects to engage with smaller-scale instances of medical tourism. Barbados's experience to date with medical tourism raises important considerations of the role that facility scale plays in shaping considerations of both the health equity and economic impacts of the sector.

The private hospital being developed by AWC is only the latest instance of medical tourism planning in Barbados. Perhaps not coincidentally, the government administrators of the original St. Joseph Hospital that previously occupied the AWC site had hoped to export services to the American market in the 1980s, having explored the feasibility of tapping into internationally portable private insurance to help sustain the facility. Likewise, Project Care, a private hospital project on Barbados's west coast that was advanced in the mid-2000s, incorporated medical tourism in its plans from the outset in order for the facility's intended range of services to be possible. For these latter two projects, medical tourism was needed to support the original goal of a full-service tertiary hospital located in a small island setting. Conversely, it has been reported that one contributing factor to the delay of the AWC project is changes to its original patient composition projection, one that now plans for a larger share of local patients than the island's population can provide. Taken together, these examples indicate that medical tourism projects in low-population, small island settings have difficulties not found in more populated locales. Indeed, the international medical tourism development narrative commonly fails to clearly articulate the relatively peripheral role of medical tourism for the vast majority of medical facilities hosting international patients, where the local population provides the clinical and financial foundation for operations and medical tourists are a minor source of additional income.

The rapid growth of the BFC sits in sharp contrast to the consistent delays and shortfalls seen in larger medical tourism projects in Barbados. The clinic's success bears out Connell's (2013b) observation that medical tourism in the Caribbean is likely best suited to niche elective treatments. While Connell (2013b) outlines the many formidable barriers to the development of medical tourism among the small island states in the Caribbean, including the high rates of health worker emigration, reliance on foreign private investment, and the propriety of structuring medical facilities to be dependent on the inherently volatile tourism market, we believe that many of these challenges can be most concisely addressed through the question of appropriate developmental scale.

When the impacts of medical tourism development are examined at a smaller scale, both the sector's rewards and its risks shrink correspondingly. While the offshore model of medical tourism being advocated for in Barbados seeks to sidestep many ethical concerns of medical tourism by limiting the resources shared between medical tourism facilities and the domestic health system, it is not clear how successful it will be in doing so given the inevitable overlaps that can emerge in the form of shared personnel, medical emergencies, and follow-up treatment. Even if the offshore approach to medical tourism successfully limits the health equity risks, it will also significantly limit the economic benefits accruing to host countries. In contrast, replicating the BFC's approach by developing small outpatient clinics specializing in exporting elective treatments would not significantly impact the day-to-day operations of the existing health system and could widen the range of specialties (albeit noncritical ones) available in small island states like Barbados. Last, in terms of regulation, a small-scale approach would also pose far less of a regulatory burden for small island countries. While private third-party accreditation organizations such as Joint Commission International have been advanced as the regulatory cornerstone of medical tourism, professional associations and Ministries of Health ultimately bear the responsibility for a jurisdiction's standards of care. Large, hospital-scale medical tourism projects would impose significant burdens on the modest regulatory resources of small island states that smaller projects would not.

Offshore Versus Local Developments

The ownership and financing of medical tourism facilities is another key consideration for small island states due to the impact that facilities controlled by external interests can have on such small places. A variety of styles of ownership of medical tourism facilities exist, ranging among foreign-run, privately owned hospitals, small private facilities drawing on both local and medical tourist markets, public facilities offering some medical tourism services, and hybrid versions incorporating elements of several approaches. Here, the "local versus foreign" debate parallels the "small versus large scale" debate. In order for the industry to develop at a larger scale, there must almost certainly be a reliance on foreign investment and capital. Public discussion around these different types of development, discussed in greater detail in the following section, illustrates the continued debate as to what degree of foreign ownership and control is desirable for a prospective medical tourism industry in Barbados.

The foreign-owned, privately run model of medical tourism, exemplified in Barbados by the AWC project, has faced opposition from local health care providers and owners of local private health care clinics, who have pushed back against foreign hospitals as a threat to the sustainability of their practices. These same providers and private clinic owners may favor a small-scale, local model of medical tourism sector development whereby local businesses provide some services to both locals and medical tourists, as does the BFC. Our work in Barbados has shown that networks of local professionals are key stakeholders that have strong opinions about the benefits and drawbacks of local versus foreign ownership. Some of these opinions may be legitimately focused on unintended impacts on local health systems, while others may be more focused on an aversion to competition and protection of vested interests.

Another key question pertaining to sector development centers on whether new Barbadian medical tourism facilities will hire foreign or local workers. While medical tourism facilities can offer local employment, which governments often tout as a (if not *the*) benefit of sector development, the drawing off of local professionals into the private medical tourism sector may negatively impact the public sector. Conversely, if foreign doctors and health care professionals are brought into Barbados to practice on international patients, unresolved questions around licensing and even immigration law arise. It remains to be seen whether these impacts on the labor supply would negatively impact local public care in a country like Barbados, if they will ultimately provide access to much-needed specialized care for local residents, or both in some combination.

An overarching concern in the development of medical tourism in Barbados and elsewhere relates to the conflict between what is perceived as rigorous regulation that demonstrates best practice and instills confidence in investors and consumers versus "red tape" regulation that hinders progress in expanding medical tourism–sector activities. Negotiations among various industry stakeholders and the Barbadian government in relation to regulation and policy has been perceived as a barrier to investment in cases such as the AWC development and as necessary to protect from the loss of resources used to support ultimately failed projects such as the Four Seasons hotel, a project that was halted due to insufficient financing after the government had already invested resources in the project. The Four Seasons project demonstrates potential risks governments face in facilitating foreign investment if the project does not go through as planned and the government is left with wasted resources and unusable land where construction began, an especially relevant concern in small island states with limited land for development. The challenge of balancing regulation with incentives in seeking foreign investment is an omnipresent challenge, particularly for small island states that may be in competition with each other in attracting the same pool of foreign investors, as in the case of medical tourism in the Caribbean. However, well-designed regulation can also build trust and confidence in the Barbados brand, appealing to foreign investors. Well-designed regulation for new medical tourism developments must take into consideration whether they occur under foreign or local ownership. Current regulatory infrastructure in Barbados is more suited to local ownership, although if a significant increase in medical tourism occurs, revisions will be needed.

DISCUSSION

The case of medical tourism sector development in Barbados serves to highlight the tensions inherent in small island state development. Contradictions between the need for foreign involvement while pursuing self-sufficiency have challenged small island state development planning, as tensions emerge between promoting local entrepreneurship and industry diversification and relying on foreign investment that limits local control. The pursuit of medical tourism in the Caribbean demonstrates how small island states navigate these tensions. In this section, the inherent tensions in Barbados's medical tourism planning as informed by Lewis's development model are considered in relation to regional competition, scarcity of local capital, and import substitution.

Regional Competition

While the economic strategy of "industrialization by invitation" detailed by Lewis emphasized the development of comprehensive and complementary economic sectors across the Caribbean as a whole, states in the region are wary of cooperation that may infringe on their self-determination and abilities to protect their own national interests (Downes, 2004). While newly developed regional bodies intend to enhance the competitiveness of the region in the global market and increase trade between countries to achieve economies of scale, regional trade and integration is limited by the presence of overlapping service-based industries. To optimize their economic development, nations such as Barbados must navigate tensions between prioritizing regional integration and fostering or maintaining a competitive edge, including in the medical tourism sector, over neighboring countries with similar exports (ECLAC, 2012).

The foreign–local, large–small binaries outlined in the previous section are relevant to navigating the challenges that Caribbean nations like Barbados face in balancing regional integration with regional competition. The countries of the Caribbean Basin already have a nascent regional health care system, with patients seeking care in neighboring islands, Cuba, and Miami through private-payment (effectively medical tourism) and cross-border care arrangements. Were the governments and/or care providers of the region to coordinate their planning, new health infrastructure in the Caribbean could be of a larger scale that can support a wide range of specialties. At this regional scale, the patient catchment would permit an approach to medical tourism as is found in Thailand and Malaysia, serving as a small additional stream of patients rather than as an unpredictable cornerstone (Ormond, 2011). More importantly, such regionally integrated multispecialty facilities would more closely reflect the health needs of the local population and thereby be more likely to meet the health infrastructure development promises advanced by medical tourism proponents (ECLAC, 2012).

If individual Caribbean countries are drawn to foreign investment offers like the AWC project in Barbados, opportunities for regional health system coordination may be compromised or overlooked in light of the presence of opportunities for new industry development "knocking at their door." In fact, foreign investors in medical tourism projects may actually be shopping around the different countries in the Caribbean to find their ideal regulatory environment, potentially creating a race-to-the-bottom environment that increases the pressure for islands to change their regulatory environment to appease foreign investors (Snyder et al., 2013). As a result, Caribbean countries such as Barbados that are seeking to expand their medical tourism sectors may be challenged to develop rigorous regulation in the context of regional competition despite the fact that regulation is necessary to protect the very brand necessary to appeal to investors and consumers, as described previously.

Local Capital

The different approaches to developing medical tourism in a small island setting illustrate the core challenges regarding asymmetric resource capacity that spurred Lewis's thinking around industrialization by invitation. Given the large cost of establishing new hospitals, large medical tourism projects in countries like Barbados will, as a matter of necessity, be dependent on private foreign investment. This poses a significant challenge to small island states seeking to achieve the larger goal of building economic capacity in their health services sector while not allowing their inherent vulnerability to be exploited. Given the considerable risks associated with large-scale projects, especially in what is a new and untested sector, the Barbadian government's conservative approach to scaling up their medical tourism sector in pursuit of foreign investment in this sector thus far is consistent with the ethos of industrialization by invitation. However, while the Barbadian government shows interest in scaling up the medical tourism industry on the island, development efforts focusing on the creation or renovation of small local clinics using local resources has been demonstrated to be the most feasible in the case of the BFC (Connell, 2013b). Given the significant risks large-scale medical tourism poses to health system functioning, the challenge of balancing incentives to attract international investment with ensuring benefits for the local population, and the long-term economic advantages of local participation and control, small island states might most productively focus their efforts on existing, excess local capacity in the private health sector wherever possible rather than compete among themselves for foreign investment in an unproven domain.

Import Substitution

Considerations for developing medical tourism in order to diversify and expand local health services in Barbados may recognize the sector's potential to serve as a form of import substitution. Increased options for medical care on the island would provide a source of economic activity, with patients able to pay out of pocket locally for services they currently must access outside Barbados (ECLAC, 2012). With a small local population to provide the number of cases necessary to provide full-time employment of certain medical specialists and maintain their skill set, medical tourism may help build adequate demand to justify the local supply of new medical specialties.

The benefits of import substitution in Barbados and elsewhere in the Caribbean can only be realized if local citizens have access to the medical resources made possible by medical tourism. Medical tourism projects, almost exclusively found in the private health care sector, may serve to realize the health equity concerns raised by medical tourism if their growth is not accompanied by initiatives to improve the health status of the local population and/or their access to clinically equivalent health services locally (Hopkins et al., 2010). Overall, the considerations of import substitution that have been raised in Barbados contribute an additional economic goal that demonstrates the unique contexts in which small island states are considering developing their medical tourism sectors.

CONCLUSION

In this chapter, we have drawn on our ongoing research in Barbados to provide an overview of the core tensions that emerge in developing a medical tourism industry that is beneficial to the country. Tensions between developing a sector that is foreign versus locally operated and characterized by small- versus large-scale operations are informed by contextually relevant economic development considerations that are faced by small island states, namely regional competition, sources of capital investment, and import substitution.

Barbados's existing tourism infrastructure and strong reputation for lawfulness and safety and its English-speaking professional medical practice arguably make it well-positioned to diversify its tourism product using medical tourism activities (Worrell et al., 2011). However, its development could mirror the race-to-the-bottom regulatory environment in the Caribbean, where many proximate small island states jockey for foreign investment in emerging sectors. This type of race-to-the-bottom competition for investment in the medical tourism industry could mitigate the realization of hoped-for benefits from this industry's development. However, with a relatively narrow scope of options for economic diversification, navigating the tensions that emerge in medical tourism policy making may prove worthwhile for small island states in terms of their economic development and health service improvement if the implementation of the sector is carefully done and regulated, particularly by critically assessing existing estimates of the global patient market and its composition. Industry scale and foreign involvement are central tensions yet to be negotiated in the process of developing a robust, beneficial—and arguably equitable—Barbadian medical tourism sector.

ACKNOWLEDGMENTS

Our research in Barbados has been supported by numerous grants and trainee awards from the Canadian Institutes of Health Research (funding reference numbers: GSD-121694; FSS-133134; FRN 119355).

REFERENCES

Andrian, L., Mercer-Blackman, V., Presbitero, A., & Rebucci, A. (2013). *Vulnerability, debt and growth in the Caribbean: A fan chart approach.* Washington, DC: Inter American Development Bank. http://publications.iadb.org/bitstream/handle/11319/5990/Debt%20and%20Growth%20Technical%20Note.pdf?sequence=1

Barbados Fertility Centre. (2014). Why BFC? Our clinic. Retrieved from www.barbadosivf.com/why-bfc/our-clinic/

Bishop, M. L. (2010). Tourism as a small-state development strategy. *Progress in Development Studies, 10*(2), 99–114.

Bishop, M. L., Girvan, N., Shaw, T. M., Solange, M., Kirton, R. M., Scobie, M., Mohammed, D., & Anatol, M. (2011). *Caribbean regional integration.* University of the West Indies Institute of International Relations. Retrieved from www.normangirvan.info/wp-content/uploads/2011/06/iir-regional-integration-report-final.pdf

Campbell, B. J., Kissoon, N., Syed, N., & Fraser, H. S. (2008). Health human resource planning in Barbados and the Eastern Caribbean States: A matter of sustainability. *West Indian Medical Journal, 57*(6), 542–548.

Campling, L., & Rosalie, M. (2006). Sustaining social development in a small island developing state? The case of Seychelles. *Sustainable Development, 14*(2), 115–125.

Chee, H. L. (2007). *Medical tourism in Malaysia: International movement of healthcare consumers and the commodification of healthcare.* Asia Institute Working Paper 83. Retrieved from http://papers.ssrn.com/sol3/papers.cfm?abstract_id=1317163

Clarkson, B., & Craigwell, R. (1997). *An analysis of the service sector in Barbados.* Central Bank of Barbados. Retrieved from www.centralbank.org.bb/WEBCBB.nsf/vwPublications/18E4E10F3754656B0425785E0049C383/$FILE/WP2007v2–03.pdf.PDF

Collinder, A. (2013). Views collide on medical tourism market. *The Gleaner.* Retrieved from http://jamaica-gleaner.com/gleaner/20130913/business/business1.html

Connell, J. (2013a). Contemporary medical tourism: Conceptualization, culture, and commodification. *Tourism Management, 34*(1), 1–13.

Connell, J. (2013b). Medical tourism in the Caribbean islands: A cure for economies in crisis? *Island Studies Journal, 8*(1), 115–130.

Downes, A. S. (2001). *Economic growth in a small developing country: The case of Barbados.* Latin America and Caribbean Economics Association. Retrieved from www.lacea.org/country_studies/barbados.pdf

Downes, A. S. (2004). *Arthur Lewis and industrial development in the Caribbean: An assessment.* University of the West Indies Cavehill. Retrieved from www.cavehill.uwi.edu/salises/about-us/sir-arthur-lewis/arthurindus.aspx

ECLAC. (2000). The vulnerability of small island developing states of the Caribbean. ECLAC. Retrieved from http://www.eclac.cl/publicaciones/xml/8/8118/G0588.html

ECLAC. (2012). *Development paths in the Caribbean*. ECLAC. Retrieved from www.afd.fr/webdav/shared/PORTAILS/PAYS/ALC/pdf/Etude-CEPALC-Develop ment-paths.pdf

Eden, C. (2012). The rise of medical tourism in Bangkok. BBC. September 4. Retrieved from www.bbc.com/travel/feature/20120828-the-rise-of-medical-tourism-in-bangkok

Erikson, D. P., & Lawrence, J. (2008). *Beyond tourism: The future of the services industry in the Caribbean*. Centre for International Governance Innovation. Retrieved from www.thedialogue.org/PublicationFiles/Beyond_Tourism.pdf

Farrell, T. (1980). Arthur Lewis and the case for Caribbean industrialisation. *Social and Economic Studies, 29*(4), 52–75.

Gonzales, A., Brenzel, L., & Sancho, J. (2001). *Health tourism and related services: Caribbean development and international trade*. Regional Negotiating Machinery. Retrieved from www.carib-export.com/login/wp-content/uploads/2009/08/Health%20Tourism.pdf

Griffith, R., Waithe, K., & Craigwell, R. (2008). The significance of foreign direct investment to Caribbean development. *Journal of Public Policy Analysis, 2*(1), 3–18.

Hopkins, L., Labonté, R., Runnels, V., & Packer, C. (2010). Medical tourism today: What is the state of existing knowledge? *Journal of Public Health Policy, 31*(2), 185–198.

Horowitz, M. D., Rosensweig, J. A., & Jones, C. A. (2007). Medical tourism: Globalization of the healthcare marketplace. *Medscape General Medicine, 9*(4), 33.

Johnston, R., Crooks, V. A., Snyder, J., Fraser, H., Labonté, R., & Adams, K. (2013). An overview of Barbados medical tourism industry. Department of Geography, Simon Fraser University. Retrieved from www.sfu.ca/medicaltourism/publica tions.html

Kirton, W. (2013). The medical tourism niche. *The Nation News*, August 30. Retrieved from www.nationnews.com/articles/view/the-medical-tourism-niche/

Labonté, R. (2013). Overview: Medical tourism today: What, who, why and where? In R. Labonté, V. Runnels, C. Packer, & R. Deonandan (Eds.), *Travelling well: Essays in medical tourism* (pp. 6–42). Ottawa, ON: University of Ottawa Press.

Lunt, N., Jin, K. N., Horsfall, D., & Hanefield, J. (2014). Insights on medical tourism: Markets as networks and the role of strong ties. *Korean Social Science Journal, 41*(1), 19–37.

Mainil, T. (2011). The discourse of medical tourism in the media. *Tourism Review, 66*(1), 31–44.

Mercer-Blackman, A. L., Presbitero, V. A., & Rebucci, A. (2013). *Vulnerability, debt and growth in the Caribbean*. Inter-American Development Bank. Retrieved from www.iadb.org/wmsfiles/products/publications/documents/38056899.pdf

Ministry of Finance and Foreign Affairs. (2005). *The national strategic plan of Barbados 2005–2025*. Government of Barbados. Retrieved from www.sice.oas.org/ctyindex/BRB/Plan2005-2025.pdf

Nussbaum, K. (2011). World-class hospital to open in Barbados to serve global medical tourism market. CNW. www.newswire.ca/en/story/725457/world-class-hospital-to-open-in-barbados-to-serve-global-medical-tourism-market

Ogawa, S., Park, J., Singh, D., & Thacker, N. (2013). *Financial interconnectedness and financial sector reforms in the Caribbean*. International Monetary Fund. Retrieved from www.imf.org/external/pubs/ft/wp/2013/wp13175.pdf

Ormond, M. (2011). Medical tourism, medical exile: Responding to the cross-border pursuit of healthcare in Malaysia. In C. Minca & T. Oakes (Eds.), *Real tourism* (pp. 143–161). Abingdon: Routledge,.

Smith, K. (2012). The problematization of medical tourism: A critique of neoliberalism. *Developing World Bioethics, 12*(1), 1–8.

Snyder, J., Crooks, V. A., Turner, L., & Johnston, R. (2013). Understanding the impacts of medical tourism on health human resources in Barbados: A prospective, qualitative study of stakeholder perspectives. *International Journal for Equity in Health, 12*(2). Retrieved from www.ncbi.nlm.nih.gov/pmc/articles/PMC3600002/

Turner, L. (2007). First world health care at third world prices: Globalization, bioethics and medical tourism. *BioSocieties, 2*(3), 303–325.

Worrell, D., Belgrave, A., Grosvenor, T., & Lescott, A. (2011). An analysis of the tourism sector in Barbados. *Central Bank of Barbados Economic Review, 37*(1), 49–75.

Zappino, V. (2005). *Caribbean tourism and development: An overview.* European Centre for Development Policy Management. Retrieved from http://ecdpm.org/wp-content/uploads/2013/11/DP-65-Caribbean-Tourism-Industry-Development-2005.pdf

13 Casino Tourism
How Does Entrepreneurship Change Macao?

IpKin Anthony Wong and Ricardo Chi Sen Siu

INTRODUCTION

Macao, the world gaming capital, has a gambling history dating back in the 19th century. The initial development of the gaming industry in Macao was sparked by a rapid contraction of Macao's transshipment hub between China and Europe since Hong Kong opened as a port run by the British government in 1842. Due to Macao's small geographical area and the short-term tenure of the Macao-Portuguese governments, Macao's economy lacked business opportunities. In order to energize the local economy, the government approved the gaming business in 1847 despite the absence of any formal regulation. However, between the middle of the 19th century and the middle of the 20th centuries, the gaming industry was largely controlled by a small number of power groups that were chasing short-term profits instead of aiming for the industry's long-term development for this tiny Chinese enclave, then measuring around 10 to 15 km². By following simple business rules of thumb to gain gambling money from the Chinese community, they focused on routine procedures rather than innovation. This was how the gaming business operated for more than a century (for details, please see Eadington & Siu, 2007; Liu, 2002; Siu, 2006).

Innovative Mindset and Long-Term Vision

Modern-day Macao's casino gaming development has undergone a radical change only in the early 1960s, thanks to a legendary entrepreneur Stanley Ho. Following the formal promulgation of the first piece of gaming legislation (Decree Law 1496) by the 119th governor of the Macao-Portuguese government in 1961, a new gaming monopoly license was granted to the Sociedade de Turismo e Diversoes de Macau (STDM) in 1962. The company was led by casino tycoon Stanley Ho, who brought a number of advancements to the gaming industry. Under his personal ambition and entrepreneurship, Macao's gaming business was launched into a new era. In developing and solidifying his family-owned casino empire, Stanley Ho innovatively materialized and reinforced the progress of casino gaming as a dominant industry in Macao's economy, which allowed this tiny island city to be crowned the "Oriental Monte Carlo" in the last quarter of the 20th century.

Stanley Ho's success did not come overnight but through a strong dedication to his career, entrepreneurial flair, and risk-taking ability. Born and raised in Hong Kong from a wealthy family, Stanley endured a series of challenging life events, as his father went bankrupt in his early childhood. He believed that education was the key to improving one's social status; hence, he studied assiduously and became the first student in Hong Kong to earn a university scholarship from a Class D (i.e., the lowest level in high school education) student. He started his career by working in a trading firm in Macao. Through his business acumen and ability to speak different languages, he moved up the ranks and became a partner of the firm when he was 22 years old. To earn his fortune, he took the risk of smuggling luxury goods into China during World War II. Using this fortune, he then opened a construction company, which benefited from the postwar construction boom in Hong Kong (McCartney, 2010). Through the social reputation and network of his first wife, who was a member of an esteemed Portuguese family, Stanley Ho's initial partnership with the STDM allowed the firm to win the gaming monopoly license in 1962. Thereafter, his willingness to allocate gaming profits over time to modernize the Macao economic society undoubtedly warranted his close links with various governors of the local government; these in turn gained him related favorable policy deals for the development of his gaming empire in Macao (more details follow).

To develop Macao as a casino tourism destination, Stanley Ho began to invest in building the necessary tourism infrastructure. First, as a response to Macao's particular geographical setting, which might curb the efficiency of visitor arrivals from neighboring regions (largely the rapidly growing middle-income class from Hong Kong), the casino monopoly undertook voluntary works to dredge silt from the city's shallow inner harbor, which was located in the west coast of the Pearl River Estuary. In addition, Ho founded the Shun Tak Shipping Company and introduced a high-speed jetfoil fleet, which was able to shorten the ride between Hong Kong and Macao from more than 3 hours to around an hour (Liu, 2002). Indeed, the proactive measures and investment undertaken by the gaming monopoly in improving the efficiency of Macao's external transportation system over time helped to improve tourist flow to Macao. It was also essential to the success of the casino business.

Moreover, given the underdeveloped internal infrastructure and related tourism facilities, as well as the narrow scope of internal demand, the gaming monopoly also offered to reinvest its gaming profits to enhance the real hosting capacity (e.g., construction of ferry terminal and connecting roadways in town, hotels) and comprehensiveness (e.g., provision of good-quality restaurants, entertainment, and tourism facilities) of this industry. Furthermore, to enlarge the physical land area of this tiny city-state, the gaming monopoly also provided financial supports to related land-reclamation public projects. During its 40-year monopolization of the casino business, from 1962 to

2001, its direct and indirect contributions through STDM have improved Macao's tourism industry. It also allowed the absolute size of Macao's land area to expand significantly (Siu, 2006).

Apart from building the necessary infrastructure projects, which were critical to Macao's long-term casino tourism growth, a landmark casino hotel—Hotel Lisboa—was constructed and opened in 1970. Named after the capital of Portugal, this property is the home of an iconic casino of Macao: Casino Lisboa. In addition to casino gaming, comprehensive modern hospitality services including luxury hotel rooms, restaurants, and simple forms of entertainment were integrated into this single property for both tourists and local residents. Hotel Lisboa was developed as a flagship of the city's casino industry as well as a landmark of Macao proper. Stanley Ho further improved the attraction and tourist-carrying capacity of this tiny island city over time by proactively reinvesting gaming profits in various tourism and hospitality facilities such as hotels and restaurants. These endeavors helped to conjure a positive image of the city and benefit the gaming industry. As a result, approvals were obtained from the local government and community for the further development of this socially controversial casino gaming business. Consequently, with all these ingredients strategically stitched together, a prosperous foundation was laid for the progress of Macao's casino tourism in the period between the 1970s to the middle of the 1980s.

Political Entrepreneurship and Stagnation

Although Stanley Ho's entrepreneurship and innovation in the gaming industry led to prominent success, being a monopoly has its downside. Following the Sino-British Agreement in 1984 and the Sino-Portuguese Agreement in 1987, which approved the return of sovereignty of Hong Kong and Macao to the Chinese government in 1997 and 1999, respectively, Stanley Ho foresaw the changes looming in the business environment. In response to the Macao-Portuguese government's short-term approach to related economic and social policies prior to returning to China, the gaming entrepreneur reacted to the changing political context with a view to protect his own monopoly status. Ho took several strategic moves in the middle of the 1980s to retain his monopoly power, leading to lock-in effects of business routines, as detailed in what follows.

For example, in the 1980s, the monopoly initiated a novel but self-centered business strategy by contracting its casino gaming business to some highly or totally independent third parties that ran their own gaming business within its properties through some specially assigned gambling rooms (also called "VIP rooms"). This was done rather informally because, by law, the monopoly was not allowed to subcontract its casino business to any third party. Under related agreements, the monopoly was entitled to a certain portion of the gross gaming revenue (GGR) as derived from the gambling rooms. By that time, it was specified by law that the casino license holder was prohibited from offering credit, although this was a common measure to attract high-end gamblers. However, the government did not check the credits offered by other third parties to casino players. Besides, to obtain the rights to operate in a gambling room, an interested party/operator had to guarantee a considerable amount of monthly gaming turnover. The introduction of the gambling-room business model was an innovative and optimal-choice strategy by the monopoly to reach out to potential high rollers. This arrangement not only allowed the gaming entrepreneur to achieve a considerable volume of gaming turnover with minimum business efforts and resources (e.g., marketing efforts and avoiding possible bad debts from the casino credits) over time; but most importantly, it also guaranteed a stable and increasing gaming tax (which was levied on GGR) submitted to the government, thus securing its monopoly position.

Gambling is often associated with negative consequences, with various forms of irregular and underground economic activities (such as crime, money laundering, and public corruption); Macao is no different. A considerable volume of cash and related credits running through the gambling rooms did lead to a vicious cycle affecting the progress of Macao's casino tourism in the 1990s. Aside from the increasing GGRs as reported and the expenditures spent by the gaming monopoly in lobbying the government and the local community (e.g., contributing to various social welfare programs and creating job opportunities for local residents), little innovation for business progress was found in this period. Indeed, service quality deteriorated remarkably during this period. Due to poor management, some casino dealers even took away part of the winning chips from players on the gaming tables as tips, despite the disagreements and complaints from the players (Brady, 1998).

Gambling also brought social problems to Macao. Fights had widely been reported among a powerful triad of groups over rights to control the gambling-room business. They also bribed the local police, which led to serious social chaos in the 1990s. The *Wall Street Journal* highlighted Macao's uncontrolled casino situation as "mayhem" (Brady, 1998). Meanwhile, the Hong Kong government warned its residents to be cautious when visiting Macao. Owing to the uncontrolled gun shooting, kidnapping, and setting of fires in the city in the second half of the 1990s, Macao acquired an image of notoriety. As a result, performance of the industry was largely affected in the second half of the 1990s. Reported GGR even fell from US$1.82 billion in 1998 to US$1.63 billion in 1999, and the progress of the industry was stagnant.

THE CHANGING GAME IN THE NEW MILLENNIUM

On December 20, 1999, Macao was formally returned to China, and the Chinese government resumed its sovereignty over Macao by granting it status as a special administrative region (SAR) of China. In order to revitalize

Macao's casino industry and further develop its casino tourism, the city decided to terminate the casino industry's monopoly structure and invited world-class casino entrepreneurs to bid for three new casino licenses through a global tendering process that took place between the end of 2001 and the beginning of 2002. The Macao SAR government further expressed and sent clear messages to potential bidders about public interests impinging on new casino operators to construct comprehensive casino tourism facilities instead of sole-casino gaming fixtures. Despite the chaos experienced by the industry in the second half of the 1990s, opportunities associated with this exclusively approved casino jurisdiction in China drew the attention of most if not all major casino entrepreneurs around the world. These included MGM, Venetian, Wynn, Harrah's, and Caesars from Las Vegas; Crown from Australia; and Sun City from South Africa. Based on 18 out of a total of 21 qualified firms that submitted tenders, three new licenses were granted in February 2002. They included Sociedade de Jogos de Macau (SJM), which is a wholly owned subsidiary of the former casino monopoly; Steve Wynn's Wynn Resort from Las Vegas; and Galaxy JV, which is a joint venture between Las Vegas tycoon Sheldon Adelson's Sands and well-known Hong Kong entrepreneur Lui Che-woo's Galaxy Entertainment Group.

In an attempt to accelerate the gaming industry's pace of growth and success, the Macao SAR government further approved a partner of each of the three casino license holders to make individual investment under their own respective brand names. That is, three sublicenses were approved based on the original three licenses. Hence, a total of six independent casino operators were approved to enter the market. This is referred to as the "3 + 3" arrangement. Indeed, following the approval granted to Sands as an independent sublicense holder from the Galaxy in December of 2002, a joint venture between Las Vegas casino giant MGM Resorts International and local entrepreneur Pancy Ho (daughter of Stanley Ho) obtained a sublicense from SJM in April 2005. Finally, the third sublicense, under Wynn, was granted to Melco-Crown. This was a joint venture between a local company named Melco, which is owned by another local entrepreneur, Lawrence Ho (son of Stanley Ho), and well-known tycoon James Packer's Australian-based Crown Resort in September 2006.

A New Arena for the World-Class Casino Gaming Entrepreneurs

The prolonged social disorder and mayhem in the 1990s, triggered by the VIP–room business model created by the former gaming monopoly, came to an end after Macao was returned to China. The partial liberalization of the casino gaming industry provided new business opportunities with a new arena for the world-class gaming entrepreneurs to effect their innovative ideas for the integrated development of casino gaming with tourism and other related service sectors, as is explained in what follows. For example, the success of the Las Vegas Sands was marked by the innovative mind of its founder—Sheldon Adelson—to integrate casino gaming with other hospitality services, especially conventions and exhibitions, shows, and retail businesses. He was also the first in Macao to build a Vegas-style casino—the Sands Casino—in May 2004. The casino was overwhelmingly successful, and its US$265 million construction cost was paid off by the profits generated from the casino in just 9 months (Cohen, 2014). The success of Wynn Resort was largely accredited to the personal vision of its founder, Steve Wynn, to position casino tourism as the premium segment of the industry by emphasizing high-end retail outlets and high-quality hospitality services.

With respect to the Galaxy Entertainment Group, the company did not possess any experience in the operation of casino gaming before it obtained the casino license; however, the company was able to leverage its talented management, the contextual mindset of its leaders, and its experiences in the entertainment business for the Chinese community to assure its capability and competencies to be an active player in this game, with a strong market position. Melco-Crown and MGM, on the other hand, leveraged the distinctive competencies from their entrepreneurial leaders' innovative mindsets, as well as the casino gaming experience and management expertise from their joint venture partners—Crown Resort and MGM Resort, respectively—to create unique positions in the industry. Last, even though firms were locked into the long-established business routine (i.e., the VIP–room model), intensified industry competition also awoke the wholly owned subsidiary of the former gaming monopoly (i.e., SJM) to rebuild its market position through new and innovative investments in another feature property, Grand Lisboa, as well as new casino hotels like Ponte 16, named for visitors to recall Macao's history as a transshipment hub.

These casino operators spent a vast amount of money to develop their casino properties. As summarized in Table 13.1, total capital investment being spent by the six casino operators (in the construction of new "property and equipment") in the first decade since the partial liberalization of the casino industry was more than six times the total amount of investment as proposed/specified in the three original contracts. These investments paid off: while Macao only cashed in gaming revenue of US$2.7 billion in 2002, the amount reached US$45.1 billion in 2013. Macao is also the second most desirable and popular destination for mainland tourists (Xola Consulting, 2008), only after Hong Kong; and it welcomed about 30 million tourists in 2013. Evidently, the long-term vision and proactive planning of these gaming entrepreneurs have formed a new ground for the redevelopment and success of Macao's casino tourism.

Materialization of New Ideas

For the gaming industry in Macao to succeed, the availability of land and capital funds is a necessary but not sufficient condition. Indeed, market-oriented entrepreneurship is an indispensable factor that amalgamates and transforms the physical and financial resources into economic commodities

Table 13.1   Contract-Specified Amount and Accumulated Amount of Investment Made by Each Licensed Casino Operator in "Property and Equipment" in USD (millions)

License holders (approved in Feb. 2002) Sublicense holders	SJM	MGM	Galaxy	Venetian	Wynn	Melco-Crown	Total
Total amount of investment as specified respectively in the 3 contracts granted in Feb. 2002	592		1,100		500		2,192
Accumulated amount of investment as of 2008	1,228		834	5,236	907	2,108	10,313
Accumulated amount of investment as of 2009	1,306		924	4,927	1,098	2,787	11,040
Accumulated amount of investment as of 2010	1,221	689	1,596	5,503	1,075	2,672	12,757
Accumulated amount of investment as of 2011	1,130	639	2,249	5,250	991	2,655	13,914

Source: "Total amount of investment as specified respectively in the 3 contracts granted in Feb. 2002": *Macao Daily News* (in Chinese), February 15, 2002, B3. SJM: aggregate value of "property, machinery and equipment" in the Consolidated Balance Sheet of SJM's 2009 and 2011 *Annual Report*. MGM: aggregate value of "property and equipment" in the Consolidated Financial Statements of MGM (China)'s 2011 *Annual Report*. Galaxy: aggregate value of "property, machinery and equipment" in the Consolidated Balance Sheet of Galaxy's 2008, 2010, and 2011 *Annual Report*. Sands: net value of value of "property and equipment" in the Consolidated Balance Sheet of Sands (China)'s 2009 and 2011 *Annual Report*. Wynn: aggregate value of "property, equipment and construction in progress" in the Consolidated Financial Statements of Wynn (Macao)'s 2009 and 2011 *Annual Report*. Melco-Crown: net value of value of "property and equipment" in the Consolidated Balance Sheet of Melco-Crown's 2008, 2009 and 2011 *Annual Report*.

in demand. Although Macao's land area expanded significantly as the gaming monopoly invested part of its profits to reclaim land continuously for this island city, a large portion of the land was in fact left idle instead of being utilized for productive usage in the 1990s. For example, the largest single piece of reclaimed land, Cotai, did not receive any comprehensive development plan when it was ready for use by the end of the 1990s. It is worthwhile to note that shortly before the liberalization of the casino industry, an informal proposal was called for to build a Hello Kitty Land in this piece of vacated land (Macau Tripping, 2008), but it was turned down owing to uncertainty about its potential business turnover. Despite the minimal public and business interest in developing this piece of land, Sheldon Adelson of Sands was the first to take a proactive and strategic move to construct his comprehensive flagship property—the Venetian—into a mega-integrated casino resort there. The initiatives from Sheldon Adelson and other entrepreneurs have turned this piece of land into the Cotai Strip, which is a mini version of the Las Vega Strip. The Venetian, opened in summer 2007, was crowned as the sixth-largest building in the world by floor area and the largest single-structure hotel building in Asia. In addition, the property has two large shopping malls with comprehensive middle- and high-end retail shops, and it is well equipped to host large-scale conventions and exhibitions. These offerings are in line with the public interest to develop the retail and MICE industry in Macao.

Other newcomers also foresaw the casino gaming boom in Macao and have explored new avenues for innovation and business opportunity. With respect to Lawrence Ho, this young entrepreneur did not only actively construct his gaming business empire like his father had, but he also made a landmark move by building his Melco-Crown's flagship property—City of Dreams—along the Cotai Strip. He also invested USD$250 million to create a feature show—the House of Dancing Water—in 2010. The show is the largest and most spectacular water-based, high-tech entertainment show in the world. It utilizes innovative ideas by mixing various cultural elements (particularly those germane to Chinese culture) to attract customers. The popularity of the show and other entertainment facilities in City of Dreams has allowed Lawrence Ho and his Melco-Crown to witness an increasing volume of patrons and a solid ground for the firm's competitiveness and sustainable growth.

At the same time, entrepreneur Lui Che-woo's Galaxy Entertainment Group was making its own market inroads. Possessing service experience in the context of the Chinese entertainment business but with an innovative mindset, Lui put special effort into building his flagship casino hotel, Starworld, and mega-casino resort, Galaxy Macau. Opened in 2011, Galaxy Macau, renowned as "the New Palace of Asia," is an impressive property that draws different types of visitors. The property has the world's largest sky-top wave pool (4,000 m2), constructed with the latest technology. It features three signature hotels tailored to different accommodation needs. It also provides an array of entertainment options, including its Fortune Diamong show, Laserama laser show, 10-screen 3D Cineplex cinemas, and ample shops and restaurants. These offerings may explain why the Galaxy Entertainment Group could command an increasing market share with a solid ground that allows the firm to differentiate and gain a competitive edge over its rivals in Macao. In turn, Lui Che-woo and his family's efforts in developing Macao's casino industry definitely add to the success of Macao's casino tourism.

These entrepreneurs, with their efforts in creating various unique themed casinos, innovative service offerings and attractions, and a wide range of world-class shopping outlets, as well as emphasizing high-quality hospitality services, have allowed the gaming industry as a whole to achieve a stage benefitting from external economies of scale. Throughout this process, the role of entrepreneurship in stitching together the right components and commercializing the right packages of entertainment services to the market clearly fashions Macao's casino tourism to reflect the city's unique setting.

THE CONTEXTUAL ASPECT OF ENTREPRENEURSHIP IN MACAO

As discussed, the liberalization of the casino gaming industry in 2002 triggered dramatic development in casino tourism in Macao. This development was largely supported and pushed by favorable policies designed by the Chinese and the Macao SAR governments. For example, although casino gaming is currently prohibited in mainland China, continuation and further development of this industry in Macao is confirmed by the Chinese government under its One Country, Two Systems policy. Likewise, inclination policies (e.g., the aforementioned "3 + 3" decision and related policies in infrastructure construction and tourism promotion) undertaken by the Macao SAR government have also facilitated the development of the city's casino gaming and tourism.

However, business success also requires an innovative mindset as well as an in-depth understanding of the contextual aspect of the Chinese culture and Macao's unique sociocultural and geopolitical environment. In fact, although world-class entrepreneurs brought innovations and changes to casino tourism in Macao, they inevitably posed challenges to the constraints of the status quo. Indeed, foreign casino operators realized that Chinese gambling behavior was significantly different from that in Las Vegas and other parts of the world. Hence, the phenomenal growth of the gaming industry in Macao also relied heavily on casino operators' vision, strategic planning, and efforts in adopting business models that fit the local market and business environment. Understanding the local context also allows these operators to address the Macao government's interests and related regulations.

For example, while patrons in Las Vegas often perceive casino gaming as a leisure and entertainment activity, many Chinese customers in Macao perceive it as a means to test luck and as an avenue to gain money. Chinese gamblers prefer table games, especially baccarat, whereas gamblers in Las Vegas prefer slot machines. Chinese perceive greater excitement and entertainment at table games due to the fact that they perceive having more control in such games and better chances to win against the house. Table games also allow them to show off their wagering skills and gambling achievement, as well as to socialize with dealers and other gamblers (Lam, 2007;

Liu & Wan, 2011). Chinese gamblers have a strong belief in feng shui and believe that the architectural style of the casino could alter their luck. They prefer gold and red colors because these symbolize fortune and good luck. Gamblers also like staying at a particular table and with a specific dealer if they bring luck to them, but they would also hop around in an effort to change their luck. Another major difference between Chinese gamblers in Macao and gamblers in other parts of the world is that the gaming revenue is primarily contributed by VIP high-roller gamblers. About 60% to 70% of Macao's casino GGR is contributed by this type of gambler, although they are far fewer in number than the mass-market gamblers. Gaming revenues are also subject to seasonal fluctuation that closely mimics Chinese holidays and travel patterns (Wong, 2011).

The aforementioned contextual differences challenged the status quo, which compelled international gaming entrepreneurs to adjust their strategies in order to align better to the unique Chinese gambling culture. For example, Wynn Resort's reddish casino theme was highly appreciated by the Chinese because it is a sign of fortune. The Venetian utilizes its golden interior to attract gamblers. Signage and casino information are available in both English and Chinese. Some casinos even use Simplified Chinese and Mandarin as the primary medium. Some casinos even use Simplified Chinese and Mandarin as the primary medium. The casino operators adjust their food and beverage (F&B) strategies to offer more Chinese food, such as Canton, Beijing, and Shanghai dishes, to suit the taste of Chinese gamblers. They also provide a video screen to record the sequence of win/lose patterns for baccarat players.

Beyond the mass market, new casino operators also notice that, within the unique contextual settings of Macao, significant business turnover (in terms of GGR) could be derived from junket operators (for gambling rooms) that focus on the VIP segment. Despite a number of controversial and legitimate issues that concern overseas regulators such as those from the United States, Australia, and Singapore regarding the practice of Macao's VIP–room casino gaming, new casino operators react strategically by developing their relationships and business models with the junket operators to ensure business turnover without breaking the related laws in Macao and in their home countries. For example, U.S. gaming operators may modify their deals with the related junket operators through various forms of commission instead of sharing the GGR from the business, as the latter is not allowed in the United States. In addition, to be congruent with the government's interests to better develop the mass market and to fully utilize the existing junket operator system, active arrangements are adopted by casino operators (evident since 2011) to expand the premium mass market as a new growing segment (details of this segment are beyond the scope of this chapter; for a general description of it, see Fong & Lu, 2013, pp. 21–24).

In the business world, innovative ideas and the willingness to take risks on the part of entrepreneurs are largely framed by unique sociocultural and geopolitical contexts. These factors are especially important for casino operators in running their businesses in Macao. For example, rigid government regulations for the gaming industry compelled casino entrepreneurs to adjust their business strategies in response to the business context in Macao and Chinese society in general. While a shortage of labor has long been felt in the local economy (for example, in the first quarter of 2014, the unemployment rate was 1.7%, and the underemployment rate was 0.4%), restrictive labor immigration practices imposed by the government to protect the local labor force have posed significant challenges to the casino operators. In addition, while the SAR government sets a quota to allow an average of 3%percent annual growth between 2013 and 2022 in respect to the industry's gaming tables, an informal cap may also be practiced by a gaming operator if it is not actively promoting more nongaming leisure and entertainment for the development of Macao's casino tourism.

Savvy gaming entrepreneurs have made earnest endeavors to cope with these issues. For example, they have proactively applied new technologies to soften part of the labor shortage pressure. Applications of these new technologies include jumbo baccarat and other electronic table gaming machines that can serve up to 50 gamblers at a time, either with a live or an electronic dealer. Since electronic gaming machines (except for those with live dealers) are not restricted to the cap at the time of writing, it allows operators to expand their hardcore gaming market and reduces their need for labor. In addition, gaming operators foresaw the opportunity presented in the premium mass segment of the mass market to push the growth of this segment since 2011. Furthermore, to respond to the government's request to diversify the gaming industry, gaming entrepreneurs have created more entertainment, providing a greater variety of hospitality services and unique attractions to tourists.

ENTREPRENEURSHIP AND MACAO'S CASINO TOURISM

A huge amount of capital has been invested to build state-of-the-art casino tourism facilities in such landmark properties as the Venetian, Sands Cotai Central, MGM Grand/One Central, Wynn Resort, Galaxy Mega Resort, and City of Dreams, among others. Over a period of 11 years since the city liberalized its casino gaming, a total of 24 new casino resorts/hotels with unique designs and themes have been built. The concentration of mega-casino resorts and the development of new and integrated establishments have also created an ample supply of nongaming leisure entertainment options such as shows and events, restaurants, accommodations, shopping outlets, spas, and family and kid playrooms to publicize and push the city's casino tourism development. For example, the provision of unique wonders tailored to stimulate various tourist demands: these include the world's best artificial beach inside the Galaxy Resort, the House of Dancing Water at the City of Dreams, the lotus flower–like iconic architecture of the Grand Lisboa casino, the Grand Praca and Butterfly Reinvention at MGM, the Rising Dragon/Golden Tree performance at the Wynn, the Grand Canal and Gondola ride at the Venetian, and having dinner with DreamWorks cartoon characters at the Sands Cotai Central. These unique and signature entertainment options are jointly creating a new chapter in Macao's gaming industry.

In addition, some casinos provide tourists with surprises such as live entertainment, streetmosphere, and a festival-like atmosphere that are free and public to casino patrons, so that tourists could easily find themselves indulging within a casino complex but outside the typical casino site. The casino's architectural design, which combines grandiose artifacts and breathtaking scenes, often gives tourists visual surprises and exceptional experiences (Wong, 2013). As a result, tourists like to sightsee at the casinos and take photos to make their experience last. All those features and the ongoing investment in new projects will continue to offer tourists experiences that go beyond hardcore gambling. In fact, recent research has shown that tourists visit Macao for a number of reasons, and casino gaming is just one of the motives (Wong & Rosenbaum, 2012). Tourists also like to seek novel entertainment, socialization, and escape and relaxation opportunities while they sojourn at casinos. Hence, contemporary casinos function not only as places for gambling but also as places for engendering unique and memorable tourist experiences that can hardly be replicated in other destinations.

Recent research (Wong, 2013) suggests that tourists' service experience derived from casinos plays a critical role in enhancing their satisfaction and the casino's brand equity, resulting in higher inclination to revisit those properties and Macao. Casinos, especially integrated casino resorts, have become a "must-go" attraction to tourists. This may explain why the tiny island city welcomed millions of tourists to a small strip of land that now only measures about 30 km².

WHO LEADS THE CHANGES AHEAD?

Throughout the process of Macao's casino tourism development, radical changes and the vitality of the industry were influenced by the visions and entrepreneurial attributes of the gaming operators. Given the unique contextual settings of Macao and the Chinese culture, as well as intensified competition at the global and regional levels, the dynamic function of entrepreneurship will be one of the necessary conditions (along with related public policies and the external economic environment, among other factors) to ensure sustainable growth of the industry in the foreseeable future. To this end, the gaming entrepreneurs' innovative mindset and effective application of technology are vital propellers.

Different from the period of monopoly, recent interaction and competition among Macao's existing world-class casino operators have established a solid foundation (e.g., data presented in Table 13.1), which has led to a new virtuous cycle in the development of the city's casino tourism in the 21st century. Indeed, the enormous changes that have been experienced by the industry in the first decade following the liberalization of the gaming industry augur further changes. The industry's portfolio, with its new and unique tourism and hospitality offerings, and including numerous appealing leisure and entertainment options, could easily be imitated and replicated by other regional rivals, such as the casinos in Singapore, South Korea, and Manila (Philippines), as well as the upcoming mega-casino resorts in Taiwan and Japan.

The promising interest of the Chinese government to construct the Pearl River Delta as one of the polycentric mega city regions in China could further help Macao to develop as the "World Tourism and Leisure Centre" in this region (Macao Trade and Investment Promotion Institute, 2014). It should motivate the six existing gaming entrepreneurs to continue their contribution to Macao's casino tourism. For example, while being a pioneer in the long-established ways of the gaming business and hence being less active in investing in the casino resort concept, Stanley Ho and his SJM finally launched its record USD$3.85 billion Lisboa Palace in Cotai in February 2014 (Lai, 2014). As compared to Hotel Lisboa and Grand Lisboa, opened in 1970 and 2007, respectively, this new property is a truly mega-casino resort. Taken together, the entrepreneurial spirit and characteristics of the various casino operators and their visions in building a number of unique and innovative themed properties have changed the nature of casino gaming and tourism in Macao. Their proactive and contextual visions in cultivating casino tourism in the growing Asian (particularly the Chinese) market have made this tiny Pearl River Delta city bright and gained worldwide acknowledgment.

To conclude, this chapter has discussed and explained the importance of initiative and the proactive mindset of entrepreneurs, as well as the support of government and local community, to the economic success of a small island city and subnational island jurisdiction like Macao. With its clear resource limitations (land, labor supply) and unique sociocultural and administrative contexts, it has represented a challenge to the conventional business model. In turn, entrepreneurship as an organizing and risk-taking factor has assembled and coordinated the right components for the development of a specific service industry. The unlikely story of Macao as a casino tourism destination is a vivid case of the exercise in "creative political economy" (Baldacchino, 2009, p. 6): it may serve as a valuable example to other island cities, states, and territories.

REFERENCES

Baldacchino, G. (2009). *Island enclaves: Offshoring, creative governance and subnational island jurisdictions*. Montreal, QC: McGill-Queen's University Press.
Brady, D. (1998, May 29). Mayhem in Macau: The joint is jumpin' at the Hotel Lisboa. *The Wall Street Journal*, p. 1.

Cohen, M. (2014, May 13). Time of sands. *Inside Asian Gaming,* pp. 10–21.

Eadington, W. R., & Siu, R.C.S. (2007). Between law and custom—examining the interaction between legislative change and the evolution of Macao's casino industry. *International Gambling Studies, 7*(1), 1–28.

Fong, K., & Lu, D. (2013, January 18). Macau gaming—2013 outlook: Structural growth should drive multiple expansion. Hong Kong: J.P. Morgan, Asia Pacific Equity Research.

Lai, T. (2014). Cotai to cost SJM HK$30 billion. *Macau Business Daily.* Retrieved from http://macaubusinessdaily.com/Gaming/Cotai-cost-SJM-HK30-billion

Lam, D. (2007). An observation study of Chinese baccarat players. *UNLV Gaming Research & Review Journal, 11*(2), 63–73.

Liu, P. (2002). *Aomen Bocaiye Zongheng ["An Overview of Macao's Gaming Industry" (in Chinese)].* Hong Kong, China: Joint Publishing.

Liu, X. R., & Wan, Y.K.P. (2011). An examination of factors that discourage slot play in Macau casinos. *International Journal of Hospitality Management, 30*(1), 167–177.

Macao Trade and Investment Promotion Institute. (2014). Regional co-operation. Retrieved from www.ipim.gov.mo/macao_exhibition_detail.php?tid=294&type_id=156&lang=en-us

Macau Tripping. (2008). Updated Cotai map—Wynn Cotai, MGM Cotai, Mega-Box, Hello Kitty and more. Retrieved from www.macautripping.com/tripping/post.php?p=179

McCartney, G. (2010). Stanley Ho Hung-Sun: The "king of gambling." In R. Butler & R. Russell (Eds.), *Giants of tourism* (pp. 171–180). Cambridge, MA: CABI.

Siu, R.C.S. (2006). Evolution of Macao's casino industry from monopoly to oligopoly: Social and economic reconsideration. *Journal of Economic Issues, 40*(4), 967–990.

Wong, I. A. (2011). Forecasting Macau's gaming revenue and its seasonality. *UNLV Gaming Research & Review Journal, 15*(1), 87–93.

Wong, I. A. (2013). Exploring customer equity and the role of service experience in the casino service encounter. *International Journal of Hospitality Management, 32,* 91–101.

Wong, I. A., & Rosenbaum, M. S. (2012). Beyond hardcore gambling: Understanding why mainland Chinese visit casinos in Macau. *Journal of Hospitality & Tourism Research, 36*(1), 32–51.

Xola Consulting. (2008). *Chinese travelers: Trends for adventure companies and destinations.* Retrieved from www.xolaconsulting.com/chinese_tourism_trends.pdf

Part 4
Other Intangibles

14 Software and Electronic Gaming Industries in Malta

Mario Aloisio

INTRODUCTION

Economic diversification is often quoted as being a key to sustainable economic growth, particularly for small island states with no natural resources and where economies of scale are difficult to achieve. For many countries, financial services and information and communications technology (ICT) have typically provided the incentives for continued economic development. More recently, many jurisdictions have concentrated their efforts on expanding the gaming sector, in particular electronic gaming (e-gaming). Malta is among those countries that has been actively exploiting this niche since 2004 and is now doing so with some success. The benefits reaped through e-gaming have been largely built upon the earlier achievements of the software and ICT industries, which have expanded rapidly.

This chapter describes the development of the software industry in Malta and how and why, the e-gaming sector has grown rapidly, contributing substantially to the economy. It accounted for 1.1% of Malta's gross domestic product in 2005, rising to 2.6% by 2012 (Xuereb, 2013).

Starting an industry or targeting a new niche is essentially an exercise and a challenge in governance and entrepreneurship. The appropriate legislation and infrastructure must be in place, the right skill set needs to be available and in suitable numbers and the right balance often needs to be found when tackling delicate matters such as liberalization, privatization and oversight. Organizations (such as Malta Enterprise, the Malta Information Technology Agency and the Malta Communications Authority) set up by government to specifically regulate and oversee the various services and industry sectors require the competence to nurture such nontraditional markets, while the private sector needs to be able to act quickly to ensure that opportunities are not missed.

HISTORICAL AND INDUSTRIAL CONTEXT

In the late 1980s, faced with the prospect of foreign competition and the "new global economy" based on advanced technology, Maltese policy makers set out to devise a strategic plan that would propel Malta into the information age, transforming the island's economy from merely depending on manufacturing and tourism into a service-oriented market. At that time, attention was focused on at least two key areas—offshore banking and financial services (Baldacchino & Fabri, 1999)—and high-tech, value-added industries such as pharmaceuticals and informatics. At the same time, a series of measures was taken to continue to promote investment by attracting foreign companies to Malta's shores. In particular, the emphasis was on foreign investment that aimed principally to increase the export market but simultaneously did not compete with sectors that were already well served by local businesses. In this vein, a Technopark was built; an Industry Development Act was enacted offering excellent tax incentives for foreign, export-oriented firms; the Malta Council for Science and Technology (MCST) was set up; and an overhaul of the telecommunications infrastructure was undertaken to enable organizations to conduct business more effectively (Bonnici, 2000).

Concurrently, science and information technology (IT) education was promoted at all levels: it was quickly recognized that, without a steady and sufficient supply of IT graduates, the vision of turning Malta into a hub of ICT excellence would not be realized. Apart from making the teaching of basic IT skills compulsory in primary and secondary schools and encouraging young people to study ICT by providing valuable bursaries, a number of IT courses targeted for adults were offered in the hope of winning the battle against the digital divide. The latter courses were either free or heavily subsidized. Additionally, in the late 1990s and early 2000s, strategic alliances with IT market leaders such as Microsoft, Hewlett-Packard, Cisco, Oracle and SAP were also sought as a way of boosting the local ICT sector.

These policies, coupled with a well-defined IT strategic plan and other factors such as a stable political environment, had a positive effect on information technology, which began to expand rapidly. This led to a corresponding substantial growth in software development and firm formation. New niche markets began to appear that software companies could tap into. Opportunities for companies—both local and foreign—to do IT business seemed optimal, particularly at the turn of the millennium with Malta's then-imminent accession to the European Union (EU), which would open a vast market of 400 million consumers. Indeed, in the decade 1995 to 2005, close to one hundred new ICT firms were formed, most still operating in mid-2014. Many of these include software developers offering services ranging from small custom applications to fully integrated systems. A software industry was in the making.

While these government initiatives have been conducive to the growth of software development in Malta, a number of local firms had already established themselves. Additionally, although a national IT Strategic Plan in 1993 referred to software development, the Maltese government never set out with the express intent of developing an indigenous software industry.

The latter thus emerged initially on private initiative, as a result of professional entrepreneurship. It was helped by the diffusion and acceptance of computer technology in the mid- to late 1980s and, only later, by the generation of the right input factors in the form of public policies.

ORIGINS

Software development in Malta did not see its humble beginnings until the late 1970s, when a handful of computer service companies were set up to offer time-sharing and turnkey solutions. As happened elsewhere, small, powerful computers began to infiltrate the local market, leading to a greater demand for software. This accelerated the software development process, and, within less than a decade, programming had become an important business activity. New advances in information technology, including the Internet, telecommunications and mobile telephony, created further demand for new applications. With market liberalization in the late 1990s, foreign software firms were also attracted to Malta's shores, adding further to the software scene. Although Malta initially lacked the technical capabilities and was slow if not late in adopting computers, the need for (and the development of) software in Malta from about 1980 followed much the same general pattern as that in many other countries.

To speak of a software industry in Malta may sound inappropriate in view of Malta's small size: a population of 420,000 on a land area of just 120 square miles. But the increase in software output in recent years—complemented by an investment in Malta by a number of foreign software firms—has been significant, so that software is now justly becoming another industry, even if tiny by international standards. Apart from the reasons already given, this rise in software production in Malta is the result of a number of factors: the creation of the Government Computer Centre in the early 1980s, followed by the establishment of the Management Systems Unit, Malta Information Technology and Training Services and the Malta Information Technology Agency, all of which provided training opportunities for aspiring civil servants as well as spearheading the procurement of IT projects to private companies; the liberalization process starting in the late 1990s; government incentives for small to medium-sized enterprises (SMEs), which also attracted a number of foreign firms and promoted interest in local company start-ups; the building of an advanced telecommunications infrastructure (the lack of which previously had put off companies doing computing business); the development in the early 1990s of the Malta Government Network (MAGNET); the recent emphasis on tertiary education in the sciences and ICT; and the continuing demand for software by organizations that have come to understand the importance of computerization for efficiency and competitiveness and by new markets such as web and database hosting and e-gaming.

ORIGINS OF E-GAMING

E-gaming in Malta has its origins with the publication of amendments to the Department of Public Lotto Ordinance (L.N. 34 of 2000) to regulate offshore betting offices and permit online betting, following which the first betting license was issued in 2001. These regulations, which licensed only betting, attracted an estimated 60 companies between 2000 and 2004, 42 of which operated successfully.

In 2001, the Public Lotto Ordinance was replaced by the Lotteries and Other Games Act (of 2001). The latter repealed a number of other game-related acts and established the Lotteries and Gaming Authority (LGA). In 2004, the act was revised to define the structure and role of the Authority more precisely; it also included provisions for games "through a means of distance communication." Subsidiary legislation titled "Remote Gaming Regulations" was published in April 2004 (L.N. 176 of 2004), in which the new laws for various types of remote gaming were laid out. In a nutshell, the 2004 legislation aimed to achieve the following:

- Be technology neutral, that is, apply to all types of technologies (Internet, mobile, telephone, fax and game devices)
- Be game neutral, that, apply to all types of games (betting, P2P, online casino, community games, etc.)
- Shift from regulating the games to regulating the means of carrying out gaming
- Establish a safe environment for players
- Give operators a competitive edge

In March 2005, on the initiative of the Lotteries and Gaming Authority, the Malta Remote Gaming Council (MRGC) was launched to bring together remote gaming operators, data carriers, ISPs and professional services providers. The aim was to give all stakeholders the opportunity to meet new challenges backed by the inherent advantages of collective effort. Currently, the MRGC's corporate members number 51, of which 34 are gaming companies and 17 are service providers (MRGC, 2014).

ICT AND SOFTWARE FIRMS: STATISTICAL PROFILE

Software-related statistics, such as the number of software companies operating in Malta in any given year, the number of workers employed in software-related jobs and software revenues, have not been available. No detailed statistics have been kept either by government departments or by industry analysts. However, the number of ICT firms increased tenfold, from about 20 firms in 1985 to circa 200, by 2005 (Aloisio, 2010). As one might expect of a small island, the vast majority of these enterprises are small: about 80%

employ fewer than 10 persons and have low turnovers. Just over a third of these firms are involved in software development and related services. The small firms are often set up by IT professionals who leave other private companies or by new computer graduates. Spin-offs—companies spawned from bigger ones—also account for some of these firms.

It has been estimated that in 2005, the ICT sector employed around 6,000 people (Malta Enterprise, 2006b): that is equivalent to some 4.3% of total employment. Percentage-wise, these statistics are higher than those applicable to India, Germany, the UK or the United States (Arora & Gambardella, 2005; Commander, 2005). By 2010, ICT employees stood at about 7,900 (Camilleri, 2011).

SOFTWARE INDUSTRY STRUCTURE AND CHARACTERISTICS

In comparison to other countries, the top software firms operating in Malta are small. This is to be expected in view of Malta's small size and the relatively young age of the industry. Nevertheless, most of the top 20 firms operating in Malta are notably Maltese owned, staffed and operated.

Yet it has taken anything between 20 to 30 years for local software companies the like of Computime, Megabyte and Shireburn to grow to employing between 20 and 50 persons each. On the other hand, foreign firms (e.g., Crimsonwing) or those that have had an overseas connection (e.g., 6pm) have grown more rapidly (Aloisio, 2010). The latter companies would have targeted a bigger market and were therefore able to expand more rapidly. Thus, while the software industry has traditionally been seen as fertile ground for innovation and small-scale entrepreneurship, "it is not easy to develop an activity [referring to software] to a meaningful size" (UNIDO, 1993, p. 10). Moreover, while niche firms are typically stable and profitable businesses, a key to growth is breaking out of niche markets and focusing on large projects. This, however, requires considerable expertise at both the managerial and technical levels.

Remarkably, most of the Maltese indigenous software firms are start-ups: they were created in the late 1970s and early 1980s when the industry was nonexistent. In many cases, the founding directors were either computer science or engineering graduates (e.g., the brothers Thomas and Carmel T. Galea, who founded Megabyte) or persons with previous computer and management experience, which was often gained by having worked in data processing departments of large organizations (e.g., the late Harry Restall, founder of Intercomp). Some founding directors (e.g., John Degiorgio of Shireburn and Alex Attard of former BDS, respectively) had qualifications unrelated to computers yet have been highly successful in their ventures, a perfect example of nimble Maltese entrepreneurship.

Software companies have gone far from the early days, when relatively small vertical applications such as insurance billing and retail software were the norm. While the development of custom vertical applications for local niche markets continues to be an important source of income, many of the small local firms have had to diversify and specialize in certain application areas. The type of specialized work that is carried out by some firms and the technology tools that are used for some of the projects may also be inferred from the adverts for software engineers that regularly appear in the local press, describing not only the prerequisite qualifications but also some of the projects companies are involved in. Relatively young companies like Ixaris and Ascent—both set up by current and former full-time University of Malta lecturers—are examples where computer science theory—from neural networks and fuzzy logic to distributed transactional systems and computer security—is also being put into practice. With a base in London and an R&D office in Malta, Ixaris specializes in secure Web-based services, while Ascent is more applications-oriented, having produced software packages such as vehicle routing and production process optimization. Specialization is, of course, one strategy for survival: it is a way of deepening competencies and differentiating oneself from other firms. Currently, there is a growing interest in so-called serious games development, with at least four institutions, including the University of Malta, offering relevant courses or study modules to cater to industry demands.

FACTORS CONTRIBUTING TO THE SOFTWARE INDUSTRY'S GROWTH

The initial success of many of the top indigenous companies owes much to the lack of any competition from foreign software firms until the early 1990s. Although the market was not protected as such by policies that specifically aimed at discouraging foreign competition, the early situation was akin to a protected market. At that time, IT in Malta was still in its infancy, with many businesses still not having computerized. There was thus much scope for the new software firms to do business by exploiting the hitherto untapped local market. The advent of the PC and the fall in price of computer hardware led to an increase in computer installations that translated into more business for the software companies.

Government procurement, although initially not a policy specifically adopted to boost the software industry, was another stimulus for growth. A handful of start-up companies strengthened their position when they secured government contracts offered by tender. Megabyte's first substantial government contract, won in 1989 and involving the computerization of the public lotto system, is a case in point. This project provided an opportunity for the company to expand its workforce and simultaneously use some of the project contract funds for research and development, building on its expertise. Often, one government contract would lead to another, as when, shortly afterward, Megabyte was entrusted with another government project, that involving the national identity card system.

The overhaul of the telecommunications system by the Maltese government in the 1990s also opened up opportunities for aspiring software firms. The number of internet service providers (ISPs) and companies offering Web services shot up in this period. With a good telecommunications infrastructure in place, companies could now be in direct contact with their clients and transact their business online, while those seeking to expand their line of business could also promote their products and services on the Web. For example, an ICT-Usage of Enterprises Survey by Malta's National Statistics Office (NSO) has revealed that, in 2003, as many as 90% of the enterprises surveyed marketed their products on their own website (although other facilities made available on the website, such as access to product catalogues and providing after-sales support, rank much lower; NSO, 2006, Table 1.14, p. 9; Table 2.13, p. 31). Now, although designing and launching one's own website can be a relatively trivial task, professional-looking, highly-interactive and intelligent-based websites require more than just a basic knowledge of Web design, particularly if this entails large database access involving security features. Procurement thus became important, evident from the relatively high number of new entrants in the late 1990s specializing in Web design and hosting. Mobile telephony and its associated technology also created opportunities for new software firms. While not a prerequisite to software growth, the new telecommunications infrastructure has facilitated the growth of the IT industry; it has also enabled foreign companies to take up e-gaming in Malta.

Traditionally, local companies have tended to concentrate their effort in the local arena, producing software tailor-made to local customers' needs, and only later ventured into the global marketplace, if at all. The Internet has changed a lot of that, partly (if not chiefly) because a company with its own Web page has an immediate global presence, lessening some of the problems associated with both marketing and distribution. Thus, whereas the older firms had practically no choice but to tackle the local market, most newer firms have been more adventurous and ambitious in attempting to immediately target the open global market. One of Malta Enterprise's roles has been to provide new local firms with access to contacts abroad. Some of these new entrants have reportedly quoted Malta Enterprise as being instrumental in their initial success.

Finally, Malta's accession to the EU in 2004 did bring new challenges to local industry; but it has also allowed some firms, particularly SMEs, to benefit from various EU initiatives such as bilateral trade treaties (concluded by the EU with the rest of the global market) and access to funding and the means to participate in EU–funded research projects. Some companies, for example Icon Studios, have already made use of these funds (ICON, 2014).

FACTORS CONTRIBUTING TO E-GAMING'S SUCCESS

The rapid uptake of e-gaming in Malta has not happened by chance. Contributory factors include relatively low official fees and gaming taxes; fairly straightforward yet thorough and cost-effective application procedures for obtaining the requisite license; a regulatory e-gaming scheme that is not too restrictive but simultaneously aims at protecting both operator and client; a good selection of service providers, including many competent and experienced software and law firms; and a sound telecommunications infrastructure. In addition, Malta's EU membership, its stable political climate, its proximity to major European gaming centers, its reputable history of finance, banking and commerce, its skilled and multilingual labor force and a reasonably strong economic environment are good reasons many operators have chosen Malta to establish and run remote gaming companies.

CONSTRAINTS

The Maltese software industry has experienced some constraints, particularly in the initial stages of its development. These include poor access to finance and skills; low levels of research and development; limited access to markets and information about markets; and a low demand and high rates of piracy in the domestic market. Other factors may have retarded the development of software in Malta, including the very small domestic market and the lack (in the early years) of an informatics or computer industry policy (UNIDO, 1993). Again, the first three constraints are applicable to local game developers who, for example, still find it hard to acquire funds (Games Audit UK, 2012).

Finance is particularly vital to software companies, which may have a lot of capital invested in incomplete projects at any point in time. If financial institutions are unwilling to provide the necessary financial support, then these companies will find it difficult to operate. New entrants, in particular, require start-up financing; a lack of suitable financial products and incentives may well put off prospective companies, therefore missing opportunities for new businesses.

Securing a loan or obtaining a significant overdraft has traditionally proved difficult in Malta, although in recent years, this has become somewhat easier, with the main banks now regularly advertising 'soft loan' schemes for start-up companies. Brincat (2001) has reported, for example, that in 2001, start-ups were still finding it difficult to obtain bank loans because of lack of security. Government incentives for small business enterprises in general have also been minimal: local software firms have not been treated any differently, that is, they have not been granted special status or incentives. Again, however, government aid has tended to improve over the years. In 2004, a national agency called Malta Enterprise (ME) was set up specifically to promote trade, investment and industrial development and to help new companies. This agency caters for all types of companies but, owing to the importance now attached to the ICT sector, it also has an ICT section geared at supporting computer firms. (ME assumed the roles previously held by IPSE [Institute for the Promotion of Small Enterprises], the MDC [Malta Development Corporation] and METCO (Malta External Trade Corporation).

The proportion of small firms in an economy tends to grow with decreasing country size. In Malta, the fragmented market and lack of economies of scale are the result of a micro local market and weak exposure to foreign contract work. Software companies (and, indeed, other SMEs) therefore need to consolidate their position through a combination of strategic vision, better management, higher standards and increased efficiency. Again, up until quite recently, incentives and the stimuli needed to help the small enterprises to realize this vision were practically nonexistent.

Apart from the small size, the relative immaturity of the local business market makes it difficult for Maltese software firms to develop new products or achieve scale economies. After the government, the largest domestic customers for software in Malta are the state-owned enterprises, most of which have now been privatized. Additionally, not all of them source their solutions locally.

Beyond the issue of scale economies, Malta's small size negatively affects the software industry in other ways. For example, unlike those countries where the native language is not English, Maltese software companies do not enjoy what has been termed a continuing "natural protection" arising from the nation's language. While there is sometimes a need to configure software to the native Maltese language, this requirement is very limited: not only is Malta small, but English is widely understood and spoken and is the preferred language of business and commerce.

A second example is that of legacy systems. Again, owing to the small market, few companies have had big computer installations typical of mainframe (or large miniframe) systems, and therefore the opportunities to specialize in providing services for legacy systems are extremely limited. In fact, only one Maltese company offers such a service: Philip Toledo Ltd, the oldest IT provider and systems house on the island.

An injustice that local software (and other) firms have faced for many years when competing with foreign firms operating locally is the fiscal incentives foreign firms have enjoyed. In order to attract foreign investment, the Industrial Development Act of 1988 granted all foreign companies in Malta and meeting certain criteria a 10-year tax holiday in which no corporate tax was paid during 10 consecutive years of operation (Fenech, 2002). This placed local companies—which typically had to pay a hefty corporation tax of 35%—at a gross disadvantage. Partly for this reason, this act was significantly revised in 2001. Under a new Business Promotion Act, no distinction is made between foreign-owned companies and Maltese firms, and the export-linked incentives for foreign firms have been removed, thus placing Maltese firms on a level playing field. Eyeing imminent EU accession, this revision also made the new Act EU compliant, since preferential treatment offered to nonlocal firms is illegal within EU single market law (Malta Enterprise, 2006a).

The Business Promotion Act of 2001 classifies ICT as a priority sector and accordingly includes a number of incentives ICT companies can benefit from. They include reduced rates of corporate tax (as low as 5%); tax credits of up to 65% on expenditure on investment of a capital nature; competitive rates of rent for company premises; low-interest loan financing; loan guarantees; and financial assistance for training of employees (up to 80% of costs involved).

E-GAMING'S POTENTIAL THREATS

A gaming sector can positively contribute to a country's economy. Yet it also has the potential of tarnishing the reputation of the jurisdiction. An issue revolving around gaming, especially betting, is player protection. For example, cases have been reported of gaming companies using players' funds to their advantage: by not separating the players' winning deposits from the operators' own funds, some companies "borrow" the players' money to cover operating costs whenever the companies run out of cash (Caruana, n.d.).

Worst-case scenarios involve gaming companies going bankrupt, shutting down their websites and preventing the players from making their own withdrawals. Malta's current regulations provide some degree of player protection by obliging operators to keep players' funds separate from the operators' own funds, but there remains scope for improvement (e.g., the setting up of player protection trusts).

Player protection is also important from a social perspective. Issuing game permits without proper legislation and regulation and aggressively promoting gaming could encourage people to spend more money on gaming instead of investing it or spending it on necessities, placing family livelihoods at risk. (Note, however, that Maltese licensed remote gambling companies are *not* allowed to sell their services to Maltese residents.)

Another concern is money laundering. There have been cases in which companies licensed by the regulator used remote gaming accounts in the regulator's jurisdiction for the transfer of fraudulent funds. In Malta, in 2013 alone, there were 29 alleged offenses reported to the police and the Financial Intelligence Analysis Unit (FIAU) for investigation (Vella, 2014). Moreover, FIAU can carry out due diligence on all applicants and undertakes regular system audits.

MANPOWER, EDUCATION AND TRAINING

In 1987, the University of Malta (UoM)—the main and only public university on the island—started offering data processing management and information systems (and, later, computer science and computer engineering) diploma and degree courses. Until then, the technical capability of local programmers and systems analysts had been acquired mainly through knowledge transfer and experience; by tapping expertise from the extensive Maltese diaspora living in places like the UK, the United States, Canada and Australia; by following long-distance courses or by attending overseas institutions. Entities like the government's former Swatar computer center and the Management Systems Unit (MSU) were instrumental in this respect. The Malta Information Technology and Training Services (MITTS) also offered a number of computer-related courses at various levels, some specifically aimed at management and others more suited to programmers. By the turn of the millennium, the NCC international diploma program run by MITTS had become a very popular full-time or part-time evening course, particularly as it was offered on a part-time (in addition to full-time), evening basis, but partly also because the Employment and Training Corporation (ETC) was offering "traineeships," as it called them, for those interested in following this course. (The NCC is the UK's National Computing Centre, the leading UK corporate IT body set up in 1966.)

The UoM remains the primary body offering the most comprehensive (in both depth and breadth of the subjects offered) range of IT–related courses in Malta. The Malta College of Arts, Science and Technology (MCAST), set up in 2001, has also been actively engaged in tailoring certificate and diploma courses to suit industry's needs. Between them, UoM and MCAST have sustained an annual IT graduate growth rate of 6% between 1997 and 2007 (Aloisio, 2010). At more than 0.12%, the proportion of IT graduates in the Maltese labor force had already exceeded that in places like India, Brazil, Germany, the United States and the UK by 2004 (Arora & Gambardella, 2005; Commander, 2005; World Bank, 2005).

A number of additional private training centers (as well as other educational institutions) have played a crucial role in providing computer education, particularly when it comes to programming and the use of software applications. These private centers have often specialized in key areas of training, usually by type of product. Thus, for example, if one wanted to specifically obtain first-hand experience in the use of Oracle products and database programming, a relatively short but intensive course at one of these private training centers is likely to prove more beneficial in the short term than perhaps the more general (and more theoretical) module offered by the university as part of an undergraduate course. Also, some of these centers and a number of private and church schools were among the first educational institutions to offer computer studies at secondary and postsecondary level in the 1980s, before computer studies became a compulsory subject in schools.

BUSINESS LINKAGES, OFFSHORING AND OUTSOURCING

Malta's strategic geographical position in the middle of the Mediterranean combined with a mild, sunny climate are natural advantages that have attracted a number of foreign companies and their expatriate staff to either (re)locate in Malta or start joint ventures with Maltese firms. More important reasons for choosing Malta include the Island's historical ties and trade relations with North Africa and the Middle East, a stable political environment, the widely spoken English language, a legal framework that is very much based on the European system and, more recently, a steady supply of suitably qualified personnel. An advanced state-of-the-art telecommunication system now facilitates all types of IT-related business. The technology penetration rate (Internet use, mobile telephony) is very high, and telecommunications access costs are now comparable to those of many advanced European countries (NSO, 2007). Malta's "network readiness" has been ranked 27th out of 122 countries (World Economic Forum, 2008) and 29th out of 100 countries in terms of global talent competitiveness (Digital Malta, 2014).

A frequently quoted reason for outsourcing and offshore work is to offer relatively low wages. Companies contemplating offshore outsourcing are often cautioned to weigh any potential benefits carefully because of hidden costs, a change of government policy, or a rapid upward trend in the outsourcing country's economy that could result in a substantial increase in local personal income (Carmel & Tjia, 2005). However, companies have rarely had to give up on offshore work. As regards Malta, relatively low income continues to be a main factor in attracting foreign investors. Although salaries in Malta have consistently increased in real terms from about the late 1980s onward, these increases have often been marginal, rarely exceeding 3% per annum of average yearly salaries. Salary increases in IT-related jobs have generally tended to be slightly higher than average; but the present salary scales still lag behind developed American or European states while being higher than those in emerging competitor economies like China, India, South Africa, the Philippines, Mexico and Russia.

It is only in the past 15 years or so that international software companies have discovered and started using Malta as an offshore site. Local talent is high; Maltese employees are considered to be hard working, ambitious and flexible; and IT graduates have been on the increase. Malta's leading foreign software company, Crimsonwing—which in October 2007 decided to go for a listing on the Malta Stock Exchange because of rapid growth—has always maintained that a key to its success has been its predominantly Maltese staff: "a young-at-heart, dynamic and professional workforce with a wealth of experience" (*The Malta Independent*, 2007). Similar sentiments have been expressed by other global companies operating in Malta.

Moreover, given the absence of economies of scale, even if Maltese companies have been successful locally, the domestic market is too limited to offer real opportunities for expansion. Maltese firms have therefore either collaborated with foreign firms to tap the overseas market or outsourced work directly to foreign clients. Strategic partnerships with foreign firms can offer local companies the prospect of entering into the export of software development and at the same time showcase the local company's full potential. This was the case with Makeezi—a Maltese firm specializing in rapid application development (RAD) deployment using Magic Software eDevelopment—which partnered with a UK firm to develop a World Wide Web–enabled software solution for the logistics and distribution channels of John Menzies, a leading UK operator (*The Malta Financial and Business Times*, 2001).

Over the years, in addition to diversifying their product or service offerings, companies have also sought to expand via mergers, the prime reason being the integration of different capabilities or technologies. Mergers need not necessarily involve foreign firms: two notable companies, Megabyte and the former BDS (Apple's former sole representative in Malta) have long merged with larger, well-established local firms to strengthen their positions. Following these mergers, both companies have experienced rapid growth.

Finally, accessing and using higher skill levels in developing countries and emerging economies has been one of the more recent trends of and fundamental approaches to offshoring. In recent years, global industry players such as IBM, HP, Oracle, Cisco and Microsoft have shown interest in doing business in Malta. It is conceivable that some of these companies will eventually set up an R&D base there. Presently, their main role has been to form strategic alliances with leading local ICT firms. These alliances can benefit all parties involved: thus, in 2001, Enemalta (Malta's state-owned and -operated electricity authority) and Microsoft Eastern Mediterranean, together with Computer Solutions (who are Microsoft technology partners) signed an agreement that enabled Enemalta to standardize all its IT requirements on a single and unified Microsoft platform. Hailed as one of the largest enterprise-scale agreements of its kind in Malta (it involved about 500 networked PCs), the move was part of Enemalta's overall business strategy to identify the right technological framework in order to rationalize its operations.

CONCLUSION

The software industry constitutes perhaps the first example of a successful high-tech indigenous industry in Malta. Tracing its roots to the mid-1980s, the industry has grown steadily since then and is now a sizeable employer of manufacturing and services. Critical mass may have been achieved in the early 2000s or more recently, but it is conceivable that the industry will continue to grow.

In absolute terms, the industry is tiny in comparison to that in other countries (owing to Malta's micro size and the limitations of scale economies); but, taken as a percentage (e.g., IT graduates or software employees per working population), it compares favorably even with some of the more advanced nations.

Government's main initiative in trying to place Malta on the international ICT map has been the widely publicized Smart City project in collaboration with Tecom Investments of Dubai (Zammit, 2006). Although it was generally welcomed, concerns about the scale of the project have raised fears of a possible brain drain whereby highly qualified and experienced professionals would be lured away from local firms to their bigger multinational counterparts, simultaneously pushing up local salaries and further disadvantaging small indigenous firms. Given that this project aimed to create some 5,500 jobs, two thirds of which were knowledge based, some have argued that foreign workers would be required, the supply of locally skilled personnel being insufficient to fill the anticipated positions. In any case, the project got delayed by some years, and the quoted number of jobs will probably only be created in the long term (Balzan, 2009; Micallef, 2012; Stagno-Navarra, 2009).

With regard to the e-gaming industry, there is scope for further expansion. Within the EU, Malta was the first EU member state to provide jurisdictional services to interactive gambling firms. And within the EU, only Malta and the UK have laws permitting and regulating e-gambling on their statute books (European Commission, 2006, p. 1400). While gaming in general has so far contributed positively to the economy, Malta still has very few indigenous companies involved in the actual creation of e-gaming systems (Games Audit, 2012). An important recommendation for Malta to continue to exploit this sector is therefore to have educational institutions train youngsters to acquire the right skills for game development.

Finally, Malta has come a long way from the time when the first computer center and some other government entities were managed by expatriates, when every purchase of a computer needed a license and a declaration by the purchaser that no worker would be made redundant as a result of the purchase, when doing an overseas telephone call meant calling in person at one of the branch offices of Telemalta (the former telecommunications incumbent) and when information technology policy was unheard of. Today, Malta can boast of an advanced telecommunications infrastructure, a state-of-the-art data center, operational ICT strategies and—importantly— qualified Maltese personnel and decision makers at all levels of management. It is a tribute to entrepreneurship, to those who, in spite of—or as a result of—Malta's small size have quickly responded to market opportunities and allowed the software industry and the e-gaming sector to grow to the size they now command.

REFERENCES

Aloisio, M. (2010). *Computing in Malta: Adoption of a technology in a small island state*. PhD dissertation, University of Warwick, UK: Department of Computer Science.

Arora, A., & Gambardella, A. (Eds.). (2005). *From underdogs to tigers: The rise and growth of the software industry in Brazil, China, India, Ireland, and Israel*. Oxford: Oxford University Press.

Baldacchino, G., & Fabri, D. (1999) The Malta Financial Services Centre: A study in microstate dependency management? In M. P. Hampton & J. P. Abbott (Eds.), Offshore finance centres and tax havens (pp. 140–166). Basingstoke, UK: Macmillan.

Balzan, S. (2009, October 7). Smart City: Malta's latest white elephant? *Malta Today*. Retrieved from http://archive.maltatoday.com.mt/2009/10/07/t6.html

Bonnici, J. (2000). A profile of Malta's manufacturing sector. In C. Vella (Ed.), *The Maltese islands on the move* (pp. 47–54). Malta: National Statistics Office.

Brincat, I. (2001, May 24–30). Lack of security hindering start-ups from getting loans. *Malta Business Weekly*.

Camilleri, B. (2011). *Information and communications technology (ICT) in Malta*. The Economic Market and Research Unit, Malta: Malta Enterprise.

Carmel, E., & Tjia, P. (2005). *Offshoring information technology: Sourcing and outsourcing to a global workforce*. Cambridge: Cambridge University Press.

Caruana, C. (n.d.). iGaming: Trusts to the players' rescue. www.fff-legal.com/igaming-trusts-to-the-players-rescue/

Commander, S. (2005). *The software industry in emerging markets*. Cheltenham, UK: Edward Elgar.

Digital Malta. (2014). INSEAD: Global Talent Competitiveness Index 2013. Retrieved from http://digitalmalta.gov.mt/en/Pages/Performance/INSEAD/INSEAD-Global Talent.aspx

European Commission. (2006). The impacts of Internet gambling and other forms of remote gambling on the EU gambling market. In Swiss Institute of Comparative Law, *The economics of gambling* (pp. 1399–1426). Brussels: European Commission (Internal Market). Retrieved from http://ec.europa.eu/internal_market/gambling/docs/study5_en.pdf

Fenech, E. (2002). *Manufacturing SMEs: Their role in the Maltese economy and the implications of the new Business Promotion Act incentives*. B. Accountancy (Hons.) Thesis, Msida, Malta: University of Malta.

Games Audit UK. (2012). *A digital gaming strategy for Malta*. Retrieved from www.maltaenterprise.com/sites/default/files/publications/adigitalgamingstrategyfor malta_-_report.pdf

ICON. (2014). ICON entrusted with TAKEOFF's marketing, branding and web development. Retrieved from www.icon.com.mt/content.aspx?id=383939

Lotteries and Other Games Act. (2001). Act XXIV of 2001, Chapter 438 of the Laws of Malta.

Malta Enterprise. (2006a). *The Business Promotion Act in brief*. Malta: Malta Enterprise.

Malta Enterprise (2006b). ICT Malta: Malta—a centre of quality for the ICT industry. Malta: Malta Enterprise.

The Malta Financial and Business Times. (2001, 12 September). Maltese IT company involved in multi-million GBP software project. Retrieved from www.business today.com.mt/2001/0912/local14.html

The Malta Independent. (2007, 21 October). Crimsonwing to go for local listing. *The Malta Independent*, p. 46. Retrieved from www.independent.com.mt/articles/2007-10-21/news/crimsonwing-to-go-for-local-listing-198538/

Micallef, M. (2012, June 10). In it for the long haul at Smart City. *The Times of Malta*. Retrieved from www.timesofmalta.com/articles/view/20120610/interview/In-it-for-the-long-haul-at-Smart-City.423507

MRGC. (2014). Malta Remote Gaming Council. Retrieved from www.mrgc.org.mt/index.asp

NSO. (2006). *ICT-usage of enterprises survey*. Malta: National Statistics Office.

NSO. (2007, February 16). News Release. Retrieved from http://nso.gov.mt/statdoc/document_file.aspx?id=1935

Remote Gaming Regulations. (2004). Subsidiary Legislation 438.04 of Lotteries and Other Games Act, Malta.

Stagno-Navarra, K. (2009, October 7). Smart City top chief reassures. *Business Today*. Retrieved from www.businesstoday.com.mt/2009/10/07/t1.html

UNIDO. (1993). *Software industry: Current trends and implications for developing countries*. Vienna, Austria: United Nations Industrial Development Organization.

Vella, M. (2014, 29 April). Remote gaming accounts in Malta used for money laundering. *Malta Today*. Retrieved from www.maltatoday.com.mt/business/business_news/38441/remote_gaming_accounts_in_malta_used_for_money_laundering#.VA58–8InHzI

World Bank. (2005). Total labor force. Retrieved from http://data.worldbank.org/indicator/SL.TLF.TOTL.IN/countries?page=1

World Economic Forum. (2008). Global information technology report 2006–2007. Retrieved from www.weforum.org/en/initiatives/gcp/Global%20Information%20Technology%20Report/index.htm

Xuereb, M. (2013, July 13). Gaming boom helped to "shake off recession." *Times of Malta*. Retrieved from www.timesofmalta.com/articles/view/20130713/local/Gaming-boom-helped-to-shake-off-recession-.477725

Zammit, S. (2006, 27 March). Heads of agreement of SmartCity@Malta signed. MaltaMedia Online Network. Retrieved from www.maltamedia.com/news/2005/bf/article_9404.shtml

15 Jersey, a Small Island International Finance Center

Adapting to Survive

Michael Entwistle and Michael J. Oliver

INTRODUCTION

This chapter considers the case of Jersey as a small island territory that has adapted to changing circumstances over many centuries and is now one of the most successful small international finance centers in the world. We evaluate a model to describe the economic life cycle of an island, using empirical evidence of the development of Jersey's finance industry. We then consider the necessary conditions that have enabled the development of Jersey as an international finance center and the reasons for its phenomenal success in this field, including the contribution of the Islanders' innovation and ingenuity. Finally, the discussion considers the current challenges to offshore finance and concludes with a speculation on the possible futures for the industry in Jersey.

Jersey is the largest of the Channel Islands, an archipelago that comprises three other main islands—Guernsey, Alderney and Sark—and a number of islets and reefs. The island of Jersey is located in the English Channel, some 100 miles south of Britain and about 12 miles off the west coast of Normandy, France.

To understand the development of Jersey as an international finance center, it is necessary to appreciate the historical, geopolitical and social context of the island (Everard & Holt, 2004). Before the Norman conquest of England in 1066, the Channel Islands were part of the Duchy of Normandy, part of what is now northern France. After the invasion, however, the Crown of England and the title of Duke of Normandy were not amalgamated under King William I. In 1204, King John of England lost his territories in continental Europe, but the Islands elected to remain as the remnants of the Duchy of Normandy, loyal to the English Crown. In return, the king granted the Islands the privileges of having their own separate legislative assemblies, the right to observe customary Norman law, to administer their own judicial systems and to set their own taxes (States of Jersey, 2014a).

This remarkable measure of autonomy remains the foundation of the Islands' unwritten constitutional relationship with the United Kingdom; they are neither part of the metropolitan UK nor a colony or Overseas Territory but a Crown Dependency. Moreover, the Islands are not part of the European Union but have a special relationship, as defined in the UK's 1972 Treaty of Accession to the European Economic Community. As a consequence, the EU has very limited legislative competence in respect of Channel Islands affairs.

Baldacchino (2010) explores the implications of jurisdictions that enjoy "in-betweenity"—in other words, being in neither one place nor another—and are able to take advantage of and manipulate their position "in limbo" in the geographical, socioeconomic and legislative milieu in between other jurisdictions. In this way, the Channel Islands have been able to benefit from their unique relationships with the UK and the EU not by being part of either but by exploiting specific niche opportunities that are a characteristic of many "offshore" jurisdictions.

THE ECONOMIC LIFE CYCLE

Island Analysis (2014, p. 60) has proposed the paradigm of an "island life cycle," which describes the "observed economic, social, and environmental life cycles through which island communities progress repeatedly over periods of time." The island life cycle comprises four sequential stages: building; fine tuning, stress/crisis and reinvention. Various islands can be plotted in their respective stages within the cycle. The author proposes that islands can move between these stages and manage the impact of the stress/crisis stage.

The concept of an island life cycle has been developed by Island Analysis Ltd. based on their research of social, environmental and economic indicators, together with government strategies and policy, from a wide range of islands worldwide. This chapter considers whether the paradigm accurately describes the life cycle of an island economy—particularly in the case of a "monoculture" economy, when the whole economy of an island is heavily dependent on a single industry or product. A similar concept has been developed in relation to a tourist-area life cycle (Butler, 1980). However, rather than the cross-jurisdictional contemporary comparison with other islands carried out by Island Analysis, we evaluate the life cycle model by drawing on and analyzing empirical evidence within one island industry: financial services in Jersey. This is followed by a consideration of the extent to which this model might accurately reflect the evolution of this industry.

DEVELOPMENT OF THE JERSEY ECONOMY

Over time, various island states and territories have been able to demonstrate the characteristics of innovation, adaptation and change in response to various challenges and to compete effectively, both with other small or "microstate" jurisdictions and with larger jurisdictions that have greater capacity and resources (Baldacchino, 2011). Jersey is no exception: its ability to respond to changing circumstances is graphically illustrated by the historical transition of the Channel Islands' main industries, initially from cod fishing and knitting in the 17th century to ship building and agriculture in the 18th century (Ommer, 1991; Podger, 1962; Syvret & Stevens, 1998), then in the 19th century to tourism and, nowadays, international finance.

Baldacchino (2006) describes the characteristics of a "PROFIT" economy as one typology among a number used to analyze the economies of subnational island jurisdictions, which, through creative diplomacy and flexible policy, wrest local control from metropolitan powers and deploy policies regarding people (immigration), natural and environmental resources, overseas management (diplomacy), finance and transport (Oberst & McElroy, 2007, p. 165). For reasons discussed in what follows, Jersey would be classified as a preeminent example of a PROFIT economy.

The creation of a finance industry in Jersey required certain conditions: jurisdictional autonomy, tax neutrality, the common law legal system, a stable government, regulatory specialization, administrative convenience, a strong economy enabling investment in critical infrastructure and transport links and proximity to one of the major global finance hubs in the City of London (Capital Economics, 2013). These are the minimum requirements, analogous to the basic physiological and safety factors in psychologist Maslow's (1943) classic hierarchy of needs. However, Maslow identified further higher-level needs that must be satisfied to achieve greater work motivation: *esteem*, including confidence, achievement and respect and *self-actualization*, for example creativity, problem solving and innovation. Beyond the minimum requirements, by analogy with Maslow's motivation theory, it is argued that the success of Jersey's finance industry owes much to the higher-level motivators: the reputation-building initiatives, innovation and creativity of the island's government and the entrepreneurship of private-sector businesses.

The ability of Jersey's government to create its own laws, adjudicated by an independent judiciary, and to set its own taxes created an environment in which Jersey has developed a competitive business environment for the finance industry. This "rich seam of jurisdictional capacity" (Baldacchino, 2010, p. 188) is illustrated by the legislative and policy initiatives introduced by the Jersey authorities.

Jersey has always maintained a low-tax regime and, following the Napoleonic Wars, from 1815, many retiring navy and army officers were attracted to Jersey to eke out their military pensions without paying British taxes. Jersey income tax had been introduced in 1928 and subsequently increased from 2.5% to a standard 20% in 1940. After the First and Second World Wars, the island provided an escape and solace from higher UK taxation, and in the 1950s, many who had lived and worked in the former British Colonies sought to resettle to a secure and stable jurisdiction, nearer to the UK but without a UK tax liability.

In 1961, a key decision was taken by the States of Jersey to repeal certain antiusury provisions in ancient legislation dating back to 1771. This enabled the setting of market interest rates and immediately attracted the establishment in Jersey of some major UK merchant banks, creating a favorable environment for the future development of the international finance industry.

Through the 1960s and 1970s, Jersey's legislature implemented measures that increased confidence in its financial institutions, including protection for investors, antifraud measures and licensing of institutions. Thus, when the UK introduced exchange controls in 1972, Jersey became increasingly attractive to banks wishing to set up off shore. Some important policies were introduced during this period that have generally continued to serve the island well: limiting licenses for new business to only the top tier of well-regulated institutions, ensuring that businesses maintain the good reputation and respectability of the island and deliberately *not* introducing banking secrecy legislation such as in Switzerland.

A leading innovator during this period was Colin Powell, CBE (no relation to the former U.S. Secretary of State). He was appointed in 1969 as Economic Adviser to the States of Jersey, a post he held until 1992, when he became Chief Adviser to the States. He is the author of the *Economic Survey of Jersey* (1971) and numerous articles on the island's economy and is currently engaged in writing a definitive history of Jersey as an international finance center. In 1981, he was appointed to the position of Chairman of the Offshore Group of Banking Supervisors; he was co-chair of the Basel Committee Cross-border Banking Working Group and is now an advisor on international affairs to the government of Jersey. Much of the economic and policy advice Colin Powell provided to the States of Jersey during his career laid the foundations of the finance industry that exists in the island today. One area of expertise in which Jersey specialized was the formation and administration of trusts. The enactment of a trust law in 1984 reinforced Jersey's leading position in this area and set a standard that many other jurisdictions have subsequently followed. Jersey continued to use its legislative autonomy to bring in further legislation that enhanced the island's reputation and commercial competitiveness: for example, the Security Interests Law in 1983, the Collective Investment Funds Law in 1988, the Bankruptcy (Désastre) Law in 1990 and the Companies Law and Banking Business Law in 1991 (Powell, 2015).

However, low taxes, stable government, respectability, comprehensive legislation and effective regulation alone may be necessary but are not sufficient for securing success and prosperity. They need to be complemented by sound domestic policy innovation, flexibility and ingenuity, as well as a dynamic private sector.

When in 1998 the UK government commissioned an independent review of the regulation of the finance industries in the Crown Dependencies, the report noted,

> The Islands owe the success of their finance centers to their substantial constitutional independence in domestic affairs, their political stability

and their continuing willingness, evident throughout their history, to adapt to changing world conditions. These are the vital factors from which all else flows.

(Edwards, 1998, p. 32)

The Edwards report further noted (ibid., p. 36) that key elements in the success of the offshore finance industry included the following:

- *Innovation and flexibility.* The offshore centers are sometimes better able than the larger centers to test out innovative financial products such as new insurance or investment vehicles. They can respond flexibly and quickly to the changing needs of international customers and markets. In the larger centers, the ramifications of change are typically wider.
- *Regulation.* The offshore centers may also be able to lead the way in certain areas of regulation.

While demonstrating the importance of factors such as reputation, expertise and sound regulatory systems, this report also highlighted the significance of flexibility and innovation and the government/industry "partnership."

An example of such flexibility was the creation of a framework under the Collective Investments Funds (Jersey) Law 1998 to provide for "unclassified funds." The requirements applicable to an unclassified fund are broadly the same as for a "recognized fund," but there is less legislation governing their structure and operation, and they may be regulated to an extent and in a manner appropriate to the nature of the particular fund following scrutiny of the proposal. This is intended to facilitate innovation by the industry while still protecting investors and the island's reputation as an international finance center.

A further example of the innovative government/industry partnership is provided by the establishment in 2001 of Jersey Finance, a nonprofit organization, funded by members of the local finance industry and the Jersey government. The organization promotes Jersey as an international financial center of excellence, and its objectives include "[to] actively represent the finance industry's needs and concerns with regards to legislation, regulation and other key areas of innovation that can enhance our jurisdictional product offering" (Jersey Finance, 2014).

The chief executive of Jersey Finance, Geoff Cook, has identified recent initiatives in the industry–government partnership that support Jersey's lead in international finance: a "future-proof" model in relation to the EU's Alternative Investment Fund Managers Directive (AIFMD) enabling managers to access both EU capital and non–EU markets—landmark legislation that provides Jersey trusts with a tangible advantage over competing jurisdictions—and changes to company law that increase the attraction for international investors. According to Cook, "First priority was to ensure that government, the financial regulator and the industry join forces more effectively to foster the commercial environment needed for success" (*Finance Review*, 2014, p. 2).

Jersey Finance has pioneered developments in new areas such as Islamic financial services and is promoting the potential to be an early adopter of clean energy and other technologies, positioning Jersey to become one of the top "CleanTech" jurisdictions of the future. And in 2014, Jersey became the first jurisdiction in the world to launch a regulated virtual currency fund, the Global Advisers Bitcoin Investment Fund (GABI), enabling corporate investors such as pension and insurance companies to invest in Bitcoin (States of Jersey, 2014b). According to Morel (2014, p. 62), "the launch of GABI was used by Jersey's government as an opportunity to welcome cryptocurrency to the island, adding that this is only as long as it falls within Jersey's existing regulatory framework." The potential for cryptocurrency is not only to provide an asset for investment but also to create a new finance sector that complements Jersey's conventional finance industry.

The commitment of the island's government to working in partnership with the finance industry to foster innovation is indicated by Jersey's Chief Minister, quoted in the Jersey Financial Services Industry Policy Framework (States of Jersey, 2014c): "Jersey is rated as one of the most stable and successful international financial services centres in the world and, working together responsibly, the government, the regulator and industry have the ability to continue to drive excellence and innovation in everything we do."

The innovation of the finance industry and its ability to adapt itself to change are also key to its success. Robert Luetkehaus, a business development officer for Moore Stephens Fund Administration in Jersey, highlights the strengths and flexibility of the workforce as follows:

> . . . what makes Jersey stand out is not just the tax efficiency but the expertise of the professional community in the island. Where this experience really tells is in reacting to new legislation, restrictions and regulation. Practitioners in Jersey have a proven track record in managing complex and specialized structures through regulatory change; they have prospered where other jurisdictions have struggled to come to terms with changes and updates. Recent updates and reactions to issues such as Basel III[1] and AIFMD, plus disclosure agreements such as FATCA,[2] show that the Island's financial sector retains a nimbleness that serves it well.
>
> (*Finance Review*, 2014, p. 8)

Innovation in the finance industry is synergistic with developments in information and communications technology (ICT). For example, Ernst and Young (EY) in the Channel Islands has developed a novel Web-based tool to assist banks and trust companies in Jersey and other jurisdictions to comply with the complex FATCA requirements. In another example, InfrasoftTech in Jersey has developed a mobile application, the M-Wallet Solution, which is designed to make everyday financial transactions fast and cashless. Anil Mookoni, vice president of InfrasoftTech, claims,

> We predict that within the next three to five years more people will manage their finances via their handheld devices . . . To be successful in the 21st century, businesses need to continue to innovate, use new technologies and identify ways of improving the customer experience.
>
> (*Finance Review*, 2014, p. 19)

A further example of synergy between the finance and ICT sectors is the Jersey-based company Foreshore. This company provides data center, disaster-recovery, hosting, managed services and a range of other cloud-based services that support the finance sector in Jersey and also a growing e-commerce industry operating from Jersey. Graham Hughes, chief executive of the parent company, Sure, says,

> As Jersey looks to strengthen its economy through diversification and, at the same time, the finance sector broadens its horizons by entering markets as far afield as South America and the Far East, Island businesses need to know they can rely on global connectivity along with reliable cloud services and back-up facilities that reside in Jersey but which can be used around the world on a 24/7 basis.
>
> (*Finance Review*, 2014, p. 6)

The empirical evidence considered here, describing the development and adaptation of Jersey's international finance industry, strongly argues the case that Jersey Islanders have the capacity to be creative and enterprising. Building on the advantages of the unique constitutional relationships with the UK and the EU, legislative and jurisdictional autonomy, low taxation and a stable government, Jersey men and women have added the key elements of enterprise and innovation to create a highly competitive and successful international finance center.

IMPORTANCE OF THE FINANCE INDUSTRY TO JERSEY

The importance and size of the finance sector to Jersey's economy is massive: 40% of gross value added (GVA) by sector was attributable directly to financial services in 2012. That proportion would be even larger if indirect economic activity, like ancillary business services, rental and construction, is included (States of Jersey, 2013, p. 2). Some critics have argued that the domination of financial services has led to the crowding out of other industries ("Dutch disease") and has led to an overdependence on finance, or the "capture" of the state by the industry. The central charge is that

> As the OFC [Offshore Finance Center] developed in Jersey during the 1970s and 1980s, its dynamism was such that it rapidly became the dominant industrial sector, and ultimately gained control of the island's political economy, thereby acting as a "cuckoo in the nest" . . . the considerable number and variety of tax/regulatory haven devices introduced by the States of Jersey in recent years demonstrate the extent to which small legislatures can be captured and used by financial capital.
>
> (Christensen & Hampton, 1999, pp. 186–187)

Although the finance sector has long dominated Jersey's economy, its share of GVA has actually fallen from a peak of 53% in 2000. Since 2008, the GVA of the finance sector has declined by 31%, and the GVA of the nonfinance sector has declined by 7%. In 2010, the combined nonfinance sector of the economy overtook finance in its contribution to GVA for the first time in at least a generation.

From an economic perspective, we should note that the concept of overdependence is a slippery one, and how it should be quantified is unclear. At what point does the composition of economic activity in a microstate imply an overdependence? Perhaps the crucial point is whether an industry is stable and sustainable over time. As the preceding section showed, the finance sector grew as a result of a combination of factors, and the decline of the traditional sectors in Jersey (particularly agriculture and manufacturing) over the last 30 years is part of a longer period of decline. As the global finance crisis (GFC) of 2008 has shown, financial services are as vulnerable as any other sector to contraction as well as expansion. Baldacchino (2011, p. 241) compares the growth and decline of an island industry sector with surfers of the ocean waves:

> . . . the life cycles of economic opportunity rarely align themselves with the life cycles of economic actors . . . so somehow, such actors are riding multiple economic waves, successively and/or simultaneously, like so many intrepid ocean surfers . . . and hopefully coming out on top to face another day, and another wave.

The growth of financial services has dominated Jersey's economy; but the growth of the finance industry over time does not necessarily prove that the state has been captured, and from a political and economic perspective, the argument is perhaps more complicated than Christensen and Hampton (1999) acknowledge.

ECONOMIC DIVERSIFICATION

Some of the academic literature on islands (e.g., Briguglio, 1995; Briguglio et al., 2009) tends to focus on their economic vulnerability, typically with an open economy based on a "monoculture" industry or a narrow range of products, which can be highly susceptible to market fluctuations and external change. In such circumstances, island entrepreneurs have to be nimble and adaptable to survive; they must either modify and refine their product in order to compete effectively or, in the extreme, reinvent to launch a new economic product.

In many small islands, there have been efforts to promote greater economic diversification, including a move away from export products to service- and knowledge-based industries (Briguglio et al., 2006, p. 17) to ameliorate the inherent vulnerability of single-industry economies. In Jersey, economic diversification has been embraced through the reinvention of existing industries such as tourism to create a more "niche" tourism product, for example focusing on short breaks, cultural and sporting events and "eco-tourism" such as cycling holidays (States of Jersey, 2014d), the launch of new information technology initiatives such as "Digital Jersey" (Digital Jersey, 2014a) and a forthcoming international aircraft registry (Jersey Aircraft Registry, 2014). The Digital Jersey initiative is a key driver for economic diversification, not only in promoting skills development, financial technology and cryptocurrency sectors but also providing a focal point ("the Hub") for startup businesses to meet, develop and collaborate. Within the first few months of the Hub opening, it had been used by 78 businesses, impressive evidence of entrepreneurial spirit (Morel, 2014, p. 24).

In addition, diversification of the financial services industry has included the development of a number of distinct sectors, which are interconnected but not entirely interdependent on each other: these include banking, funds management, private wealth management and company and trust administration, with the supporting legal and accounting services. Recognizing that there will invariably be peaks and troughs in the life cycle of any one particular industry sector, the aim in managing such industry sectors in a diversified economy might be like the trick of spinning plates, to ensure that even in times of global recession, they do not all slow down at the same time. According to Island Analysis (2014, p. 60),

> The recent years of "fine-tuning," followed by "stress/crisis" in several of the islands featured in the *Monitor*, have also reinforced the importance of economic diversification in island economies. This is a high priority for most island governments as a route to reduce the risk of a future economic and social stress and crisis in their community.

Work by Briguglio and colleagues (2009) on the economic vulnerability and resilience suggests that small, often island jurisdictions can succeed if they adopt policies conducive to good economic, social, political and environmental governance. As discussed earlier, Jersey has historically met numerous challenges in all these areas. Despite this, there are two well-known characteristics (which are more akin to challenges) for small island states and territories that give cause for concern in Jersey as it has adapted to survive. The first concerns the limited diversification of the economy, and the second is the restrictions on institutional capacity: that is, the high fixed costs associated with providing public services. Both characteristics add intensity to the "stress/crisis" stage of the Island Analysis paradigm and make reinvention both a necessity and a challenge.

The authorities have frequently stressed the importance of economic diversification in Jersey in the pursuit of sustained economic growth (States of Jersey, 2005, 2012; Policy and Resources Committee, 1995). The 2005 Economic Growth Plan set a target for economic growth of 2% per annum between 2005 and 2009. Over the economic cycle (taken from 2000 to 2007), excluding finance-sector profits, the growth of GVA was 1.5% per annum. However, a substantial proportion of GVA is made up of finance-sector profits, which declined by about 30% over the economic cycle, so the compound annual growth rate for the entire economy was 0.1%. The 2012 Economic Growth and Diversification Strategy did not promise to raise the rate of economic growth but instead offered a "wider basket of indicators" to judge the success of economic policy that included employment, unemployment, average earnings, Islanders' perceptions of quality of life and public safety and level of crime.

Unfortunately, the compelling case for moving the economy away from undue reliance on the finance industry has often been beset by confused objectives: the mantra that governments cannot pick winners is often in conflict with micromanagement—the tension between *laissez-faire* and necessary government intervention. The consequence has been lack of engagement with the key issues required to raise productivity in the nonfinance sector and ephemeral political support that ebbed and flowed according to the fortunes of the finance sector. In short, because the profits in the finance sector were healthy until the GFC, the efforts to diversify the economy can at best only be described as piecemeal and haphazard. The onset of the GFC changed this, but policy makers were slow to react. This was largely because they believed the downturn in the finance sector to be temporary, but as the international community began to adopt a more aggressive stance to activities in offshore finance centers, policy makers in Jersey were forced to prepare for the worst.

A recent analysis of Jersey's economic health (Demos-PwC good growth index) identified the lack of progress on diversification as a key issue for Jersey's future development:

> . . . perhaps because of the quality of life which has been enjoyed for many years by Jersey residents, there was concern expressed that there

may be a sense of complacency creeping in, with insufficient desire to make the changes some felt to be necessary if megatrends such as technological advances and the digital revolution are not to bypass them.

(Jones, 2014, n.p.)

The importance of diversifying the economy in the event of future financial crises and a range of external threats (from more draconian regulation to further loss of business to other financial centers) cannot be understated. Since the 1970s, Jersey's economy has moved from "low-value-added" activities (e.g., tourism and agriculture) to "high-value-added" activities (financial services). The impact of this transition has diminished over the last decade; and, in real terms, measured by GVA, the entire economy has not grown.

CHALLENGES TO THE FINANCE INDUSTRY IN JERSEY

It is not hard to see why policy makers are reliant on financial services to generate economic growth and why they are wedded to promoting finance unless and until it can be replaced by a similar wealth-producing industry. To this end, Jersey Finance tasked consultants McKinsey & Company to produce a report on the future of the financial services industry. McKinsey began work in October 2012 and consulted with a large number of stakeholders. Although the report was never released (at a cost of £1m to the public purse, the decision not to publish was curious), the recommendations were fed into a new Financial Services Industry Policy Framework, which was published in April 2014. It was shaped around four key priorities: sustain the core, enhance enablers, capture adjacent growth and reposition and build new capabilities.

In essence, sustaining the core implies protecting Jersey's existing business in financial services. The finance industry is made up of five subsectors: banking, trust and company administration, fund management, legal and accountancy. The banking subsector is the most important of the five in terms of employment and profitability. The total Jersey labor force is more than 56,000, of whom more than one fifth (12,400 employees) work in the finance sector (Jersey Labor Market Report, June 2013). Banking accounted for almost half of total employment within financial services (the fallout in employment from financial services since 2008 has been dramatic, with a decrease in employment of more than 1,000). In 2013, banking accounted for 79% of the total net profits of Jersey's entire financial services sector (a similar proportion from the mid-1990s until 2008).

Despite the publication of the Industry Policy Framework, two big challenges remain. First, the most successful part of the finance sector has been the banking subsector; but 6 years of record low interest rates have reduced profits considerably. Economists expect only very gradual increases in rates over the next 3 years, and that would mean a decade of historically low interest rates. The sterling value of deposits in Jersey declined by more than a third between 2007 and 2013, and the authorities hope that the measures stemming from the new Policy Framework will encourage a range of new banks to deposit funds in Jersey, which might counter this contraction. Concerns have been expressed that, by relaxing the constraint on limiting banking licenses for only those in the world's top 500, standards might slip (Burrows, 2014).

Second, the sustained verbal attack on offshore jurisdictions in the wake of the GFC has been added to by increasingly complex legislation relating to regulation and supervision. This includes the EU Savings Tax Directive the U.S. Foreign Account Tax Compliance Act and the proposed OECD standards for automatic information exchange. To counter the verbal criticism that Jersey was a problem for the international financial community, Capital Economics (2013) produced a report that showed the opposite, including evidence that Jersey helps the UK generate around £2.3 billion in tax revenue each year and supports 180,000 British jobs. Jersey continues to work very hard with counterparties in other jurisdictions to guarantee that any international legislation does not have a disproportionate effect on the island relative to other offshore centers. However, various commentators, even those supportive of offshore finance, concede that the future for offshore finance is very uncertain (Kurdle, 2013). Although some would argue that the growth in the number of compliance jobs in finance is a positive sign of a recovery in financial services (there was an increase of 160 full-time-equivalent staff across the finance sector engaged in compliance in 2013 compared to 2012), the majority of this activity was a cost to business. Jersey already has a high cost base, and the danger for the island is that if business is made more expensive, profits will be further squeezed and customers will choose cheaper jurisdictions for doing business.

In the past, levels of government expenditure have been predicated on a thriving financial-services sector. The challenges for the authorities in not securing high levels of income from this or other sources are considerable. The latest financial forecasts at the time of writing suggest that income receipts will be significantly down over the next two years, which will require tax rises and cuts in public expenditure (States of Jersey, 2014e). The growth of public expenditure in Jersey has become a source of concern over the last decade (States of Jersey, 2014f). It is difficult to find comparable data on the levels of expenditure in small island states, but the work of Cas and Ota (2008) from a 42-country sample (of which 26 were islands) illustrates a wide range of total government expenditure. This ranged from 19.5% of GDP (the Bahamas) to 68.4% of GDP (Micronesia), and some countries had levels of public debt ranging from 31.8% of GDP (Trinidad and Tobago) to 297.6% of GDP (São Tomé and Príncipe). By comparison, up until the GFC, Jersey's public finances appeared to be very sound, with no external indebtedness and no public debt. A decade before the GFC, the average level of States expenditure was a little more than 13.5% of GVA and, although it had grown particularly fast between 2000 and 2005, it was better managed between 2005 and 2008. In recent years, the level of States expenditure has increased because of the recession; and expenditure in 2013 was probably around 20% of GVA.

There were concerns in Jersey by the mid-2000s that fiscal policy was becoming procyclical—that is, spending was increased in booms and reduced in downturns. The retrenchment was not particularly severe because income streams returned; but the fiscal expansionism exacerbated the economic upswings. In turn, this threatened the cost base of the island: government expenditure added to demand, which contributed to inflationary wage and price pressure. To counter this, a Stabilization Fund was created in 2006, and monies were transferred to the fund from the Consolidated Fund (essentially the States of Jersey's current account). The purpose of this was twofold: first, to prevent the States spending money that was in the Consolidated Fund and second, to have a source of funds to be used in an economic downturn. (Jersey also has a Strategic Reserve, often referred to as the "rainy day" fund, which was to be used in exceptional circumstances to insulate the island's economy from severe structural decline such as the sudden collapse of a major island industry or from major natural disaster). A Fiscal Policy Panel was created, which commented on the States financial position and forecasts; it made recommendations whether money should be added to or taken out of the Stabilization Fund. A recent policy paper has sought to strengthen the fiscal framework further (States of Jersey, 2014g).

DECLINING PRODUCTIVITY

While curbing the growth of public expenditure is a significant challenge, another is the slow rate of growth of productivity. Higher productivity should lead to several positive outcomes for an economy. First, as workers are more efficient, businesses make more profit and can reinvest this into their business, leading to a virtuous circle of internal growth. Second, businesses can afford to pay higher wages. Third, it leads to increased competitiveness and enables firms to compete more effectively in global markets. Finally, cost savings by firms are passed on to consumers in the form of lower prices, which in turn encourages demand, more output and increases in employment.

Jersey's productivity problem has recently been identified by the Fiscal Policy Panel (2013) as significant, but it was recognized as a problem more than a decade ago by the then chief executive of the States that, outside of financial services, productivity in Jersey's private sector was in danger of faltering. This was followed by an initial series of publications on productivity by the Economics Unit that linked to an anti-inflation strategy and first Economic Growth Plan. Since then, the debate about productivity has faded. This is unfortunate. It should be stressed that the best proxy Jersey has for measuring productivity is GVA per full-time equivalent employee (FTE). Overall, GVA per FTE has fallen by about 14% in real terms over the period 1998 to 2012: in the finance sector, it has decreased by just over a third (34%).

Although in current income terms, GVA per FTE in the finance sector is almost double the average of all other sectors, there is no room for complacency for two reasons. First, as finance is such a big contributor to Jersey's GVA, with falling productivity, standards of living in Jersey will fall. Second, productivity cannot be looked at purely in terms of the domestic economy: faltering productivity should be examined by a comparison to what is happening in other jurisdictions. Stark differences in productivity across countries account for a substantial amount of the differences in average per capital income; over time, country X will become poorer relative to other countries (Hall & Jones, 1999; Jones & Romer, 2010).

In the banking subsector, there has been a significant fall in productivity of around 6% per annum since 2000. Although some have argued that this is due to the low-interest-rate environment and that profitability and productivity will return to banking when interest rates are raised, the fall in productivity began before the implementation of unconventional monetary policy in 2009. As is recognized by outside experts, including McKinsey, the adverse market trends for the finance sector include ongoing external and regulatory challenges, not all of which can be quantified. This suggests that any significant renewal in productivity growth and output is not a forgone conclusion.

CONCLUSION

To conclude on an optimistic note, however, in recent years, there have been two new developments in Jersey that could unleash important productivity gains. First is Digital Jersey, which has a very ambitious business plan for 2014 (Digital Jersey, 2014b). Second is the money being spent by Education, Sport and Culture in its "Vision for IT in Education 2013–2015, 'Thinking Differently'" (States of Jersey, 2014h).

The life cycle paradigm provides a useful analytical tool to describe the evolution of the finance industry in Jersey. However, it is not evident that such a model is necessarily predictive of the outcome—that is, that stress/crisis is inevitable and leads to the need for radical reinvention of the economy. With regard to Jersey's finance industry, it is necessary to give further consideration to the current challenges facing the industry. This chapter speculates whether "fine tuning" might reorient the industry, enabling the development of alternative products or structures, or whether there needs to be a more radical drive for innovation, reinvestment and rejuvenation to reinvent the economy of Jersey, perhaps developing the fields of information and communications technology. Perhaps Jersey's PROFIT economy needs to evolve in response to new business opportunities as and when they arise. Jones (2014, n.p.) summarizes the dilemma faced by Jersey:

Although having a unique identity forged by history, and with a proud population and a distinctive way of life—the Jersey way—the challenge for the Channel Islands is in many ways similar to other places which are already doing well: trying to find the keys to unlock their growth potential without impacting a way of life which has proved attractive to many over successive generations.

NOTES

1. "Basel III" is a comprehensive set of reform measures, developed by the Basel Committee on Banking Supervision, to strengthen the regulation, supervision and risk management of the banking sector.
2. The U.S. Foreign Account Tax Compliance Act.

REFERENCES

Baldacchino, G. (2006). Managing the hinterland beyond: Two ideal-type strategies of economic development for small island territories. *Asia Pacific Viewpoint, 47*(1), 45–60.

Baldacchino, G. (2010). *Island enclaves: Offshoring strategies, creative governance and subnational island jurisdictions.* Montreal, QC: McGill Queen's University Press.

Baldacchino, G. (2011). Surfers of the ocean waves: Change management, intersectoral migration and the economic development of small island states. *Asia Pacific Viewpoint, 52*(3), 236–246.

Briguglio, L. (1995). Small island developing states and their economic vulnerabilities. *World Development, 23*(9), 1615–1632.

Briguglio L., Cordina, G., Farrugia, N. & Vella, S. (2009). Economic vulnerability and resilience: Concepts and measurements. *Oxford Development Studies, 37*(3), 229–247.

Briguglio L., Persaud, B., & Stern, R. (2006). *Towards an outward-oriented development strategy for small states: Issues, opportunities and resilience building. A review of the small states agenda proposed in the Commonwealth/World Bank Joint Task Force report of April 2000.* 2006 Annual Meetings. Singapore: World Bank Group/International Monetary Fund.

Burrows, D. (2014). Breaking the rules? *Business Life, 33*(July/August), 40–43.

Butler, R. W. (1980). The concept of a tourist area cycle of evolution: Implications for management of resources. *The Canadian Geographer, 24*(1), 5–12.

Capital Economics. (2013). *Jersey's value to Britain: Evaluating the economic, financial and fiscal linkages between Jersey and the United Kingdom.* London: Capital Economics. Retrieved from http://jsy.fi/1cHSddE

Cas, M. S., & Ota, R. (2008). *Big government, high debt, and fiscal adjustment in small states.* IMF Working Paper, WP 08/39. Retrieved from www.imf.org/external/pubs/ft/wp/2008/wp0839.pdf

Christensen, J., & Hampton, M. P. (1999). A legislature for hire: The capture of the state in Jersey's Offshore Finance Centre. In M. P. Hampton & J. A. Abbott (Eds.),

Offshore finance centres and tax havens: The rise of global capital (pp. 166–191). Basingstoke, UK: Macmillan.

Digital Jersey. (2014a). Digital Jersey. Retrieved from www.digital.je/

Digital Jersey. (2014b). Digital Jersey strategy business plan 2014. Retrieved from www.digital.je/news/strategy-business-plan-for-2014

Edwards, A. (1998). *Review of financial regulation in the Crown Dependencies.* Cm 4109-I. London: The Stationery Office. Retrieved from www.gov.uk/government/uploads/system/uploads/attachment_data/file/265705/4109.pdf

Everard, J., & Holt, J.C. (2004). *Jersey 1204: The forging of an island community.* London: Thames & Hudson.

Finance Review. (2014). *Jersey Evening Post* supplement, September 3, 2014: Jersey. Retrieved from http://edition.pagesuite-professional.co.uk/digitaleditions.aspx?tab=0&pid=ecff7f14-e27e-4253-b977-e42997ddb0dc

Hall, R., & Jones, C. (1999). Why do some countries produce so much more output per worker than others? *Quarterly Journal of Economics, 114*(1), 83–116.

Island Analysis. (2014). *2014 Island Monitor 1.* St. Peter Port, Guernsey: Island Analysis Ltd.

Jersey Aircraft Registry. (2014). Jersey aircraft registry. Retrieved from www.jar.je/

Jersey Finance. (2014). About Jersey Finance. Retrieved from www.jerseyfinance.je/about-jersey-finance

Jersey labor market report. (2013, June). States of Jersey statistics unit. Retrieved from www.gov.je/Government/Pages/StatesReports.aspx?ReportID=978

Jones, C.I., & Romer, P.M. (2010). The new Kaldor facts: Ideas, institutions, population, and human capital. *American Economic Journal: Macroeconomics, 2*(1), 224–245.

Jones, N.C. (2014). Good growth: an island story. PwC public sector matters blog. Retrieved from pwc.blogs.com/publicsectormatters/2014/05/good-growth-an-island-story.html

Kurdle, R.T. (2013). *The future of offshore finance as a global policy problem.* Paper presented to seminar on Deconstructing Offshore Finance, University of Oxford, September 2–3.

Maslow, A.H. (1943). A theory of human motivation. *Psychological Review, 50,* 370–396.

Morel, K. (2014, September 10). Both sides of the (Bit)coin. *Business Life.* www.businesslife.co/Features.aspx?id=both-sides-of-the-bitcoin

Oberst, A., & McElroy, J.L. (2007). Contrasting socio-economic and demographic profiles of two, small island, economic species: MIRAB versus PROFIT/SITE. *Island Studies Journal, 2*(2), 163–176.

Ommer, R.E. (1991). *From outpost to outport: A structural analysis of the Jersey-Gaspé cod fishery, 1767–1886.* Montreal, QC: McGill-Queen's University Press.

Podger, A. (1962). Jersey's shipbuilding industry. *Annual Bulletin of La Société Jersiaise, 18*(part 2. St Helier: Société Jersiaise), 229–241.

Policy and Resources Committee. (1995). *Strategic policy review, 2000 and beyond, Part 1.* St. Helier: States of Jersey.

Powell, G.C. (1971). *Economic survey of Jersey.* States of Jersey, St. Helier, Jersey: Bigwoods.

Powell, G.C. (2015). *History of Jersey as an international finance centre.* St. Helier: Ashton and Denton Publishing.

States of Jersey. (2005). *Economic growth plan 2005.* St. Helier: Policy and Resources Committee. Retrieved from www.statesassembly.gov.je/AssemblyPropositions/2005/36737-29324-1942005.pdf

States of Jersey. (2012). *Economic growth and diversification strategy.* St. Helier: Council of Ministers. Retrieved from www.statesassembly.gov.je/AssemblyPropositions/2012/P.055-2012.pdf

States of Jersey. (2014a). Jersey's relationship with the UK and EU. Retrieved from www.gov.je/Government/JerseyWorld/InternationalAffairs/Pages/Relationship EUandUK.aspx

States of Jersey. (2014b). First regulated Bitcoin investment fund welcomed. Retrieved from www.gov.je/News/2014/Pages/CryptoCurrency.aspx

States of Jersey. (2014c). *Jersey financial services industry policy framework.* Retrieved from www.gov.je/SiteCollectionDocuments/Government%20and%20 administration/P%20Financial%20Services%20Policy%20Framework%20 20140402%20LO.pdf

States of Jersey. (2014d). Tourism strategy 2012 consultation green paper. Retrieved from www.gov.je/Government/Consultations/Pages/TourismStrategyConsultation. aspx

States of Jersey. (2014e). Draft budget statement 2015, States of Jersey. Retrieved from www.gov.je/Government/Pages/StatesReports.aspx?ReportID=1080

States of Jersey. (2014f). *Draft 2015 budget.* Corporate Service Scrutiny Panel, S.R.12/2014.

States of Jersey. (2014g). *Updating Jersey's fiscal framework.* States of Jersey, R.102. Retrieved from www.statesassembly.gov.je/AssemblyReports/2014/R.102-2014. pdf

States of Jersey. (2014h). *Vision for IT in education 2013–2015: Thinking differently.* Retrieved from www.gov.je/SiteCollectionDocuments/Education/ID%20 Thinking%20Differently%2020131015%20JB.pdf

Syvret, M., & Stevens, J. (1998). *Balleine's history of Jersey.* Chichester, Sussex: Société Jersiaise. Phillimore and Co. Ltd.

16 Tuvalu
Entrepreneurship and the Dot TV Phenomenon

Godfrey Baldacchino and Colin S. Mellor

INTRODUCTION

Tuvalu is the world's smallest and most isolated independent developing archipelago. Upon gaining independence from the United Kingdom in 1978, it was the world's third-poorest country. The current population of Tuvalu is around 11,000 persons (United Nations Population Fund, 2014). The country has an exclusive economic zone (EEZ) that covers an oceanic area of at least 270,000 square miles (700,000 km²) but a total land area of just 9.9 square miles (25.6 km²; Bell et al., 2011, p. 251). This consists of three reef islands and six atolls, each of which typically has one or more sizeable islands and often many islets. Tuvalu is situated some 620 miles (1,000 km) to the north of Fiji in the Pacific Ocean, between latitude 6–11° South and longitude 176–180° East. The dispersed and minute population, its isolation from its neighbors, and the scant natural resource base severely limit Tuvalu's prospects for economic development in any conventional economic growth sense. Tuvalu does not promote tourism, which in any event would be very restricted by poor air access to the country. Access by air travel is from Nadi, Fiji to Funafuti, the capital, with three flights a week operated by Fiji Airways, using an ATR 72–600 aircraft, with a capacity of 68 passengers. The islands have an inadequate quality and stock of tourism accommodation: there is one hotel with 12 rooms, plus some modest guesthouse-style lodging available. There are also poor interisland transport facilities. For a short period in the 1980s, Tuvalu had an interisland sea plane service, the *Sea Bee*; this was an excellent service but proved commercially unviable, and it quickly folded. That leaves two interisland passenger/cargo vessels based at Funafuti, the *Nivaga II* and *Manu Folau* (Tuvalu Islands, 2014a). They provide services throughout the island group, along with occasional visits to Fiji, Kiribati, and Tokelau (Tuvalu Islands, 2014b).

To compound these challenges, Tuvalu is among those countries expected to suffer the greatest impacts of climate change, including complete disappearance in the worst-case scenario. In fact, like the other small atoll archipelago states of Kiribati, Marshall Islands, and Maldives, Tuvalu's main rationale for visibility in international fora of late has been its strident campaign to make the world aware of some of the dramatic consequences of global warming and sea level rise. The highest point in the country is around 15 feet (4.6 meters) above sea level (on Niulakita Island). Widespread tidal and storm surge flooding is a common occurrence, and inundation from tropical cyclones and tsunamis has been devastating from time to time. In October 1972, Hurricane Bebe struck Funafuti atoll, including the main island of Fongafale; 90% of the houses and trees were washed away, the airport was covered by sea water to a depth of 5 feet (1.5 meters), five fatalities were reported, and a hurricane bank of coral rubble some 10 feet (3 meters) high was created on the ocean side of the island, which remains the highest point of land on Funafuti atoll (Fitchett, 1987; Terry, 2007, p. 118).

To some extent offsetting these problems, Tuvalu has the advantages of a strong and resilient culture, a broadly egalitarian society, close family ties, strong democratic principles, and a record of prudent fiscal management. As an almost whimsical aside, it must be about the only country in the world that has a prison with no encircling walls (Flickr, 2013), there being quite literally nowhere to run or to hide. Overall, Tuvalu has an excellent record of meeting its people's basic needs since independence in 1978, with near-universal access to basic health services and formal education. Life expectancies are on a par with those in some middle-income countries. It is well on track to achieve the Millennium Development Goals (MDGs) for 2015 (Government of Tuvalu, 2011a; Pacific Islands Forum Secretariat, 2010). How has such a small, resource poor, archipelago nation achieved such enviable development results?

THIS CHAPTER

This chapter explores this conundrum, with a special focus on the role of the Dot TV phenomenon. Through a striking combination of happenstance, gamesmanship, and political initiative, which is detailed in what follows, Tuvalu acquired exclusive rights to the Internet domain name *.tv* and has been able to capitalize on the potential financial value of this unique Internet resource. Revenues from leasing this highly desirable Internet domain name to international investors have resulted in a significant financial boost to the whole country. Combined with other considerations related to its economy, government, society, and cultural inclinations, the subsequent result has been that, despite all the evident challenges, Tuvalu has socioeconomic indicators that are the envy of many developing countries. Extreme poverty is effectively nonexistent, literacy rates are close to 100%, and both educational and health indicators are decent.

The term *governpreneurship* (Hisrich & Al-Dabbagh, 2012) is used in this chapter to describe an entrepreneurial flair that is not nested in the private sector. Instead, it refers to the combination of inventiveness, ingenuity, and entrepreneurial spirit adopted by governments—often with the guidance of seasoned and trusted senior public servants—to maximize their revenues from sources of wealth derived from their sovereign status. Small (often island) polities can, in principle, better operationalize this suite of resources by virtue of their easier societal access to decision makers and their ability to take snap decisions, enact policies, and/or pass suitable legislation rapidly and flexibly in order to actuate potential opportunities as they arise (Azzopardi, 2004; Pirotta et al., 2001). There is here an understanding of jurisdiction as a resource (Baldacchino and Milne, 2000) and of government as having the good sense of deploying this resource creatively, albeit at times controversially.

Some of the ways in which jurisdiction has been exploited commercially by small states and territories—flags of convenience, passport sales, citizenship schemes, phone sex lines—continue to raise concerns (Kelman & Shreve, this volume). Crocombe (2007, pp. 163–168) dismissed these antics as "selling sovereignty and integrity," part of the kit of desperate measures taken by chronically vulnerable jurisdictions that perceive that they realistically have no other development choices to consider. Yet, cannot these policy decisions be also considered and condoned as expressions of creative governance, a fuller exploitation of political geography for economic or strategic gain (Payne, 2009, p. 285; Prasad, 2009, p. 53)? Tuvalu has very limited opportunities for economic growth in any conventional sense. In these circumstances, the country has little alternative to maximizing its national revenues by exploiting to the fullest all possible sources of wealth, including those derived directly from its sovereign nation status, with the Tuvalu government thus manifesting governpreneurship. As detailed in what follows, Dot TV is a significant source of such wealth to the sovereign state of Tuvalu.

WHAT'S IN A NAME?

Tuvalu is the name of the former Ellice Islands (named after a British politician and merchant who owned the cargo of the ship *Rebecca*, from which the first known British sighting of the islands took place in 1819). It became a part of the former British colony of Gilbert and Ellice Islands, which gained independence on October 1, 1978. At a referendum prior to independence, Tuvalu voted to be separate from the Gilbert Islands. There were strong reasons for this; ethnically, Tuvaluans are Polynesian, whereas the people of the Gilbert Islands are primarily Micronesian (McIntyre, 2012). The two island groups are quite separate geographically, thus somewhat justifying the split. Moreover, the British administrators evidently found the Ellice Islanders to be better public servants than their Gilbertese subjects, partly because of the disruption of Gilbertese development by the Japanese occupation during the Second World War, no doubt to the chagrin of the latter (McIntyre, 2012, p. 138). After independence, the Gilbert Islands became Kiribati, which is simply the word *Gilberts* spelled in the local language. However, the Ellice Islands name was dropped entirely, and the word *Tuvalu* was adopted for the country. This word in the local language can be translated as *eight standing together*, meaning the eight main islands in the country. References to the islands as *Teatu Tuvalu* (cluster of eight) existed even prior to independence (e.g., Roberts, 1958). In the Tuvaluan language, *valu* is *eight*, and *tu* means *our* or *ours*, and combined, the word implies *eight together, eight standing together*, or even *eight traditions* (in the context of *unity in diversity*). Some observers have claimed that *Tuvalu* was the traditional name of this group of islands and atolls, though there is little evidence to support this (Countries and their cultures, 2015). In any event, the name Tuvalu was adopted and, as we will see, this choice of name became the source of considerable wealth to this tiny country.

The irony is that Tuvalu actually consists of *nine* islands, not eight. Tuvalu has three reef islands (Nanumaga, Niutao, and Niulakita) and six atolls (Nanumea, Niu, Nukufetau, Funafuti, Nukulaelae, and Vaitupu). However, one island (Niulakita) was considered so small as to not be counted and was reportedly uninhabited until some settlers from Niutao Island arrived in 1949, a move supported by the British Lands Administrator at the time as a means of reducing population pressure on Niutao. Niulakita has reportedly been uninhabited from time to time since then. However, the Tuvalu National Population Census for 2002—the latest census results available—reported 35 residents on Niulakita.

In any case, had the name chosen for the new country been *nine standing together*, in the local language this would probably have been a combination of *tu* meaning *together*, and *iva*, meaning *nine*, such that the name might well have been something like *Tuiva*. The key point here is that, either way, the name of the country started with *T* and contained a *v*, and no other country or subnational jurisdiction—whether Tajikistan, Tanzania, Thailand, Timor-Leste, Togo, Tonga, Trinidad & Tobago, Tunisia, Turkey, or Turkmenistan, even including Taiwan, Transdnistria, or Tibet—has the same combination and sequence of these two letters.

The country might well be described as an excellent example of *primitive socialism* or perhaps even *island socialism*. There are strong social networks that provide needed support to underprivileged citizens, in part through church groups, wealthy local benefactors, and nongovernmental organizations (NGOs) and in part by a strong tradition of sharing among citizens. The country has a unicameral parliament but no political parties; simply put, some individuals in politics are able to build factional groupings, but once a joint decision is made, the leaders and people of Tuvalu generally remain united. In addition, the country has no formal unemployment (Mellor, 2003, 2004); this is because effectively all citizens can revert to subsistence activity whenever they choose. This condition has been aptly described as "subsistence affluence" (Fisk, 1982). What this means in the case of Tuvalu is that, without formal employment, people can nevertheless readily engage in fishing; gathering seafood such as crabs (including the truly delicious coconut crabs); gathering birds for food, especially seabirds; growing pigs, chickens, ducks, and vegetables; harvesting taro, *pulaka* (swamp taro), bananas, breadfruit, coconut palm products (including nuts for eating, drinking, and making copra, fronds for weaving, and fermented coconut juice, *toddy*, for drinking); harvesting *pandanus* (pandan) flowers and nuts for cooking and fronds for weaving; gathering firewood; and making handicrafts, typically from sea shells, and dying and weaving coconut palm and pandan fronds, such as decorative ornaments of many kinds, necklaces, bracelets, baskets, dishes, displays and pictures, and a wide variety of mats, which are generally recognized as among the finest examples of such traditional Pacific Islands handicrafts. Some of these activities yield a modest cash income for purchasing other necessities (typically imported goods such as matches, tobacco products, alcohol, tea and coffee, canned and frozen foods, fruits, cooking and eating utensils, clothing, and the like). In addition, many families will have at least one family member in formal employment, thus providing some cash income to the family. Another family member may also be abroad, working as a seaman or earning an income in places like Australia and New Zealand; in either case, a transfer of remittances or goods in kind (cargo) to the home family can be expected (Dennis, 2003; Mortreux & Barnett, 2009).

ORIGINS OF THE DOT TV PHENOMENON

To put the dot com phenomenon in proper context, one must note that Tuvalu's link to telecommunication technologies can only be described as paltry. There is only one state-owned radio station, Radio Tuvalu, which broadcasts in English and Tuvaluan several hours a day on FM on Funafuti, and AM on the eight outer islands, then takes *BBC World Service* via satellite and *Radio Australia* via shortwave. Expensive local telephone services are provided through state-owned Telecom Tuvalu. Ironically, there is no domestic television station in Tuvalu, not even in Funafuti. Satellite television is available, with various families having subscriptions to Fiji TV, a Sky Pacific satellite pay-TV service. The Government Information Technology Office is the main local Internet service provider, using modems and, increasingly, local-area WiFi delivery. The available bandwidth is only 512 kbit/s uplink and 1.5 Mbit/s downlink. All Internet access is satellite facilitated, and work is underway to extend Internet access to all outer islands. Well-connected and savvy visitors can find WiFi hotspots around the Taiwanese-funded government building that dominates the southern Funafuti skyline, across from the tiny Funafuti International Airport and its suggestive destination code: FUN.

Country code top level domain names (cctlds), popularly known as country codes, were allocated in the early 1980s by the Internet Assigned Names Authority (IANA). The first registered cctlds in 1985 were .us, .uk, and .il. It is not surprising that Tuvalu acquired the cctld of .tv. At the time, of course, few (if any) people, including in Tuvalu, would have realized the potential financial significance of this domain name. However, before long,

Tuvalu was being courted by a procession of potential buyers of this domain name (Boland & Dollery, 2005), and it was rapidly realized by the leaders of Tuvalu that they had acquired, through no initiative of their own but by virtue of their sovereign rights as an independent country, a potentially valuable financial resource in their Dot TV domain name (Raskin, 1998). On advice from a consultant assigned by the International Telecommunications Union (ITU), Tuvalu established a Top Level Domain Task Force and a carefully laid-out bidding process for the eventual selection of a marketing partner for its much-coveted, two-letter, top-level Internet domain suffix, .tv, desired by almost every major television broadcasting corporation in the world (Ogden, 1999, pp. 454–455). This was a deliberate attempt to maximize the benefit to the country of this unexpected financial resource. Anton Van Couvering, then president of Net Names, who had been assigned by the ITU to consult with Tuvalu on how to profit from its country code, stepped down as a consultant in order to become a bidder for .tv through his company, Net Names (Hackney, 2011, n.p.).

Jason Chapnik, a 28-year-old entrepreneur from Toronto, Canada, now appears on the scene. Mr. Chapnik, who was president of Information.ca, came up with the idea of registering names within the .tv domain as early as 1994. "We started brainstorming," Chapnik recalled. "If we could have dot-anything, what would we want? We made lists; dot-info, dot-law. Once we hit on dot-tv as a concept, we knew we had it" (*Chicago Tribune*, 2000, n.p.). But securing the rights to the .tv domain from the Tuvalu government was no shoo-in. Mr. Chapnik sent written proposals and spent months researching and making contacts with the Tuvalu government. By 1997, others people had come up with the same idea and were doing their own lobbying. By 1998, the Tuvalu government had narrowed the prospects down to three companies. At that point, Mr. Chapnik and his wife, Jodi, took a vacation and went to the islands to make their pitch in the flesh. Late in 1998, after months of negotiation, Tuvalu made its decision. "I think my wife won it for us," Mr. Chapnik noted. "Family is very important to them. Coming down with my wife and not business partners spoke volumes to them" (Black, 2000, n.p.).

According to the deal, Tuvalu was to receive US$50 million over a 12-year period. But Chapnik was unable to raise the money; at that point, Idealab stepped in directly, and Tuvalu agreed to license its cctld to Idealab for US$1 million per quarter, adjustable for inflation, with a US$50 million cap over 10 years (Boland and Dollery, 2005). Additionally, the Tuvalu nation received a 20% equity in the administering company. In August 2000, Idealab announced the three most expensive sales in .tv history; Free.tv, China. tv, and Net.tv were each sold for US$100,000 for the first year and an additional percentage for each year following. In January 2002, Idealab sold its Dot TV International unit for US$45 million to VeriSign Inc., a substantial American Internet company, which is the domain administrator for .com. Tuvalu's share of the sale amounted to about US$10 million, which was received as a lump sum. VeriSign initially held the rights to market .tv for 15 years, until the end of 2016 (Hackney, 2011, n.p.).

Tuvalu's up-front payment of US$10 million from VeriSign in 2002 was fortuitous. At that time, the Australian dollar was worth about 50% less than the US$. This was a major financial windfall for the country, which uses the Aus$ as its currency. In addition, Tuvalu was guaranteed US$2.2 million per year, plus 5% of all .tv revenues exceeding US$20 million per year. This arrangement has since been extended for 5 additional years, to the end of December 2021, on reportedly better financial terms for Tuvalu. Precise financial details, however, are not in the public domain at this time (Berkens, 2012; Hayes, 2006, pp. 113–116).

Meanwhile, notable .tv sites include: ABC.tv (American Broadcasting Corporation); Blip.tv (Blip belongs to Makers Studios, a global leader in short-form video); MLB.tv (U.S. Major League Baseball uses this site for streaming live baseball games); TNT.tv (a large cable TV station owned by Time Warner); MTV.tv (European MTV, a Viacom International company); Exercisetv.tv (a physical exercise show on Time Warner Cable and Comcast Cable); Skateboard.tv (an action sports network); WFN.tv (World Fishing Network); and Yes.tv (an independent Pan-Asian sports media company). By June 2014, .tv was well placed as having the tenth-largest number of registrations for a cctld or a generic top-level domain (gtld), duly following .com, .tk, .net, .org, .info, .biz, .co, .mobi, and .me in popularity. Between them, these 10 domain names accounted for 176.2 million domain name registrations, 63% of total global registrations (VeriSign, 2014).

THE ECONOMIC AND FINANCIAL SIGNIFICANCE OF DOT TV FOR TUVALU

As indicated earlier in this chapter, Tuvalu is resource poor in any conventional economic sense. Traditional economic growth models (based on the development of natural resources, labor, capital, comparative advantage, and technology) are not applicable to the country in any meaningful way. During the 1980s, this led to new economic models being developed for such small, mainly island, and acutely resource-poor countries. Particularly suited is the MIRAB model, referring to migration, remittances, aid, and bureaucracy in a national economy (Bertram & Watters, 1985; 1986). More whimsically perhaps, this same concept has been described as the MIRAGE model: migration, remittances, aid, and government expenditure. Tuvalu, along with the Cook Islands, Niue, Tokelau, and Kiribati, was one of the five island states and territories originally designated as MIRAB/MIRAGE economies. This model is not without criticism; for example, it overlooks the real opportunities for tourism development and other niche industries. Possibly the best examples of these alternative economic development paths are the "small island tourist economy" model or SITE (McElroy, 2006), exemplified by the Maldives and its massive tourism development, and the "personnel attraction, resource management, overseas engagement, finance services, and transportation" model or PROFIT (Baldacchino, 2006), exemplified by Singapore and its repertoire of provisions that include a vast service industry plus niche manufacturing. The latter appears more likely to take off in countries that are otherwise devoid of conventional economic resource endowments.

These models appear to be applicable to Tuvalu and are certainly useful as an analytical framework. It would appear that there might well be possibilities to develop some niche tourism markets, including diving, adventure tourism, and ecotourism, in Tuvalu. Obviously, these would require some supporting infrastructure investment; so far, Tuvalu is arguably one of the world's five least-visited nations, with some 1,200 annual visitors (*The Windsor Star*, 2014). Also, there could well be possibilities to develop an industry in some specialist marine products, such as pearl farming, seaweed farming, and high-value seafood exports, such as fresh fish, crustaceans, and aquarium fish. Clearly, there are serious logistic challenges that would need to be overcome here to get any fresh and perishable produce to market within critical time periods. Possibly, high-end Pacific-style fashion clothing might be an interesting opportunity. In the longer term, offshore drilling for oil and gas and seabed mining for valuable minerals might also prove attractive. Nevertheless, while various studies have looked at these opportunities, to date, nothing has materialized.

With a strong maritime tradition, Tuvalu's main tangible export remains skilled labor: approximately 15% of adult males work as seamen on merchant ships of various countries around the world, contributing about Aus$10 million annually to its economy (Shen & Binns, 2012; Wu, 2013). The main natural export product is frozen fish, followed by copra. Beyond these items, and for the immediate future, the Tuvalu government is focused on maximizing its revenues from sovereignty-conferred rights. These include revenues from fishing in Tuvalu's extensive Exclusive Economic Zone, revenue from the leasing of the .tv Internet domain name, and interest accruing from the Tuvalu Trust Fund (TTF), set up with initial one-time deposits by the governments of the United Kingdom (Aus$8.5 million), Australia (Aus$8 million), New Zealand (NZ$10.0 million), and Tuvalu itself (Aus$1.6 million) upon securing independence (International Trust Fund for Tuvalu, 2008).

OTHER SOVEREIGNTY-RELATED REVENUE GENERATORS

The Tuvalu government has dabbled in a range of other sovereignty-related initiatives, including passport sales, sales of Tuvalu telephone numbers to phone sex operators, an international shipping register, fishing rents, philatelic sales, and numismatic sales, with occasional modest success, though none as dramatic, durable, and lucrative as Dot TV.

Until 2000, the Tuvalu Trade Mission in Hong Kong was actively marketing *passports* at US$11,000 for individuals or US$22,000 for a family of up to four members (Field, 1997). Although citizenship was not included, holders were granted permission to reside in Tuvalu. Disappointing returns and bad publicity convinced the government to end the practice (Tuvalu Travel Guide, 2014).

The lease of Tuvalu's +688 *international telephone dialing code* to phone sex operators in 1996 was a cause of some revenue but also much embarrassment to the deeply religious community; the contract, then worth Aus$2 million a year, was cancelled in 2000 (Tuvalu Travel Guide, 2014).

Tuvalu also has a *shipping registry*, set up in 1987 and headquartered in Funafuti, with its international operations based in Singapore (Wu, 2013). It has more than 300 ships or 1.3 million gross tons in the registry, which places it somewhere in the middle of world rankings by size. Tuvalu, as a seafaring nation, is, however, not listed as a "flag of convenience" by the International Transport Union, and its registry is reportedly well regarded by major international players in the shipping industry. Nevertheless, any net revenue from this source is modest at best; it is not reported separately in the country's national accounts.

Tuvalu receives a payment—based on 5% of the value of the fish catch or a minimum of $10,000 per vessel—for the *licensing of fishing vessels* from distant-water fishing nations (DWFNs), mainly by virtue of the multilateral treaty on tuna fishing that the U.S. government has signed with various Pacific countries, including Tuvalu (Bolland & Dollery, 2005, pp. 14–15). Fishing access fees are now the second-largest source of capital for the Tuvalu government (Siaosi et al., 2012).

Philately was quite successful for some time in the early 1980s until the Tuvalu government took an ill-advised decision to expand the number and volume of new stamp issues, hence turning off serious stamp collectors; it also found itself embroiled in a scandal in which stamps were deliberately being printed with errors and then sold at exorbitant prices (Cannon, 2014).

Finally, Tuvalu has done reasonably well from the sale of *collector coins*, minted in Australia in gold and silver. Designs feature such characters as Optimus Prime and Megatron from the *Transformers* blockbuster movie (World Mint Coins, 2009) and the American buffalo (SilverTowne, 2014).

Consequently, for the immediate future, revenue prospects for the Tuvalu government lie almost completely in the hands of fishing revenue, TTF distributions, and funds received from its .tv leasing, in addition of course to sporadic aid disbursements, domestic tax revenue, and remittances sent to Tuvalu households. Government's intent to continue to pursue such forms of creative sovereignty-related initiatives is clearly stated in the current National Action Plan 2015 (Government of Tuvalu, 2011a, 2011b).

In financial terms, revenues from .tv are firmly established in the annual budget of Tuvalu. The precise amounts vary from year to year, depending especially on the exchange rate between the US$ and the Aus$ (which is used by Tuvalu). This source of revenue is likely to remain a significant contributor to the government budget for the foreseeable future. In any case, these disbursements are an extremely welcome addition to Tuvalu's tiny $US14 million-or-so annual budget. The revenue has allowed the government to introduce electricity on the outer islands, create scholarships for its citizens, and fund a new scheme to evacuate serious medical emergency patients to Fiji for treatment. Funds were also deployed to pave the main roads on Funafuti, fixing a persistent dust problem afflicting locals living along the main atoll road. The single runway of Tuvalu's international airport was also extended and asphalted. The revenue has also been used to fund Tuvalu's membership of the UN, which requires annual fees of around US$20,000.

FUTURE PROSPECTS FOR DOT TV

Predictions in the Internet industry are notoriously difficult to make given its fast-moving nature, fickleness, and close links to rapidly changing technology. Some industry observers are pessimistic on the future of .tv, suggesting that more specific and cheaper domain names would be more popular in the future (Davidson, 2010). The IMF has noted that as Internet technology "ages," there may be a long-term risk to Dot TV revenues (IMF, 2011). Others feel that .tv is here to stay, as evidenced by a recent major sale of a video-streaming website using the .tv Internet address: Twitch.tv, "where 60 million gamers watch other gamers" (BBC News, 2014). In fact, it is even suggested we could be on the cusp of a .tv boom (Cohen, 2014). As simply observers with modest IT skills and knowledge, we do not feel strongly qualified to buy into these predictions. We do, however, note that, to the best of our knowledge, there are no impending new telecommunication technologies in the offing that could replace the Internet or, for that matter, television. Hence, short of some truly amazing technological changes impacting the future of the telecommunications industry, ".tv" seems likely to be a solid figure in the future telecoms landscape in the coming decades. Under these circumstances, Dot TV should remain a significant source of wealth for Tuvalu.

CONCLUSION

The Dot TV cctld continues to be operated by VeriSign via its subsidiary, .tv Corporation International. It is marketed as an open cctld since its registration is open outside of Tuvalu and it is marketed around the common abbreviation for "television." Entities involved in animation, film and television, and bloggers and websites that feature video content, are its primary users. Other open cctlds include Colombia's .co (popular with technology start-ups), Montenegro's .me (with its wide appeal, especially with verbs as names), Moldova's .md (appealing to medical doctors), Turkmenistan's .tm (for businesses with trademarks), and Niue's .nu (which means "new" in all Scandinavian languages).

With a dispersed and minute population, its isolation from its (also small) island neighbors, and a meager natural resource base, Tuvalu's prospects for development in any conventional "economic growth" sense are extremely limited. Tuvalu is also recognized as one of the world's most environmentally vulnerable countries, with the ongoing threat of rising sea levels as a result of climate change. A severe drought event obliged the government of Tuvalu to declare a state of emergency on September 28, 2011, after the nation had suffered a lack of adequate or sustained rainfall lasting more than 6 months. Desalination units had to be flown in from Australia and New Zealand, and supplies of fresh water had to be delivered by ship (BBC News, 2011; Perry, 2011).

In these circumstances, the Tuvalu government really has little alternative to playing the smart governpreneur, maximizing its national revenues by exploiting to the fullest all possible sources of wealth derived from its sovereign status. Through a striking combination of happenstance, gamesmanship, and political initiative, as well as a constructive cooperation among politicians, canny public servants, and visionary expatriates, Tuvalu has acquired exclusive rights to the Internet domain name .tv and has been able to capitalize on the potential financial value of this unique Internet resource. The Tuvalu government has been able to generate substantial revenues from leasing this highly desirable Internet domain name to international investors, resulting in a significant financial boost to the country and complementing other sovereignty-based revenue generators. Meanwhile, the existence of this domain extension and the associated lease contracts provide some welcome additional weight to the argument that, even should Tuvalu find itself submerged with sea level rise, legal implications preclude the possibility of it ceasing to exist as a sovereign state (Scholten, 2011, p. 3).

REFERENCES

Azzopardi, R. M. (2004). Small islands and economic viability. In *Islands of the World VIII conference, changing islands; changing worlds, Kinmen Island, Taiwan*. Retrieved from www.academia.edu/6333151/Small_Islands_and_Economic_Viability

Baldacchino, G. (2006). Managing the hinterland beyond: Two ideal-type strategies of economic development for small island territories. *Asia Pacific Viewpoint, 47*(1), 45–60.

Baldacchino, G., & Milne, D. (Eds.). (2000). *Lessons from the political economy of small islands: The resourcefulness of jurisdiction*. New York, NY: St. Martin's Press.

BBC News. (2011, October 7). Australia, New Zealand in airlift to drought-hit Tuvalu. Retrieved from www.bbc.co.uk/news/world-asia-pacific-15210568

BBC News. (2014, November 5). Twitch: Where 60 million gamers watch other gamers. Retrieved from www.bbc.com/news/technology-29900788

Bell, J.D., Johnson, J.E., & Hobday, A.J. (Eds.). (2011). *Vulnerability of tropical Pacific fisheries and aquaculture to climate change*. Noumea, New Caledonia: Secretariat of the Pacific Community.

Berkens, M. (2012, February 25). VeriSign renews contract with Tuvalu to run. TV registry through 2021. The Domains. Retrieved from www.thedomains. com/2012/02/25/verisign-renews-contract-with-tuvalu-to-run-tv-registry-through-2021/

Bertram, G., & Watters, R.F. (1985). The MIRAB economy in South Pacific micro-states. *Pacific Viewpoint, 26*(3), 497–519.

Bertram, G., & Watters, R.F. (1986). The MIRAB process: Earlier analyses in context. *Pacific Viewpoint, 27*(1), 47–59.

Black, J. (2000, September 4). Tiny Tuvalu profits from web name. *New York Times*. Retrieved from www.nytimes.com/2000/09/04/business/tiny-tuvalu-profits-from-web-name.html

Boland, S., & Dollery, B. (2005). *The value and viability of sovereignty-conferred rights in MIRAB economies: The case of Tuvalu*. Working Paper Series in Economics, No. 9/2005. Armidale, NSW: School of Economics, University of New England.

Cannon, B. (2014). Tuvalu and the leaders of the world: A philatelic scandal. Retrieved from www.tuvaluislands.com/stamps/LOW_story.htm

Chicago Tribune. (2000, September 18). Isle clear survivor of net stampede: Tuvalu sitting pretty after 1998 sale of .tv rights to entrepreneur. Retrieved from http://articles.chicagotribune.com/2000–09–18/business/0009180217_1_jason-chapnik-tuvalu-domain

Cohen, N. (2014, August 27). As online video surges, the .tv domain rides the waves. Retrieved from www.nytimes.com/2014/08/27/business/media/a-newly-valuable-virtual-address.html?emc=edit_th_20140827&nl=todaysheadlines&n lid=37589315&_r=0

Countries and their cultures. (2015). Tuvalu. Retrieved from www.everyculture.com/To-Z/Tuvalu.html

Crocombe, R. (2007). *Asia in the Pacific islands: Replacing the West*. Suva, Fiji: Institute of Pacific Studies, University of the South Pacific.

Davidson, K. (2010, November 1). Tuvalu's Dot.tv domain code likely to drop in value. Retrieved from www.radionz.co.nz/international/pacific-news/193393/tuvalu%27s-dot-tv-domain-code-likely-to-drop-in-value,-says-consultant

Dennis, J. (2003). *Pacific island seafarers: A study of the economic and social implications of seafaring on dependents and communities*. Noumea, New Caledonia: Secretariat of the Pacific Community.

Field, M.J. (1997). Tuvalu joining passport sale business. *Tuvalu News*. University of Hawai'i at Manoa, USA: Center for Pacific Islands Studies. Retrieved from www.tuvaluislands.com/news/archived/1997/1997–10–31.htm

Fisk, E.K. (1982). Subsistence affluence and development policy. *Regional Development Dialogue, 3*(1), 1–12.

Fitchett, K. (1987). Physical effects of Hurricane Bebe upon Funafuti atoll, Tuvalu. *Australian Geographer, 18*(1), 1–7.

Flickr. (2013). Tuvalu Prison. Photo taken on September 14, 2013. Retrieved from www.flickr.com/photos/ryan_roxx/9924470835/

Government of Tuvalu. (2011a). *Tuvalu, Millennium Development Goals, progress report 2010/2011*. Funafuti, Tuvalu: Government of Tuvalu.

Government of Tuvalu. (2011b). *Te Kakeega II mid-term review: Action plan 2015*. Funafuti, Tuvalu: Government of Tuvalu.

Hackney, R. (2011, February 7). The history of the Dot TV extension. TLD Investors. Retrieved from http://tldinvestors.com/2011/02/the-history-of-the-dot-tv-extension.html

Hayes, M. (2006). Dot TV: Remote Tuvalu adapts media to its ways. In L. Duffield & J. Cokley (Eds.), *Journalists coping with and crafting media information in the 21st century* (pp. 101–136). Sydney, Australia: Pearson Education.

Hisrich, R. D., & Al-Dabbagh, A. (2012). *Governpreneurship: Establishing a thriving entrepreneurial spirit in government.* Cheltenham, UK: Edward Elgar.

IMF. (2011). *Tuvalu: Staff report for the 2010 Article IV consultation. Country report 2011/46.* Washington, DC: International Monetary Fund. Retrieved from www.imf.org/external/pubs/ft/scr/2011/cr1146.pdf

International Trust Fund for Tuvalu. (2008). *Agreement concerning an international trust fund for Tuvalu.* Revised edition. Retrieved from http://tuvalu-legislation.tv/cms/images/LEGISLATION/SUBORDINATE/1987/1987–0001/Agreement concerninganInternationalTrustFundforTuvalu_1.pdf

McElroy, J. L. (2006). Small island tourist economies across the life cycle. *Asia Pacific Viewpoint, 47*(1), 61–77.

McIntyre, W. D. (2012). The partition of the Gilbert and Ellice Islands. *Island Studies Journal, 7*(1), 135–146.

Mellor, C. S. (2003). An economic survey of Tuvalu. *Pacific Economic Bulletin, 18*(2), 20–28.

Mellor, C. S. (2004). *Tuvalu labour market review.* Working Paper No. 1/2004. Suva, Fiji: The University of the South Pacific, Pacific Institute of Advanced Studies in Governance, Employment and Labour Market Studies.

Mortreux, C., & Barnett, J. (2009). Climate change, migration and adaptation in Funafuti, Tuvalu. *Global Environmental Change, 19*(1), 105–112.

Ogden, M. (1999). Islands on the Internet. *The Contemporary Pacific, 11*(2), 451–465.

Pacific Islands Forum Secretariat. (2010). *Pacific regional MDGs tracking report.* Suva, Fiji: Pacific Islands Forum Secretariat.

Payne, A. (2009). Afterword: Vulnerability as a condition, resilience as a strategy. In A. F. Cooper & T. M. Shaw (Eds.), *The diplomacies of small states: Between vulnerability and resilience* (pp. 279–285). Basingstoke, UK: Palgrave Macmillan.

Perry, N. (2011, October 27). Tuvalu's fresh water crisis deepens. *Washington Times.* Retrieved from www.washingtontimes.com/news/2011/oct/27/tuvalus-fresh-water-crisis-deepens/?page=all

Pirotta, G. A., Wettenhall, R., & Briguglio, L. (2001). Governance of small jurisdictions: Guest editors' introduction. *Public Organization Review, 1*(2), 149–165.

Prasad, N. (2009). Small but smart: Small states in the global system. In A. F. Cooper & T. M. Shaw (Eds.), *The diplomacies of small states: Between vulnerability and resilience* (pp. 41–64). Basingstoke, UK: Palgrave Macmillan.

Raskin, A. (1998). Buy this domain: Tuvalu's .tv stands to radically upgrade the country's $10 million GDP. *Wired*, September, 106–110. Retrieved from http://archive.wired.com/wired/archive/6.09/tuvalu.html

Roberts, R. G. (1958). Te atu Tuvalu: A short history of the Ellice Islands. *The Journal of the Polynesian Society, 67*(4), 394–423.

Scholten, H. J. (2011). *Statehood and state extinction: Sea level rise and the legal challenges faced by low-lying island-states.* Unpublished L.L.M. thesis. Groningen, the Netherlands: Rijks Universiteit Groningen.

Shen, S., & Binns, T. (2012). Pathways, motivations and challenges: Contemporary Tuvaluan migration to New Zealand. *GeoJournal, 77*(1), 63–82.

Siaosi, F., Huang, H. W., & Chuang, C. T. (2012). Fisheries development strategy for developing Pacific Island countries: A case study of Tuvalu. *Ocean & Coastal Management, 66*(1), 28–35.

SilverTowne. (2014). 2014 P Tuvalu silver American Buffalo 1oz high relief proof in OGP. Retrieved from www.silvertowne.com/p-24121–2014-p-tuvalu-silver-american-buffalo-1oz-high-relief-proof-in-ogp.aspx

Terry, J. P. (2007). *Tropical cyclones: Climatology and impacts in the South Pacific.* Tokyo, Japan: Springer.

Tuvalu Islands. (2014a). Funafuti: Manu Folau and Nivaga II at port. Retrieved from www.tuvaluislands.com/uq/gallery/slides/10_ManuFolauNivagaIIatPort.html

Tuvalu Islands. (2014b). About Tuvalu. Retrieved from www.tuvaluislands.com/about.htm

Tuvalu Travel Guide. (2014). Tuvalu economy: Innovations. Retrieved from http://tuvalu.southpacific.org/tuvalu/innovations.html

United Nations Population Fund. (2014). UNPF Tuvalu country profile. In UNPF, *Population and development profiles: Pacific island countries* (pp. 74–78). Suva, Fiji: UNPF Pacific Sub-Regional Office. Retrieved from http://countryoffice.unfpa.org/pacific/drive/web__140414_UNFPAPopulationandDevelopmentProfiles-PacificSub-RegionExtendedv1LRv2.pdf

VeriSign. (2014). Innovation: Domain name industry brief. Retrieved from www.verisigninc.com/en_US/innovation/dnib/index.xhtml

The Windsor Star. (2014, February 18). Travel top 5: World's least-visited nations. Retrieved from www.windsorstar.com/travel/travel+world+least+visited+nations/9520400/story.html

World Mint Coins. (2009). Transformers: Optimus Prime 1oz silver proof coin. Retrieved from http://worldmintcoins.com/2009-australian-coins/transformers-optimus-prime-1oz-silver-proof-coin

Wu, S. Y. (2013). The Tuvalu ship registry. *Baltic and International Maritime Council Bulletin, 108*(4), 36–38. Retrieved from https://www.bimco.org/en/Products/BIMCO_Bulletins/BIMCO_Bulletins_Digital_Issues/2013_04/~/media/Products/BIMCO_Bulletins/Web/2013_04/pdf36.ashx

Part 5
Island Entrepreneurship
A Personal Testimony

17 Being a Small Island Entrepreneur— Making Cheese from Bruny Island, Tasmania

Nick Haddow

INTRODUCTION

I am often asked the question "why did you start a cheese factory on Bruny Island?" It is a good question. To start with, there are no dairy farms on Bruny Island. Bruny Island has no history of cheese making or any other form of value-added food production. It is also quite remote, being located off the south coast of Tasmania, the least populated of all Australian states. It is relatively more expensive to live and work on Bruny Island, and it is difficult to find and retain staff. Indeed, the reasons not to start a small business on Bruny Island, perhaps any island, far out weigh the reasons for it.

My answer is always the same: despite the challenges that running a small business on a small island brings, I am convinced that my business would not have been as successful if had been located somewhere more "sensible." Many of these challenges were unknown to me when I started my business, and that is probably a good thing. Would I do it again? Absolutely!

BACKGROUND

Bruny Island is an island off an island (Tasmania) off an island continent (Australia). However, this is not a case of diminishing returns. Bruny Island is about 90 km long from north to south but as narrow as 100m wide in some places. Correctly speaking, Bruny Island is actually two islands that are joined by a long, narrow, sandy isthmus that is colloquially referred to as "the Neck." It has a permanent population of around 700 people; however, this number swells to more than 3,000 in the summer months, when the island becomes a destination for tourists and holiday makers. There are four main settlements on Bruny Island: Dennes Point is on North Bruny, while Adventure Bay, Alonnah and Lunnawanna are on South Bruny.

The island has a mixed land use. It is primarily a holiday destination, with many holiday homes (called "shacks" locally) owned by residents of Hobart—Tasmania's capital city and only a 40-minute drive and a 20-minute

ferry ride away. Recently, it has also had a tourism boom, with many interstate and international tourists attracted to its proximity to Hobart, its natural assets and, increasingly, its reputation for high-quality food and wine
experiences. Although the argument for a permanent bridge to the island is
raised regularly, the island is well serviced by the vehicular ferry.

The rugged beauty of Bruny Island is seen as something of a microcosm
of Tasmania as a whole, and visitors can experience many of the natural
assets Tasmania is famous for: long, empty beaches, rugged coastlines, a rich
biodiversity of native plants, birds and animals and beautiful walk-through
native forests.

After tourism, agriculture is the second-largest economic industry on
Bruny Island. North Bruny has large grazing tracts that are primarily used
for the production of wool and lambs. Across Bruny Island, there are large
native hardwood forests that have been logged for timber up until recently,
when the Tasmanian timber industry has suffered something of a collapse
due to a combination of economic forces, inefficient production quotas and
pressures from environmental groups. This downturn has also resulted in
the complete stoppage of logging on Bruny Island, where as well as the
aforementioned reasons, there was considerable local community pressure
to cease logging due to the negative message it was perceived to be sending
to tourists. Moreover, the inbuilt additional costs of transporting the logs
off the island to the nearest mill, located a 2-hour drive away, made the cost
of timber harvesting on Bruny Island even more economically unfeasible
than in most other locations in Tasmania.

Bruny Island is also typical of most islands in that it has a strong and active
local community that is both united and disparate at the same time. Stakeholder bodies such as the Bruny Island Community Association, Bruny Island
Tourism, the Bruny Island Primary Industries Group and the Bruny Island
Environment Network represent various factions within the community.
These groups often oppose each other over specific developments; however,
the community at large is strongly parochial and protective of those who live
and work on Bruny Island.

Because of its strong community, access to the amenities of a capital city,
good local services, comparatively inexpensive land and housing, and excellent natural assets, Bruny Island has become a very popular destination
for people to migrate to, especially interstate residents looking for a "sea
change" experience. This especially applies to older people who no longer
have the considerations of schooling or careers to contend with, resulting
in the region's aging population. The flip side of this is that these people are
often educated, wealthy, cultured and with considerably rich life experiences. It is said that Bruny Island boasts the highest density of PhDs per
capita of any region of Australia. These "blow-ins"—of whom I am one—
add diversity to the population but can themselves be the source of friction
with those who claim a greater ownership of Bruny Island because they have
descended from real "islanders."

BACKGROUND ON BRUNY ISLAND CHEESE CO.

Within the first few minutes of arriving on Bruny Island, I knew that this was somewhere I wanted to live.

My partner Leonie and I had been living in Tasmania for a year after having moved from the Japanese island of Hokkaido. Our first experience of Tasmania was a difficult one, and we found it hard to manage a satisfying transition from a privileged expatriate lifestyle to an isolated and economically depressed rural community that was quite closed and hard to break into.

I was working for another cheese company on a dairy farm that had been run by the same family for five generations (something that is quite rare in Australia, where European settlement has existed for little more than two centuries). As much as it was an honor to be the custodian of this product for a short while, the working conditions were challenging. Perhaps it was this adversity that gave rise to thoughts that Leonie and I could make cheese for ourselves one day, even though at that time we had no idea where that might be.

Seven months into that job, we were so exhausted and disenfranchised that we had actually decided the best course of action for us was to return to the familiar and go back to Japan. Realizing that we had seen very little of Tasmania, we made an effort to use whatever free days we had to tour around the island state. It was on one of these weekends that we drove south, through the quaint capital of Hobart, and farther down the d'Entrecasteaux Channel that separates Bruny Island from the mainland of Tasmania. We were knocked over by the beauty of this region and started entertaining ideas that we might stay.

On our return to the north of the state, we began looking for property in the area. It was not long before we stumbled upon the notice of a small farm on Bruny Island in an area called Great Bay that was up for sale. It was, shall we say, very well photographed. We put in an offer, it was accepted, and in that moment we fulfilled a dream that neither of us knew we had: to live on a small island. Bruny Island Cheese Co. began the following year with a very humble launch.

We started making cheese from a rented premises that we shared with another cheese maker (who was also our landlord and who grew to become very resentful of our successes and eventually found reason to evict us, forcing us into building a cheese factory for ourselves). For the first couple of years, we made cheese using a few plastic tubs we had bought at a $2 shop, some PVC pipes I had cut into short lengths, and a few baker's trays I had stolen from the back of a local supermarket. We transported the milk in 20-liter buckets in the back of our VW Kombi next to our dog, and we sold the cheese (illegally) from an antique display fridge in our lounge room. We worked from 6 a.m. until 6 p.m. making cheese and then went and worked in a bar until midnight to make enough money to buy enough milk to do it all again the following day.

It is almost impossible to reconcile how that same business grew and morphed into what it has become today.

Since those early days, we have grown continuously. I am not necessarily a believer that a business must grow in order to be successful, but in our case, the growth has been largely organic rather than strategic. I have always been motivated by the simple act of making people happy through my cheeses, and that has largely driven the growth of my business. Owning a small business is a pretty self-indulgent exercise at times, as it allows you to do exactly what you want to do rather than be forced to go in directions that might not be where you want to go.

There are much better places to start a small business, making a hand-made and highly perishable product, than a small island off the south coast of Tasmania. It is tempting to say that *despite* our location, we have achieved success in our business. I suspect, though, the truth is that we have been successful *because* of our location.

THE GOOD AND BAD OF RUNNING A BUSINESS ON A SMALL ISLAND

There are plenty of great things about living and running a small business on Bruny Island. But there are also a lot of challenges.

The purpose of many of the small businesses that exist on Bruny Island is intrinsically linked with their location. These include the tour operators that guide visitors around the island's natural assets, both on land and around its coast. Bruny Island Cheese Co. is different in this respect. Other than its name, it has no need to be located on Bruny Island. In fact, financially speaking, it would be better off to be located on the Tasmanian mainland, closer to its market, its source of milk and a greater staff pool. Despite this, whenever I have been faced with the choice of investing further in our infrastructure on Bruny Island or developing the business in another, financially beneficial location, I have always elected to invest further on Bruny Island.

The Ferry Factor

One of the biggest challenges (and additional costs) that we face on a daily basis is access to and from Bruny Island. Bruny Island is only connected to the mainland by a ferry. The ferry is privately owned and operated and only runs during daylight hours. The good thing about this is that when it stops at night, Bruny Island really does feel like an island—there is very little traffic, and the noise of cars driving along the main road disappears and is replaced by the soothing sounds of nature.

The ferry unites the island community in its displeasure about the cost, inconvenience and quality of the ferry service. Many residents of Bruny Island consider that the ferry should be an extension of the roads, which are owned and maintained by the Tasmanian state government and are free for all to use. They resent having to pay to use the ferry to access their homes, shacks or businesses.

It was economic forces that led to the island's ferry service being sold by the government to private operators. The benefit of such a move is an improvement in quality of facilities and service. The problem is that there is hardly any likelihood that the service is going back to public ownership. Another problem is that there is no alternative to getting to Bruny Island other than this privately owned ferry service.

Residents are, however, subsidized. It costs a standard car $26 to make the crossing. It costs residents only half of that amount. If you work on Bruny Island but do not own property there, you do not qualify for the discount. This is a particular burden for some of my staff that commute to the island from their homes in Hobart up to five times a week. Inevitably, I end up having to subsidize the cost of travelling to the island for them in order to attract a high caliber of staff. Again, there is very little alternative to this scenario: if I want to employ experienced staff, the population of Bruny Island is limited, so I must look to the large population centers off the island, and these staff cannot be expected to forgo a significant percentage of the weekly salary on ferry fares. Furthermore, for businesses such as mine that operate larger vehicles such as trucks, the cost increases exponentially with the size of the vehicle.

Commuting is not the only way a privately owned ferry adds to the cost of having a business on Bruny Island. Tradespeople on the Island call it the "ferry factor": the cost of bringing goods *to* the island and, in our case, also *off* the island. It is estimated that simply being on Bruny Island adds approximately 5% to 10% to the cost of doing business due solely to the ferry costs. Anything that our business requires needs to be brought onto the island. We use a small truck to collect our milk from our farms (located on the Tasmanian mainland, as there is no dairy farming on Bruny Island: another good reason to not start a cheese factory there!). Our truck leaves Bruny Island at least three times a week to collect milk and make deliveries. This activity alone costs the business some US$7,000 every year. Add to that the cost of freighting additional goods, the subsidizing of staff and general ferry use, and that cost more than triples, becoming a significant cost burden for our small business and, importantly, one that is not borne by our competitors.

An additional cost associated with the ferry is that relating to its timetable. The ferry operates approximately hourly with a couple of hours break in the middle of the day so that the crew can eat their lunch. This leads to gross inefficiency and the associated cost, another that does not have to be carried by competitors. For example, it is common that I will have a meeting in Hobart. If that meeting is at 9.00 a.m., the only possible ferry connection is the one leaving at 7.00 a.m., meaning I would need to leave at home 6.40 a.m. in order to get to the ferry on time. In other words, my travel time becomes almost 2.5 hours for a trip that should only take an hour. This scenario happens several times a day for my business, with staff commuting to Bruny Island or travelling off the island making deliveries or conducting meetings, all waiting for a ferry rather than working productively. This is a serious cost to my business and one we have estimated to be worth approximately US$20,000 every year.

But it is a moot point. The counterargument is either to relocate off Bruny Island or build a bridge to Bruny Island. Both scenarios would have adverse affects on my business.

Staff Retention

Another great challenge I have to my business is the procurement and retention of quality staff. This challenge cuts both ways: there is definitely some attraction to living on Bruny Island for some people. The problem is, these are not always the people that I am seeking. Rental properties on Bruny Island are difficult to come by and, because of the size and property distribution of the island, there may often be at least a 30-minute drive from and to our workplace. These properties are also comparatively expensive, with the owners preferring to keep their homes vacant for the highly lucrative summer months, when they can get up to eight times the rental income in a week for short-stay holiday accommodation than they can get from long-term rental.

Bruny Island Cheese Co. being a highly specialized business, I often require staff with a very specific skill set. In a population of 700 residents, this is often difficult, despite practicing a policy of employing as many islanders as possible. Inevitably, I advertise for these positions interstate and internationally. Because of the reputation my business has built, these positions are often sought by excellent candidates with a high degree of experience. When interviewing applicants, one of my strong considerations is how well a candidate will cope with living and working on an island and in a small community. To gauge this, I need to understand their personal circumstances, private lives and histories to a far greater degree than I would if my business was located on the mainland. It is often not the starry-eyed candidate that is the issue in the end but his or her partner or children who might not be able to find employment or education to a standard they expect or are used to, causing stress, disharmony, resentment and ultimately frustration and resignation.

Shipping Products, Sourcing Supplies

Access to markets is another issue with being on a island. Of course, all businesses have this issue: a cheese factory in Sydney would still need to get its product to its customers in Melbourne or Perth. However, we face this additional issue of first having to get our product off Bruny Island. The vast majority of our customers live on the Australian mainland, and to reach them, we usually rely on air freight from Hobart airport. Although the freight service we pay for is called Door-to-Door, this is a misnomer: there is no freight company that will collect freight from Bruny Island, stating that the cost is prohibitive, even to any large multinational company. The cost still needs to be borne by us, and we need to drive an hour and a half to the airport to deliver our freight.

Access to suppliers is the same issue. Almost everything my business purchases, consumes or sells needs to be brought onto Bruny Island. Our biggest item is milk. There are no dairy farms on Bruny Island, so milk needs to be brought onto the island. As I have mentioned, freight to Bruny Island is extremely limited (especially perishable freight), so this requires our own truck and driver. The cost of bringing goods to the island is considerable, and often, in the course of operating a small business on an island, when a key consumable runs out, the cost of going to get it and bringing it back is often greater than the cost of the item itself.

These challenges are all costs that are unique to island life. We do not really talk about them much; we just accept them as a given and an integral part of where we live. But the reality is that they are costs that our competitors do not have, and that means we are at a financial disadvantage. So, in light of the success my business has had, there must also be some advantages to being located on an island.

The Island Advantage

It is possible that our timing was especially fortuitous, but when we started Bruny Island Cheese Co., it coincided with a resurgence of interest in the provenance of food and the quality of artisan produce. Tasmania as a brand, a destination and a producer of high-quality food was also experiencing some ascendency. As a result, it was easy to attract publicity, as our story ticked several of these boxes at once. Being aware of this confluence of interests was also critical, because it allowed us to position ourselves better with regard to any media interest.

Underlying these points of interest was also the key factor that we were located on an island. This presented the media with the added benefit that they were covering an exotic and isolated location, providing even more interest and "wow" factor for their readers or viewers. The publicity we attracted in the early years of business played a critical role in developing our brand and establishing a strong market presence.

One of the interesting facets of conducting a business on an small island is the self-limiting factor that our location brings. Economies of scale need to be achieved to be efficient and profitable, and the scale of production we need to maintain might need to be higher on Bruny Island than elsewhere because of the inherent additional costs of being on Bruny Island. However, these built-in challenges and costs also restrict the size and type of businesses that can be successful in that environment. Islands tend to favor small businesses, which can respond more nimbly to the nested challenges. Often these businesses are very small, owner-operated outfits practicing artisan techniques and creating high-value products which can absorb the additional costs. These are interesting businesses making interesting products and are very much in line with the natural brand heft that islands possess.

The test for businesses located on an island, then, is how to align themselves with the island brand and, in doing so, how to leverage the benefit of their location to counteract some of the challenges that come with island living.

The impression that has traditionally typified the brand of many small island communities, including Tasmania and Bruny Island, is that the size and isolation of an island occurs at the expense of economic scalability, market access and procurement of suitably experienced and qualified staff.

However, this impression belies the reality that many small islands around the world boast strong economies underpinned by brand values that recognize the opportunities that their island status brings them. High-value agrifood production, niche and experiential tourism, information technology, arts and finance are the hallmarks of these standout island economies as well as more traditional commodity industries, such as mining, forestry, manufacturing and agriculture, which have recognized the importance of innovation, social license, environmental credibility and global best practice to remain sustainable in both their market and their community.

Islands have a strong, natural competitive advantage. Their naturally implied brand evokes a sense of nature and naturalness. They are destinations set apart from the rest of the world, intriguing and naturally innovative. Because their economic model is often based around the manufacture of high-value, niche products, islands are also synonymous with quality. Bruny Island is no different in this respect, and it was important to the success of my business to realize the opportunities that our location presented as well as the challenges. In truth, our approach was to ignore the challenges (they were fixed and unavoidable) and concentrate on the opportunities.

Our name was the first way in which we embraced our location. It was essential that our name contained the words Bruny Island. Really, it was just the word "island" that seemed important, because the feelings it evokes are very much aligned with the feelings we wanted to create with our cheese: special, out of the ordinary, natural, exclusive, handmade.

The style of communication reinforces these values at every opportunity as well. Communication is essential to our business success. To start with, we are geographically isolated from our market, so we need to communicate with potential clients in order to bring them into our world. Second, the types of products we make do not seek to replicate European cheeses: we do not make brie or cheddar. Instead, we make cheeses that are informed by and are unique to their environment, and they are named appropriately, with names such as 1792, Oen, Tom and Otto, names that require some explanation. Our communication style naturally reflects the personality of the business; it is very relaxed but authoritative. We use images and video to a large extent, as that also helps us to reinforce the brand values. Many of these images and videos are not specifically about our cheeses or our business but often show different aspects of Bruny Island, again underlying the point that our business and our location have a symbiotic relationship. Indeed, the suggestion is that there would not be one without the other.

The authentic voice and tone we use in our videos and written communication not only strengthens our points of difference but also further proves to the consumer that we are a bit different and that difference can be explained by the fact that we live and work on a small island. We present ourselves as assertive but laid back, bombastic but relaxed. These are perhaps my own personality traits as well as those of Bruny Island; but, then, perhaps that explains why I was attracted to the island in the first place.

MARKET ACCESS

In 2003, when we started Bruny Island Cheese Co., we assumed a typical business model for my industry. That is, we made the product and largely relied on others, notably wholesalers and distributors, to sell our products for us. Our cheeses were in all the best shops and restaurants in Australia, and we were going places. The ultimate prize in this model was export, and we also went down that path, with almost one third of our production ending up in the United States in our third year. And at the same time we were sending cheese overseas, we were declining local enquiries due to an inability to fill orders. In 2005, 90% of our production was being sold through wholesale, or export/distributor channels, with the remainder being sold by us direct to consumers at events, farmers' markets or through our Cellar Door shop. We thought that demand outstripping supply was the pinnacle of success. The problem was, despite all this success, we were going broke.

The only part of the business that was making any money was our Cellar Door—our shop at our cheese factory on Bruny Island. When we first built our cheesery on Bruny Island, it was a little-known destination to anyone outside of Tasmania. Despite this, we allowed some space for the on-site sales of our cheese to anyone who wanted to drop by. In fact, we had such low confidence in that being a strong stream of revenue that the place was designed so that the shop could be serviced by the staff making cheese.

Two key events happened at that time. The first was I received a card from a gentleman in New York who very kindly wrote to compliment me on the quality of our cheese. As an artisan producer on the other side of the world, getting this kind of compliment was incredibly special. Except, over the next few weeks, it started to really get under my skin. I had failed in a fundamental objective of my business—I no longer had a direct relationship with my consumers—the vast majority of my cheese was now being sold via third parties to shops that I had no connection with and, more importantly, who had very little connection with Bruny Island Cheese Co. My cheese was now being represented by people who almost certainly had not been to Bruny Island, had not met me or understood why I do what I do and why I chose do it on an island off the south coast of Tasmania.

The other significant event that happened at that time was the people that visited our cheesery on Bruny Island from elsewhere in Australia were saying things like, "We love your cheese. Can we buy it anywhere when we get home?" Of course, given that our production and distribution network was very small (and we were exporting a great big chunk of it), the answer was inevitably no. But these were people who had already tried our cheeses and liked them, they had been to see us on Bruny Island (no small feat) and they had heard our story, directly from us. In other words, they were already invested in the brand and were already over the line in terms of wanting to buy it again. These were people that I wanted to have a direct relationship with and who cared enough about what they ate to come to Bruny Island, meet the cheese maker, and hear what he had to say about his products and business.

As a direct result of both these events, we started investigating ways we could send cheese directly to customers around Australia. This had not been done by anyone before. Given the huge distances and low population density, Australia has very poor logistics infrastructure, and no refrigerated door-to-door freight exists. We set about developing a packaging solution that allowed us to keep cheese cool enough for the time it took to transport.

And so the Bruny Island Cheese Club was started. We began collecting the email addresses of our customers in Cellar Door and began to write to them directly. Our customers were suddenly no longer the middlemen of the sales chain; they were the people who were actually eating our cheese. We were suddenly able to communicate directly with our consumers and let them know what was going on at Bruny Island Cheese Co. We could now take them on a journey that included not only information about the cheeses but also a broader dialogue about Bruny Island and what it meant to be living and working there. This was something that resonated with our customers, as not only had they already been there and made a connection with the place, but it was also a world that was different from their own and was therefore interesting and alluring.

We were also able to market our cheeses directly to them by putting together special offers that we would send directly to them. We very quickly got skilled in building attractive email campaigns using the imagery of our cheeses and our locations. We now use embedded video to a large extent as a way of truly (well, digitally) bringing our customers back to Bruny Island. I am just as likely to be seen talking about our cheeses while standing on a beach or from the top of a mountain looking down on Bruny Island as I am in a maturing room full of cheeses. All of these environments are significant and relevant to the cheese, and linking the sense of us being on an island to our cheeses helps to reinforce our point of difference.

What we have been able to achieve through the Cheese Club, given the geographical challenges that we face, astounds me. We are based on a small island off the south coast of Tasmania, and our customer base is spread all over Australia—often in some very hard-to-reach places. We claim that we can get a box of cheese, in great condition, to anywhere in Australia within 3 days (most orders are delivered in less than 30 hours). "Cheese Clubbers" live anywhere from down the road (yes, we have members on Bruny Island!) to gas rigs in the Gulf of Carpentaria, several thousand kilometers (and three "islands" away).

Compared with packing up a large order and sending it to the United States, the Cheese Club is a lot of hard work. Technology has helped but, comparatively, we still spend a large amount of time per customer. Each order is packed separately and dispatched to a unique location, often with very specific delivery instructions that require tracking and follow-through. However, through the Cheese Club, we can now have a continuous dialogue with the people who are eating our cheese and, importantly, they have one with the people who are making their cheese. Our customers provide instant feedback on what we are doing. They encourage and support us in a way that would not be possible through a traditional sales model.

The Cheese Club has grown since its inception in late 2007 to almost 15,000 members today. It is now 40% of our total sales. We do not advertise and insist that people should become members only after they have had some contact with us. That could be in the form of tasting our cheese at an event or market, coming to Bruny Island to our cheesery or "meeting us" vicariously through another Cheese Club member. By far, the strongest source of new Cheese Club members is our Cellar Door on Bruny Island.

We could not have been more wrong with our predictions of how popular our Cellar Door was going to be and how much of a significant part of our business it has become. Today, after multiple investments totaling several hundred thousand dollars, it accounts for 38% of our total revenue. We have added a wood-fired bakery to the cheesery and are currently building an on-site microbrewery to add to our customer experience. Providing a quality experience at the Cellar Door level is vital to a fruitful longer-term relationship with our customers through the Cheese Club. Incorporating an authentic island experience into this is also vital. Our service style is aligned with the island values previously discussed: individualistic, relaxed, quirky, generous, different.

We also now have a shop in Hobart, our largest nearby city and the capital city of Tasmania, that replicates our Cellar Door experience for those visitors unable to get to Bruny Island or for the locals who want to access our cheeses more conveniently. Interestingly, replicating our Bruny Island service style in the city is more challenging and often feels inauthentic once we are no longer "on the rock."

We also have a busy calendar of events around Australia, including participation in a weekly local farmers' market and food and wine events in every city of Australia. It is important that we utilize our own staff for these events in order to give a true experience and be able to discuss not just our cheeses but our island with genuine knowledge. Our location is a constant subject throughout our dialogue when discussing our cheeses: as much because people are interested and intrigued as we are keen to inform them of Bruny Island.

CONCLUSION

All of these retail channels have been born out of necessity. We need a bold solution to the issue of being able to access our market, and fortune, it seems, really does favor the bold. We need to invent ways to build and access markets and at the same time build the shortest possible distance between us and our consumers. We need to be able to tell our story directly to those who wanted to hear it. We need to be able to engage with our customers in the same authentic style long after they have left Bruny Island; we need to be able to, and we can, take them back there occasionally through our dialogue and our products. Today, almost 90% of our production is sold by us directly to our consumers.

Part 6
Epilogue

18 Conclusion
A New Paradigm
Léo-Paul Dana

OUT OF THE RUBBLE

It is no secret that I have a passion for islands and that I have spent long periods on various islands studying island entrepreneurship (see Dana, 1990, 1999, 2002, 2003). Hence, I was delighted when Professor Godfrey Baldacchino invited me to write this conclusion. I have great respect for him and for his work. And I like his editorial of this collection that leads off with the words, redolent with meaning: "Vulnerable, resilient, but also doggedly perseverant and cleverly opportunistic." Perhaps because I was born on an island and I reside on an island (New Zealand's South Island), I can therefore feel a canny affinity and relate to his words. As Godfrey mentioned in his introduction to this book, New Zealand is among the world's seven island states with populations between 1 and 5 million.

In New Zealand's South Island, I experienced vulnerability to seismic activity first-hand. With the earthquakes of 2011, I lost my mother after falling bricks crushed her; I lost my business as the building that housed it crumbled with the quakes; I lost my home as my house broke into three and the Crown took the garden and orchard on which I had toiled over a decade; I lost friends and neighbors. During the hundreds of seismic aftershocks, we had no power and no running water. For weeks, my access to the world was via the local Red Cross computer, shared with hundreds of others. To my village, water was trucked in; not far away, neighborhoods were more vulnerable: isolated with no road access and dependent on airlifts.

At the time of writing this conclusion, in late 2014, Christchurch is still devastated. Some downtown areas look like photographs of Berlin in 1945. Yet I have witnessed resilient people persevere with opportunistic strategies. Money was made showing visitors remains of former mansions and newly homeless people sleeping in vehicles. While others were reading about dark tourism (Foley & Lennon, 1996; Seaton, 1996), I witnessed it. Indeed, my island is a superlative case of a vulnerable and resilient but also doggedly perseverant and cleverly opportunistic people and society. Such themes are probably generalizable, with the residents of most small islands possibly occupying the extreme end of a range of subjects.

When natural disasters have struck the United States, people from Mexico and elsewhere were employed to rebuild. In Christchurch, a tiny population base limits the availability of skills. And our remoteness complicates matters, given that our closest neighbor—Australia—is almost four hours away by jet plane. Whereas Mexicans have walked or driven to the United States, getting into New Zealand is a totally different matter. There is something special about islandness and being small, along with the often-associated attributes of remoteness and being at the periphery, although these factors can be opportunities, qualities that permit some island-based businesses to emerge, thrive, and survive.

In the introductory pages of this volume, Godfrey emphasized the inherently limited domestic markets of small islands; in South Island, we suffered from limited supply of material to rebuild after the earthquakes; shortages led to price increases. Isolation made us vulnerable, as did the absence of economies of scale. We can come back to the haunting words of Maria Amoamo, "fragile, small, peripheral and dependent . . . within a discourse of 'vulnerability'" (2011, p. 69). But this volume has much more to offer.

Traditionally, islands were fragile, small, peripheral, dependent, and vulnerable. And they still may be so, but with an important caveat. The paradigm has changed. Island economies around the world are no longer as dependent on traditional, subsistence-based farming and fishing coupled with mining or monoplantation agriculture (Baldacchino, 2007). Yes, in former times, islands were transformed by colonists into wholesale tobacco and sugar plantation economies, and this was very profitable to the colonizers with the use of slave and indentured labor. But wages have risen and protected access to markets has collapsed, giving rise to new models of island development. I have considered tourism in the British Virgin Islands and banking in the Caymans (Dana, 1987), among other cases (Dana, 1995).

A RICH VARIETY OF MODELS

The present volume exposes us to an even greater variety of models. In Chapter 2, Ilan Kelman and Cheney M. Shreve explore dark entrepreneurship, quite different from traditional, subsistence-based farming and fishing coupled with mining or monoplantation agriculture. These authors discuss activities such as the sale of passports and citizenship by Dominica, the Marshall Islands, Nauru, Samoa, Tonga, and Vanuatu; the processing of waste, as does Batam Island; holding asylum seekers, as do Christmas Island, Nauru, and Papua New Guinea; human trafficking, as reported in Bijagos Islands (Guinea-Bissau), and Cape Verde; flag-of-convenience registry, as is possible in the Marshall Islands and Tuvalu; and others, including child sex tourism in Phuket, Thailand. Quite far removed from subsistence-based farming and fishing coupled with mining or monoplantation agriculture!

O'Rourke (2002) suggested that emigration can be an effective policy mechanism for a country to raise its living standards, and this is the theme of Chapter 3, in which Keith Nurse focuses on the diasporic economy. Indeed, many people leave their homes to work overseas, and they send remittances to family members. The transferred funds contribute to the development of country of origin, mainly boosting its domestic demand. Among other figures, Nurse shows that, in 2012, remittances represented 25% of Haiti's GDP. After an absence from their island of origin, many people return as tourists, sometimes with new family members and/or friends. This diasporic tourism can be good and sustainable for an island economy, and exports are increased when individuals take away niche, nostalgic, and specialty goods.

The Finnish (but Swedish-speaking) autonomy of Åland has long been an island of academic interest (Brown, 1921; Padeldorf & Andersson, 1939). In Chapter 4, Katarina Fellman, Jouko Kinnunen, Bjarne Lindström, and Richard Palmer revisit this fascinating island. These authors explain that, although the challenges of economic development for small islands are considerable, Åland has developed into a modern service economy with a high standard of living, low unemployment, and a growing population. Here, per-capita GDP is close to US$40,000 (PPP), about 16 % higher than that in Finland. Obviously, the economy of Åland is not based on subsistence farming and fishing, coupled with mining or monoplantation agriculture. The authors of the chapter explain that the triple keys to success: (i) turning the dependence of seaborne transportation into an economic asset; (ii) focusing on place-based branding and high-quality production instead of scale economies; and (iii) making creative use of the economic opportunities that the island's special political status entails.

Several decades ago, O'Dell (1939) observed the unique knitting patterns on Fair Isle. In Chapter 5 of this book, Richard W. Butler focuses on Fair Isle, still known for its specific style of knitting. Local entrepreneurs produce knitwear, the demand for which exceeds supply. The Internet provides details to potential buyers for this local industry that generates considerable income, making this activity both economically and culturally important.

In Chapter 6, Gestur Hovgaard provides us with a case study set in the Faroe Islands, an 18-island archipelago that is an autonomous country within Denmark, with home rule since 1948. Whereas the Faroese people traditionally depended mainly on traditional fishing for their economic survival, modern Faroese aquaculture began in 1947. In this chapter, Hovgaard tells us that, today, Faroese fisheries and aquaculture are the basis for the production and export of high-quality Faroese fish products, representing 95% of merchandise exports and some 20% of total Faroese GDP.

The author of Chapter 7, James E. Randall, focuses on biosciences: a new economic driver on Prince Edward Island, which has come a long way from *Anne of Green Gables*. Randall discusses Diagnostic Chemicals Limited (DCL) and its successor, BioVectra Limited. Here is an example of a knowledge-intensive set of economic activities gaining some leverage over the potatoes, mussels, and lobsters for which the island has been traditionally known.

Williams (2011) has noted that the internationalization of local firms contributes to the prosperity of small island economies. In Chapter 8, Karen L. Orengo Serra and Sopheap Theng take us to the French Caribbean jurisdiction of St. Barthélemy, off the shores of St. Martin. Here, a small hospitality firm has internationalized successfully, positioning itself as a global luxury brand.

In 1938, LYSI Ltd. was established in Iceland, and this firm is the subject of Chapter 9, written by Gylfi Dalmann Aðalsteinsson and Runólfur Smári Steinþórsson. This firm is at the forefront of knowledge on the production of marine lipids, which are omega-3 fatty acids. A key provider of vitamins and nutrition for people and livestock, the enterprise now has a global reach.

Woodruff (2007) noted that reliance on imported fuel strains budgets. On many islands, expensive fossil fuels are still required to make electricity. But now there is an alternative. Chapter 10 by Carola Betzold focuses on biofuel made from the ubiquitous coconut in the Solomon Islands.

In Chapter 11, Michael Lujan Bevacqua and Hermon Farahi investigate the changing colonial context and cultural decolonization of Guam's tourism industry, pointing to a potential renaissance of local culture and pride.

Krystyna Adams, Rebecca Whitmore, Rory Johnston, and Valorie A. Crooks take us to the Caribbean and the small, sovereign, island state of Barbados in Chapter 12, where they study medical tourism. This is a profitable health service niche that exploits a tourism reputation, location, a salubrious climate, and medical expertise.

IpKin Anthony Wong and Ricardo Chi Sen Siu take us to a former fishing village in the Pearl River Delta: Macao, composed of the peninsula of Macao and two small islands: Coloane and Taipa. In Chapter 13, the authors focus on casino tourism in this special administrative region of China, and they note that gaming revenue generated here was about seven times that of Las Vegas in 2013. Beyond subsistence indeed!

Mario Aloisio describes the development of the software industry in Malta in Chapter 14. He discusses how and why the e-gaming sector has grown rapidly, contributing substantially to the local economy.

In Chapter 15, Michael Entwistle and Michael J. Oliver consider the case of Jersey, the largest of the Channel Islands, whose citizens are subjects of the British Crown, but not of the United Kingdom. This small island territory has adapted to change and perseveres among the world's most successful small international finance centers. The authors link this success to innovation and ingenuity among residents, plus just-as-creative legislation.

And while local culture remains strong in the small island community of Tuvalu, there is a fair degree of brinkmanship in place in how that small archipelagic state and its government go about exploring and exploiting the various niches that their location and their sovereignty offers. We get welcome insights into this practice of governpreneurship from Chapter 16 by Godfrey Baldacchino and Colin S. Mellor.

Finally, while some academics write about entrepreneurs, entrepreneur Nick Haddow wrote his own chapter about being founder of the Bruny Island Cheese Co. on an island with no dairy farms. Bruny Island is remote, off the southeast coast of Tasmania, itself off the main island continent of Australia. Bruny has no history of cheese making or any other form of value-added food production. Furthermore, the author reports that it is difficult to find and retain staff. Yet Haddow has succeeded, and he tells us how in his own inspirational words.

A FUTURE THAT BECKONS

What do all these chapters have in common? They show us that times have changed. Once upon a time, islands survived with subsistence-based farming and fishing coupled with mining or monoplantation agriculture. But that paradigm is passé. Nowadays, entrepreneurs on islands around the world are still vulnerable—possibly they have always been so, and possibly they may always remain so—but they are also resilient, doggedly perseverant, and cleverly opportunistic. The time has come for a new and more constructive and optimistic paradigm of island economies, with biosciences, finance, software, and niche tourism at least as important as the more traditional and historical practices. The paradigm needs to change not just for providing that added dose of confidence in what can be accomplished but also—as this book does so well—for more properly recognizing and celebrating what has been and is being, done.

REFERENCES

Amoamo, M. (2011). The mitigation of vulnerability: Mutiny, resilience and reconstitution: A case study of Pitcairn Island. *Shima: The International Journal of Research into Island Cultures, 5*(1), 69–93.

Baldacchino, G. (Ed.). (2007). *A world of islands: An island studies reader*. Charlottetown, Canada, and Luqa, Malta: Institute of Island Studies, University of Prince Edward and Agenda Academic.

Brown, P.M. (1921). The Åland Island question. *The American Journal of International Law, 15*(2), 268–272.

Dana, L.-P. (1987). Entrepreneurship and venture creation: An international comparison of five Commonwealth nations. In N.C. Churchill, J.A. Hornaday, B.A. Kirchhoff, O.J. Krasner, & K.H. Vesper (Eds.), *Frontiers of entrepreneurship research* (pp. 573–583). Wellesley, MA: Babson College.

Dana, L.-P. (1990). Saint Martin/Sint Maarten: A case study of the effects of politics and culture on economic development. *Journal of Small Business Management, 28*(4), 91–98.

Dana, L.-P. (1995), Public policy and entrepreneurship in the Caribbean: Nine styles of policy. *Journal of Private Enterprise, 10*(2), 119–141.

Dana, L.-P. (1999). The social cost of tourism: A case study of Ios. *Cornell Quarterly, 40*(4), 60–63.

Dana, L.-P. (2002). Sustainable development in the Maldives: The Dhivehi context of entrepreneurship. *International Journal of Entrepreneurship and Innovation Management, 2*(6), 557–565.

Dana, L.-P. (2003). The challenge of exporting fresh food from the Chatham Islands to markets overseas. *British Food Journal, 105*(1/2), 9–22.

Foley, M., & Lennon J. (1996). JFK and dark tourism: Heart of darkness. *Journal of International Heritage Studies, 2*(2), 198–211.

O'Dell, A. C. (1939). *Historical geography of the Shetland Islands*. Lerwick, Shetland: T. & J. Mason.

O'Rourke, K. H. (2002). Globalization and inequality: Historical trends. In World Bank, *Annual World Bank Conference on Development Economics 2001* (pp. 39–67). Washington, DC: World Bank.

Padeldorf, N. J., & Andersson, G. A. (1939). The Åland question. *The American Journal of International Law, 33*(3), 465–487.

Seaton, A. V. (1996). From Thanatopis to Thanatourism: Guided by the dark. *International Journal of Heritage Studies, 2*(4), 234–244.

Williams, D. A. (2011). Impact of firm size and age on the export behavior of small locally owned firms: Fresh insights. *Journal of International Entrepreneurship, 9*(2), 152–174.

Woodruff, A. (2007). *An economic assessment of renewable energy options for rural electrification in Pacific Island countries*. Technical report. Suva, Fiji: Pacific Islands Applied Geoscience Commission (SOPAC).

Index

For Product Safety Concerns and Information please contact our EU
representative GPSR@taylorandfrancis.com
Taylor & Francis Verlag GmbH, Kaufingerstraße 24, 80331 München, Germany

www.ingramcontent.com/pod-product-compliance
Ingram Content Group UK Ltd.
Pitfield, Milton Keynes, MK11 3LW, UK
UKHW021606240425
457818UK00018B/409